2 Litchfield Road
Londonderry, NH 03053
Meetinghouseofnhdems@gmail.com

THE CHILDREN OF NAFTA

David Bacon

THE CHILDREN OF NAFTA

LABOR WARS ON THE U.S./MEXICO BORDER

UNIVERSITY OF CALIFORNIA PRESS
Berkeley Los Angeles London

University of California Press
Berkeley and Los Angeles, California

University of California Press, Ltd.
London, England

Library of Congress Cataloging-in-Publication Data

Bacon, David, 1948–
   The children of NAFTA : labor wars on the U.S. / Mex-
ico border / David Bacon.
       p.   cm.
   Includes index.
   ISBN 0-520-23778-1 (cloth alk. paper)
   1. Alien labor, Mexican—United States.   2. Mexican
Americans—Employment.   3. Migrant labor—Mexican-
American Border Region.   4. Quality of work life—
Mexican-American Border Region.   5. Labor movement—
Mexican-American Border Region   6. Canada. Treaties,
etc. 1992 Oct. 7.   7. Mexican-American Border Region—
Economic conditions.   8. Mexican-American Border
Region—Social conditions.   I. Title: Labor wars on the
U.S/Mexican border.   II. Title.

HD8081.M6 B33 2004   331.1'0972'1—dc22

Manufactured in the United States of America

The paper used in this publication meets the minimum
requirements of ANSI/NISO Z39.48-1992 (R 1997)
(*Permanence of Paper*). ♾

CONTENTS

INTRODUCTION / 1

1 Grapes and Green Onions / 19

2 Putting Solidarity on the Table / 42

3 Tijuana's Maquiladora Workers / 60

4 Han Young / 80

5 Build a House, Go to Jail / 121

6 The Strategic Alliance / 151

7 Duro Means Hard / 185

8 Mexico's Wars over Privatization / 223

9 Transplanted Expectations / 251

10 The World of the Border Has Changed / 285

EPILOGUE: THE CONFRONTATION TO COME / 313

INDEX / 325

INTRODUCTION

I was a union organizer for twenty years. In part, I followed in the footsteps of my parents, both of whom were labor activists in the 1930s and 1940s. My father helped organize bank employees and publishing workers in New York City, a notable achievement given that few workers in either industry have succeeded in joining unions in the decades since. My mother, a librarian, must have belonged to at least three unions in the course of that career, not counting the Book and Magazine Guild, in which she was active at the time I was born.

So unions run in the blood. Strikes must have been explained to me at a very young age; I have no memory of learning about them. I always just knew—you don't cross picket lines.

The world of labor into which I was born—permeated by the radical, left-wing, socialist movement centered in New York City—was very different from today's world of work. The culture of that earlier world was based on the ideals of European immigrants, ideals that were shared with the city's African Americans and Puerto Ricans. Together, they insisted that a vision of the future that didn't involve eliminating racism was no vision at all.

My parents' generation stood by their internationalism, often paying a high price amid the xenophobia and hysteria of the cold war. Paul

Robeson, the great people's singer of the past century, was their model of cultural understanding. He made it a matter of principle to sing songs from almost every corner of the earth, each performed in its original language. But this generation's ideal of mixing cultures on a world scale also had its blind spots inside our own borders: despite their growing numbers (even then), the cultures of immigrants from Mexico, Latin America, and Asia were largely invisible.

Thus began the intellectual odyssey of many of my own generation. We sought to use those class instincts we had inherited as tools to understand a far different world. My own journey took me through years as an organizer for the United Farm Workers, the United Electrical Workers, the International Molders Union, and a handful of others. I went from factories to fields and back, from New York and Oakland, where I grew up, to the small farmworker towns of rural California and Arizona. It was a journey from English to Spanish, from "Solidarity Forever" and "Which Side Are You On?" to "De Colores" and "La Huelga en General." I entered a world where people moved beyond picket lines, where strikers built *plantones*, tent encampments, at plant gates. It was the world of the hunger strike and the boycott.

The farmworkers movement taught me Spanish, and I saw it teach other workers English; still others learned how to read. Many of today's unions and social justice movements do not value such teaching highly enough. Communication is the basic survival skill for all organizers; any organization that plans to grow must teach it. This was the school where I learned the importance of the voice. It's not just the message that matters, I discovered, but who is able to speak it, what words they know how to use, and which worldview those words reflect.

I left the farmworkers' movement with empty pockets after four years on the union's salary of five dollars a week plus room and board. At first, I went to work in the fields; like many farmworkers, I told myself that I would be there just for a while, long enough to save a little money and find another job. I found that picking strawberries fast enough to earn a living required more than experience, dexterity, and the will to ignore the pain of a back bent for hours at a time (none of which I had).

There was an additional job requirement, fulfilled by many of my co-workers, who had journeyed from small towns in Mexico and the Philippines: economic desperation, the sting of the whip. When I went on to pick wine grapes, normally a pretty good job in farm labor, I barely made minimum wage. In the self-mocking way Mexicans laugh at themselves, my crew called itself the *relámpagos*, the lightning bolts. We were the slowest of fifty crews in the Almaden vineyards, and I was the slowest *relámpago* of all—the only white guy.

Unable to make a living at farm work, I went back to the city in the late 1970s, to the electronics plants of Silicon Valley. Another lesson in changing demographics awaited me there, in the huge factories where tens of thousands of immigrants labored on the wafer fab, test, and assembly lines, segregated by sex, race, and immigration status. Years in the plants eventually landed me on a blacklist, the result of standing up for the union in an industry that prides itself on having none. More organizing jobs followed, one after another. Each seemed designed to demonstrate that the "global economy" wasn't just a phrase describing a macroeconomic abstraction but in fact was a day-to-day, hour-to-hour reality experienced by millions of people.

As a foundry organizer, I saw waves of Mexican workers replace African Americans in some of the heaviest, dirtiest jobs imaginable—and then saw both groups of workers dumped into the street when foundries closed and production moved south across the border or west across the Pacific. I helped fight a desperate rearguard battle to build unions among tens of thousands of immigrant Chinese women sewing clothes in San Francisco sweatshops, while friends tried to do the same among even larger numbers of Mexican and Central American garment workers in Los Angeles. Thousands of those jobs went south, too.

I received a firsthand education in the global economy. It convinced me that the most important changes brought about by globalization have taken place at the bottom of the economy, not at the top. People who can't make a living as coffee farmers in Veracruz become farm laborers picking grapes in Delano, or die crossing the border's Desierto del Diablo in the attempt. Mexican workers won a nineteen-month strike at a Watsonville, California, frozen food plant, only to see other Mexicans hired to fill their jobs a few years later, when the company moves production a thousand miles south to Irapuato.

All my organizing jobs led south, to the border. I worked for the United Farm Workers in California's Imperial Valley, visiting the homes of farmworkers who lived across the line in Mexicali and San Luis. During union organizing drives with the United Electrical Workers among electronics and other factory workers in San Jose and Los Angeles, people often went home to their families across the border once their resources ran out in the north. When Mexican sewing workers organized in Santa Rosa, Napa, and Los Angeles, their factories closed and left town. Some reopened in Tijuana and Ensenada, just hours away from their former locations. Here at the border, globalization unfolds in its most concentrated form.

At the end of the 1980s, as the debate began over the North American Free Trade Agreement (NAFTA), the importance of the maquiladora industry—foreign-owned factories in Mexico that use low-wage labor to manufacture products for export—and the movements of workers in these border plants became increasingly obvious to workers in the United States. What's more, their own interest in these developments grew, as they saw for themselves the results of the free trade policies that had been treated as holy sacrament for decades.

On the border, I found a long history of working-class social movements, encompassing not only a chronicle of exploitation but also a tradition of powerful resistance. At key moments, some of these movements—such as the Cananea miners' strike of 1907, which heralded the coming of the Mexican Revolution—changed the world far beyond their immediate environs. Today, with more than a million workers in thirty-eight hundred factories, the border is a region where the movements of the poor are shaking the economic pillars of the free trade economy. Yet, just as most of the organizing campaigns among workers in the United States go unreported, the history of the border's social movements is also untold.

And just as those reporting on Silicon Valley have focused on life among a relatively thin top layer of engineers and managers, ignoring the vast majority on the production lines, those reporting on the U.S./Mexico border have often had a similarly distorted focus. In the mainstream press, these reports on life at the border are dominated by visions of a Wild West of drug runners and shootouts. Much of the reporting is manipulated by the boosterism of the maquiladora industry and its adulation of new plants and jobs. And not coincidentally, now that the bottom has fallen out of both countries' economies, another form of tunnel vision has become prevalent—accounts of jobless workers as economic victims, powerless to alter the terms of their own exploitation.

The border has been treated as an area bereft of its own social history, especially any history of social struggle. Those movements that surge from below—workers trying to wrest survival from low-wage factory jobs, squatter communities holding onto their land even as their leaders are jailed and they are threatened with eviction—have a history as unrecorded as that of the strikes in which I was an organizer. The voices of the people who understand the consequences of globalization most directly, and who can speak with the authority of their own experience, are unheard. And the absence of this history in the public debate poses a critical question: How can people take control of the economic forces that determine the parameters of their lives if their responses are invisible and their experience unavailable to others in the same situation?

A NOTE ON SOURCES

A decade ago, I left my work as an organizer and embarked on an effort to document the social upheavals in which I had been not only a witness but also an active participant. That effort has resulted, in part, in this book. Its purpose is to record what has previously gone unrecorded, to help fill in the empty space that belongs to the history of social struggles along the border. It is the product of reporting on the ground. In writing it, I tried to get as close as possible to the people involved and the movements they organized. It therefore embodies both the strengths and the weaknesses of such an effort.

It is overwhelmingly based on my own experience. I describe what I saw and what I heard from workers and activists. This book thus necessarily reflects their experience as well as their analysis of the events in which they have been central actors—the strikes at Han Young, the occupation of the land in Cañon Buenavista, the election campaign rallies in Tijuana and San Quintin.

When the U.S. and Mexican governments reordered their economic priorities to develop industry and encourage investment on the border, the consequences could not be summed up neatly in a collection of statistics. Understanding what the weakened rule of law in Tijuana has meant for the wages and rights of workers is impossible without an account of the Han Young strikes, not as viewed by the city authorities or the factory owner, but as viewed by the people who organized them. Because of the particular role the border now plays in the economic life of North America, these consequences are felt far beyond Tijuana. The broken union drive at Plasticos Bajacal and the strikes at Han Young had a direct impact on the lives of workers in Los Angeles. The employers' proven ability to suppress strikes and keep wages low was a key motivation, for instance, in the relocation of hundreds of jobs from the Price Pfister plumbing supply plant in Los Angeles's San Fernando Valley to the outskirts of Mexicali. What's more, Price Pfister workers—who went on a hunger strike for days, protesting the relocation of their jobs—were well aware of this.

The point isn't simply to understand the fact that jobs move, but to understand the impact this movement has had on the thinking of the people who are affected by it on both sides of the border. It is consciousness, and the action and organization based on it, that creates social change.

The documentation contained in this book has therefore attempted to trace the development of that consciousness. Some of my earliest documentary efforts predate the NAFTA debate; they are based on the first trips by California union activists to find their counterparts in Mexico and on campaigns that ensued after strikes and plant closures in Watsonville and Stockton, California. The surge of border activity that coincided with the NAFTA debate then produced further efforts to document and report these struggles.

A great deal of the documentation I've produced over the years takes the form of photographs. The images of the bus rallies in Mexico City and the strikers in Tijuana facing down the police are visual evidence of the determined resistance to economic "reform" in Mexico. They are convincing in a way that words alone can't convey. Photographs of the children working in Mexicali's green onion fields add another dimension to an understanding of who pays the price for free trade. Exhibitions of many of these photographs have been organized by labor studies centers in the University of California system, by the Service Employees International Union, by the German union IG Metall, and by the London-based International Committee for Trade Union Rights. Although the publication of most of these photos must be deferred until another day, the images reproduced in this book provide some idea of the broader work.

Some of my most exciting experiences in documenting the border upsurge have been radio broadcasts on KPFA, the Pacifica station in Berkeley, where I began a weekly half-hour show, "Labor and the Global Economy," during the week of the fraudulent, open-ballot election at Plasticos Bajacal that smashed the workers' independent union. Our first broadcast sent the voices of these workers, even as they were being threatened by thugs from the company's preferred union, out to thousands of listeners throughout northern California. As the show evolved into a segment of the station's early morning drive-time program, commuters from Fresno to Silicon Valley had the chance to hear the story of the Duro election, the Han Young strikes, and other highlights of the border struggle, through the voices of participants, often by cell phone as the events were unfolding. Tapes of those interviews have provided many of the quotations contained in this book.

But the most lasting and widely circulated accounts of these events have been articles published by newspapers and magazines over the past decade. Pacific News Service, where I've been an associate editor for ten years, has published articles about almost every major battle, including some in the voices of border workers themselves. For a few years, the *San Francisco Chronicle* carried my dispatches describing strikes and land invasions, its coverage eclipsing even that of its rival in Los Angeles. Generally, however, weekly newspapers have been more open to publishing accounts of border rebellion, especially the *LA Weekly*, the *San Francisco Bay Guardian*, and the now-defunct *LA View*. National progressive magazines, including *The Nation, The Progressive, Z, The American Prospect*, and *In These Times*, have carried stories as well. The labor press also deserves credit for taking a far greater interest than the mainstream media in the progress of strikes and organizing in the maquiladoras and community fights in border barrios. Notable are the publications of the United Auto Workers, the International Longshore and Warehouse Union, the Newspaper Guild, and the former Oil, Chemical and Atomic Workers.

Writing and taking pictures is the way I make a living. I'm grateful to all these publications and their editors for providing the resources that have enabled me to spend these years traveling on the border, reporting what I've seen. Much of the material developed in covering these stories and writing these articles has found its way into this book.

As I've worked to accurately portray the economic context for events on the border, I've often found that employers in Mexico are not unwilling to provide important information; some, such as the management of ITAPSA, Plasticos Bajacal, Duro Bag, Hyundai, and Grupo Mexico, have clearly stated their position on the labor conflicts in their operations. The maquiladora association itself provides estimates of employment and other useful statistics. Church-based institutions such as the Center for Reflection, Education, and Action and the Interfaith Center on Corporate Responsibility keep careful track of the living standards of maquiladora workers in various border cities. For economic analysis, I often refer to Alejandro Álvarez Bejar, who teaches as a member of the economics faculty at the National Autonomous University of Mexico. Álvarez has spent a lifetime studying the impact of neoliberal economics on Mexican working people. He and his brother Raúl (a student leader in the uprising at Tlatelolco and a witness to the subsequent massacre) are widely respected activists in the country's progressive community. The economic effects of NAFTA have been consistently documented by Sarah Anderson of the Institute for Policy Studies and by the research department of the AFL-CIO, both located in Washington, D.C.

It is Mexico's good fortune that newspaper ownership in that country is still much less concentrated than it is in the United States, allowing Mexicans to enjoy a much wider variety of political viewpoints than readers of newspapers north of the border, where monopoly is creating a kind of bland ignorance. In particular, *La Jornada*, Mexico City's left-wing daily, contains excellent economic reporting and analysis, which is useful for anyone wanting a broad picture of the Mexican economy. Although some of the newspapers in border towns are shrill mouth-pieces for local political bosses and their friends who run the maquiladoras and the captive unions, there are some valiant exceptions. Mexican reporters, including Raymundo Ramos at Ciudad Laredo's *El Mañana* and Araceli Domínguez, who covered the Han Young strikes for Tijuana's *El Mexicano*, made considerable sacrifices to cover border struggles. In addition, the Mexico City magazine *Trabajo y Democracia Hoy* (Work and democracy today), published by the Centro Nacional de Desarollo Social (National Center for Social Development), is a good source for economic information about Mexican workers and for debate over current issues in the Mexican labor movement.

U.S. writers have also made important contributions to our understanding of the complicated history of Mexican labor. First among them is Dan LaBotz, not only an activist in democratic movements in the unions of both countries but also the author of the excellent *Mask of Democracy: Labor Suppression in Mexico Today* (Boston: South End Press, 1992), a history of the Mexican labor movement to the early 1990s. Some of the subsequent history is recounted in Dale Hathaway's *Allies Across the Border: Mexico's "Authentic Labor Front" and Global Solidarity* (Boston: South End Press, 2000), an examination of the crucial relationship forged between the United Electrical Workers and the Authentic Labor

Front (La Frente Auténtica de Trabajo), one of Mexico's most important independent unions.

The labor history of Mexico and that of the United States have many parallels. Both labor movements were strongest in the 1930s and 1940s. The main institutions organized during that period—the CIO (Congress of Industrial Organizations) in the United States and the CTM (the Confederation of Mexican Workers, Confederación de Trabajadores Mexicanos) in Mexico—owe their origins to Communists, socialists, and other radicals. In both movements, however, left-wingers were purged from positions of power during the cold war. Examining these histories is not the aim of this book, although I do try to assess the impact of NAFTA and the border labor war on putting the cold war to rest. Nevertheless, an honest and open examination of these histories— one organized by the formal labor institutions of both countries—is a necessary step both in coming to terms with the past and in trying to recover a radical vision for the future, which might be capable of inspiring workers to make the sacrifices needed to rebuild each country's labor movement.

As compared to the United States, democratic and progressive labor activists in Mexico had a stronger influence on labor's politics and direction, although they also paid a higher price. Some insight into that history and, by implication, into the potential for a movement with much more radical objectives is offered by *Mi Testimonio: Memorias de un Comunista Mexicano* (Mexico City: Ediciones de Cultura Popular, 1978), the autobiography of Valentín Campa, the railroad workers' leader and a founder of the Confederation of Mexican Workers. Campa was jailed for years for leading a national railway strike with Demetrio Vallejo and then ran as the Communist candidate for president after his release from prison.

Cross-border movements of labor activists and radicals have been an important part of the political life of both Mexico and the United States for more than a century; early high points include the activities of the Flores Magón brothers and the uprising in Cananea. A good account both of the movements themselves and the mechanism created to suppress them is W. Dirk Raat's *Revoltosos: Mexico's Rebels in the United States, 1903–1923* (College Station: Texas A&M University Press, 1981).

In the more recent past, the left-wing and progressive labor culture of Mexico was profoundly affected by the massacre of the students at Tlatelolco in 1968. Many authors have provided accounts of those events, including Elena Poniatowska, in *La Noche de Tlatelolco: Testimonio de Historia Oral,* 2d ed. (Mexico City: Biblioteca Era, 1997); and Raúl Álvarez Garin, in *La Estela de Tlatelolco: Una Reconstrucción Histórica del Movimiento Estudiantil del 68* (Mexico City: Editorial Grijalbo, 1998).

The important experience of the workers at the Kuk Dong (Mex Mode) plant, briefly described in Chapter Seven, is presented more fully by Professor Huberto Juárez Núñez of the Benemerita Autonomous University of Puebla, in *Rebelión en el Greenfield* (Puebla: Benemerita Universidad Autónoma de Puebla, 2002), published with the assistance of the AFL-CIO.

A moving account of the lives of today's Mexican migrants coming to the United States is Rubén Martínez's story of the Chávez family, three of whom died when a van carrying them from the border left the road in Riverside County in 1996; see *Crossing Over: A Mexican Family on the Migrant Trail* (New York: Henry Holt, 2001).

NAFTA's effects, and the reasons for them, have obviously been the subject of intense debate since the treaty was passed. Three of the most thorough examinations are Robert Scott, Carlos Salas, and Bruce Campbell, "NAFTA at Seven: Its Impact on Workers in All Three Nations," a briefing paper published by the Economic Policy Institute (Washington, D.C., 2001); Sarah Anderson and John Cavanagh, "Rethinking the NAFTA Record," a report published by the Institute for Policy Studies (Washington, D.C., 2002); and John R. MacArthur, *The Selling of "Free Trade": NAFTA, Washington, and the Subversion of American Democracy* (Berkeley: University of California Press, 2001).

THE VOICES IN THIS BOOK

The Children of NAFTA is not intended as a survey of all the strikes and social movements on the border during the period it covers (roughly from 1988 to early 2003). Rather, it concentrates on a few key move-ments and events, partly because I was often there to witness them and to interview participants. It can therefore give expression to the voices of the people who organized these movements—an important goal in itself, for it can provide readers not only with an account of the partici-pants' experience but also with their assessment of the lessons they learned. In other words, rather than producing a survey with more breadth, I've opted for greater immediacy and depth.

This book seeks to examine these basic questions: How has the development of the border, and the transfer of production to Mexico from the United States, affected the lives of people at the grassroots? What social movements have they organized in response? Because the cross-border movement owes so much of its origin to the negotiation of NAFTA, the book looks particularly at the social struggles organized in the wake of that treaty and weighs NAFTA's effect on labor on both sides of the border. And because the treaty's proponents promised that it would help to protect workers' rights, the book focuses especially on those strikes and organizing efforts that shed light on the fate of com-plaints made under the agreement.

The experience of the past decade has particular relevance because the Bush administration in late 2002 won fast track negotiating author-ity to extend NAFTA through the rest of Latin America, in a new treaty creating the Free Trade Area of the Americas. The experience on the U.S./Mexico border is not so specific that it would apply only to the North American continent. It is in fact illustrative of the overall conse-quences of neoliberal development policies, which affect dozens of countries around the world. The defects of the original treaty, and its carefully crafted tilt toward the concerns of profit-making and against any measures that might enhance the security and well-being of most people, will be multiplied many times over as the NAFTA model is extended southward.

The book begins by looking at agriculture, a generally unrecognized area of border development, through the eyes of farmworkers them-selves. Chapter One, "Grapes and Green Onions," describes the experience of southern California laborers who saw their jobs move south across the border and recounts the impact of this loss on their union. Some California farmworkers did attempt to investigate the motives behind the job flight. What they discovered—the extensive use of child labor in northern Mexico—represents a return to a past that thirty years of strikes and boycotts in the United States had sought to end.

The following chapter, "Putting Solidarity on the Table," then outlines the book's general arguments about the impact of neoliberal development on the Mexican economy and the challenges that neoliberal policies pose to unions and workers globally.

The next three chapters turn to direct reporting of life in Tijuana, describing the history of labor and community organizing in Baja California in the post-NAFTA period. The desperate economic situation of most workers and the first organizing efforts in response are recounted in Chapter Three, "Tijuana's Maquiladora Workers." The following chapter covers the two seminal Han Young strikes. More than any other social struggle on the border, the Han Young battles highlight the way neoliberal policies, designed to foster foreign investment, have undermined the laws that have historically protected workers, farmers, and the poor. The fifth chapter, "Build a House, Go to Jail," examines the same problem as it affects farmworkers who produce tomatoes and strawberries for the U.S. market. It shows not only that discrimination against indigenous Mixtec, Triqui, and Zapotec migrants from Oaxaca has become part of the neoliberal agenda but also that these indigenous groups have created unique cross-border organizations in their struggle for political and social rights.

Chapters Six and Seven examine two of the most important cross-border movements organized as a result of NAFTA. Chapter Six, "The Strategic Alliance," outlines the evolving relationship between the United Electrical Workers and the Authentic Labor Front, the most extensively developed relationship between a U.S. union and a Mexican union. Their experience poses important questions about the possible goals of such relationships. The chapter also describes the extraordinary sacrifices workers made in pursuing this alliance, especially at the ITAPSA and Friction Brake plants. Chapter Seven, "Duro Means Hard," takes a look at the other principal vehicle for cross-border campaigns over the past decade: the Coalition for Justice in the Maquiladoras. It describes the personal history of the group's current director, Martha Ojeda, who organized the historic battle at Sony's plants in Nuevo Laredo. It also details the lengthy efforts by workers at Custom Trim and Auto Trim, the Duro Bag Company, and Mex Mode to build independent unions, as well as organizing attempts in Torreon and Baja California Sur, and the implacable opposition they faced from authorities on all sides. Both chapters inevitably arrive at bitter conclusions about the efficacy of the North American Agreement on Labor Cooperation, NAFTA's infamous labor side agreement, after assessing the many futile efforts to make the treaty function as promised that took place during these campaigns.

Chapter Eight, "Mexico's Wars over Privatization," examines the broader changes in Mexico's economy and labor movement that form the political context of the border struggles. It recounts key battles in which workers sought to stop privatization, with its consequent job losses and gutting of labor agreements. It focuses on the strike at Cananea's copper mine as well as the long fight of Mexico City's bus drivers and the imprisonment of their union leaders. The description of the privatization of Mexico's ports is especially timely, given current speculation, in the aftermath of the recent West Coast longshore dispute, that shipping companies might seek to bypass unrest in U.S. ports by shipping through Mexico's privatized facilities.

Chapter Nine, "Transplanted Expectations," looks at another way in which NAFTA and cross-border activity have influenced U.S. labor—through the influence on U.S. unions of newly arrived Mexican and Central American immigrant workers. It is hard to overestimate the importance of this demographic transformation of great parts of the U.S. workforce and the resulting changes in the politics of U.S. unions. The story of one immigrant, Tony Castillo, highlights the sources of the progressive ideas that many immigrants bring north as well as the efforts some immigrant labor leaders have made to affect the politics of their home countries. As the history of the organizing drive at the ConAgra beef plant in Omaha, Nebraska, makes clear, these demographic changes not only create new possibilities for cross-border cooperation but also hold the potential for the survival of many U.S. unions.

Chapter Ten draws all these strands together. It first assesses the impact that NAFTA and a decade of cross-border activity have made on Mexico's labor movement. The analysis offered is that of leaders who have been involved in many of these cross-border efforts, including Benedicto Martinez of the Authentic Labor Front; María Estela Ríos Gonzalez, formerly head of Mexico's National Association of Democratic Lawyers (Asociación Nacional de Abogados Democráticos) and now counsel to Mexico City's mayor; and Francisco Hernández Juárez, the head of the new independent labor federation, the National Union of Workers (Unión Nacional de Trabajadores). Turning to the United States, Stan Gacek, who heads the section of the AFL-CIO's Department of International Affairs responsible for relations with Latin American unions, also examines the impact of NAFTA and cross-border organizing. This chapter then argues that the cross-border movement has helped U.S. labor to move beyond the failed policies of its cold war years and find a new basis for international labor solidarity—which could be a decisive move forward, toward an internationalism capable of challenging corporate globalization.

Finally, an epilogue examines the most recent problems confronting border workers. The continuing murders of women in Juárez point out how little the political authorities in either country value the lives of women maquiladora workers. At the same time, the current economic recession is now being used to exert further downward pressure on wages. A recent company campaign that threatens border workers with job relocation, especially to China, echoes the same threats U.S. workers have heard from their own employers for years. Anti-Chinese hysteria, however, also obscures the reality that unemployment on the border is caused by the shrinking U.S. market, to which the region's economy is tightly tied. These events demonstrate that the workers' movement along the border now faces problems perhaps even greater than those encountered in the immediate post-NAFTA period.

CHILDREN OF NAFTA

This book is called *The Children of NAFTA* for several reasons. It begins by investigating child labor on the export farms of the Mexicali Valley. The relocation of production from the United States, which NAFTA accelerated, created the conditions that bring children into the fields there and elsewhere in northern Mexico. NAFTA on its own did not create the poverty that forces families to depend on the labor of their children, but the treaty made such poverty deeper and more widespread. These children working in the fields, therefore, are indeed children of NAFTA.

But some of the most progressive developments among workers in both countries, especially as described in the last chapter, also owe their origins to NAFTA. After all, but for the treaty, interest among U.S. workers in their co-workers south of the border would have remained low, as it had been for decades. The organizations that have been built in response to the debate over free trade—from the Coalition for Justice in the Maquiladoras to the alliance between the United Electrical Workers and the Authentic Labor Front to Enlace—are also rightly children of NAFTA, as are the many activists who have labored to build these groups.

And, like it or not, the inhabitants of all three countries—the United States, Mexico, and Canada—are now bound together by strong economic forces. These forces may have been set in motion by development policies coming from the world's largest corporations and the governments who defend their interests. But unbinding ourselves by stopping trade, putting up walls against immigrants, or returning to nationalistic labor movements incapable of seeing beyond their narrow interests is neither possible nor desirable. The key questions are who controls the process, who benefits, and who pays. The challenge to progressive social activists is winning sufficient political power to control these forces and using that power to reorder economic priorities. In that sense, then, we are all children of NAFTA.

· · ·

This book would be incomplete without recognizing that my own family members have become children of NAFTA, too. My wife, Lillian, and my three beautiful daughters, Miel, Yolanda, and Miki, all supported and helped me in the weeks and months I spent on the road over the past decade and in the many hours of labor required to produce the documentation from which this book was drawn. I thank them for that, from the bottom of my heart, as I thank my many other *compañeras* and *compañeros* who made this book possible.

1

GRAPES AND GREEN ONIONS

THE CASTILLOS LOSE THEIR UNION

NAFTA repeatedly plunged a knife into José Castillo's heart.

He felt its first thrust on almost the same day the treaty took effect. He lost his job.

That New Year's Day, in 1994, the Zapatistas took up arms in southern Mexico, denouncing NAFTA's marginalization of poor Mayan farmers in the Lacandon jungle. Video cameras closed in on their ski masks and ancient rifles, uplinking to satellites a new iconography of the underside of the global economy. Three thousand miles north, on the desert fringe of southern California, Castillo and a thousand other Mexican farmworkers were also being pushed to the social margins. They offered an equally haunting icon of the impact of free trade, but unemployed Mexicans in California have less media appeal. No one from the *Times* or CNN noticed.

NAFTA then inflicted a second wound: its promised benefits failed to materialize. According to U.S. president Bill Clinton and labor secretary Robert Reich, a safety net—including retraining and extended unemployment benefits—was ready to catch the unfortunate few whose out-of-date skills made their jobs expendable. José Castillo and his wife,

Ingracia, found this promise to be like the hot wind that blows around their home in the Coachella Valley—elusive, empty, and incapable of sustaining life.

But the third thrust was the cruelest. To understand this, you must know that José and Ingracia are veterans of the union wars that swept the California fields for three decades. They are the ones called *de hueso colorado*—all the way "to the marrow of their bones"— they are Chavistas, followers of César Chávez.

They lost their union.

"I felt like I lost my child." Ingracia's voice aches at the memory of the change that turned their world inside out and threatened the meaning that their struggle for dignity had given to their lives. Their story is part of the real history of NAFTA, about its consequences for working people on both sides of the border.

Because the Coachella Valley is so far south, only a couple of hours north of Mexico, its grape harvest comes in at the beginning of the season, in late May. By bringing their grapes into supermarkets before anyone else, valley growers always commanded premium prices; during the early 1990s, they were accustomed to receiving twenty dollars or more for a twenty-two-pound box in May. By July, when the harvest moved north to the San Joaquin Valley, the price usually dropped by half.

General Augusto Pinochet was the first to threaten that privileged position. Looking for exports to revive Chile's economy after the 1973 fascist coup, he discovered a winter market in his patron country. Even today, supermarket shelves in the United States are filled with Chilean grapes when the Coachella harvest starts.

But the real blow to the Coachella growers came from Mexico. U.S. ranchers like Delano's Jack Pandol, who began growing grapes in Chile under Pinochet, later began planting in the Sonoran Desert, south of Arizona. The year after NAFTA dropped restrictions on importing Mexican grapes into the United States, 7 million boxes flooded across the border. Coachella Valley's harvest was 10 million boxes that same season, only slightly more than the Mexican imports. And, to make matters worse for Coachella growers, the Mexican harvest starts at the same time. Their profitable position vanished overnight.

Since NAFTA, hardly any new fields of grapes have been planted anywhere in the Coachella Valley. Heaps of dry dead vines, their roots torn from the earth, point at the sun—sentinels of a dying industry.

The Bluestone Farming Company was one of the first to start tearing up its grapes. On January 6, 1994, Bluestone sent a letter to the Castillos and hundreds of other workers, informing them that the company was quitting the business of growing table grapes. By that time, however, the company was only a shell of its former self, a far cry from the days when its huge vineyards, spreading out across the desert, belonged to Lionel Steinberg.

Steinberg's enterprise, the David Freedman Company—or simply Freedman, as workers called it—is legendary in the United Farm Workers Union (UFW). It was one of the world's largest grape growers through the 1960s and 1970s, and it became the early home of the union.

While other grape growers fought the UFW with everything from lawyers to the gloved fists of strikebreakers to bullets, Steinberg was the exception. Perhaps ironically, his different attitude made him a very wealthy man.

By 1970, grape growers in California had been squeezed for five years by the UFW's fight for union recognition and its first grape boycott, a social movement that had become a symbol of economic justice in the minds of millions of people. The boycott had spread across the country, keeping growers' grapes locked up in coolers instead of filling supermarket shelves.

Steinberg broke ranks with the other growers and signed the first contract ending the historic grape strike, which had begun in 1965. Other growers followed suit. But when those same growers signed sweetheart contracts with the Teamsters union in 1973, in an effort to break the UFW, the farmworkers struck again. The renewed boycott once more squeezed off the sales of table grapes.

Steinberg, however, stayed with the UFW. Socially conscious consumers were trained to look for boxes of Freedman grapes, with the

UFW's black eagle stamped prominently on the side. Steinberg sold when no one else could, and he got a higher price.

In 1973, the Castillos were strikers. But a decade earlier, when the union began, they had not been Chavistas. After coming north from Mexico at the beginning of the 1960s, José Castillo became a seasonal laborer. Like most farmworkers of that era, he was unemployed and hungry much of the year. But then he got a job as a year-round permanent employee on the big grape ranch of Mr. Karahadian.

With a dream of stability seeming closer to reality, he went back to Mexicali, a hundred miles south across the border. There, he married Ingracia, a woman from his home state of Jalisco, and then brought her back to the vineyards in the desert. Mr. Karahadian rented a house to them on the company ranch, a privilege commonly granted to permanent employees. And, in return, the Castillos were loyal workers.

"Those were hard times. We never had any breaks," Ingracia says. "I remember that I would bring food to work hidden in my clothes, and I would eat a little when I thought no one was looking. Today there's cold water to drink when we work, but in those days there was nothing. When women wanted to go to the bathroom, we'd just have to go find a place to hide ourselves in the vines. These were all things we had to battle for—time to eat, water to drink, bathrooms. We never had unemployment insurance before. We just had to work and work and work. As soon as one job ended, I had to find another one right away."

In June of 1965, the first grape strike started in Coachella. Filipino workers across the valley walked out, seeking to raise wages from $1.10 an hour to $1.25. When the harvest moved north into the San Joaquin Valley around Delano, the Mexican workers organized by César Chávez and Dolores Huerta agreed to join the fight. The two streams of migrants— the old Filipino *manongs* (a term of respect because of their age), who had been organizing field labor upheavals since the 1920s, and the vast wave of Mexican workers who had been flooding California fields since the 1940s—came together, and the United Farm Workers union was born.

"I remember that I was very afraid," Ingracia recalls. "We were so green then. I'll never forget it. We were working in a field on Fifty-Seventh Avenue, which is just a dirt road. When the organizers first showed up and started talking to us from the road, we went running into the field so that we wouldn't be able to hear what they were saying, about how good the union was. We went running into the vines. We didn't want to have anything to do with the union."

This, of course, made Mr. Karahadian very happy, and he told his workers to run and hide whenever the organizers showed up. But as the strikes ground on, year after year, Karahadian's losses began to temper his enthusiasm for fighting the union.

José remembers: "In 1970, Karahadian couldn't sell his grapes because of the boycott. One morning, very early, he came out and told us he wanted to talk to us. We were all at the labor camp. At that time, we were all still very against the union, because we were with him. We always believed whatever the boss told us. 'Don't sign anything. I'm with you. You're with me.'

"But when the boycott beat him, he said, 'I don't want to go broke. I'm going to sign with Chávez. You have four days. If you don't sign within those four days, you'll be out of here.' From that time onward, we saw how he had used us, and we never believed him again. First he'd hidden us inside his vines, and then he'd just made us a meal on a plate on the table."

In the three years that followed, the Castillos and the other grape workers in the valley realized that the union organizers had been right: the union was good for the workers. They might have been drawn in by the growers' involuntary defeat, but once they learned how to make the union work, they discovered that their contracts provided benefits, job security, and a newfound freedom from discrimination.

Despite the UFW's tumultuous history of strikes and boycotts, most grape workers had only those three years of UFW contracts by which to judge the union. Yet it was enough to win their loyalty for the two decades of struggle that were to come.

When the UFW grape contracts expired in 1973, "one night, Mr. Karahadian signed with the Teamsters," Castillo explains. "The next morning, he told us, '*Señores*, I'm with the Teamsters now, and for me it's the better choice. You have four days to sign up.' But this time, a worker at the ranch named Hilario stood up, and he said to Karahadian, 'If you've made what's the best choice for you, well, we have too.' And he pulled a great big union flag out from under his shirt, and that's how the strike started there. And so Karahadian threw us off his property, into the street."

The Castillos took their children to stay with José's mother in Mexicali. Ingracia and her sister pulled their crew out on strike, in a scene made famous in the UFW's film *Fighting for Our Lives*. By the time the strike reached Delano in midsummer, it was one of the largest farmworker strikes in U.S. history. The Teamsters union, still two decades away from reform under Ron Carey, furnished goons who beat up strikers on the picket lines. In rural, grower-dominated counties, the sheriffs either looked on approvingly or arrested strikers and carted them off to jail. Ingracia still remembers vividly a priest telling her that her own arrest was an act of conscience and that God was on the side of the poor.

But when Juan de la Cruz and Nagi Daifullah were gunned down on the picket line, César Chávez called off the strike. The union sent some of the strikers to reorganize the grape boycott in cities across the United States and Canada, but most went back to the fields to find work, having spent months on the picket lines. And they discovered the unpleasant reality of the blacklist.

For grape workers like the Castillos, Freedman was the only company where the union still had the right to dispatch workers to the job—and it was the only company that would hire them. For twenty-one years, that right kept them employed—José as a permanent worker, Ingracia as a seasonal one—and provided stability for their family. It helped them buy a house in a pleasant neighborhood in Coachella. Their children went to college, a rare achievement for farmworkers.

It was the blacklist that made Freedman the vibrant heart of the union.

The workers at Freedman, despite their many skirmishes with Steinberg over work rules and grievances, looked at the company almost as if it were their own. "All the people who had the consciousness that the union was a good thing were concentrated there," José asserts. "And with that consciousness, Freedman was very well organized. Lots of workers would tell us it was the best place to be. It had the best benefits, and it had job security. In other companies, if you weren't working, you were afraid to even leave the house to go on an errand, because they might call you to give you work. In Freedman, we knew when we were going in to work and when we would leave. We didn't have to please anyone today to get work tomorrow."

When Governor Jerry Brown signed California's Agricultural Labor Relations Act in 1975, the vote at Freedman to decide whether or not workers wanted the union was a celebration, whereas at most other companies it was like a war. More than nine hundred workers voted for the UFW at Freedman. Only fourteen voted against it.

As the years passed, Steinberg's son, Dilly, left farming and went to Hollywood to become a songwriter. Lionel finally sold most of the ranch to new investors, including Prudential Insurance, who renamed it Bluestone Farming Company.

When Bluestone closed, the Freedman workers applied for benefits under the NAFTA-related Trade Adjustment Assistance (TAA) program. A bone thrown to workers during the debate over the treaty, NAFTA-TAA extends unemployment benefits and pays for retraining for workers who can demonstrate that NAFTA cost them their jobs.

Hundreds of workers at Bluestone depended on getting seasonal work every year thinning and picking grapes and pruning, tying, and girdling the vines. But the California Employment Development Department (EDD) ruled that, out of the entire workforce, only forty-three people were eligible for benefits—everyone except the permanent year-round workers was disqualified. José got a little extra money as a result, but not much.

EDD's rationale was that the company's layoff notice was dated January 7, a few days before the seasonal crews would have been called to begin pruning vines. Because they were on layoff and not yet actively working at the time of the notice, EDD held that they didn't qualify. Ingracia and hundreds of other workers received no benefit at all from NAFTA-TAA, although no one—not EDD, the U.S. Labor Department, or even the company itself—disputes that Mexican grape imports allowed under NAFTA caused the company to close.

EDD will not discuss the case, but its claim of confidentiality seems an odd objection. The EDD office does virtually nothing to let workers know that the program even exists. The workers laid off from Bluestone had to discover it for themselves, and they subsequently took on the burden of collecting money and buying radio time to ask potentially eligible workers to come forward and apply through the union.

In Coachella, José Castillo was unemployed for a year after being laid off. He applied at all the other grape companies but never got a call. He finally found work at a golf course.

Ingracia was hired, with a number of other Chavistas from Bluestone, by Bagdasarian, a big nonunion grape grower. But when the supervisor of their crew found out that they were all ex-Freedman workers, their jobs suddenly disappeared.

According to Gus Romero, the UFW representative in the valley at the time, "The safety net just wasn't there to catch them."

In fact, EDD seemed much more interested in holding down the number of claims, to avoid embarrassing California governor Pete Wilson. The governor, of course, had claimed that NAFTA would produce hundreds of thousands of jobs, although his administration's own statistics were proving the opposite.

Wilson wasn't the only public official facing embarrassment. Many congressional representatives, including some liberal Democrats, had been wooed and won by the same job promises. While the agreement was being debated, corporate executives of companies belonging to USA•NAFTA, the business coalition formed to back the agreement, walked the halls of Congress, wearing red, white, and blue neckties. They made extravagant claims that U.S. exports to Mexico would add 100,000 jobs in its first year alone. Yet even these boosters could document only 535 U.S. jobs actually created by the agreement in 1994, a figure also cited in "NAFTA's First Year: Lessons for the Hemisphere," a December 1994 report edited by Sarah Anderson et al., sponsored by the Alliance for Responsible Trade, the Citizens Trade Campaign, and the Trade Research Consortium.

Except for NAFTA's boosters, everyone else also documents a hemorrhaging of jobs. In the first year of the treaty, the U.S. Department of Labor received claims for NAFTA-TAA from 34,799 workers, including those from Bluestone. In only the first five months of 1995, another 34,000 applied. These applications had to be certified both by the U.S. Department of Labor and by state unemployment offices. Like EDD, the Department of Labor had a vested interest in keeping the numbers of certified claims low, since President Clinton had also promised thousands of new jobs in order to get the treaty through Congress.

In California, 3,457 workers applied for NAFTA-TAA in the year and a half after the treaty went into effect. This number is very low, in the opinion of many employment experts, because most workers who lose their jobs are not aware of the program. The unemployment office and employers themselves do little to publicize it. Unless workers have a union, few are knowledgeable enough to apply. Further, the applications of people like the seasonal workers at Bluestone simply aren't counted.

Nevertheless, of the 3,457 laid-off California workers who did apply during that period, only 914 were certified by the U.S. Department of Labor.

California's experience was echoed in Kingstree, South Carolina, when Baxter International laid off 830 workers after sending their jobs out of the country. The Department of Labor certified the claims of 120 of those workers, agreeing that their jobs had gone to Mexico. But it asserted that the rest of the jobs had gone to Asia, and it therefore rejected the claims of 610 workers.

In Eatonstown, New Jersey, fifty workers at Allied Signal lost their
jobs in March 1994. When they applied for NAFTA-TAA, they were
also rejected, even though some of them had actually been sent to train
their counterparts at the company's plant in Monterrey, Mexico, and
Mexican managers had been trained in New Jersey. Allied Signal workers had reason to be bitter. The CEO of their company, Lawrence
Bossidy, was the chair of USA•NAFTA. While NAFTA was being
debated on the floor of Congress, Bossidy had directly denied, on television, any intention of moving Allied Signal jobs south.

The production of many well-known manufactured items shifted to
Mexico in 1994. The list includes KeyTronic computer keyboards (277
jobs lost in Washington), Matsushita televisions (295 jobs in Illinois), Nin-
tendo games (136 jobs in Washington), Oxford shirts (435 jobs in Geor-
gia), Sara Lee sweatshirts (245 jobs in Georgia), Woolrich sportswear (500
jobs in Pennsylvania and Colorado), and Zenith televisions (430 jobs in
Missouri). California companies certified by the U.S. Department of
Labor for NAFTA-related layoffs include Formglas, Canon Business
Machines, Xentek, Baltimore Aircoil, A&W Brands, ITT Cannon,
Kyocera International, American Metal Products, Plantronics, Bluestone,
Hughes Aircraft, and Amphenol.

And one other—Boscovich Farms.

South of Riverside, in Perris, the workers at Boscovich had to fight their
way into the NAFTA-TAA program. No one keeps count of all the
farmworkers who have, for whatever reason, lost their jobs. But only
Bluestone and Boscovich workers applied for NAFTA-TAA—because
they had an organization to help them. At Bluestone, workers had the
UFW. Boscovich farmworkers never had a union. But they did have the
Hermandad Mexicana Nacional, the Mexican National Brotherhood, a
grassroots community organization that fights for civil rights and social
services.

Over the years, some of the 170 Boscovich workers who cultivated
and picked green onions in the Perris Valley had participated in community campaigns organized by the Hermandad. The biggest had been

the fight with the city council to rename the town library after César Chávez.

On January 17, 1995, all the Boscovich workers received letters saying that the company was ending its operations in Perris and was laying them off. They knew that the Hermandad office was the place to go.

In the local newspaper, Phil Boscovich, vice president of Boscovich Farms, blamed the water district, claiming that it was taking back land for the Domenigoni Valley Reservoir, land that had been leased by the company. The district, according to Boscovich, wouldn't guarantee a continued flow of water to irrigate the land that was left.

Workers knew, however, that Boscovich, with offices in Oxnard, California, also farmed in Arizona and in the Sonoran Desert below the border. "We got really suspicious," recalls Luz María Ayala, who directs the Hermandad's Perris office, "when we saw irrigation pumps being taken out at night and driven away on trucks."

In 1993, Ayala had traveled to Washington, D.C., with a delegation led by legendary civil rights leader Bert Corona, to lobby against NAFTA. She understood the effect the treaty would have and anticipated that she would see its results in her own community. She didn't have to wait long.

Ayala, her husband, Antonio (a fellow Hermandad coordinator), and Jesús González, a retired Boscovich worker, decided to follow the trucks. Their search led them to San Luis Río Colorado, a small farmworker town at the eastern edge of the Mexicali Valley, just across the border from Arizona's Gila River Valley. There, they found onion packing sheds—and workers who told them about Boscovich's operations. Armed with that information, Ayala went to the U.S. Department of Labor. Eventually, Boscovich personnel manager John Bautista admitted that the lost production had gone to Mexico, and the Department of Labor agreed.

Even then, the Boscovich workers had to fight against the EDD office in nearby Hemet, which they say mistreated them. "EDD never told anyone about TAA," Ayala says. "They think that because farmworkers are immigrants from Mexico, we have no right to unemployment [benefits]. If we hadn't fought for TAA, if we hadn't made our own investigation, we would have received nothing."

But Ayala explains that the fight was about more than TAA. "We're trying to wake people up, to make them more conscious, so there'll be a change. We're Mexicans and immigrants, but we live here now. We have to take care of this country. No one else is doing it."

CHILDREN IN THE FIELDS

From a distance, Muranaka Farms' green onion field, in the heart of the Mexicali Valley, looks almost festive. Dozens of large colored sheets are strung between pieces of iron rebar, providing shelter from the sun and rippling in the morning breeze. The soft conversations of hundreds of people, sitting in the rows next to great piles of scallions, fill the air. The vegetable's pungent scent is everywhere.

Small toddlers wander among the seated workers, some of the children nursing on baby bottles and others, their faces smeared with dirt, chewing on the onions. A few sleep in the rows or in little makeshift beds of blankets in the vegetable bins.

A closer look reveals that the toddlers are not the only children in this field. As the morning sun illuminates the faces of the workers, it reveals dozens of young girls and boys. By rough count, perhaps a quarter of the workers here are anywhere from six or seven years old to fifteen or sixteen. The crew foreman, who doesn't want to reveal his name, says it's normal for his three-hundred-person crew to be made up of families, including many kids. He says they work for Muranaka Farms.

The year is 1996. NAFTA has been in effect for more than a year.

This field is where Muranaka transferred its onion harvest, after shutting down its operation near Oxnard and Coachella. The surrounding valley here is dotted with other farms, also runaways from southern California.

Gema López Limón moves slowly down the rows. She has a slight limp, which makes her steps careful and deliberate. She is a stranger to the families seated here in the dirt, but she's obviously not a very threatening one.

She stops next to María, a child who is working alongside her mother, and talks to her softly. María is twelve years old. "My grandmother told me this year that we didn't have enough money for me to go to school," she explains. "At first, I stayed home to take care of my little sister, but it was boring, and sometimes I was scared being by ourselves all day. So I came to work here. We need the money."

López takes careful note of what María says. López is a well-known investigator of child labor in Mexico, a professor in the school of education at the Autonomous University of Baja California in Mexicali. She has an easy way with children. They talk to her as if she is a relative, or someone who has just come over from the next field.

López moves on down the row.

Honorina Ruiz is six years old. She sits in front of a pile of green onions in the same field. She notices López coming toward her, but she keeps working, grabbing onions from the top of her pile to make a bunch. In a little gesture of self-consciousness, she pulls her sweater away from her face.

Her hands are very quick. She lines up eight or nine onions, straightening out their roots and tails. Then she knocks the dirt off, puts a rubber band around them, and adds the bunch to those already in the box beside her. She's too shy to say more than her name, but she's obviously proud to be able to perform a task at which her brother Rigoberto, at thirteen, working near her, already excels.

López talks to Honorina's mother for a few minutes and then moves on again.

In another onion field about a mile away, López finds another crew. Here Lorena, also twelve, works in an even larger group of five hundred people. She's here with her sisters Lupe and Cynthia; her mother, María; and her little brother Agustín, who at four years old is too young to work. Lorena says she's been coming to the fields every year for seven years, beginning at the same age as Honorina. "I finished first grade in primary school," she tells López, "but then I left." Her mother adds that she tried to send Lorena back to school, "but what I can earn here by myself isn't enough for us to live on, so she had to come help us."

According to foreman Samuel Cerna, this field, in Ejido San Quintan, is being farmed by Mario Cota. Cerna explains that Cota farms only in the Mexicali Valley but has work for the crew for seven months of the year. All the onions are packed in ice and sent to California and Great Britain. Although Cota would not be interviewed, the secretary in his office reports that he contracts with three U.S. growers and that he denies that children work in his fields.

That this denial is not very convincing is in large part a result of the work done by López and a small core of human rights activists over the past five years. In her tours of the fields, López is often accompanied by another well-known opponent of child labor, Federico García Estrada, who in 1996 was the human rights prosecutor for the state of Baja California. Other Mexican states have human rights commissions. But in Baja California, human rights violations have the status of offenses, meriting a separate prosecutor's office.

García and the lawyers and other personnel who work with him have won broad popular support for that office. It hasn't made this tall, lanky lawyer very popular with the conservative National Action Party (PAN, Partido de Acción Nacional), which governs Baja California. But the support he has garnered among the people has made him a voice to be respected.

Together, López, García, and their *compañeros* are trying to mobilize public pressure on the Mexican government to enforce its own child protection laws.

Child labor is not legal in Mexico, any more than it is in the United States. Article 123 of the Mexican Constitution proclaims that children under the age of fourteen may not work and limits the work time of those between the ages of fourteen and sixteen to six hours a day. Article 22 of the Federal Labor Law also prohibits the employment of children younger than fourteen and permits those between fourteen and sixteen to work only by special permission, if they have already completed their mandatory education.

But according to López, child labor is growing, as a result of the country's successive economic crises and the rise in export-oriented agriculture. Joint ventures between Mexican and U.S. growers, producing for the U.S., European, and Japanese markets, "are achieving greater competitiveness at the cost of children working in the fields," she observes. "We're creating a workforce without education, condemned to the lowest wages and to periods of great unemployment."

Although no official statistics are collected on the number of these working children, the Mexican government's Secretariat of Labor and Social Forecasting estimates that eight hundred thousand children under the age of fourteen work in different sectors of the economy. Based on the 1990 census, the Secretariat of Public Education guesses that more than 2.5 million children between the ages of six and fourteen do not attend school.

According to López and García, three thousand children work in the green onion harvest in the Mexicali Valley. Beginning in October and running through June, the season coincides with the school year and has a dramatic impact on school attendance. While the population of the valley grows—the city of Mexicali itself now boasts more than six hundred thousand inhabitants—the number of children in rural schools decreases almost every year.

The Alfredo A. Uchurtu primary school draws its students from Ejido Veracruz II, in the heart of the green onion district. Teacher Pedro González Hernández is another seasoned veteran of the fight to keep children out of the fields. It's a fight they're not winning, he says. Of the 252 students who registered at Uchurtu in September 1996, more than 40 were no longer coming to school at all by the end of the season.

González talks while seated at his desk in front of a room full of second graders. As he cuts decorations out of red construction paper for the classroom, he punctuates his points with jabs of the scissors. "Attendance began to fall in 1987, when the school had 363 children," he recalls. "That's the year we had the first economic collapse."

In rural Mexico, the word *maestro*, or teacher, is more than a job title. It's a sign of the respect conveyed by rural communities, which view teachers as leaders and spokespersons. For the best teachers, like González, the title is a badge of social activism. Schools are resources communities must fight for. Teachers, who are some of the lowest-paid workers in Mexico, typically use part of their salaries to buy supplies like notebooks and pencils. They are also the people who collect whatever statistics exist on rural communities, especially concerning children.

Of the sixteen boys in Uchurtu's sixth grade, seven come to class only two or three times a week, as do three of the eleven girls. "For these children, we've tried to devise a kind of study they can do at home," González says. "It will never be as good as actually attending class, but at least it's some alternative."

Even in May, the temperature in the Mexicali Valley climbs to 100 degrees, and the afternoon heat radiates up from Uchurtu's playground. A few trees provide shade for the school's ten low-slung buildings, which look a little like the portable classrooms often seen in the United States. Some of the buildings aren't used anymore because of declining enrollment, and nighttime vandalism of the empty structures created a problem for the school. But the community found a family to live in one of the unused buildings, and the problem disappeared. González believes that keeping the school's appearance from deteriorating helps to maintain the morale of the students and makes the school more attractive to them.

Teachers in Baja California have tried other ways to keep children in school. They convinced the state government to offer stipends of 118 pesos a month, plus food coupons, to rural children who would otherwise have to work. Twenty-five kids at Uchurtu get the *beca*, and all of them are still in class. But there aren't enough stipends, and rumors persist that children of government functionaries take some of them. The schools were slated to begin serving breakfast to the children, but the program has been held up by red tape.

"We have to admit," González concedes, "that not only can't they come, but that often they don't want to. With all the problems they've had in keeping up, when they do come, they face a lot of blame."

Presiliano Martínez, a rural teacher at the Escuela Aquiles Serdán in neighboring Colonia Elias, cautions that "if you scold the children for the times when they don't come to school, then they just don't come back at all." But Martínez doesn't agree with González about formulating curricula for part-time attendees. "They must come every day," he asserts. He seems less an activist and more a man trying to hold on to the educational values and principles of his own youth.

Martínez's school once had a teacher for each of six grades. Now there are only three teachers. Aquiles Serdán is older than Uchurtu and has a large, ornate adobe building with the name proudly emblazoned above the door. But the building is unused, and the actual classrooms are smaller, cinder block boxes.

At a countryside crossroads in Colonia Madero, a third school sits in the corner of a ploughed field. The furrows come up to the edge of the two small buildings. This school has been abandoned entirely. "The people went away, looking for work, and the school was left without children. At last, the teacher had only two left, and they closed it," a neighbor told López.

"We realize that what drives the children into the fields is that the wages their parents receive [aren't] enough to support the family," González comments bitterly. "We're not dreaming we can end this. But we have to do something."

The companies pay 80 or 81 centavos (11 cents U.S. in 1996) for a dozen bunches of onions. For an adult, this can amount to 50 pesos on a good day. A young child might produce twenty or thirty dozen bunches—half the total produced by an adult.

Workers in the fields report that the growers don't raise the piece rate from year to year, despite big price increases for groceries. In January 1995, the price of a gallon of milk was 7 pesos. It rose to 15 pesos a year later, and to 17.50 in 1997. A gallon of milk that year cost almost half a day's wages for an adult. In 1995, the price of a chicken went from 4 to 10 pesos. A kilo (two pounds) of beans used to cost 3.50 pesos; in 1997, it cost 9.

At the height of the season, families sometimes stay out in the fields until dark, just to earn enough to eat. "We start work," Lorena says, "at

five-thirty in the morning, and we work at least until four." Adults and
children work the same hours. There is no overtime pay, except for
work on Sunday. When children start out working with their families,
they work under a parent's employee number. But by the age of twelve
or thirteen, according to López, children usually have their own number and are paid separately.

The Mexicali Valley extends south from the southern borders of California and Arizona. It is the southern end of the same valley that rises
to the San Gorgonio Pass, 50 miles north of Coachella and 150 miles
north of Mexico. It's all an irrigated desert; without the water of the
Colorado River, there would be no farms on either side of the border.

Despite the cloth shelters in the fields, the temperature gets brutally
hot during the day in the late spring, and in the winter it can go down to
freezing. In the Muranaka and Cota fields, one portable bathroom was
provided for the whole crew. A metal drum on wheels held drinking water.

Conditions for workers in the Mexicali Valley resemble those suf-
fered by farmworkers in California before the era of the United Farm
Workers, as the Castillos describe. This makes the valley a magnet for
California growers.

Boscovich Farms, with headquarters in Oxnard, is only one of a number of U.S. row crop producers who now have operations in Mexico.
Growers from Salinas and Watsonville who also farm green onions in
the Mexicali Valley include Fresh Choice, Frank Capurro, VegaMix,
and Nunes Farms. Arizona-based Phoenix Vegetable Growers has
moved across the border, as has Muranaka, which also comes from
Oxnard.

According to Juan Pablo Hernández Díaz, president of the Agricultural Association of Vegetable Producers of the Mexicali Valley (Asociación Agricola de Productares de Hortalizas del Valle de Mexicali),
most U.S. growers contract with a local Mexican grower, providing
chemicals and loans, agreeing to distribute and sell the boxes of green
onions at the wholesale market price. A few U.S. companies, Hernández
says, run their own Mexican operations or have formed joint ventures
with Mexican growers.

Carisa Wright of Muranaka Farms explains that the company farms on both sides of the border, mostly on its own, but sometimes by contract. In Mexico, it has operations in the Mexicali Valley, in Sonoita in Sonora, and in Maneadero, farther down the Baja peninsula. The company's vegetables, which include green onions, spinach, radishes, cilantro, parsley, kale, leeks, and beets, are processed in the packing sheds of the Empacadora Toluca in the heart of the green onion district.

Wright describes Muranaka's operations in Mexico as profitable and expanding. She declined to provide figures, but Mexican observers calculate that gross receipts to a grower from a hectare of green onions may reach 25,500 pesos (3,600 dollars in 1996). Some ten thousand hectares of the Mexicali Valley are planted in green onions, which can be planted and harvested twice a year. Sometimes the onions alternate with another vegetable, such as radishes. "Most of our operations are labor intensive, so we do save money on labor costs by comparison with the U.S.," Wright admits.

Muranaka management would not answer questions directly about their use of child labor. A letter from the company states that "as far as we know, our growers comply in the fullest with Mexican federal and state labor laws to the best of their abilities" and that, therefore, workers "are over the minimum legal working age."

At Fresh Choice, Greg Flood explains that the company doesn't consider itself responsible for the employment practices of the Mexican growers with whom it contracts, although he asserts that both his company and its Mexican partner obey all Mexican laws. He travels to the Mexicali Valley at least ten times a year. He has seen very young children, of nursing age, with their parents in the fields, which he attributes to the lack of child care. To him, the situation is similar to that of a hardware store owner who brings a son or daughter to work in the store.

Tom Nunes of the Nunes Company, a large vegetable grower in Salinas, uses the same Mexican contractor as Fresh Choice. The Mexican grower grows and packs the green onions in ice and sends them to the Nunes coolers in Salinas and Yuma. Nunes sells the onions at market prices and then deducts the cost of seeds, cartons, loading, and customs duties, as well as a charge for selling the onions, which he estimates at about a penny per bunch. What's left belongs to the Mexican grower.

Asked whether he would consider charging an extra penny a bunch to his customers, in order to raise the wages paid to field workers, Nunes responds that "a penny is what we charge for selling them. There's no incentive for us to do that." He adds that he can't tell his Mexican partner how to run his business.

"There are no green onions grown now in the U.S. in the winter, because they can't compete with the price of those grown in Mexico," Nunes says. "I wouldn't go over there if this competition didn't exist. It was a problem before NAFTA to some extent, but what's really causing this is the devaluation of the peso. What people are [earning in Mexico] is nothing. The power of the market is stronger than all of us."

Hernández, the president of the producers association, agrees that devaluation was a shot in the arm for the Mexican industry, which he says was in danger of disappearing. In 1996, he estimated, the green onion harvest in the Mexicali Valley had a wholesale value of $50 million—about 12 million cartons selling for three to five dollars apiece, with the Mexican growers receiving one to two dollars for each box.

Hernández considers the crop a boon to the valley's residents, claiming that it has provided nearly year-round employment since growers began planting green onions in 1966. Before that, workers were employed only during the cotton harvest, which provided jobs for a few months in the summer. In the off-season, they had to leave the valley and migrate to follow other crops. At the beginning of the 1990s, however, the cotton harvest failed. Families began to migrate again, and Hernández says that families began going hungry again, too.

To Hernández, the problem of child labor stems from the lack of child care. "We could prohibit parents from bringing their children to the fields," he says, "but then we'd have a bigger problem. Kids would be left by themselves."

He admits, however, that Mexico's worsening economic crisis left parents feeling that there was no future for their children. "If there are no jobs for educated people," he asks, "or what an educated person can earn is less than what a family earns in the fields, what kind of future is there? When parents see engineers selling tacos for a living, why should they invest money they don't have anyway in sending their kids to school?"

"What makes our country attractive to U.S. growers," López responds, "are low wages. We're told that if we make our country attractive enough for foreign investment, transnational corporations will come here to invest in greater productivity. Supposedly, that will lift us out of poverty. But does it? That investment produces wealth we never see. Meanwhile, we're stuck with miserable economic conditions."

Mexicali Valley agriculture, dependent on exports and the U.S. market, is a showcase for this economic policy, called structural adjustment, which is promoted by the Mexican and U.S. governments and the International Monetary Fund. The policy uses depressed wages to attract investment. To keep wages low, the government finds subsidies, López says. Some are indirect, such as meals for rural children and the stipends that keep them in school. But the government also directly subsidizes some costs for growers, such as the expense of water for irrigation, which is much cheaper in Mexicali than it is just across the border in the Imperial Valley.

"What we need," López concludes, "is to produce food first for people to eat in Mexico, where people are actually hungry. No one eats these green onions here. If we have extra capacity to produce food after feeding ourselves, we can export the rest to the U.S. or anywhere else. These foreign companies bring jobs here to the fields. But what kind of jobs are they? They're jobs with no future."

Rural teacher González argues that structural adjustment also means that Mexicans lose control over the rules of their own society. "Our laws say one thing, for instance, about child labor, but the reality is another, and everyone knows it. The companies may create jobs, but they [should] pay [higher wages] so it doesn't have these consequences for children."

The analysis developed by López, González, García, and activists on the border is not simply rhetoric. They demand solutions. In March

1996, López went to Mexico City, bringing her accusations before the second International Independent Tribunal Against Child Labor. She brought children from the fields with her, to make sure that the human face of child labor wasn't lost.

"Trade agreements like NAFTA promised protections for workers," López testified. "But they don't prohibit child labor—they regulate it."

The tribunal brought witnesses from eighteen countries to the huge auditorium of Mexico's largest hospital, the social security health complex located in the capital. The explosive testimony of children made headlines in Mexico City newspapers and sparked earnest television commentaries. It was a high point, after years of documenting the hardships in the green onion fields.

The tribunal concluded that the economic forces responsible for the growth of child labor in Mexico had had the same effect in many countries. The number of working children globally has climbed to more than 150 million. In a document issued after three days of formal hearings, tribunal judges called for the ratification of the International Labour Organization's Convention 138, which outlaws labor by children of mandatory school age.

One of the principal organizers of the tribunal noted that international support for the convention was weakening under the impact of the marketplace. María Estela Ríos González, then president of Mexico's National Association of Democratic Lawyers, leveled accusations of hypocrisy at supporters of the free market. "They oppose every kind of regulation on business, especially where the labor of children is involved," she declared.

To weaken the International Labour Organization's blanket prohibition of child labor, the United Nations formulated another convention in 1989. Convention 32 leaves it up to each government to determine the age at which child labor is permitted and to regulate the circumstances under which children work. Many countries that refused to ratify Convention 138 have adopted the U.N. approach.

"Instead of saying that we should recognize that child labor exists, and therefore regulate it, I believe it should be eliminated," Ríos says.

"We cannot substitute the labor of countless children for the inadequate income of their parents. For all the history of humanity, adults have been the protectors and nurturers of children. Now we have children nurturing and protecting the adults. We are robbing them of their own future."

2

PUTTING SOLIDARITY ON THE TABLE

THE IMPACT OF NAFTA

When Luz María Ayala and the workers from Boscovich Farms followed the irrigation pumps from the company's Perris Valley property to the green onion fields on the other side of the border in Mexico to investigate the disappearance of jobs, they were responding to one of the raw realities of a globalized economy. Employers today can move production between the United States and Mexico much more freely than at any time in the past. And the Mexican economy has been transformed to make the process even easier—NAFTA itself is only part of much larger, overarching economic changes.

The Boscovich workers resisted simply becoming victims of these changes. As much as they could, within the confines of forces over which they had no control, they sought to take action to change their situation. At the very least, they believed, they were owed the promised legal benefits, to ease the wrenching transition they faced as their jobs disappeared.

To get those benefits, they had to cross the border. They had to find out where the production had gone, had to prove that their jobs still existed even though they themselves were no longer employed to perform them. That trip to the border transformed them from victims into actors, participants in a new movement of workers, unions, and communities who are grappling with this new reality and trying to change it.

On the Mexican side, Gema López Limón left her office on the campus of the University of Baja California to venture into the same green onion fields of the Mexicali Valley, a heartbeat away from the border. There, she documented the other side of the picture—the new jobs created when Boscovich and other growers moved production south. Like the workers from Perris, she was unwilling to allow herself or the children she found in those fields to simply become victims. Rather, she brought child workers to Mexico City to force her government to confront the reality of who, exactly, made up the labor force in this part of the new, export-driven economy.

From both directions, north and south, the border is like a magnet attracting activists. The movement of production and the new conditions it imposes on workers have become material forces bringing together activists from each side.

In addition, the border symbolizes the nature of the new economic reality. Production and jobs can move across it easily, but the people who perform those jobs cannot. The border, an imaginary line in the sand for most of its two-thousand-mile length, enforces vast differences in both standards of living and social and political rights.

Nowhere is this more visible than at the iron wall that divides Tijuana from San Diego. Though separated by less than a dozen miles, these two cities exist in completely different worlds.

When it rains in downtown San Diego or in its middle-class suburbs, the asphalt streets become shiny. The runoff is swiftly channeled down the storm drains and spills out into the Pacific Ocean.

In the hills of Tijuana, just a few miles south, rain creates a particularly sticky kind of mud called *barra*. Huge clumps cling to the shoes of anyone who sets foot in it. Cars traveling down the little dirt streets, where hundreds of thousands of Tijuanecos live, are immobilized. If vehicles start to move downhill at all, even at a snail's pace, they lose traction in the mud and slowly slide into another car, or a wall, or a hole in the road. And there they sit until the street dries out again.

When it rains, many of the tens of thousands of workers who pour into the maquiladoras every day begin their trip to work with a long trek through the mud to the nearest paved road to wait for a bus; others face an even longer walk, all the way to the factory. Most workers don't have cars.

The difference between one side of the border and the other is the difference between mud and sidewalk, walking and riding, poverty and wealth. The difference reflects the fact that, as Eduardo Badillo of the Border Region Workers' Support Committee (CAFOR, Comité de Apoyo Fronterizo de Obreros Regionales), points out, "a worker in Tijuana earns the same in a whole day's work [as] even an undocumented worker earns in an hour, just a few miles north."

"The increase in maquiladora production is unquestionable," says Harley Shaiken, professor of education and geography at the University of California at Berkeley and director of UCB's Center for Latin American Studies. "It's a great paradox that it's expanded so much while the rest of the Mexican economy was collapsing. But these factories combine first world quality with third world wages, all right next to the U.S. market. The productivity of maquiladoras rivals plants in the U.S. That's a very powerful incentive to companies to build factories along the border."

When the maquiladora program began in 1964, it was heavily restricted. From the end of the Mexican Revolution in 1920 through the early 1970s, the Mexican government had encouraged economic development by Mexican producers, making products for sale in Mexico. Foreign investment was strictly limited. The original intent of the maquiladora program, in fact, was focused on absorbing workers on the border who found themselves unemployed at the end of the bracero contract-labor program, which had brought thousands of temporary Mexican workers into the United States over the years.

Under pressure from an accumulating foreign debt, however, Mexican economic policy began to change. Government businesses were sold to private investors. U.S. companies were allowed to own land and factories anywhere in Mexico, without Mexican partners. Prices on basic goods were decontrolled, and government subsidies on food and services for workers and the poor were cut back or ended altogether. In 1998, the government dissolved CONASUPO, a system of state-run stores that sold basic foodstuffs such as tortillas and milk at subsidized low prices. At the same time, price supports for small corn growers were also ended.

Mexico was a laboratory for the economic reforms that have transformed the economies of developing countries, moving those countries away from policies that encourage national development and toward ones that open up the economy for transnational investors. Today, the Mexican economy looks nothing like it did twenty years ago.

"For the Mexican government, the revenue from maquiladora production is pivotal," Shaiken explains. "Maquiladoras furnish the second largest source of foreign exchange for the Mexican economy, after oil. This has created a culture in which anything favoring maquiladora production is emphasized, while the human cost is not addressed. The Mexican government has created an investment climate which depends on a vast number of low-wage earners. This climate gets all the government's attention, while the consumer climate—the ability of people to buy what they produce—is sacrificed."

The 1994 North American Free Trade Agreement was part of that process, designed to make it easier for foreign companies to move money and goods across the border. But relying on foreign investment didn't produce a stable economy. Instead, panicked U.S. speculators began selling off Mexican government bonds at the end of 1994. The newly inaugurated president, Ernesto Zedillo, trying to prevent a flood of money back to the north, was forced to devalue the peso almost immediately after he took office. From 3.1 pesos/dollar, the value of the peso fell immediately to 5.7. Interest rates climbed to 30 percent, as Zedillo agreed to a package of reforms mandated by the International Monetary Fund (IMF) as the price for a $20 billion bailout, organized by U.S. president Bill Clinton. Instead of producing growth and prosperity, Mexico lost a million jobs, by the government's count, in 1995, the year after NAFTA went into effect.

IMF conditions for the bailout included further privatization of national enterprises, measures to hold down inflation, and the use of oil revenues to guarantee repayment, making them unavailable for economic development. The Task Force on Trade of the AFL-CIO commented that the bailout provided "protection for speculative investors who placed more than $75 billion in Mexico."

No similar effort was made to help ordinary Mexican workers, who paid for the crisis with a steep decline in their standard of living. Prices rose at a government-estimated annual rate of 42 percent in 1994. A worker at the Zenith television factory in Reynosa, across the border from Texas, earned an average weekly wage of 135 pesos, worth $19.27. Daily bus fare to work alone was 3.5 pesos. That year, maquiladoras displaced tourism and oil as Mexico's top dollar earner, and their workforce grew by 6.2 percent, to six hundred thousand.

As predicted by NAFTA opponents, U.S. corn exports to Mexico in June 1994 increased 525 percent over the previous year, further undermining small Mexican farmers who grow corn for domestic consumption. At the same time, production of tomatoes by large-scale corporate farms in Mexico for export to the United States increased. One Florida grower, Regency Packing, finally declared bankruptcy in the face of this competition, leaving more than a thousand U.S. workers without jobs. Florida Rural Legal Assistance lawyer Rob Williams explained that retraining programs wouldn't help these workers because there are no other jobs in the area. "Retraining for what?" he asked. Laid-off tomato pickers "go to a big parking lot and wait for a bus to come and take them to the fields. If they're lucky, they can get on a bus."

Other companies began deliberately shifting production to Mexico, and U.S. job losses began to mount. The Zenith plant in Missouri, the last television factory in the United States, had once employed as many as four thousand workers. In 1987, its workforce agreed to an 8.2 percent wage cut to keep the plant open. "The story going around the plant was, if you didn't give them wage concessions, they were going to move to Mexico," remembered Lionel Hudspeth, a line inspector. The company left anyway, closing its doors to the remaining four hundred workers on

February 24, 1995. Zenith is now one of the largest maquiladora employers on the border.

The same intimidation was used by the Leviton Company in Rhode Island, which threatened to move production of electrical outlets to Mexico. As a result, members of the International Brotherhood of Electrical Workers agreed to a contract with a wage freeze for two years and twelve-hour shifts paid at straight-time rates.

According to "NAFTA at Seven," a 2001 report by the Economic Policy Institute, "NAFTA eliminated 766,030 actual and potential U.S. jobs between 1994 and 2000 because of the rapid growth in the net U.S. export deficit with Mexico and Canada." In "Rethinking the NAFTA Record," published by the Institute for Policy Studies, Sarah Anderson and John Cavanagh report that between the time NAFTA took effect in 1994 and May 2002, the U.S. Department of Labor certified 403,000 U.S. workers for NAFTA-TAA benefits because the treaty cost them their jobs.

The picture wasn't any brighter for Canadians, who had the additional disadvantage of living under the U.S./Canada Free Trade Agreement for four years before NAFTA came on line. During that entire period, the official unemployment rate in Canada did not drop below 10 percent. In 1995, Canadian manufacturing employed 365,000 fewer people than in 1989, a drop of 18 percent. Ontario alone saw almost seven hundred permanent plant closures during the same six-year period.

In an analysis of NAFTA's impact after its first full year, the Institute for Policy Studies pointed to three factors causing job loss in the United States. First, a $3.9 billion U.S. trade surplus with Mexico in 1992 turned into a $2.1 billion deficit in the first two months of 1995 alone. Auto imports increased by thirty-six thousand cars, while the peso devaluation, which made U.S. goods in Mexico more expensive, practically wiped out auto exports from the United States.

Second, exports don't always produce jobs. In the five industries that account for most exports to Mexico—electrical equipment, machinery, transportation equipment, chemicals, and primary metals—more than

1.5 million jobs disappeared from 1980 to 1995, while exports by these industries increased.

Third, NAFTA in fact accelerated the export of capital rather than the export of goods and services. Foreign investment in Mexican plants and equipment, mostly from the United States, grew by $8 billion in the first half of 1994. General Electric's Mexican plants alone increased their sales in 1994 by 18 percent, to $1 billion. CEO Jack Welch told *Business Week* that General Electric's future would lie in Mexico.

"The last year and a half is the proof that the North American Free Trade Agreement is a bad model for development," concluded Harry Brown of Albuquerque's Interhemispheric Resource Center in 1996. "We need to do more than knock down tariffs."

Clearly, NAFTA alone can't be blamed for Mexico's economic crisis and the devaluation of the peso, for U.S. trade-related unemployment, or for the continuing lack of protection for workers, communities, and the environment along the border. But critics of the agreement point out that NAFTA liberalized trade without changing social and political conditions.

In the wake of Mexico's economic crisis, the northbound stream of workers from Tijuana across the U.S. border not only has continued but grown. The ten-foot iron wall separating Tijuana from San Ysidro spreads east along the border—a potent symbol of the U.S. government's attitude toward poor Mexicans, denying hungry people the same free passage NAFTA extended to money and goods. While a river of trucks also travels north, bearing the products of the border factories, Mexican workers who are caught in the United States, trying to find a better standard of living than the maquiladoras are willing to support, are deported back to the south, in a reverse flow.

The border crossing on Tijuana's Otay Mesa is next to one of the largest concentrations of maquiladoras on the border. Here, hour after hour, bus after silver bus, each bearing the Border Patrol seal, pulls into the customs and trade zone from the north. Each bus discharges a long line of people, mostly young men and women in jeans, T-shirts, and tennis shoes. They slowly shuffle back into Mexico, in front of a line of

National Guard troops in camouflage uniforms, automatic rifles posted at port arms.

The border has become NAFTA's symbol. In Tijuana, it's not hard to see the price of free trade. Maquiladora development lays waste to entire communities, and workers who want to change terrible conditions in the factories face enormous difficulties.

Yet the border isn't only a showcase for NAFTA's victims. It is also the birthplace of a new strategy of cross-border organizing. In an economy in which the production and capital of transnational corporations traverse borders with impunity, as though national barriers don't exist, cross-border solidarity has become crucial to unions and communities on both sides, to the preservation of millions of jobs, and to achieving a standard of living commensurate with the vast wealth produced.

THE CONTEXT OF THE CROSS-BORDER MOVEMENT

Cities like Tijuana and Juárez recall scenes of Detroit or Pittsburgh during decades past. Hundreds of thousands of workers stream through factory gates each shift change—a human wave that pours into communities of cardboard houses and dirt streets, where the expectation of a better life is on a collision course with harsh economic reality. The ability of workers to cooperate across the border here, which decades ago was primarily an ideological question, has now become one of survival.

During the decades following World War Two, U.S. unions exhibited little concern about conditions in Mexico. But as U.S. plants began to close and companies moved south, interest in the Mexican labor movement grew. The campaign against NAFTA provoked a profound debate among workers across the United States, a debate that surged up from union halls and workplaces, prodding U.S. workers into an extensive reexamination of their relations with their Mexican counterparts. Coalitions of unions, churches, community organizations, and environmentalists began to look for ways of establishing new relationships with Mexican workers and activists.

In Mexico during the same postwar period, workers were tied to an official, corporatist union structure. Most Mexican unions functioned as a support apparatus for the government's political and economic policies. But as those policies have come to depend increasingly on using low wages to encourage foreign investment, more militant trends in Mexican labor have grown stronger to challenge them.

Through bailout and loan conditions, the U.S. government enforces a low-wage policy on the Mexican economy, with the Mexican government's active cooperation, in order to encourage maquiladora construction. As a result, labor conflicts have broken out in plant after plant for the past decade, from one end of the border to the other. And as those conflicts have grown more frequent and intense, a movement to support the workers involved has been painstakingly organized to the north, in the United States and Canada.

This cross-border solidarity movement goes beyond providing immediate material support for embattled workers. As maquiladora-style production transforms the economies of developing countries such as Mexico, this movement in response has become a proving ground for a new model of international relationships between the workers and unions of various countries.

Today, solidarity across the U.S./Mexico border is developing in many regions, among different groups of workers, using a variety of strategies. These new cross-border campaigns share a general democratic and grassroots character that differentiates them clearly from labor's old top-down, cold war approach to international relations. One of their great strengths is that they give a voice to workers themselves.

Links between labor in both countries have become an important source of support for independent (non-government-affiliated) unions in Mexico. Meanwhile, the ties binding Mexican unions to their government's pro-investment policies are unraveling, giving rise to a new movement that proposes greater democracy and a fight against declining living standards. Mexican workers fighting for economic development that gives people a better life instead of impoverishing them are beginning to see some U.S. unions, churches, and community activists as potential allies.

Cross-border solidarity is not really new. The Flores Magón brothers planned the first battles of the Mexican Revolution with supporters from the Industrial Workers of the World in St. Louis and Los Angeles. Jailed by the U.S. government on political charges, they paid with imprisonment and death in Leavenworth prison. During the 1930s, in the heady days when the largest industrial unions in U.S. history were being organized, Vicente Lombardo Toledano and Latin American labor radicals built ties between progressive union federations from Canada to Central America.

These traditions were largely forgotten after World War Two. Instead, the international apparatus of the AFL-CIO promoted the defense of U.S. cold war foreign policy and corporate interests, along with domestic hostility to immigrants and radicals. As a consequence, when NAFTA created a crisis that called for a common front of labor in the United States, Canada, and Mexico, U.S. workers and unions had to start building it from scratch.

U.S. labor's involvement in cold war foreign policy and its anti-immigrant positions had not created a legacy of good relations across the border, however. Solidarity activists today confront a great deal of well-deserved suspicion in Mexico as a result. But a new leadership in the AFL-CIO in recent years has at least proclaimed a more internationalist ideology and put forward a new set of guiding principles.

The AFL-CIO's cold war stance was unable to cope with the globalization of corporate activity, compromised as it was by its defense of free trade and U.S. foreign policy. Today, this stance is being challenged by a new alternative—solidarity from below. This newest vision of what the labor movement could become is being born not in an office in Washington or even in the streets of Seattle, but in shantytowns along the border.

This vision is a product of profound movement from labor's rank and file. Throughout two decades of wrenching industrial restructuring, plant closures, relocations, and the growth of the low-wage service sector, U.S. workers have developed a deeper understanding of the need for solidarity. Many realize that they cannot successfully confront transnational corporations within the borders of the United States alone.

This change in consciousness, driven from below, is having a profound effect on labor's political direction. The aftermath of NAFTA taught millions of U.S. workers that government policies enforcing privatization and pro-corporate economic reforms at home and abroad lead to job losses. Challenging those policies will surely require cross-border cooperation and greater political independence.

Security is not national, but international.

THE CHALLENGE TO COLD WAR IDEOLOGY

Despite the end of the cold war, U.S. military, economic, and political intervention around the world continues to grow. At home, the military budget consumes the hopes for a radical reordering of economic priorities. The idea of a peace dividend is all but forgotten, as peace itself recedes farther away than ever on the global horizon.

In the wake of the attacks on the World Trade Center and the Pentagon on September 11, 2001, national security has become a pretext for the Bush administration to attack unions, strip away the rights of immigrants, and pursue an openly pro-corporate economic agenda. Fast track trade authorization to extend NAFTA throughout Latin America, which President Clinton failed to win from Congress, was presented by President Bush as a step in fighting terrorism abroad. His bullying succeeded. And a war in Iraq was justified by the new doctrine of "preemption"—the assertion that the United States is entitled to take military action against any country it views as a potential threat, even in the absence of any kind of overt aggression or threatening military action.

Although U.S. unions and workers increasingly challenge globalized production and free trade, many continue to accept the idea that a common national interest abroad should unite all segments of U.S. society, including labor and capital. National security, workers are told, is an overarching common bond.

But in a world divided between rich and poor, in which the security of the few is obtained and ensured at the expense of the many, the real question is—security for whom?

Do countries have a right to control their own economic development in the interest of their own security? Or should guaranteeing a free market, and unlimited opportunities for corporate profits, override national interests when economic decisions are being made?

The transformation of national economies around the world is forcing unions and workers everywhere to debate the meaning of international working-class solidarity—to ask who has the right to economic security. The cross-border solidarity movement is at the cutting edge of this debate.

These questions simmered in the U.S. labor movement throughout the Reagan administration's interventions in Central America, but they broke out into the open following the passage of NAFTA. In large part, the debate was forced onto the floors of union halls, into the sanctuaries of church congregations, and before the city councils of industrial communities by the job losses that followed the treaty's implementation. In addition to the lost jobs, workers were also facing increasing intimidation and coercion, according to Kate Bronfenbrenner, professor of labor studies at Cornell, who notes that documented instances of employer threats to move production out of the country if workers organized a union have more than doubled in the United States since NAFTA went into effect.

Insecurity for U.S. workers has led neither to more jobs in the United States nor to greater security for Mexicans, despite the promises of both governments. More than a million Mexican jobs were eliminated in 1995 alone, by the Mexican government's own count, even with the increased numbers of workers employed in maquiladoras.

Well before NAFTA's passage, the disparity between U.S. and Mexican wages was growing. Mexican salaries were a third of those in the United States until the 1970s. They are now less than an eighth, according to Mexican economist and former senator Rosa Albina Garabito. United Auto Workers international representative Steve Beckman estimates that since the 1981 debt crisis Mexican wages have dropped to as low as a twelfth or a fifteenth of U.S. wages, depending on the industry—even during a period in which U.S. wages have declined in buying power.

Over the past two decades, the income of Mexican workers has lost 76 percent of its purchasing power. Under pressure from foreign lenders, the Mexican government has ended subsidies for basic necessities, including gasoline, electricity, bus fares, tortillas, and milk; and prices have risen dramatically. The government estimates that 40 million people live in poverty, with 25 million in extreme poverty. And although it claims that unemployment is less than 6 percent, the country's new independent union federation, the National Union of Workers (Unión Nacional de Trabajadores), puts the number at more than 9 million people, or a quarter of the workforce.

These results are largely the product of the economic reforms imposed on Mexico by the IMF, backed up by conditions required by U.S. bank loans and bailouts. The most fundamental of those conditions, even beyond ending subsidies and opening the Mexican economy to imports, has been privatization of Mexican state enterprises and other policies designed to encourage foreign investment.

In countries like Mexico, with a mixed economy in which socialism was put forward as an eventual goal of economic development, a large percentage of workers historically have been employed by state enterprises. A majority of Mexican industrial workers worked for the government until economic reforms began transforming the economy in the 1970s. The greatest strength of the country's organized labor movement traditionally lay in the state sector.

Although three-quarters of the workforce in Mexico belonged to unions three decades ago, fewer than 30 percent of workers are union members today. In the state-owned oil company, Pemex, union membership still hovers at 72 percent. But when the collateral petrochemical industry was privatized over the past fifteen years, the unionization rate fell to 7 percent. New private owners reduced the membership of the railway workers union from ninety thousand workers to thirty-six thousand in the same period.

Loan conditions enforced by the IMF and the World Bank reflect U.S. economic policies, which encourage high unemployment to keep pressure on wages. U.S. and IMF loans are not available for social benefits—in fact, their conditions require ending the subsidies that finance such benefits. Instead, the loans are made for infrastructure improvements to encourage investment.

Those conditions required Mexico to reduce the money available for rural credit—driving people into the cities, while opening up the market for imports of food. At the 1996 World Food Summit in Rome, U.S. agriculture secretary Dan Glickman boasted that the United States "is the leading supplier of food to the world," where farmers "plant for world demand instead of for government programs." For the United States, "the private sector is the great untapped frontier in the world war on hunger."

To drive the point home, the U.S. position at the summit declared that "the United States believes that the attainment of any 'right to adequate food' or 'fundamental right to be free from hunger' is a goal or aspiration to be realized progressively that does not give rise to any international obligations." At the insistence of the United States, point four of the summit's plan of action was dedicated to the pursuit of "a fair and market-oriented world trade system," which, it admitted, may cause "short term negative effects" on the world's poorest countries.

No wonder poor corn farmers in Chiapas joined the Zapatista rebellion. What alternative did they have, with U.S. corn imports flooding the Mexican market? The free market, it appears, is the goal—not feeding the hungry or enabling people to stay on the land.

Privatization opened up important sectors of Mexico's economy to transnational corporate investment. Even more important, it reduced the state's ability to control that economy and to use that control to further social goals other than profit-making, such as promoting strategic industries, subsidizing prices for farmers and workers, or maintaining social benefits, higher wages, and unionization.

While economic reform has its price, not everyone pays. Almost invariably, workers at privatized enterprises have faced huge layoffs and wage cuts, as new private owners seek to cut labor costs to increase their profits.

U.S. labor has also faced protracted struggles against privatization, but the state-controlled sector of the U.S. economy has always been very small, even compared to many other capitalist countries. Never-theless, "the loss of social benefits in the U.S. is comparable to what's happened to us," says Benedicto Martínez, general secretary of Mexico's Authentic Labor Front, the Frente Auténtica de Trabajo. "It's all a prod-uct of the same global policy."

Progressive Mexican labor leaders assert that Mexico has the right to pursue economic development in its own interest. And to achieve eco-nomic development that benefits all people, there must be an alternative to becoming a low-wage export platform, with increasing social and economic inequality enforced at the point of a gun.

But to win the right to pursue that alternative, "there has to be a political change here—things can't go on as they are," Martínez empha-sizes. "There has to be an answer which includes economic develop-ment. We're more indebted than ever, despite the fact that our debt has been paid many times over. The Mexican government is simply enact-ing agreements imposed by the U.S., and, as a result, more plants come here because of the advantages they get. These things affect all of us. We have to have a broader concept of solidarity."

Mexican unions aren't the only ones pointing out this problem. Labor movements globally debate the same question.

"Governments are told that workers' rights and economic develop-ment are a zero-sum game, that improving workers' lives slows devel-opment," explains Zwelinzima Vavi, general secretary of the Congress of South African Trade Unions. "In the pursuit of profit, they are told to remove worker protections, and then use that as an inducement for investment. But development is a wider concept. . . . Development can't exist with mass unemployment and poverty."

Unless the international trade structure is changed drastically, national development alternatives, based on rising wages and production for a domestic market, will not be possible. "The struggle by unions, social jus-tice groups, and environmentalists is about more than just winning a seat at the table, or a 'social clause,' or environmental rules," declares a Cana-dian Labour Congress statement issued just before the Seattle demonstrations against the World Trade Organization. "We're determined to change the entire trade regime."

Global inequality produces insecurity and economic desperation, which forces people from their countries of origin. According to Migrant Watch International, based in Geneva, more than 130 million people today live in countries other than the ones where they were born. Migration from Mexico to the United States is a product of that inequality.

No matter how many walls are built on the border, no matter how many National Guard troops or helicopters patrol it, workers will still cross, looking for a future. There's no more eloquent testimony to this than the deaths of the 1,420 women and men—workers and farmers—who perished in the desert during the six years between 1996 and 2002, trying to make the journey from northern Mexico into the United States, according to the Mexican Foreign Relations Office.

U.S. workers become victims of the same free trade economy, losing their jobs when their plants close or when the shrinking tax base that pays for social services leads to job cuts. And when this happens, they are told to find someone to blame workers in Mexico for taking their jobs, or immigrant workers in the United States. As a result, anti-immigrant hysteria has now become an extremely serious problem, as immigrants have become an integral part of the workforce.

This system creates severe economic insecurity on both sides of the border. The Federal Reserve Bank reported that the median yearly income for California families went from $26,700 in 1997 to $25,800 in 1998. When the median drops, it indicates that the number of poor families, earning less, is growing.

And earning this income requires more hours of work. The average work week is now forty-three hours, and rising. Latino workers work an additional five hours a week, and African American workers an additional nine hours.

According to a study by the Institute for Health Policy Studies at the University of California at San Francisco and the Field Institute, released in September 2000, employed Latinos were eleven times more likely than whites to live in poverty, and African Americans five times more likely. One reason for both growing poverty and the pronounced racial gap is that large corporations have abandoned permanent jobs. Only a third of white workers now work in traditional jobs—with permanent, full-time status, working directly for the company rather than a contractor. And only 25 percent of Latino and African American workers hold traditional jobs.

Globalization doesn't affect all people in the same way. In the United States, workers experience speed-up, runaway shops, and declining income. In Mexico, as in most developing countries, they endure superexploitation, environmental degradation, and the destruction of their traditional way of life. But the gap in living standards, enforced by U.S. political, economic, and military power, affects all workers, across all borders. As long as that gap exists, jobs will leave developed countries, and superexploitation in the developing world will increase.

This is the basic challenge to international solidarity—to look beyond the actions of individual corporations to the basic causes of poverty and economic inequality on a global scale. The new world economic order is not really so new at all, but a continuation of the imperialist system inherited from colonialism, in which wealthy industrial countries divided up the world and created a system that continues to siphon off the wealth of entire peoples and nations.

One of the most eloquent denunciations of this world economic order comes from Prime Minister Cheddi Jagan of Guyana. Jagan, a left-wing socialist, was the target of successful CIA destabilization efforts in the 1960s, when he tried to implement wide-ranging land reform and nationalization of foreign enterprises. After years out of power, he was reelected in the early 1990s and found the strings of debt wound so tightly around Guyana that he was unable to reintroduce the reforms he had initiated years before without devastating reprisals from the world financial community.

"A stop must be put to an unjust global economic order," Jagan said at the Rome World Food Summit in 1996, "which robs the south of about $500 billion annually in unjust, nonequivalent trade; an order where the south finances the rich north with south-to-north capital outflow of $418 billion in the 1982–90 period as debt payments—a sum equal to six Marshall Plans . . . [which] did not even include outflows from royalties, dividends, repatriated profits, and underpaid raw material."

Guyana itself paid $308 million in debt service from 1992 to 1995. Those funds would otherwise have gone to poverty relief, rural development, agriculture, health, and education. Jagan called the idea that privatization, free markets, and foreign investment would lead to development "a myth."

U.S. labor has an objective interest, therefore, in opposing U.S. policy in areas where it leads to a drastic decline in living standards, whether this occurs through loan bailouts in Mexico, austerity programs in East Asia, or economic reforms in Eastern Europe.

And because both Republicans and Democrats in the United States pursue essentially the same foreign and trade policies, solidarity between U.S. labor and unions in countries subjected to such reforms requires political independence—in other words, it requires that U.S. unions pursue a political agenda that focuses on guaranteeing rights and security.

Mexican workers and voters took a historic step toward their own political independence on July 2, 2000, casting aside the Party of the Institutionalized Revolution (PRI, Partido de la Revolución Institucional), the party that had governed them for seventy-one years, for its failure to follow an agenda that protected their interests. The new government of the conservative National Action Party (PAN) may also betray their hopes, but no party in Mexico can count any longer on the automatic support of workers and unions.

To confront globalization, U.S. labor needs a similar independence.

The cross-border solidarity movement, and the economic forces pushing it forward, has no choice but to demand answers to these questions from the labor movements of all three NAFTA countries, if unions are to survive on a world scale and successfully challenge the new world economic order.

Forcing these questions onto the table has been the cross-border movement's greatest contribution.

3

TIJUANA'S MAQUILADORA WORKERS

PLASTICOS BAJACAL

What is your name?
Antonio González.
Do you promise to tell the truth answering these questions?
Yes.
Where do you work?
At Plasticos Bajacal.
What union do you want to represent you?
Mexico Moderno. CROM.

This exchange unfolded on a windswept street, in a hilltop industrial park on the outskirts of Tijuana. Antonio González was voting in a 1993 union election at the Tijuana plant of Plasticos Bajacal, a division of Carlisle Plastics, a company based in Boston.

The factory is a stark, prefab concrete building in a section of the development that seems deserted. Empty streets, filled with blowing paper and dust, snake up the hillside toward the plant, arriving at a guard shack outside a metal fence.

On this particular day, three white wrought-iron tables had been carried out of the plant and set up in the street. Government clerical workers sat behind the tables, pounding away on manual typewriters.

González and his friends were escorted out of the plant, one by one,
by officials of the company-favored union, who were clad in leather
jackets and dark glasses. As each worker arrived at the tables, he or she
was greeted by José Mandujano, who headed the Junta Nacional de
Conciliación y Arbitraje for Baja California Norte, the state's labor
board.

Mandujano pointed his finger at González, as he had at many others
that morning, and the ritual of question and answer began. Human
rights representatives and observers from a handful of U.S. unions gathered around the tables. Behind the fence, company managers looked on,
noting the name and the vote of each worker.

In contrast to votes in U.S. union elections, González's vote was not
secret. He had to state his choice aloud, in a crowd of fifty people, and
then sign a written declaration affirming it on the spot.

The Mexican union election process is a product of the 1930s and
1940s, an era when strong, left-wing unions had great political power
and were incorporated into the government and its ruling party at the
time, the PRI. Workers had no need to be afraid, according to the logic
of the time, since those unions could and would defend them from any
retaliation by their employers.

It is a mark of the extent of the economic and political transformation
of Mexico—government policy encouraging foreign investment by
holding down wages, and conservative official unions defending that
policy instead of protecting workers—that what was at one time a symbol of workers' power has become instead a legal trap.

The choice facing workers in this Tijuana plastics factory was whether
or not to have a new, independent union representing them. Almost
none of the U.S.-owned maquiladora factories along the U.S./Mexico
border have democratic, worker-controlled unions. The workers at

Plasticos Bajacal not only tried to form such a union; they made their plant a symbol of the sweatshop working conditions behind the modern facades of Tijuana's industrial parks.

Plasticos workers also formed a close alliance with rank-and-file union members on the U.S. side of the border. The struggle at Plasticos took place as the U.S. Congress debated the North American Free Trade Agreement, and hundreds of thousands of labor activists campaigned against it, in an unprecedented surge of protest. During the ferment created by that campaign, this worker-to-worker support effort at Plasticos became an example of how unions and workers could create new international relationships in the free trade era—a model for uniting workers across the border instead of dividing them.

"We're at the beginning of a much bigger movement," said Javier Hernández, who was fired from the plant in April 1993 for his role in helping to start the independent union. In an interview just after the vote, he predicted, "Even if we didn't win the election here, thousands of other maquiladora workers like us are going to keep trying to do the same thing."

According to Jaime Cota, head of the Workers' Information Center (CITTAC, Centro de Información para Trabajadoras y Trabajadores Asociación Civil) in Tijuana, Plasticos workers began protesting conditions in the factory in 1992. Cota and the center provide assistance to workers in Tijuana's maquiladoras, helping them to understand their labor rights under Mexican law.

Cota recalled that the protests started when the company cut wages in 1992 and then forced people to work on the Mexican national holiday, September 16. A series of industrial accidents finally provoked a work stoppage. Jorge Barrón, a Plasticos employee, was injured when a drill bit broke and a piece of it flew into his eye. He was then forced to work for eight days without medical attention. The company did not provide goggles, and lack of medical attention cost Barrón his sight in the injured eye. Another worker, Luz Elena Corona, suffered a miscarriage when supervisors refused to allow her to rest after she complained of pain and exhaustion. They told her that she was the plant's fastest worker and insisted that she was needed on the production line.

Winter storms flooded Tijuana in January of 1993, and city authorities told the maquiladora owners to allow their workers to stay home during the emergency. "But when we went back to our jobs," Hernández remembered, "we found that for our one day of absence, the company deducted three days of our pay. We had to work two days for free." Deducting three days' pay to punish a day's absence is a common practice in maquiladoras, even though it is a violation of Mexican labor law.

Finally, company managers took another step that enraged the plant's workers even further. In the past, Plasticos had provided four vans to transport workers to and from the job. For women at the factory, who make up 70 percent of the workforce, those vans meant a lot. "We don't have any cars, and buses don't go most places. Some of us have been beaten and robbed when we walked home, especially at night," explained Leticia Mendiola, another fired worker. But the company eliminated the buses, and many women quit their jobs.

Cliff Deupree, president of Carlisle's molded products division, denied that there was any history of labor unrest in the plant. Nevertheless, in 1992, the company signed a contract with Mexico Moderno, a union affiliated with the Revolutionary Confederation of Mexican Workers (CROM, Confederación Revolucionaria de Obreros Mexicanos).

"We were here for three years without a union," Deupree said. "Then we were advised by our legal counsel that it was better to be organized. We examined the alternatives, and after talking to CROM, we invited them in. [Our attorney] talked to CROM and worked out a contract." Deupree asserted that Mexico Moderno officials held meetings with Plasticos workers at the company's invitation. "We were basically encouraging CROM and the people to get together."

Jovita Chávez, the company's attorney, said the company talked to CROM because it had been given a strike notice. Mexican labor law, she explained, permits union officials to give notice of a strike without showing support among workers.

According to Carmen Valadez, who works with Cota and Factor X, an organization of women maquila workers, CROM received political support from the treasurer (and later governor) of the state of Baja California Norte, Eugenio Elorduy. Plasticos, along with many other maquiladoras, belongs to the Centro Patronal, an employer association that has assisted other companies in signing contracts with CROM to ensure labor peace. Such agreements, in which union officials receive payment directly from the companies, are called protection contracts. Workers covered by such contracts often don't even know that they belong to a union.

While trouble was brewing in the Plasticos plant, union and community activists on the other side of the border, in San Diego, were watching the proliferation of maquiladoras with growing concern. Tijuana's population had grown from 165,000 in 1960 to 1.5 million in 1990 as a result of the expanding border factories and the migration of people from elsewhere in Mexico to fill the newly created jobs.

"Even before the NAFTA debate, we could see that there were already a million people along the border, working in conditions that would shock most workers here," explained Jelger Kalmijn, a technical worker at the University of California campus in San Diego and then president of his local of the United Professional and Technical Employees.

Plasticos was a product of the enormous movement of production south of the border that created the maquiladora industry. The plant belongs to Carlisle Plastics, a corporation with headquarters in Boston and eleven other factories in the United States, Singapore, Taiwan, and Hong Kong. In 1989, Carlisle owned a plant in Santa Ana, California, A&E Plastics, which employed more than 450 workers making plastic coat hangers for the garment industry. Ironically, its workforce consisted mostly of Mexican immigrants. When they began to organize a union, with the help of the United Food and Commercial Workers, Carlisle closed the plant, fired the workers, and moved production to Tijuana, where it opened the Plasticos Bajacal maquiladora.

Meanwhile, Kalmijn and other rank-and-file union members in San Diego began publishing a newsletter, "Fuera de Linea" (Out of line), to publicize poor working conditions across the border. When the January 1993 floods hit, they set up a food bank to give assistance to families faced with hunger. Plasticos workers were among the many who came into the food bank—and they quickly found a source of support for their nascent organizing efforts as well.

"Most of our fellow workers wanted a union, although we were all afraid that we might lose our jobs," Mendiola remembered. Their fears proved well founded. Twelve Plasticos employees were fired for union activity almost as soon as the organizing campaign for an independent union started. The company gave Mendiola a letter stating that she was laid off for lack of work. Then, when she and other fired workers got legal help, another letter was produced. This one stated that she and six others had been fired for handing out leaflets on company property during work time, urging workers to join the independent union.

Magdaleno Reyes, CROM's secretary for propaganda, defended the firings and called the fired workers lazy. "If you had people who didn't want to work, wouldn't you want to see them go?" he asked. "If everyone is more productive and works hard, then the company will produce more and everyone will be better off."

Despite the firings, Plasticos workers filed a petition with the state labor board, seeking a *registro*, or legal status, for their new union. That's when they discovered they already had one.

CROM, the existing union, had never held a union meeting at the plant. Workers had no idea that union dues were being paid in their name, since the company paid CROM directly. A representative of Mexico Moderno was on the Plasticos payroll. Undeterred, Plasticos workers found another Mexican union federation, the Confederation of Revolutionary Workers (COR, Confederación de Obreros Revolucionarios), to support them. COR loaned the workers its *registro*, the legal registration necessary for a union to participate in any legal process and to represent workers in bargaining.

As NAFTA became a household word in the United States, the San Diego activists organized the Support Committee for Maquiladora Workers to publicize events at the Plasticos plant. A steady stream of

U.S. congressional representatives and union leaders made the factory and its workers a stop on tours to collect information about labor conditions in Mexico.

On September 24, Kalmijn escorted a bus with thirty-seven leaders of the International Association of Machinists (IAM) across the border, for a meeting with Plasticos workers and a look at the plant. When the bus arrived outside the factory, Mexican plainclothes immigration police, who claimed to be acting at the request of the plant manager, arrested everyone on board. The bus was driven to a parking lot behind a liquor store close to the border and held for four hours.

"They told us that we would be charged with the crime of discussing working conditions with Mexican workers," according to Mike Day, business manager of IAM District 190 in Oakland. Finally, the bus was allowed to return to the United States. The publicity provoked by the incident led to a visit to Plasticos by a delegation from the U.S. Congress.

The San Diego committee organized more than political support; it also raised money to provide financial support for some of the fired workers. As a result, three Plasticos workers were able to organize full-time, handing out leaflets at the factory and visiting workers at home.

The provision of financial support was a controversial decision in Mexico. "The authorities say we're paid and manipulated by gringos," said Hernández, one of the three. "But we, as workers, make all the decisions. The support committee raises money, gives us publicity, and pressures the owner. Our movement at Plasticos belongs to us."

The support committee also participated in the North American Worker to Worker Network, an early coalition of unions and activists supporting work on the border. This group organized a demonstration against the firings in front of Carlisle's national headquarters in Boston. Afterward, William Binnie, Carlisle's owner, called Mary Tong, a committee member in San Diego, and agreed to provide compensation to the workers who had been injured at the Plasticos factory.

On December 1, Plasticos workers received notice from the Mexican government that an election would be conducted at the plant on

December 15, to choose between Mexico Moderno (CROM) and the independent union (COR). Although they were elated by the news, the fired workers worried that the company would pressure people into voting for CROM. "Some of our families received calls at home, saying that bad things would happen to them if we kept up our union activity," Hernández recalled. "We were told our names would be put on a blacklist and sent to the other factories here." The company denied that any blacklist exists.

The biggest barrier for the workers, however, turned out to be the election process itself. On the day of the election, many workers complained that they felt intimidated by the open voting process. Santos Lizarraga, after voting for COR, described the widespread rumors that COR supporters would be fired after the election or that the plant would close if COR won. "In the morning, everyone was saying they were going to vote for COR, but they changed because of the pressure and those guys there," he said, pointing to the CROM and management representatives around the tables.

Eustolia Velázquez also voted for COR because of the company's policy of deducting three days' pay to punish workers for one day's absence. "I've been here for four years," she declared. "I want things to get better, because so far I've gotten nothing."

The San Diego support committee organized a delegation of a dozen U.S. union members to act as observers, hoping that their presence would prevent gross irregularities. "What I saw that day left a very deep impression on me," recalls Virginia Rodríguez, an organizer for the Communications Workers of America, who was shocked by the open voting in front of company managers. "I saw one woman with tears in her eyes say she was voting for CROM. There were a lot of young workers—sixteen and seventeen years old—and you could see the fear in their faces."

After about three hundred of the plant's five hundred workers had voted, Pedro Molina, a lawyer representing the fired workers, asked that the election be suspended. About 25 percent of the votes had been cast for COR at that point. A settlement was negotiated, in which the company agreed not to retaliate against COR supporters and seven fired workers were given back pay and severance pay. Mexico Moderno's contract with Plasticos remained in force.

Mandujano, the head of the state labor board, asserted that Mexican labor law required open voting. Before becoming director of the labor board, he had been the lawyer in Tijuana for the state chapter of COPARMEX, the Mexican employers' association. The Plasticos election, he announced, "shows that Tijuana continues to be a favorable place for investment."

Leticia Mendiola, one of the fired workers, said she felt bad that people had been forced to vote for CROM. The movement for an independent union at the plant would probably suffer, she predicted, and she was right. Organizing efforts never resurfaced there—and, despite company promises, many of the workers were terminated in the months that followed.

Jaime Cota agreed with the decision to suspend the election, to avoid risking the jobs of additional independent union supporters inside. "Still, despite the defeat," he concluded, "this was the first time in Tijuana in thirteen years that workers could choose between two different kinds of unions. The people here will eventually work at other maquiladoras and carry the experience with them."

The election indeed had a profound effect on Rodríguez and the other U.S. unionists who witnessed it. She came away from her experience in Tijuana committed to organizing support for Mexican workers north of the border. "These workers are employed by U.S.-based companies, who are making tremendous profits at their expense," she said. "And since the market for what they produce is in the U.S., we can organize boycotts and take action against them on the other side, if we get organized. For workers here to have the confidence they can win, they need to know there's support for them in the U.S."

Her prediction proved to be prescient.

FEAR IN THE WAKE OF PLASTICOS

In this border city, the factories are like lords of the earth. They occupy the high points, the tops of the mesas, while the neighborhoods of the workers spread down the slopes into the valley below.

Francisco Ortiz works at Ken-Mex, a medical products plant built in Tijuana in the mid-1980s by Kendall International. He lives with his extended family in a tiny house in the barrio of Vista Alamar, below Otay Mesa. The main structure of Francisco's home is made of cinder blocks, but other rooms have been added on with whatever material came to hand. Ingenuity is the main building principle. The factories themselves, willingly or not, supply many of the materials. The inside walls of one extra room in his house are made of corrugated cardboard, salvaged from shipping cartons. A stack of wooden pallets towers in front of a house down the street, furnishing the lumber for its frame. Even the old car that is up on blocks in front of a third house has the faint blue trace of a company logo on its white doors.

A visitor to the Ortiz family, coming in from the street, passes through a gate in a wooden fence, tall enough to give a little privacy. Inside is a small dirt yard. An old couch sits under a small tree in a corner, and on most days Francisco's grandmother, eighty-three-year-old Isabela, sits there. She can't see her great-grandchildren playing around her anymore, but she can hear them arguing and laughing.

An old washing machine in the yard is a luxury most maquiladora workers don't have. Its drain hose snakes away from it, down into a hole in the dirt covered by a piece of plywood.

Inside the front door is the main room, filled with beds. A bunk bed on one side and a narrow single bed on the other leave a small space in between. A third mattress butts up against them at the end of the room. On the fourth wall, on a tall stand, is the big television Francisco won at a company raffle. "In all the years I've bought tickets for every raffle you can imagine, that's the only thing I've ever won," he says.

Francisco shares the house with three sons, who live with him in the front room. His uncle, the uncle's wife and children, and Francisco's mother and grandmother live in another room. It's hard to see how there could be space for everyone. There's even a tiny sitting room with a couch in back. On the wall, Francisco has put up the training certificates earned in the seven years he's been at the plant.

The family shares space by working different shifts. Francisco is on during the evening, until 2:00 A.M. One son works days, and another works graveyard.

"I'm a little better off than most assemblers," he acknowledges, "because I'm not on the line anymore, and I get a twenty-peso-a-week bonus for working an off shift. Assemblers at Ken-Mex make about twenty-three pesos a day, and I get about fifty." Wages in the maquiladoras are so low, and prices rise so fast, that many companies also give workers coupons for food. At Ken-Mex this year (1995), the coupons are worth about 45 pesos a week.

"The wage I make isn't enough to support my family," Francisco complains bitterly. Even combining his income with that of his two sons doesn't cover clothes or shoes. "It's just enough to eat, nothing more. We can barely afford to buy milk, and we only eat meat once or twice a month. Every day, we have to walk about forty minutes to work and forty minutes home. When we can afford the bus, it cuts the time to twenty minutes."

The neighborhood where Francisco lives is home to many of Ken-Mex's six hundred workers. Most are young, between fifteen and thirty years old. Some don't last long in the plant. Alfredo Tapia, a twenty-year-old native of Puebla, in southern Mexico, worked at Ken-Mex for only three months before landing a better job at another maquiladora. "I was making twenty-five pesos a day, and even though I'm single, I couldn't live on it," he recalls. "In addition, when the company got a big order, they would begin yelling at us on the line, to make us work faster. I got tired of it, and I left."

For older maquiladora workers, it's not so easy to find another job. María Ibarra, who lives in the same neighborhood, works at the Maxell factory, also on Otay Mesa, assembling tape cassettes and computer floppy disks.

It's difficult for her to think about her own future, she says. "I just make a little bit, and I've been there a long time. I'm too old to think about changing jobs to work somewhere else. When a person gets to be older, they have to take care of their job. Once you get to be a certain age, they don't want you anymore."

The same feeling of insecurity haunts Francisco. "When I get old," he thinks, "I'll just have the miserable amount we get from social security. When my kids have their own life, I don't know what I'll do or who will support me. Maybe I'll have to sell gum or flowers in the streets, like the children and old people."

Like Francisco, María sent her children to work in the factories. Her eldest started working at Ken-Mex when he was fifteen. "He's been there since he was small. He couldn't continue going to school because we couldn't get by on what I was earning. He had to go to work."

When she remembers that moment of giving up on his education, her breath gets short and her voice breaks. "One feels very bad, because we wanted something so different for them, that they were going to study and become something in life. But then the economy failed, and they were forced to go to work, just two more of many others." María estimates that as many as 40 percent of the workers she sees are younger than eighteen.

Even with two sons working, the Ibarras brought home only about 410 pesos a week. A gallon of milk cost 17.50 pesos, half a day's work for María. A kilo of beans cost 9 pesos—two hours. "You have to buy what you can afford, the cheapest things," she explains. "I get everything on special."

When Mexican president Ernesto Zedillo devalued the peso in January 1995, prices for groceries and basic services started to climb steeply for maquiladora workers. But the same process that made groceries more expensive made the labor of Ken-Mex workers cheaper. Victor Díaz, the plant manager, called the devaluation sad for the workers. "But it favored the maquiladoras," he explains. "Costs of operating here became much less." Kendall's profits, earned from paying pesos to workers in Mexico and selling disposable medical supplies for dollars in the United States, increased when the dollar value of the peso was cut in half. Díaz observes that, after devaluation, the cost of wages at Ken-Mex, in U.S. dollars, was equivalent to the cost in 1985.

Kendall International, famous for Curad bandages and Curity medical supplies, merged into the disposable and specialty products division of the giant Tyco conglomerate in 1994. In 1995, that division accounted for more than half of Tyco's profits—$261 million out of $514 million. In 2002, Tyco's CEO, L. Dennis Kozlowski, was paid more than $81 million in salary and stock options. Exposure of his billing the company for incredible luxuries in addition to expenses led to his resignation and indictment.

The Tijuana plant accounts for about 15 percent of Kendall's employees. It makes bandages, bags of saline solution, gloves, and supplies for operating rooms.

Business boomed at Ken-Mex, and the plant's production volume went up 50 percent in the year of the merger. Meanwhile, Tyco closed three of Kendall's twenty-one plants in the United States, moving the work to Tijuana. Díaz acknowledges that the plant concentrates on labor-intensive production, but he calls it an integrated plant, doing all the operations for each of its products.

"Although labor costs here may be a little higher than in, say, the Philippines, transportation costs less, and because the plant is so close to the U.S., the company has better control over production," he asserts.

Making Mexico attractive to foreign investors like Tyco and Kendall is the policy of both the Mexican and U.S. governments. In the first three months of 1996, 134 new factories began production along the border—three every two days. They employed 10,336 workers and represented a total investment of $126 million, according to the Mexican Secretariat of Commerce and Industrial Development. In March 1996, in Tijuana alone, eleven new plants started up in one month.

Yet maquiladora workers have not passively accepted the economic conditions that were used to attract plants to the border. At Maxell, María Ibarra and her co-workers organized a successful effort to have the company supply buses to take them to work. A group got together and went to the plant management. "And to show the company we weren't just by ourselves, we put it all in writing, and everyone signed it," she remembers. "It really lifted our spirits because even though getting a bus is not a lot, it's something. And we save enough at home to buy another container of water or a kilo of tortillas."

Despite that success, however, they feared retaliation for this kind of collective action. "Everything has to be done undercover," she explains, "because people fear they'll be fired. We can't do these things openly. People believe that if they make a fuss about the wages, they'll lose their jobs. The managers tell us that the company expects us to be obedient and submissive."

For quite a while, the defeat at Plasticos reinforced that fear. The workers were not yet ready to confront the companies again directly in another effort to bring in independent unions. Instead, the San Diego–based Support Committee for Maquiladora Workers cooperated with the Border Region Workers' Support Committee (CAFOR) in conducting health and safety training for maquiladora workers. They hoped that a semi-clandestine struggle could end some of the worst cases of exposure to toxic chemicals on the factory floors. Meetings were held for workers and residents of communities in the factory zones. Health and safety experts came from California to explain ways of recognizing health hazards and the kinds of changes that could be demanded from the companies.

To some degree, this effort succeeded. At the Sanyo maquiladora, one of Tijuana's largest, many children of the female employees had serious health problems, which the workers attributed to chemical exposure during pregnancy.

After attending the training meetings, one of the workers brought a booklet to work entitled "Is Your Job Making You Sick?" Together, she and her workmates surveyed the plant to identify possible sources of toxic exposure. They left a copy of the booklet and their survey anonymously on the desk of the plant manager. He called a meeting and asked for the names of the people responsible. No one gave him names. Then he claimed that there wasn't enough money to build a ventilation system, as the survey demanded. One worker spoke up and suggested writing a letter to the parent company in Japan. The manager backed down, and eventually a ventilation system was installed.

CAFOR also organized community residents in the neighborhoods around the factories. They focused on the neighborhood of Chilpancingo, below Otay Mesa. In 1993, in this small barrio, six children were born with a terminal medical condition called anencephaly—essentially, born with no functioning brain. In 1994, the community activists counted thirteen more children who were born with the same awful defect. In 1995, the local political boss told residents to stop the surveys, warning that uproar or protests would discourage companies from building new factories in Tijuana.

On the mesa above the community sits a closed battery recycling plant. Mary Tong, of the San Diego committee, reports that lead and heavy metal deposits have been measured in the soil there at concentrations forty thousand times over safe levels.

"We of course blame the companies for this," says Eduardo Badillo of CAFOR, "but we don't hold them alone responsible. Our own government shares the responsibility for these conditions, because it doesn't insist that the factories abide by the laws and regulations which already exist. We have a saying—these companies don't come to this side of the border to eat tacos and enchiladas, but to find cheap labor."

THE BIKINI CONTEST

Since the end of the revolution in 1920, the official Mexican trade unions, like unions in most countries, have organized massive celebrations of May Day every year. (Ironically, the United States, where May Day was born in the streets of Chicago during the effort to win the eight-hour day, is one of the few countries where the holiday goes officially unrecognized.)

The Labor Congress (Congreso de Trabajo), the umbrella federation for the official unions, was accustomed to using the Mexican May Day celebrations to pledge support for the government and the ruling PRI. But in 1996, President Zedillo asked nonagenarian Fidel Velásquez, the Labor Congress president, not to hold a demonstration. Entering the last years of his life, Velásquez, who died in 1997 at ninety-seven, agreed and refused to organize any protest against the government's neoliberal reforms and low-wage policies.

Both Zedillo and Velásquez feared that thousands of people in the streets might easily become an uncontrollable demonstration of anger at the government's economic policies. The fear was well founded. The Labor Congress threatened to expel any union that marched on May Day, a stance that only contributed to growing rifts inside the country's labor movement. And in Tijuana and other cities on the border, the growth of unofficial marches helped create the political space for discontented maquiladora workers to demonstrate.

In both 1996 and 1997, from Tijuana on the Pacific to Matamoros on the Gulf of Mexico, maquiladora workers organized demonstrations to demand a wage increase that would compensate for the fall of the peso. Huge demonstrations filled the Zócalo, Mexico City's central plaza, making the same demand.

When maquiladora workers took to the streets on May Day in 1997, their anger was undeniable. Despite fear of firings and the blacklist, workers from the plants of Sanyo, KFC Electric, Nypro, Kendall, Zettler, and others formed a thousand-strong march from the outskirts to downtown.

Tijuana's unions, however, were nowhere to be seen. Blas Manríquez, a Communist labor leader of the generation of the 1930s and patriarch of the political opposition, hotly condemned their absence. Hundreds of workers blocking an intersection in the middle of the business district fell quiet, as Manríquez, his strong voice belying an aging body, accused the government and the official unions of "conspiring together to sell Tijuana's workers to foreign companies, and selling us at hunger-level wages to boot."

Workers marched and heard similar speeches in Juárez and Matamoros. In Piedras Negras, the mayor told demonstrators that their demands were just. In Ciudad Acuña, nine hundred workers marched to the factories. In Nogales, the official demonstration was never canceled; workers used the gathering to demand a wage increase and elimination of the new 15 percent value-added tax.

The independent May Day demonstrations were ample evidence that workers felt abandoned by their union leadership. In response, they organized their own protests, finding new ways to defend themselves against government austerity policies and foreign companies, especially along the border. The marches signaled that a fundamental realignment in Mexican labor was beginning to take shape and that new relationships were developing between workers on both sides of the U.S./Mexico border.

José Delgado, an activist in the Tijuana organization of the left-wing Party of the Democratic Revolution (PRD, Partido de la Revolución Democrática), expressed this sentiment: "Today, I hope that a new labor movement will arise here, which will be more intelligent and more innovative. Already, people building independent organizations along the border are much better than the leadership of the old unions. They are more concerned about health and the use of toxic substances in the work process. Their movement is very spontaneous and makes allies with neighborhood organizations, with farmers, and with teachers and with people from across the border. Neither of our governments has an answer to the demands of these people. We will find the answer for ourselves."

"You can imagine how desperate we are, since we're so poor. Here, if you have no money, the government won't enforce the law. We really have very good laws in Mexico, but a very bad government."

As she said this, Yolanda Vásquez stood in the middle of the 1996 May Day march, on Tijuana's Avenida de la Revolución, in the heart of the old downtown. Voices poured out of bullhorns and the crowd swirled around her, while in her hands she held a placard that read "For the dignity of women in the maquiladoras." Other women stood with her, holding signs in both English and Spanish with similar appeals. One said simply, "We demand that the companies obey the law."

Vásquez, who had been a maquiladora worker for five years, was expressing an opinion heard over and over among Mexican workers in Mexico—their problem isn't the law; it's the lack of enforcement. She had discovered the truth of this opinion repeatedly during these years, as she fought battles that included sexual harassment, the closing of the plant where she worked, blacklisting, and wages that have fallen to a tenth of the minimum wage paid just a few miles away, on the other side of the border.

Vásquez was a worker at Exportadora de Mano de Obra, a maquiladora started eight years ago by National O-Ring of Downey, California, a division of a large U.S. corporation, American United Global. Dan Meléndez, a spokesperson for National O-Ring, denies that his company ever actually owned Exportadora. Nevertheless, he admitted that Exportadora's wages, personnel policies, and the work itself were controlled from Downey. The Exportadora plant employed about 180 workers, who did finishing work and inspection on rubber O-rings.

In the summer of 1996, Exportadora held its annual picnic. According to Vásquez, in the middle of the picnic, an announcement was made over the PA system that a bikini contest would be held among the plant's female workers. "It took us by surprise, because there had never been one before."

Meléndez alleges that there had been a bikini contest every year, which he called "a benefit for the workers." National O-Ring has never asked its workers in Downey to have such a contest, nor has it ever held a company picnic for them.

When Vásquez and her co-workers balked at the idea of stripping and putting on bathing suits for company managers, she was told that it was at the request of company president John Shahid, who was at the picnic. Fearing for their jobs, many women complied, and the contest was videotaped.

Later that fall, workers asked for meetings with the company to protest. They also wanted improvements in the wages and conditions at the plant. When they finally met with Shahid and asked him for a raise, he took the money he had in his pocket, about fifteen dollars, and threw it on the table. "We told him we didn't want money like that, that we wanted our pay increased," Vásquez recalls. "So he asked us what we would give him in exchange. We said we'd give him our work, like we always did. But he told us that he wanted love."

Shahid would not be interviewed. According to Meléndez, workers were told that the company had bought land and had begun building another plant. When it opened, Shahid told them, some of their demands for better conditions could be met. Meléndez says Shahid also told them that he was conducting a survey of wages in other maquiladoras, to determine whether the wages at Exportadora were too low.

The women went to the state labor board to complain about the bikini contest. A labor board investigator then asked the company for a copy of the video. When the investigator received it, however, it was blank. Enraged, he encouraged the workers to file sexual abuse charges with Tijuana's public prosecutor.

Two days after those charges were filed, the work coming from Downey dried up. The normal shipment of O-rings received for processing, two hundred boxes, was cut first to fifty and then the next day to ten. Finally, on the third day, workers were told to go home.

Meléndez accuses the workers of slowing down the work in Tijuana as a protest over their conditions. "We demanded that they increase their productivity, and when they wouldn't, we closed the plant," he claims. Since then, National O-Ring has abandoned plans to build a new plant in Tijuana and has moved the work back to Downey. The Tijuana workers earned wages comparable to about $20 a week. Meléndez wouldn't provide information about the wages paid in Downey, but California's minimum wage at the time was $170 for a forty-hour week—and, as a union plant, the company must have paid wages quite a bit higher than that.

When Exportadora workers lost their jobs, they did something new, however. With the aid of the Support Committee for Maquiladora Workers, they found a lawyer in Los Angeles, who filed suit in superior court, alleging that workers had been sexually harassed and then punished with the closure of their plant after they protested.

The suit marked the first time that workers in Mexico, aided by supporters in the United States, had filed suit in a U.S. court to defend their rights, reasoning that National O-Ring was a U.S. company, and John Shahid a U.S. resident. In an unprecedented move, the judge accepted jurisdiction, and the company immediately settled out of court, paying the workers severance.

One other factor undoubtedly encouraged National O-Ring to settle. Workers at its Downey plant are represented by the United Auto Workers. Mary Tong and AFL-CIO representative Ed Feigan, who went to the union for support, found that the UAW contract stipulated that workers could refuse to labor on materials made under substandard conditions. When the local threatened to invoke that clause, Shahid undoubtedly felt pressure as well.

Vásquez believes that their experience sent an important message to U.S. companies. "Companies like National O-Ring and people like Shahid come to Mexico to make money," she says. "They think they can do anything they want with us because we're Mexicans. Well, it's our country, even if we're poor. Not theirs."

4

HAN YOUNG

WALKING OUT TO WIN AN INDEPENDENT UNION

Each morning, as the sun rises over Tijuana, thousands of workers stream out of the city's barrios, up the hillsides to industrial parks on the mesas above. In a human flood, they surge into the maquiladoras. But on June 2, 1997, the 120 workers who usually would have gone through the doors of one factory, Han Young de Mexico, stopped at the gate instead. They huddled in knots in the street outside, their animated voices rising in the already dusty air.

Han Young's workers were on strike.

For two days, they occupied the street outside the cavernous industrial building where they normally labored. They demanded negotiations, first with their bosses and then with the authorities of the Baja California labor board. By the end of the second day, the company had agreed to bargain, itself a remarkable achievement for workers in an industry where managers have almost absolute power.

Work stoppages flare up periodically in the maquilas, and, at first glance, Han Young seemed to be just one more. But there was a crucial difference between this strike and economically motivated walkouts. At the heart of the Han Young strikers' demands was company recognition of an independent union.

Han Young de Mexico was a feeder factory for the huge Hyundai manufacturing complex, a Korea-based corporation that is one of the largest in Tijuana's vast industrial network. Han Young's workers built chassis for truck trailers and huge metal shipping containers, which were then finished in the main Hyundai plant in Tijuana. Han Young turned out twenty-six chassis a day, each selling for eighteen hundred dollars. Workers earned the equivalent of thirty-six to forty-eight dollars a week, working under some of the most dangerous conditions in a city well known for workplace accidents.

When Han Young first started production in the 1980s, its owner had signed a protection contract with a pro-government union, a *sindicato charro*. The phrase originally referred to unions led by Luis Morones, a Mexican labor leader who founded the Revolutionary Confederation of Mexican Workers (CROM) in the 1920s. Morones was famous for dressing up like a cowboy, or *charro*. A notorious conservative in the Mexican labor movement, he signed sweetheart agreements with employers; consequently, workers "celebrate" his memory by referring to company unions as "*charro* unions."

Protection contracts and *charro* unions are the primary system of labor control for foreign corporations that have built factories on the border. This system allows them to pay extremely low wages, even by Mexican standards, and to maintain dangerous and even illegal working conditions, with little fear of organized worker resistance.

Jesús Campos Linas, the dean of Mexican labor lawyers, says that thousands of such contracts in Mexico are arrangements of mutual convenience among government-affiliated unions, the government itself, and foreign investors who own factories in the country. "The government basically uses these labor federations to get votes during elections," he explains. "Companies make hefty regular payments to union leaders under these contracts and in return get labor peace."

Han Young managers, like most of their colleagues in Tijuana, made regular payments to officials of a union affiliated with the Revolutionary

Confederation of Workers and Farmers (CROC, Confederación Revolucionaria de Obreros y Campesinos), a labor federation connected to the PRI. The union held no meetings, and its representatives rarely visited the plant. Workers with complaints got no assistance—the company paid for labor peace, not for grievances and problems.

The walkout at Han Young in June 1997 was fueled by complaints about low wages and fears that the company would not pay the annual profit-sharing mandated by Mexican law. But instead of simply being a one-shot spontaneous rebellion, that strike marked the beginning of a hard-fought challenge to this protection contract system. The two-year fight that developed at this beat-up plant became not only the most important labor battle in Tijuana's history but a formative experience for workers throughout the border industry, with repercussions felt from the U.S. Congress to the Los Pinos residence of Mexico's president.

The struggle at Han Young began as one of a series of battles that engulfed Hyundai's Tijuana operations, which had been plagued by labor unrest for years. Hyundai subcontracted its operations with the most dangerous conditions—and consequently the largest number of labor disputes—to factories like Han Young. At one of those plants, Daewon, sixteen workers were fired after a walkout a year before the first Han Young strike. After the Daewon stoppage, ninety-one workers walked out at another contract plant, Laymex. Together, Laymex and Daewon workers marched to Hyundai's main factory, demanding a raise in pay.

Han Young workers heard about both these events. Emeterio Armenta, who became the leader of the first Han Young strike, lived in the barrio of Maclovio Rojas, a community built as a result of a land occupation on the outskirts of Tijuana. As Chapter Five describes, Maclovio Rojas had itself been at war with Hyundai for years over company efforts to dispossess residents and build a new industrial park on their land.

Fred Lonidier, a photography professor at the University of California at San Diego and a longtime cross-border activist, met Armenta at a community meeting in Maclovio Rojas and interviewed him over the course of a year. After getting to know some of Armenta's friends from the plant, Lonidier introduced them to Mary Tong and the San Diego Support Committee for Maquiladora Workers. "We want to even the odds faced by maquiladora workers who get into fights with factory owners and the government, and educate people in the U.S. at the same time," says Tong, the committee's director. "In a global economy, the jobs and livelihood of people north of the border can depend on the outcome of the struggles of workers south of it, at factories like Han Young."

Lonidier remembers that "over a month before the first work stoppage, Mary and Emeterio went to the workers' homes on the weekends to build support for taking on the company with an independent union. The crucial difference with dozens of other plant struggles was that action was taken only after a lot of groundwork had been done. That groundwork included a plan for a new union registration, the legal means to file correctly and appeal at great length if necessary, overwhelming support of workers and their families, plans for job actions with Mexican and international support lined up, and skill in using the media."

In an interview with Lonidier, Armenta expressed the bitterness that workers felt toward the tight relationship between Han Young and the CROC. "I talked to the union representative, Luis Parrada," Armenta explained. "I said to him, 'Listen, you come here like the clouds of January, when they are not needed. When we need you, you are never around. You only come here when you have a meeting with the Koreans, and from them you receive your check. When we need you, you are never there for us. So what are you, really? Are you the protector of the workers or of the company?' 'Well, if you were paying me, then I would help you,' he answered me. 'But you do not pay me. The one who pays me is the company.'"

The growing unrest at Han Young opened possibilities that fired the imagination of Tijuana's left-wing workplace activists.

"If workers succeed here, the formation of independent unions could sweep like a wave through the factories of Tijuana, where conditions are much like those at Han Young, and even to other cities along the border," predicted Enrique Hernández, at the time president of the Civic Alliance (Alianza Cívica), a community organization supporting maquiladora workers and barrio residents. Hernández and lawyer José Peñaflor Barrón were asked by the workers to act as their *assessores*, professionals who give advice to unions. Given the legal and political minefield confronting workers who want to organize an independent union, they must have the help of people who know how to negotiate the minefield and who can spend the huge amount of time this effort takes. *Assessores* do the work that, in the United States, might be done by both lawyers and union organizers.

When Han Young managers settled the June 1997 walkout, it appeared that the company might forgo retaliation and might even be willing to deal with representatives elected by the workers. But the workers knew that, in any case, they would have to navigate the complicated system of Mexican labor law to win formal government registration of their union. They made it clear to the authorities that they were prepared to stop work again if roadblocks were put in their way.

Nonetheless, the battle was renewed two months later, when the company moved to purge union activists. Emeterio Armenta was fired August 6, and two other key activists, Guadalupe Yañez and René Méndez, were terminated a week later. The following day, August 14, workers again shut down the plant for a day.

By striking against the firings, workers were fighting for the right of their union to exist. But they also wanted to prevent the dire consequences that usually befell workers who lost their jobs after being labeled as troublemakers. All along the border, maquiladora owners maintain a blacklist of worker-activists like Armenta. Getting fired at one plant is often the equivalent of never working in any maquiladora again.

"I was told I made the company spend too much money on things like safety equipment," Armenta recalled. "They accused me of being behind all the problems."

Armenta's firing was a decision made not only by Han Young managers but also by the network of government authorities and large corporations who determine the rules for labor relations in Tijuana. Reacting to the June strike, and acting on behalf of the maquila industry, the local labor board had insisted in early July that the company hire a new personnel director, Luis Manuel Escobedo Jiménez. Escobedo in turn began to purge the plant of the strike's leaders. Armenta accused Escobedo of "using psychological pressure to try to divide the workers and break our efforts for justice."

In the United States, Escobedo would be called a union-buster. Mexican employers haven't traditionally used such consultants, but maquiladora managers have begun to adopt the hardball tactics of U.S. labor relations.

After the June strike, Armenta and the other Han Young workers had made an additional move that threatened factory owners. They asked Mexico's most independent union federation, the Authentic Labor Front (FAT, the Frente Auténtica de Trabajo), to help them obtain a *registro*, or legal status, for their own union. For years, the FAT had been cooperating with the U.S.-based United Electrical Workers (UE) and the Teamsters union in organizing drives along the border. In addition, the FAT was one of a tiny group of Mexican labor organizations that opposed NAFTA.

Working with the FAT, Han Young workers formally petitioned Tijuana's labor board for the right to be represented by one of the unions belonging to the FAT, the Union of Workers in the Metal, Steel, Iron, and Connected Industries (STIMAHCS, Sindicato Trabajadores de la Industria Metal-Mecánica).

Maquiladora owners feared that if Han Young workers won recognition for their new union, it would give the FAT a base in Tijuana. Its presence in the midst of the city's growing labor unrest might strengthen the movement for independent unions and push wages up.

Managers and Tijuana labor authorities also had an eye on Mexico City, where, that August, some of the country's largest unions split from the government-dominated labor federation, the Labor Congress. Led by the telephone workers, the breakaway group eventually formed a new independent federation, the National Union of Workers (UNT). These unions voiced loud criticism of the government's policy of keeping wages low in order to attract investment, and they spoke out strongly against NAFTA, a watershed in the labor movement's opposition to the treaty. The FAT actively participated in the founding of the UNT.

Independent unionism also got a shot in the arm when the doddering head of the Labor Congress, Fidel Velásquez, died in June. Among all of Mexico's political dinosaurs, Velásquez had fought hardest against democratic reforms in labor.

The stage seemed set in Tijuana for a determined effort to break the hold of the old, government-affiliated unions on the million maquiladora workers on the border. Cross-border labor activists in the United States also saw that possibility. "The . . . breakup of the old union federation is only one of a number of positive developments in Mexico recently, which also include the ruling party's loss of its majority in the federal Chamber of Deputies and the election of Cuauhtémoc Cárdenas as Mexico City mayor," Tong explained hopefully. "They all open up space for the growth of independent unions and politics on the border."

MAKING WAVES IN CONGRESS

At the beginning of October, Han Young workers and the FAT finally forced the local labor board to hold an election, in which workers could legally voice their preference for which union should represent them. Similar elections have been very rare—among the million workers in the maquiladoras, only a tiny handful have been able to make that choice.

In the traditional open voting system used by Mexican labor boards, fifty-five workers publicly declared their support for STIMAHCS, the FAT union, while thirty-two favored the CROC.

"This is the beginning of the independent labor movement in Tijuana," crowed José Peñaflor, the local attorney for the workers, who acted as the FAT's lawyer during the proceedings. "This is the beachhead for democratic unions on the border."

But the election had not gone smoothly. Although voting was scheduled to begin at noon in the tiny offices of the labor board (the JNCA, Junta Nacional de Conciliación y Arbitraje) in a dilapidated building in downtown Tijuana, by 11:00 A.M. dozens of workers had already formed a long line in front of the door to the conference room where voting was to take place. More than half of them were wearing T-shirts emblazoned with the FAT union's logo. Fearing that the company wouldn't release them from work to vote, they had stopped work that morning and traveled to the JNCA office together.

When the election finally began, they trooped into the conference room one by one and presented themselves at a table where JNCA secretaries and officials were seated. Each worker was asked first for a photo ID and then for another identification paper documenting his employee status at Han Young. Finally, he was asked, "Which union do you prefer?"

A packed crowd of representatives from both the FAT and the CROC surrounded the table, listening intently. A delegation of observers from U.S. churches and unions, assembled by the Support Committee for Maquiladora Workers, jammed into the small room as well.

As secretaries typed furiously, each worker openly declared his choice. When no one else was left in line, fifty-two had voted for STIMAHCS, and only seven for the company union.

Then angry shouts broke out from the waiting area outside. A heated confrontation erupted, as a new group presented themselves to vote. To the outrage of Han Young workers, they saw their supervisors, as well as others they didn't recognize—individuals who had never been in the plant before.

The labor board representatives reopened the election procedure. After police were called, the new group was escorted into the conference room and began voting. Many had no papers identifying them as Han Young employees. Some didn't remember, until reminded by others in line, the name of the company where they supposedly worked. At least one was not asked for an ID at all. Another admitted that he had gone to work in the factory only days before. One voter, Manuel Uribe

Vásquez, admitted after casting his ballot that he was a foreman and therefore ineligible to vote under Mexican law.

As this group voted, angry Han Young workers outside chanted, "*¡Fraude! ¡Fraude!*" (Fraud! Fraud!). In the end, however, the votes of the second group proved insufficient to defeat the FAT. The total stood at fifty-five for STIMAHCS and thirty-two for the CROC.

Under Mexican law, the results of such a union election must be certified as valid and fair. Then the winner takes over the administration of the labor agreement currently in force at the plant and gains the right to renegotiate it when it expires. The FAT's victory would have given the union its first contract in a maquiladora.

Three days after the voting, on October 9, the labor board opened a hearing to determine the eligibility of the challenged voters. The FAT questioned the eligibility of twenty-five voters, including the supervisors and the workers who had been hired only days before; the CROC questioned two votes. The challenged votes were clearly insufficient to change the outcome of the election.

Nevertheless, the labor board refused to certify the results and instead began a process of postponing any action that would have allowed the union to gain its legal representation rights. And while the board found one excuse after another for inaction, the political fallout from the election snowballed.

That the election had been held at all was viewed as a strategic disaster by the maquiladora association and most government authorities. Days before voting began, CROC officials had met with the governor of Baja California, Héctor Terán Terán. The governor then forced the resignation of the JNCA chief in Tijuana, Antonio Ortiz. Tijuana newspapers quoted sources inside the labor board as saying that Ortiz was being punished for allowing the election to occur.

During the voting, the board's previous chief, José Mandujano, had shown up, representing Han Young. For many years, he had been the lawyer for the maquiladora association. During his tenure as head of the labor board, he had defeated the attempt to form an independent union at Plasticos Bajacal three years earlier. The Han Young election was administered by Mandujano's protégé, Carlos Pérez Astorga, who denied that any voting irregularities had occurred.

The authorities also took steps to undermine cross-border support for the Han Young workers. At the October 9 hearing, representatives of the Mexican Interior Ministry showed up looking for Mary Tong and Jim Clifford, leaders of the San Diego support committee. They told one reporter that Tong and Clifford would no longer be allowed to enter Mexico.

It was clear that the Mexican government was very nervous about the Han Young fight, at least in part because of the plant's role as a feeder factory for Hyundai. The state and federal governments were both looking to the giant Korean conglomerate as the linchpin of an ambitious plan of industrial development, including new container facilities to modernize the port of Ensenada and a rail link connecting it with the border plants. Such a system would have enabled shippers to circumvent the U.S. ports of San Diego and Los Angeles. Hyundai also spread rumors that it was considering building an auto assembly plant and a basic steel mill. Clearly, any failure to suppress labor unrest at one of its contract plants, authorities feared, could shatter their dreams of massive new foreign investment.

For weeks preceding the October election, the company had escalated pressure on the Han Young workers. According to one of them, Armando Hernández, Han Young's owner, Ho Young Lee, called him into a private meeting at the beginning of September. "He offered me a raise of six pesos a day [eighty-five cents] and told me that if I didn't accept it and stop the effort to organize an independent union, I'd lose my job." Hernández refused and was fired.

Other workers reported that plant manager Won Young Kang called a meeting at lunchtime on September 25, in which he told them that the factory would close if they voted for the independent union. Won denied the charge, saying, "It's not possible that the company would close. The company doesn't favor any union."

Nevertheless, on September 3, a full month before the vote, a state government representative ordered all TV stations in Tijuana to stop covering the Han Young situation. In the face of that pressure, the FAT's general secretary, Benedicto Martínez, credited the presence of U.S. observers with breaking the media blackout and shining a spotlight on the election process. "I'm glad they were here," he said. "They call them outsiders, but there are times when people need outside support."

And support didn't come only from the United States. Just before the election, the AFL-CIO moved to pressure Hyundai to insist that Han Young managers respect the election results. AFL-CIO representative Ed Feigan contacted the Korean Confederation of Trade Unions, the union for Hyundai employees in South Korea, which wrote a letter to Han Young warning against any efforts to intimidate the workers. Meanwhile, Progressive Asset Management and the Interfaith Center on Corporate Responsibility, both shareholder action groups, contacted the Korea Fund of Scudder, Stevens and Clark, a major investment house, to exert further pressure on Hyundai.

"All the maquiladora owners were worried that an independent union at Han Young would encourage workers to organize at other factories and drive up wages," said Enrique Hernández of the Civic Alliance. Despite the majority vote for STIMAHCS, the labor board continued to refuse to certify the results. Han Young managers were pleased. "Eighty percent of the workers really wanted another union, not STIMAHCS, but they weren't permitted to vote," claimed Won Young Kang.

In November, the government denied certification, and charges were filed under NAFTA's labor side agreement by the San Diego Support Committee for Maquiladora Workers, Mexico's National Association of Democratic Lawyers, and a handful of other organizations. They alleged that the labor board had illegally permitted management personnel to vote and had illegally refused to certify the election results. The complaint was filed with the National Administrative Office (NAO), an arm of the U.S. Department of Labor and the U.S. agency charged with enforcing NAFTA's labor side agreement.

At first, the charges seemed to go nowhere. In the United States, a network of union and community activists began picketing car dealerships belonging to Hyundai. Bad publicity and possible lost sales, they hoped, would force the corporation to intervene. According to Mary Tong, "under Mexican law, manufacturers are responsible for the actions of their contractors." But although Han Young produces solely for Hyundai, the corporation's representatives disavowed responsibility.

Pressure grew more intense during the November debate in the U.S. Congress over fast track legislation that would have given the Clinton administration the authority to negotiate future trade agreements, including expansion of NAFTA to other countries, without amendment by Congress. Opponents used the Han Young election as a symbol of NAFTA's failure to protect workers' rights. As the administration sought to line up support for the fast track authorization, Democratic representatives David Bonior and Richard Gephardt buttonholed members of Congress, telling them about Han Young and arguing against the bill.

In Tijuana, a small group of fired Han Young workers, seeing no progress, started a hunger strike on November 20 in front of the state government building downtown. On December 2 and 3, workers struck the plant again, and company officials agreed to talk—but the labor board refused to permit negotiations. The hunger strikers chained themselves to the doors.

With the intensifying publicity and support as the debate in Congress proceeded, the Mexican and U.S. governments grew desperate to defuse the Han Young issue. Under extreme pressure, the labor board finally agreed to a deal. If the factory's workers voted for the independent union again in a second election, and their supporters withdrew the NAO complaint, the board would certify the results. Han Young would rehire the fired workers and bargain with STIMAHCS.

On December 4, in front of the factory, thirty-two workers voted for the independent union for a second time; twenty-seven voted against it.

In the meantime, Clinton proved unable to come up with the necessary votes, even with substantial Republican support, and the fast track bill was pulled off the floor of Congress. Reportedly, when representatives from Vice President Al Gore's office called Congressman Bonior, asking what the problem was, they got a two-word reply: Han Young. (Bonior, especially, had become an important ally of the Han Young workers. Coming from Michigan, a state with a high percentage of unionized workers, especially members of the United Auto Workers, Bonior was a consistent opponent of free trade policies and an outspoken critic of NAFTA. As the Han Young battles escalated, the support committee in San Diego called him frequently to get help in pressuring the U.S. and Mexican governments.)

In Tijuana, six of the fired workers were rehired, and it seemed at first that the deal would hold. But within days it started to unravel.

A representative of another government-affiliated union, the Revolutionary Union of the Working Class (Sindicato Revolucionario de la Clase Obrera), began appearing in the factory, apparently welcomed by the company. At the same time, the managers refused to bargain with Enrique Hernández, who had been elected by workers to represent them; management would not even permit him to enter the plant.

Meanwhile, the plant began hiring new workers by the busload from Veracruz, where big layoffs in shipyards and oil fields were producing lots of unemployed welders. Independent union supporters worried that the company intended to claim once again that a majority of workers opposed the union and then push for a third election.

Not all the Veracruz workers proved to be such docile pawns, however, and the company undermined its own efforts by cheating them. Carlos Pérez Cruz, hired in Veracruz, claimed that the recruiter promised he would make 1,200 pesos a week. But his pay stub for a week in February showed that he had been paid only 558 pesos (about 31 dollars), including overtime and incentive bonus. "I'm being evicted from my room because I can't pay the rent," he complained bitterly. "I don't have enough to eat or [to] send money to my family, and I can't even go home—the fare is twelve hundred pesos. Even if I didn't eat and slept in the street, it would take two weeks to make that."

The situation grew more tense in January. Just after New Year's, a crane carrying a one-ton truck chassis almost collided with another crane, and the chassis fell. Six workers leaped out of the way, narrowly escaping death or serious injury. Torrential rainstorms struck, and leaking water poured through the roof of the plant. High-voltage cables connected to welding equipment snaked through two-inch-deep puddles, which spread across the floor, threatening shock and electrocution.

Workers struck again for a day on January 6 to force a government safety inspection. In the wake of the stoppage, the NAO complaint was amended to include allegations that Mexico was not enforcing health and safety laws at Han Young.

Filing the NAO complaint had a certain element of irony. Almost all the activists organizing workers on the border, including Tong, Hernández, the FAT, and others, were implacable foes of NAFTA. They all condemned the side agreement as window dressing, originally intended only to sway the congressional votes needed to get the treaty adopted, and predicted that it would be ineffective. The side agreement has no provisions for penalties or fines against governments that violate workers' union rights.

In filing the complaint, the activists all knew that the Clinton administration would try to use it to win credibility for its trade policy—a policy that the activists held responsible for workers' poverty and lack of rights. And, in fact, by the time of the NAO hearing in San Diego, the Han Young case had become a political litmus test. The Clinton administration planned to reintroduce fast track legislation later that spring. In addition, Gephardt and Gore were planning to face off for the Democratic presidential nomination two years later; anticipating the contest, Gore sought to blunt criticism from opponents of free trade within the Democratic Party.

"There's no question that the purpose of free trade is to create favorable conditions for foreign investment," Enrique Hernández said. "On the border, those conditions include low wages and company unions. So it's hard to give any credibility to the labor side agreement, which was just window dressing to get us to accept NAFTA to begin with. But we have to use the tools that are available to us. If the NAO case helps Han Young workers stabilize their union, and the idea spreads to other workers and plants, then I guess we'll have to pay the price of lending some credibility to a policy we oppose."

When the NAO hearing finally opened in San Diego on February 18, more than two dozen workers lined up to testify that the legal process had failed to guarantee their union rights and that the government had proven unwilling to enforce safety laws.

Even getting to the hearing wasn't easy. Although the workers had received temporary visas the day before to allow them to cross the border, Border Patrol agents at the San Ysidro crossing the next morning questioned the validity of the visas. For three hours, revolving teams of agents held the credentials for verification and refused to allow the workers to pass. Only after NAO secretary Irasema Garza personally phoned the border station did the Border Patrol let the workers proceed. Her sympathetic treatment of the workers contrasted remarkably with conduct during previous NAO proceedings, when workers and unions had been treated with indifference, bordering on hostility.

At the hearing, workers and their supporters focused mainly on health and safety issues. All previous NAO complaints had alleged that Mexico was not enforcing its laws protecting workers' rights to form their own unions. The Han Young complaint, however, had been amended to allege that the government was also failing to enforce health and safety laws. Activists hoped to make that a very expensive failure. While the side agreement fails to punish governments that don't protect union rights, it does specify a penalty for failing to enforce workplace safety. The potential fine was the equivalent of 0.007 percent of the value of Mexico's yearly trade with the United States, or about $50 million at the time.

The health and safety complaint was the brainchild of Garrett Brown, who called the working conditions at Han Young "a catastrophe waiting to happen." He should know. In his day job, Brown is a health and safety inspector for the California Occupational Health and Safety Administration.

In his private life, this soft-spoken industrial hygienist has traveled the border for years, from Tijuana to Brownsville, holding classes for

Mexican workers and teaching them how to recognize health and safety dangers at work. In the wake of highly publicized exposures of bad working conditions in the border plants, he and other health and safety activists had formed the Maquiladora Health and Safety Support Network.

As industrial turmoil boiled over at Han Young, Brown began surveying conditions in the plant, through interviews with dozens of its workers. That survey became the basis of the NAO complaint. When the two dozen workers testified in San Diego, they conveyed a horrifying sense of the working conditions they faced daily:

- Overhead cranes carried truck chassis weighing a ton or more through the plant. The controls of the cranes repeatedly malfunctioned.
- Pools of water one to two inches deep, described by a Mexican safety inspector as *lagunas* (lakes), covered the floor in some departments during winter rains. Heavy cables carrying 440 volts, some with frayed insulation, snaked through the water to industrial arc welders.
- There was no ventilation in the plant, and some workers suffered from "metal fume fever," a condition caused by welding. Ozone and ultraviolet light, which damage lungs and eyes, were other welding by-products.
- An inspection report described the bathrooms as in "bad condition and very dirty." One toilet stall door had fallen off. There was no toilet paper or hot water, and the sinks worked so poorly that they "generated many biological and pathogenic microorganisms," according to the report.

One worker who testified was Miguel Solorzano, who later was fired, along with a dozen other supporters of the independent union. Solorzano earned 64 pesos (about 8 dollars) daily; breakfast and lunch alone cost 28 pesos. "I have a physically exhausting job," he explained, "and I'm always tired because I just can't afford to eat enough." He rolled up his sleeve to show poorly healed fractures in his right forearm, the result of falling from a precarious position while welding one of the truck chassis. "They only gave me ten days off when it happened," he recalled bitterly, "and then I was forced to come back to work, even though I couldn't even close my fist. My arm still hurts."

Han Young plant manager Won Young Kang alleged that "a lot of liars" testified in San Diego. He pointed to the corner store near the plant, saying, "Even they've been robbed once or twice. So every company has its own set of problems." At the hearing, company officials showed off a table piled high with health and safety equipment they claimed was in use in the factory, but it all looked new, as though it had never been used.

Although the conditions workers described were terrible, such conditions are not illegal under NAFTA. What made the complaint possible was that the plant had been inspected eleven times in five years. Each time, inspectors from the Mexican government's Secretariat for Labor and Social Benefits (STPS, Secretaria de Trabajo y Previsión Social) compiled long lists of illegal conditions. In July, for instance, just weeks after the workers struck for two days to win an independent union, an inspection detailed forty-four illegal conditions. Han Young was given twenty days to remedy twenty-two of the violations.

STPS waited until September to send inspectors back in. At that time, they found that almost none of the conditions had been fixed.

The company got more time. No one from STPS came back to check on compliance until workers struck again in January, after the crane incident. Once again, inspectors found that the company had failed to remedy the most serious problems, many of which had been cited in July, including the lack of ventilation, the leaking roofs, poor maintenance on the cranes, a malfunctioning crane, and no written health and safety program.

Mexican law requires fines for almost all of these conditions, especially for repeat violations. No fine was ever assessed against Han Young until the day after the San Diego hearing, when the secretary of the STPS fined the company the equivalent of about nine thousand dollars.

"It's clear that the inspectors tried to document the violations," Brown points out. "But the government failed to actually enforce the law and protect the health and safety of Mexican workers."

Brown believes that efforts by the Mexican government to encourage foreign investment and maintain an economic austerity policy to please the International Monetary Fund "undermine its political will to enforce regulations against transnational corporations generating hard currency [that is] desperately needed to pay off foreign bankers."

In his travels along the border, the workers he has talked to have described the same conditions over and over again, he says. "There are thirty-eight hundred maquiladoras in Mexico, employing a million workers. Han Young is far from being an exception."

One of the workers whose case was discussed in San Diego was Norberto Cordoba, who sacrificed his job trying to end conditions so dangerous that he was afraid someone would die. In June, when his friends organized the independent union and walked out on strike, he joined them willingly, even though he had been working at Han Young only three months. "I've always been a union man," he asserted. "In Veracruz, where I'm from, I was a union leader at all the shops where I worked."

Despite being a skilled welder, Cordoba could make only 300 pesos a week in Veracruz. So he did what millions of Mexicans have done over the past three decades: he made the long trek north to the border. At Han Young, he found a job that paid him almost twice as much. Although it had a union, too, it was not like those he had known before. "I saw it was just a union for the protection of the boss," he recalled. "It did nothing for us."

When the Han Young managers made concessions to end the two-day June strike, they agreed to set up the health and safety committee required by Mexican law. In its years in Tijuana, Han Young had never permitted such a committee, and the CROC had never insisted otherwise. Cordoba was chosen by his fellow workers as one of three safety committee representatives from the new independent union. Within months, all three were fired, as Han Young moved to cleanse itself of activists.

According to Kang, "If you want to strike [in Mexico], you're supposed to have permission. Their work stoppage wasn't legal, so we fired
them." After being fired, Cordoba worked short jobs in construction,
surviving day to day, trying to send money home. He was never rehired.
Kang says the company offered Cordoba money to give up his claim to
his job and that he accepted. "That's true," Cordoba admitted. "I was
out of work for a long time, living a thousand miles from my family, who
had nothing to support them at home. I didn't know if I would ever see
the inside of the plant again. What was I supposed to do?"

Mexican employers commonly buy out workers as a way to settle the
cases of troublemakers without rehiring them. "But I want to go back,"
Cordoba insisted. "I've been part of all this. I told the company I would
even be willing to start as a new worker again, without my seniority."

Cordoba never saw the inside of the plant again. And, despite the testimony and documentation produced by the NAO hearing, NAFTA's
labor side agreement had no ability to put him back to work.

Under pressure from the hearings and the political fallout in Washington and Mexico City, the labor board finally agreed to give the independent union at Han Young the right to bargain, called the *titularidad*. But
in the legal proceedings that granted the *titularidad*, Enrique Hernández and attorney José Peñaflor Barrón, as the *assessores* chosen by the
workers, signed papers giving representation rights not to STIMAHCS
and the FAT but to a new union with a new *registro*, the October 6
Union for Industry and Commerce (Sindicato 6 de Octubre para Industria y Comercio).

Hostility had been brewing for some time between the FAT and the
Han Young workers and supporters, who complained they couldn't get
cooperation from the Mexico City FAT office about taking necessary
legal actions. On one visit to the capital, Mary Tong and Hernández
found that a press conference about the struggle was suddenly canceled,
and they came to believe that a whisper campaign was being conducted
against them among supporters in the UNT labor federation and the
left-wing opposition party, the PRD.

Seeking bargaining rights in the name of a new independent union was a decision that caused enormous controversy and bad feeling—on the border, in the United States and Mexico City, and even in Canada. FAT officials felt betrayed, and they spread the word to their supporters. But Hernández, Peñaflor, and the workers contended that they needed more resources than the FAT had been providing and that they wanted to maintain local control over negotiations and decisions.

When the struggle in Tijuana escalated, this proved to be a fateful decision. The struggle did remain locally driven; and the workers' committee, Hernández, and Peñaflor kept the structure of the union and its control in Tijuana. But it became more difficult for them to keep and build the outside support they needed to survive.

On March 22, the independent union gave the company the required sixty-day notice of its intention to strike if the company refused to negotiate. The union demanded recognition, a 35 percent wage increase, wage scales based on seniority and experience, and a profit-sharing plan in accordance with Mexican law.

In April, Irasema Garza of the NAO issued two decisions. One held that the government had indeed allowed violations of normal legal procedures by the Tijuana labor board, intended to deny the independent union the right to represent workers. The other decision found that occupational safety and health laws were not being enforced. But any potential penalties or enforcement proceedings seemed a long way away.

PULLING OUT ALL THE STOPS

As dawn broke over the hills of Tijuana on May 22, 1998, dozens of rough-clad workers began gathering in a narrow road facing the old industrial building that housed the Han Young plant, high on one of the city's mesas. An undercurrent of tension and anticipation filled the dusty street, as they awaited the beginning of the first legal strike by an independent union in the history of the maquiladoras.

From inside the plant, the sounds of machinery could be heard, operated by a workforce of three dozen laborers hired by the company over the prior two weeks. As eight o'clock approached, the hour at which their work shift would normally have started, Han Young's regular workers left the street and filed into the factory, not to turn their machines on but to turn them off.

Once they were inside, shouting matches broke out. Around the welding machines in the dim, cavernous interior, the regular workers confronted the new hires and the company's human relations director, Magdaleno Reyes. They demanded that everyone comply with Mexican labor law and leave. In a legal strike, the company cannot continue operations. All personnel must leave the premises, and the doors must be locked.

Reyes refused to order the new workers out or to go himself. Instead, he got into a shoving match and, according to the workers, hit some of them.

Finally, the regular workers left. Outside in the street, they strung the traditional red-and-black strike banners across the entrances. As the day wore on, the new hires trickled out of the factory, complaining that production couldn't continue without the strikers' skilled labor. By evening, the plant was dark and deserted.

For the following two weeks, Han Young strikers lived in the street outside the factory day and night, parking their vehicles in front of its huge corrugated iron doors. No one entered.

But throughout that time, the city's entire political establishment mobilized to declare the strike illegal and discredit the strikers. In a speech before the Baja California chapter of the employers' association, COPARMEX, the state's director of Labor and Social Services, Eleazar Verastegui, warned that the strike had been "provoked by foreign unions" who wanted to discourage investment in Mexico.

North of the border, in the U.S. Congress, minority whip David Bonior declared that "Han Young management, the Tijuana labor board, and the Mexican government are engaged in a systematic effort to deny Han Young workers their right to an independent union, through harassment, intimidation, and fraud." He called on Vice President Al Gore to communicate U.S. concern to the Mexican government, while the U.S. Labor Department announced that it was "monitoring developments very closely."

Meanwhile, Han Young managers refused to bargain, claiming that yet another government-affiliated union had claimed jurisdiction over the plant. Human relations director Reyes had long-standing ties to that union, a branch of the government-affiliated Confederation of Mexican Workers (CTM). According to Enrique Hernández, Reyes had used those connections to hire the wave of new workers before the strike.

Once the conflict started, Reyes and his powerful political allies at the CTM began moves to have the strike declared illegal, arguing that it wasn't supported by a majority of the workers. On May 27, the labor board conducted an election outside the factory, using its normal procedure in which workers declare their votes out loud, in front of company, union, and government representatives. Fifty-two workers voted to continue the strike, and sixty-four voted against it.

Hernández and attorney Peñaflor, however, alleged that forty-eight of those who voted against the strike were ineligible because they had been hired after the union gave its strike notice or had never worked at the company at all. "They were even recruiting voters at the flea market the day before the election," Hernández charged.

The labor board never required the company to produce a list of eligible voters before the strike, and now it refused to invalidate the election. "The union has to provide proof that those workers it challenged weren't eligible to vote," asserted Jesús Cosio, head of the labor board. Although a list of workers employed by Han Young on March 22 would have been easily available to Cosio from the records of the Mexican Social Security Institute, he said that he was unwilling to ask for it. "Anyone who presents themselves to vote will be allowed to do so," he declared.

The board also ruled that the strike was "nonexistent" (illegal, in Mexican legal terminology) because the strike banners had been put up fifteen minutes too early. It then took out a full-page advertisement in Tijuana's leading newspapers to announce its decision. Strikers charged that, in return for substantial payments for the ads, newspapers had to agree not to carry further stories on the strike. In fact, after the ads appeared, almost all newspapers along the border maintained a news blackout on events at Han Young.

On Friday, May 29, the board held another election in front of the plant, in which the government-affiliated CTM sought to take over the independent union's bargaining rights.

At 9:00 A.M., two dozen black-uniformed members of Tijuana's tactical squad, known as the Special Forces (Fuerzas Especiales), were deployed in front of the factory. Reyes then marched, at the head of dozens of men wearing CTM caps, up the street to the factory doors.

Before voting started, Hernández again demanded that the board require the company to produce a list of eligible voters. Cosio turned the request aside. The strikers then filed up to the table under the watchful eyes of the police, Han Young management, and CTM officials to cast their votes. After they voted and returned to their side of the police lines, a tiny group of four women stepped out of their ranks.

Although they had never worked in the plant before—and had actually joined the independent union at another factory—they presented themselves at the table to vote. The CTM supporters whistled and made rude remarks about them, but they refused to leave the voting tables. "Since you're permitting anyone to vote, these women demand the same right you've accorded to others," Hernández announced.

Board personnel were at first nonplussed and insisted that the women go away. "Everybody knows that there are no women who work in this factory," one board agent declared. But after huddling and talking it over for an hour, in the end the board was still bound by Cosio's declaration that no IDs would be required and that anyone presenting themselves would be allowed to cast a ballot. The strikers hooted at the burlesque they had made of the labor board's trick.

Then the CTM supporters voted. One voter was an eighteen-year-old youth who gave his name as Josue. In a conversation a block from the plant the day before, he admitted that he had been hired on May 15. "Reyes told us to say that we had started work before February 12 [the cutoff date for eligibility] if we were asked," he stated.

Not all the votes cast by CTM members went to the CTM. Anticipating the labor board's decision, a progressive CTM local with no corrupt ties to the maquiladoras—Gastronom Sección 22—recruited some of its members to go down and vote for October 6, the independent union.

The final total was seventy-four to sixty-five in favor of the independent union. Since no one was asked to provide proof of employment status, it was unclear what the results would have been if only the votes of eligible employees had been counted. Following the voting, Cosio stated that "we ran this election correctly, and we don't intend to change the way we do it."

The local labor board includes management and labor representatives, in addition to government officials, and at least one member had an apparent conflict of interest. The labor representative, elected at a convention of Baja California's government-affiliated unions, was Fernando Murrieta Llaguno, a past official of the CTM cinematographers' union. "I'm independent," Murrieta said. "I'm not afraid to rule against the CTM if it's doing something wrong."

The irregularities, however, proved too much for Judge Maria Lourdes Villagomez Guillon of the Fifth District Federal Court. Hours after the voting concluded, Villagomez suspended all of the board's actions against the strike and the independent union and set a June 18 date to hear evidence on the issues. Meanwhile, the strike continued.

According to Han Young plant manager Won Young Kang, the company lost forty thousand dollars during the strike's first week. "This conflict is being used by U.S. unions and political parties in Mexico who don't want us here," he charged. Those in favor of the independent union "aren't sincere," he alleged. His accusation was parroted by state labor secretary Verastegui, who claimed that U.S. unions were behind the Han Young conflict. Although no U.S. union representatives were present at either election or during the strike, that didn't stop the attacks in the press. Mary Tong was warned again by the Mexican Interior Ministry that she would be deported if she tried to attend any activity involving the Han Young workers in Mexico. And in an atrium outside the labor board's offices in a Tijuana shopping mall, CTM officials put up a huge banner declaring *"¡Mary Tong Fuera de Tijuana!"* (Mary Tong, Get Out of Tijuana!).

"The government accuses us of weakening our country," responded strike leader Miguel Ángel Sánchez. "But they're protecting foreign investors who are here exploiting us and violating our laws, when they should be protecting us and enforcing the law. If it's okay for the companies to cross the border to do this, I think it's not only right for workers to support each other across the same border, it's necessary."

Under Mexican law, no one is permitted to remove the red-and-black banners that symbolize a legal strike or to enter the factory until the dispute is settled. Nevertheless, on June 3, Tijuana authorities moved in with a massive show of force. More than one hundred members of the city's SWAT team, the Special Forces, went to the plant, where they not only tore down the red-and-black banners but burned them in the middle of the street. Police then opened the factory doors and ushered in a contingent of strikebreakers. These actions are all serious violations of Article 123 of the Mexican Constitution and the country's Federal Labor Law. State authorities also issued arrest warrants for Enrique Hernández and José Peñaflor.

At the June 18 hearing, Judge Villagomez cited the actions of the labor board in reopening the plant as serious violations of the law. In an appeal for support, Hernández and five members of the Han Young strike committee complained bitterly that "the protection which the state government is giving to foreign maquiladora investors is very obvious. The government is allowing them to trample on the Federal Labor Law and the Constitution, which protect the right to strike. In Baja California, labor justice is a dead letter."

Labor board chief Jesús Cosio responded that "there are political forces among the strikers seeking to use this dispute to their own advantage." Plant manager Kang also hinted darkly that there were "political groups" among the strikers and claimed that "they want too much money, and we already pay better than anyone else."

Strikers charged that they faced a conspiracy between the labor board, the maquiladora owners, and government-affiliated unions.

"We're challenging the system the government uses to attract foreign investment," Hernández said. "They keep wages low by encouraging corrupt unions to sign protection contracts with the maquiladora owners, guaranteeing labor peace. If our strike is successful, thousands of other workers will try to break out of that system."

Moves to crush the strike led to a backlash that could be seen in the surging growth in voter support for Mexico's left-wing opposition party, the PRD. The party had been very small in Baja California for many years. But two weeks before the June 28 municipal elections, polls estimated support at over 30 percent, and growing at 8 percent a week. Meanwhile, support for the conservative National Action Party (PAN), which had ruled Baja California and Tijuana for eight years, was dropping. The PRI, at the time Mexico's national governing party, was a distant third. Both the PAN and the PRI share a policy of encouraging foreign investment, particularly in the maquiladoras.

Most observers credited the growth in PRD support to its increasingly open sympathy for the struggle at the Han Young factory. Whereas Tijuana's labor board, the association of maquiladora owners, and Baja California's state government cooperated in trying to crush the strike, the PRD increasingly embraced the cause of maquiladora workers. The party's candidate for municipal president (mayor), Jesús Ruiz Barraza, the rector of the city's university, met with the strikers. Afterward, his campaign issued a leaflet calling for a minimum wage of 100 pesos a day in the maquiladoras, child care for the mostly female workforce, and free transportation to and from work. (Daily wages at Han Young averaged 64 pesos, and most maquiladora workers earned less.) These work-related issues were linked to demands for basic city services in the barrios, including housing, water, electricity, paved streets, and sewers.

The PRD leaflet was distributed in the neighborhoods of maquiladora workers by the thousands. Barraza spent three hundred thousand dollars on his campaign, supplementing it with a first-ever infusion of money from Mexico City. Araceli Domínguez, a reporter who had covered the Han Young strike for the city's largest newspaper, *El Mexicano*, ran for city council on the PRD ticket. She put strikers to work painting and posting her banners, and the paper promptly forced her to quit her job.

Meanwhile, the PRD began organizing its first neighborhood committees in working-class electoral precincts. Tijuana's fast-growing street sellers association, which represents thousands of migrant workers from Oaxaca, set up a PRD committee headed by its president.

"We're trying to involve our party in the life of the people," explained activist Jorge Alberto Jiménez, a worker in the social security office who passed out hundreds of leaflets. "We want to get rid of the apathy which has traditionally kept voter participation very low."

Not all of the strikers had faith in electoral politics as a solution to their dilemma, and most shared a cynicism common in Mexico about the corruption of political parties and the political process generally. Nevertheless, many strikers organized demonstrations and marches throughout the city every day. They turned the PAN's election slogan "With a heart for Tijuana" into rude chants of "Abusing workers with a heart!" and "Violating labor rights with a heart!" In the city's working-class neighborhoods, growing crowds answered back with laughter and cheers.

Mexico City mayor Cuauhtémoc Cárdenas, the PRD's candidate for national president in 1988 and 1994, held a campaign rally in Tijuana for PRD candidates, drawing two thousand people. He later met with the Han Young strikers and promised to publicize their strike in the nation's capital.

A delegation of union leaders and opposition figures then met with the undersecretary of labor in Mexico City, to protest the violation of federal labor laws in Tijuana. Afterward, the new independent union federation, the National Union of Workers, held a press conference in cooperation with PRD congressional deputies to call for support for the strike. The move marked a significant step in the breakup of Mexico's old political system, in which the major union federations were allied closely with the ruling political party.

Support for the PRD increased dramatically. Although the party had won only 10,000 votes in Tijuana in 1992 and 1995, on June 28 it received 25,800, or 9.5 percent of the total votes cast—not as large a total as the overly optimistic polls had forecast but an extremely significant increase in support nonetheless. "In the past [with vote totals like these], I would have been entitled to a seat on the city council, along with two of our other candidates," observed Aurora Pelayo, PRD president for Baja California. "But the PRI and the PAN engineered an electoral reform last year which they used to deny us any seats at all." The party did, however, win council positions in the smaller cities of Mexicali, Ensenada, and Rosarito.

"We succeeded in provoking a general debate over the conditions of workers," Ruiz Barraza said later. "While our city has grown as a result of the increase in maquiladora-generated jobs, we've become impoverished because of the low wages. Since NAFTA was signed, the whole border area has moved backward economically."

Of Mexico's 10 million permanently employed workers, more than a million work in the border factories—two hundred thousand in Tijuana alone. Increased voter participation and worker activism could prove crucial in Mexico's future national elections. "If the movement among maquiladora workers grows," says Hernández, who formerly headed the PRD state organization in Baja California, "we could win tens or even hundreds of thousands of new votes."

That prospect would certainly unbalance the country's power structure. Border political authorities and factory owners clearly viewed this potential political shift with alarm.

As the political campaign unfolded in Tijuana, activity accelerated outside Mexico. More than five hundred labor and human rights leaders in the United States and a dozen other countries signed a letter to President Ernesto Zedillo, asking that he act to overrule local actions suppressing the strike. That appeal, delivered by a delegation to the Mexican consulate in San Francisco, was fiercely attacked by Baja California state authorities, who alleged again that the strike was a provocation by U.S. unions intent on poisoning the climate for foreign investment.

Hyundai Corporation became a target of solidarity actions by West Coast longshore workers in Portland, Oregon. When the HML *Chal-*

lenger, a Hyundai-owned ship carrying the company's huge cargo containers, pulled up to the Portland docks on June 13, it was met by a picket line organized by the city's Cross Border Organizing Committee. Prominent on the picket line were two workers from the Han Young plant, Miguel Sánchez Murillo and Ricardo Hernández Hernández.

As members of the local longshore union reported to work the ship, the two strikers and their supporters explained the issues. About fifteen longshore workers already in the terminal decided to leave, and another dozen refused to cross the picket line as they arrived to work. One picketer was arrested as she sat in the road leading to the docks. Although the arbitrator called to the scene eventually ruled that the dockworkers had to go to work, the unloading of the *Challenger*'s cargo was delayed for twenty-four hours. Shipping sources estimate that such delays can cost a shipper tens of thousands of dollars.

The longshore action was followed on June 16 by coordinated demonstrations in eight U.S. cities, along with Toronto and Mexico City. Union federations in Brazil, Spain, Peru, Bangladesh, and other countries also protested the situation in Tijuana directly to the Mexican government.

For months after Tijuana's SWAT team reopened the struck plant, Hernández and Peñaflor were careful not to appear in the same place at the same time. Almost every day, members of the state judicial police came knocking on the door of Peñaflor's office seeking the two, telling the frightened secretary that they were going to be arrested at any time.

To avoid detention, Hernández moved the headquarters of the independent union out of the small hall behind the lawyer's office, to a second-floor warren of tiny rooms near the downtown jai alai court. Hernández himself kept on the move throughout the city, rarely spending much time in any one place.

But early in the morning of December 17, 1998, their efforts came to an end. A police squadron swooped down on the two as they were setting out for the state capital in Mexicali. There, they intended to file legal motions supporting the strike at Han Young, which by then had become a cause célèbre along the border.

The two were taken to the offices of the federal prosecutor and interrogated for more than five hours. They were then temporarily released but were told to return within days, when they could again face indefinite incarceration.

Both were accused of holding the Han Young factory's owner, Ho Young Lee, hostage inside the plant for an hour in June 1998, during the strike's second week. On June 2, the clerk of the city's labor board had come to the plant to insist that the workers return to work. He tore down the strike banners that workers had strung across the doors and permitted Ho Young Lee to enter and eat lunch. While he was inside, the strikers restrung the red-and-black strike flags across the doors. The prosecutor claimed that this action was an attempt to hold the owner captive in the factory, although he later left without incident. Hernández and Peñaflor described the accusation as a pretext for further legal repression.

Despite efforts by city authorities to keep the independent union movement from spreading, workers at other Tijuana factories began to join it. Both the Han Young strike and the election effectively increased the popularity of the independent October 6 Union for Industry and Commerce in Tijuana barrios. Hernández and the strikers were soon approached by workers from the closed Cobe Renal plant. The factory, belonging to Colorado-based Gambro Healthcare, assembled parts for kidney dialysis machines. Although the company had shut down the original plant, it then reopened in another location with an entirely new workforce. The plant's former workers asked for help in forcing the company to pay the severance benefits mandated by Mexican labor law and the right to get jobs in the reopened plant.

Then workers at the factory of Pennsylvania-based Axiohm Transaction Solutions Corporation also asked the independent union for help. The plant makes printer heads used in most bank ATM machines and Quick-Pick Lotto ticket machines. Inocencia Hernández, a supervisor at the factory for eleven years, said that she and her co-workers worried that they, like workers at Cobe Renal, would lose their jobs. "When you reach a certain number of years at the company, they let you go," she explained, "because they don't want to pay the increasing benefits that the law requires."

Inocencia Hernández and others collected the signatures of almost the entire workforce on a petition for workplace improvements, which she gave to the plant manager. "Three days later," she recalled, "a lawyer in the human relations department called me in and told me the company didn't need my services any longer. A policeman escorted me out of the plant, pointing a gun at my head. We were accused of planning to assassinate the plant manager and burn the factory." Six other workers were also fired. Mark Basla, Axiohm's director of corporate communications, dismissed the accusations. "Axiohm is an ethical company in its relations with all its employees," he claimed.

After the firings, Axiohm workers met with Enrique Hernández, and the independent union then filed a notice of its intent to strike with the city's labor board (the first legal step in the process of demanding representation rights). The board, however, refused to hold an election that would have allowed workers at the plant to vote for the independent union.

The close relationship between Tijuana authorities and the maquiladora managers was further challenged when the UNT organized a chapter in Baja California a few months after the May strike. Enrique Hernández became one of the group's three co-presidents. The local federation started with a combined membership of twenty-five thousand workers, and another three thousand workers in state health clinics immediately joined.

The new federation began to challenge fundamental government economic policies. When President Zedillo offered workers a 14 percent salary increase to compensate for inflation, the UNT demanded 22 percent. Along the border, the federation began to campaign for a daily wage of 100 pesos (10 dollars), double the average maquiladora salary at the time. "We are rejecting government policies which use low wages to attract foreign investment," Hernández explained.

The economic situation of the Han Young strikers was growing desperate, however. "About twenty of us found jobs in other maquiladoras, but when the bosses found out we were strikers, we were fired immediately," said Francisco Solis. "Lots of companies have computers with lists of workers like us, who they think will cause problems." Some strikers got construction work on a snowy mountaintop in a national park farther south on the Baja California peninsula, but they returned after a few days. They had no coats or jackets to withstand the cold.

"My family in Veracruz has no money because I can't send any home," Solis worried. "I'm feeling desperate because they write me that they don't have enough to eat. But I don't have enough money to return home, and there are no jobs there, anyway. The fact that more workers here in Tijuana want to join our union now is the main thing that keeps most of us going."

Then, almost exactly a year after the first legal strike, it all started again.

On April 6, 1999, the First Collegial Court of the Fifteenth District, the highest judicial authority in Baja California Norte, issued a ruling that shocked the state's political establishment. The court held that Tijuana authorities had violated the law the previous June in suppressing the strike at Han Young.

"The justice system of the republic protects [the independent union] against acts of the authorities [in declaring the strike illegal]," the court wrote. The opinion, granting the strike legal status, was signed by all three sitting judges. Gerardo Medel Torres, the new chief of the local labor board, which the year before had called the strike "nonexistent," also publicly conceded that it was legal.

In the year that followed the May 1998 strike, the Han Young plant had moved across town. The company used the move as a pretext for arguing that the old orders giving the October 6 union bargaining rights at Han Young no longer applied, that they were valid only for the old location. That illogic was rejected by the judges, who ruled that the factory was operated by the same company and was subject to the same board decisions.

Following the court's ruling, the independent October 6 union once again tied red-and-black strike flags across the gate of the Han Young factory, bringing production to a halt on May 3. Instead of respecting the high court's decision, however, city and state police immediately began trying to bring strikebreakers into the facility to resume work, even after the union obtained further court orders protecting its strike.

On May 5, a patriotic holiday in Mexico, two attorneys arrived at the struck factory accompanied by ten trucks of Tijuana municipal police. The attorneys refused to identify themselves publicly, but police commandant Armando Rascón later identified them as Marcantonio Mejía and Jesús Ibarra Estrada, lawyers for the state employers' association, COPARMEX.

The two demanded that police take down the strike banners and permit twenty workers, assembled a short distance away, to enter. At first Rascón announced that he would comply. When asked if this action would violate the state court's decision, he declared, "That doesn't matter." Rascón claimed that he had no idea whether the attorneys had a valid court order telling him to break the strike. "My orders come from the state," he said.

After television crews from local stations arrived and began filming the action, and representatives of the federal Labor Department and the local PRD began taking notes, Rascón made an about-face and told the strikebreakers to go home.

Six days later, however, more than a hundred members of Tijuana's Special Forces police detachment, joined by state judicial police, did tear down the strike flags and escort seventy people into the plant. Nonetheless, production did not resume since, according to the union, few of the new workers knew how to operate the factory's welding equipment.

The next day, Enrique Hernández, who had been elected the union's general secretary, tied the strike flags across the closed factory gates once more. "I don't care how many times they take the flags down," he declared. "We will just put them up again."

Police action wasn't confined to the streets in front of the plant. Silvestre Reyes, Miguel Ángel Sánchez, and other members of the strike committee described how state judicial police came to their homes, telling their families that they would be arrested. Reyes had been a Han Young employee since 1993, and Sánchez since 1995.

New legal charges were brought against Hernández, Reyes, and Sánchez, accusing them of illegally depriving the company of the use of its factory. The union obtained injunctions blocking all the arrests, but even after the court prohibition, city police issued new warrants against Hernández.

The Baja California courts were reluctant to enforce their own decisions. Pedro Fernández Reyes Colin, the lead judge who signed the state high court decision, said that although he had the power to enforce it, he was taking no action. "I'm not aware that any violations are occurring," he stated.

On May 13, Peñaflor, attorney for the October 6 union, filed criminal charges against state officials for failure to obey the court decisions and injunctions. Dodging the police who had been sent to detain them, Peñaflor and Hernández flew to Mexico City, where the federal Senate set up a commission to investigate the situation in Tijuana.

The state chapter of COPARMEX had encouraged Tijuana and Baja California police to defy the court rulings. On May 5, COPARMEX director Pedro Martínez and Maquiladora Industry Association head José Calleros Rivera called the resumption of the Han Young strike a threat to investment all along the border. Martínez described the strike as a "breeding ground" for links to U.S. unions and the left-wing PRD. In a Tijuana press conference, the two warned that independent unions could spread to other factories on the border in the wake of a union victory at Han Young.

Local newspapers reported that Ted Chung, president of Hyundai Precision America, Inc., had publicly called on Tijuana's mayor, Francisco Vega de la Madrid, to request federal troops to provide security in the maquiladoras. Peter Ahn, spokesperson for Hyundai Precision America, denied that Chung had made such a request. "It seems he was misquoted," Ahn said, adding that any such suggestion had come from the mayor during a visit to Hyundai's Tijuana facility. Ahn claimed that he had never been informed of the court decision declaring the Han Young strike legal.

"I've been told that there is no strike and that the plant entrance is being blocked by outsiders who never worked there," he said.

For weeks, Tijuana teetered on the brink of official lawlessness, as city and state police defied Mexico's legal system. Raúl Ramírez, member of the Baja California Academy of Human Rights, warned that "the state is in danger of violating the Constitution and the Federal Labor Law ... as it succumbs to the temptation to use force." A group of federal senators who conducted an investigation that May called the situation a growing political crisis. Speaking for the group, Senator Rosa Albina Garabito declared that "violations of the rule of law by actions of the authorities themselves betray an inadmissible contempt which we cannot tolerate.... We demand an immediate and definitive end to the repression."

Hernández, Peñaflor, and the strikers were eventually able to suppress the arrest warrants, but the strike was broken.

The plant resumed production, and the strikers again were forced to find work where they could. Most were eventually dispersed. Ironically, two years later, Hyundai began reabsorbing into its main plant the work that it had formerly given to contractors such as Han Young, Laymex, and Daewon.

STRIKERS BEATEN—COMPLAINT RESOLVED

The Camino Real is a swanky Tijuana establishment full of men in expensive business suits—a modern concrete blockhouse, garishly painted in violently clashing shades of purple and yellow. Its very appearance made it an appropriate choice for a meeting about labor conflict, and on June 22, 2000, it was the scene of a conflict that suddenly turned immediate and violent.

In Salons Uno and Dos, the hotel's largest combined hall, Javier Moctezuma Barragán, Mexican labor subsecretary, began intoning a list of rights won for Mexican workers by the outgoing Zedillo administration. Three hundred well-dressed listeners filled the auditorium's seats and lined the walls, appearing to give him rapt attention. Most wore badges with the initials of the CROC.

As Moctezuma spoke, a small group of two dozen workers entered and walked quietly down the aisle between the seats, carrying banners. Hand-painted letters on torn sheets called for *libertad sindical*—the right of workers to decide for themselves what union they wished to join—and condemned the repression of the strike at the Han Young factory.

When the group arrived at the front of the room, its leader, Enrique Hernández, looked out at the sea of hostile, angry faces as Moctezuma fell silent. Then suddenly, with no warning, men from both sides of the aisle jumped from their seats, screaming as they began beating Hernández and his companions with their fists.

Hernández took a blow to the side of his head and went down. His friends turned to flee, but the aisle behind them was full of men with CROC badges, fists flying. Hernández made it to his feet, only to be pushed toward a corner of the hall, where he was knocked down again. His head snapped back, as heavy shoes kicked his cheek. Other kickers went for the ribs. One swung a pedestal, angling for Hernández's face.

The room broke into chaos, as the advocates of *libertad sindical* were forced to flee under a rain of blows. Hernández, once again on his feet, was pushed and buffeted by fists as he backed out of the salon. Pursued by dozens of angry attackers, the workers were pushed through the hotel lobby and out the main doors. The Tijuana newspaper *La Frontera* later identified the leader of the perpetrators as Raniel Falcón, director of a youth group organized by the CROC, who was linked to the state government of the National Action Party. Hernández said they included a group of CROC-affiliated truckers.

After a few minutes, Moctezuma came out and stood halfway down the lobby stairs, while Hernández and his companions demanded that he do something to guarantee their right to be heard. The subsecretary announced that there was a "lack of space." He took a few questions from agitated reporters and returned to the salon. No invitations or guarantees of safety were forthcoming for the workers left outside.

This might have been simply one more demonstration of the problems encountered in organizing independent unions in Mexico if one important factor had not lent the situation an air of pathetic irony. The

Mexican Labor Ministry had organized the meeting, titled a "Seminar on Union Freedom in Mexico," to explain two new agreements it had signed the month before. In those agreements, it promised to protect the right of workers to form independent unions.

The case that led to one of the two accords was that of the very people beaten and left outside—the workers whose strike at the Han Young factory had been the first by an independent union in the history of the maquiladoras. Not only were these well-known advocates of independent unionism violently expelled from the meeting, but the very name of their strike and their union was so completely absent from the commentary of the assembled dignitaries that it seemed forbidden.

"They threw us out because it was impossible to maintain the pretense that the freedom to organize independent unions exists while we were present in the room, living evidence of the lie," Enrique Hernández commented bitterly.

When the North American Free Trade Agreement went into effect in January 1994, enforcing labor rights in Mexico became the responsibility of more than the Mexican government alone. All three NAFTA countries, including the United States and Canada, agreed to the North American Agreement on Labor Cooperation (the labor side agreement), in which each country pledged to enforce its own labor laws and which set up a process for hearing complaints that labor rights were being violated.

In the ensuing years, more than twenty complaints have been filed. Han Young was one of the highest-profile cases. Following the San Diego hearing in 1998, the NAO concluded that serious violations of Mexican law had occurred.

But in May 2000, U.S. labor secretary Alexis Herman and her Mexican counterpart, Mariano Palacios Alcocer, signed agreements to settle the case at Han Young and ITAPSA, a factory in Mexico City where similar violations of labor rights and health and safety laws had taken place. Mexico agreed to hold two seminars to discuss better protection for workers who were organizing independent unions and better enforcement of health and safety laws. The Tijuana meeting was the first of the two. The second seminar, scheduled for Mexico City, where ITAPSA is located, was never held, in the aftermath of the Tijuana beatings.

The agreements did not require the Mexican government to do anything concrete to change the situation of workers in either plant. "We're extremely disappointed," commented Robin Alexander, director of international affairs for the United Electrical Workers, a U.S. union that supported the FAT in its fight at ITAPSA. "We expected there would be a more significant outcome."

The UE, the FAT, and the October 6 union at Han Young had held particularly high hopes for the complaints about lack of enforcement of health and safety laws. As mentioned earlier, Mexico could have been fined a percentage of its export earnings, a potentially huge amount of money, for health and safety violations. With the settlement agreements, that possibility was removed.

The problem of lack of enforcement was particularly acute at Han Young. Although the Baja California labor board ruled the strike illegal, the Mexican Fifteenth District Federal Court overruled that decision three times and ordered the labor board to protect the workers' right to strike. Yet the board simply refused to implement those orders. Instead, Tijuana and Baja California authorities called in the police to remove the strikers' picket lines, burned their strike flags, and escorted strike-breakers into the plant.

In addition, strikers such as Julián Puente were blacklisted. "I went to Hyundai's main plant and got hired," he said. Hyundai was offering 69 pesos a day, about 7 dollars, for skilled welders. "But then one of their foremen recognized me as a striker. The human relations manager told me there was no work for me there." Like other strikers, he could find only occasional work on local construction projects.

"The settlements didn't remedy our situation at all," charged José Peñaflor. "The violence [at the June 22 meeting] has its roots in efforts by corrupt union leaders to hold onto their protection contracts. The problem is the enforcement of the law. Despite what the government says in meetings like [this], Mexico's labor policy is actually hardening.

It's clearer than ever that it won't permit any kind of independent union on the border."

"There are about six hundred fifty thousand union contracts in Mexico, but only fifty thousand of them are real negotiated agreements," explains José Luis Hernández, vice president of the UNT. "The rest are simply protection agreements. The people who benefit from them are a kind of mafia. To get rid of these agreements is going to require a virtual war."

For the U.S. Labor Department, the beatings at the Camino Real were a big embarrassment. Four department representatives attended the seminar, led by Louis Karesh, then deputy secretary and head of the NAO. "I'm disappointed to see what happened," he said, but he tried to present a positive interpretation. "I was glad to see Moctezuma came out to talk to the workers."

Later Labor Department comments were less sympathetic. "How one views what happened in Tijuana is in the eye of the beholder," Andrew Samet, deputy undersecretary for international affairs, told Larry Weiss of the Minneapolis Resource Center for the Americas. Labor Secretary Alexis Herman even wrote a letter to UE president John Hovis, suggesting that the strikers had provoked their own beatings.

During the huge demonstrations at the meeting of the World Trade Organization in Seattle in December 1999, the Clinton administration argued that free trade agreements could protect workers' rights while boosting profits for large corporations. It pointed to NAFTA's labor side agreement as proof of its claim. Vice President (and then presidential candidate) Al Gore went even further, claiming that he could guarantee the enforcement of labor rights in future trade negotiations.

Moctezuma held out the same promise to Mexican workers, declaring in his speech at the Camino Real that "NAFTA has as a purpose increasing the respect for workers' rights." Mexico has developed "a new labor culture of harmony and cooperation between workers and employers" as a result of NAFTA, he added.

But Karesh admitted that because the treaty is government-to-government, "we can't get a particular worker's job back or try to resolve cases in favor of particular groups of workers." Stating that he'd hold further dialogue with the Mexican government as a result of the beatings in Tijuana, Karesh pointed out that the Mexican government did promise two important reforms in the settlement agreements. It pledged that workers would be able to choose a union to represent them by secret ballot in future elections, a change from the current procedure requiring workers to announce their votes in public. And it agreed to publish a list of all union contracts, which would make protection contracts public knowledge for the first time, especially to those workers who labor under them.

The UNT's José Luis Hernández called the situation "absolutely absurd." Noting that Moctezuma had personally invited him to the seminar and had guaranteed that the October 6 union would be given a chance to speak and make proposals, Hernández describes the beatings as an act of treachery. "We didn't have a problem of physical space in the hall, but of political space in our country. The Mexican government signs these agreements to project a certain image, but in reality there's a lack of political will to enforce them. The government depends on this system of protection contracts, both to attract foreign investors who want low wages and because this system supports them politically."

He pointed out that the beatings took place within a few days of the July 2 national election, when the governing PRI lost to a competing party for the first time in its history.

Hernández announced to the Han Young workers that he would lay their situation before the AFL-CIO. "What's happening here affects U.S. workers too, since companies are relocating production to Mexico to take advantage of our situation," he explained. Despite the increase in nationalist rhetoric in the national election campaign, Hernández called cross-border ties important to the survival of workers on both sides. "In the last few years, it's clear to us that the AFL-CIO has a different attitude now toward Mexicans, both here in Mexico and in the U.S.," he noted. "We're cooperating and supporting each other much more now than in the past. We'd like to see the AFL-CIO take this case to the U.S. administration."

In the end, however, Robin Alexander of UE argues that unions must face the fact that the NAFTA process itself is fatally flawed. In order to protect workers' rights adequately, "we need a separate entity that has teeth, that has the power to require enforcement," she says. "It's obvious now that NAFTA won't sanction governments when they violate workers' rights and that companies can't be held accountable, either. We don't want more meetings and further study. We want real changes."

For Moctezuma Barragán, however, the situation was fine. In ending the Tijuana seminar, he complimented his audience, telling them that "in Baja California, society has a clear democratic mission, characterized by open and frank discussion."

The workers expelled from the meeting weren't in much of a position to argue.

5

BUILD A HOUSE, GO TO JAIL

CAÑON BUENAVISTA

Every day at midmorning, the phone rings in Julio Sandoval's house in Cañon Buenavista, and his daughter Florentina answers. It's the daily call from the prison in Ensenada, twenty miles away, where Sandoval has been held since December 2001.

Florentina sits at a cable-spool table talking to her dad, while her toddler, Jonathan Abel Sandoval Silva, practices his new skill of walking on the dirt floor. Meanwhile, Julio's wife, Juana, heats tortillas on a stove set up on cinder blocks, connected by a rubber hose to a big methane bottle the family has to fill twice a month. Their one large room, dim even at midday, is divided down the middle by a yellow blanket.

Over the phone, Julio gives his daughter instructions to pass on to his lawyer, and Florentina tells him the news from home. After the call, Juana and Florentina pack the three kids into an old pickup and leave for Ensenada. There, they spend the rest of the day in front of the fish taco stands on the waterfront, selling tourists the wool shoulder bags Juana weaves at home at night as well as jewelry and crafts made by their neighbors.

The Sandoval home is better than many in Cañon Buenavista. "Some of us live in cardboard houses and cook on wood fires, a very dangerous combination," Julio points out. He speaks quickly over his home phone from prison in an interview arranged by the family, his voice rising in an urgent, angry staccato. The house's exterior plywood wall still shows the charred marks of one such fire, which burned down the home next door.

These residences of the poor, scattered over a desert hillside, hardly seem much of a threat to anyone, yet Julio Sandoval has been in prison for helping indigenous migrant workers in Baja California settle in homes like these. When he was arrested, he joined Beatriz Chávez, a well-known leader of similar efforts in San Quintin, farther south down the Baja peninsula. Chávez was held in El Cereso prison from May 2001 until the fall of 2002, when the charges against her were reduced and she was released. Sandoval, however, was still in prison a year and a half after his arrest, facing a five-year term.

Their crime is an offense unique to Baja: *despojo agravado*. *Despojo*, according to Tijuana attorney José Peñaflor Barrón, "means using land or water belonging to someone else, without their authorization, in a furtive manner." This offense is on the books throughout Mexico. But in Baja the legislature created a new, more serious crime a few years ago—*despojo agravado*—which charges that a person has led or instigated others in committing *despojo*.

The law is directed against communities created by land invasions and especially targets the people who lead them. *Despojo agravado* is really a political offense. "The government is afraid of the poor sections of the population, especially the migrant indigenous people from Oaxaca, and wants control over them," Beatriz Chávez said over the phone from El Cereso before her release. "They think their only way to ensure control is by throwing the leaders of social movements among them into prison. It's a racist attitude."

Baja California authorities would not permit a reporter to go into the prison to talk to either of the two prisoners, nor would they make any public statements about the cases.

Tijuana, Baja California Norte, June 1995. A worker looks over the fence between Mexico and the United States, hoping to cross at a moment when the Border Patrol may not be looking.

La Alianza barrio, Monterrey, Nuevo Leon, August 2001. Electric wires illegally hooked up to the main line half a mile away snake into the workers' barrio of La Alianza, where the city of Monterrey provides no services. In many communities of maquiladora workers, this is the only way families can get electricity for their houses.

Coachella, California, April 1995. José and Ingracia Castillo participated in the great 1973 grape strike by the United Farm Workers. After being blacklisted, they got jobs at David Freedman, the only union grape grower at the time. Just days after the passage of NAFTA, the company decided that it could not compete with grapes grown in Mexico and went out of business. After twenty-two years there, the Castillos lost their jobs and their union. The union banner they carried for years is on the wall behind them.

Mexicali Valley, Baja California Norte, June 1996. Honorina Ruiz, six years old, ties bunches of green onions together in a field farmed by Muranaka Farms, a U.S. grower. Her mother, Esperanza, and brother Rigoberto (at right) work with her.

Tijuana, Baja California Norte, December 1993. A young worker in the Tijuana maquiladora of Plasticos Bajacal pulls plastic parts from a plastic molding machine. The parts will be assembled into coat hangers for the garment industry. Workers in this plant tried unsuccessfully to organize an independent, democratic union in 1993.

Tijuana, Baja California Norte, December 1993. Workers try to vote for the independent union in an open ballot in front of the Plasticos Bajacal plant. They are escorted to the voting table by thugs from the company-favored union and vote in front of company officials. The head of Tijuana's labor board, José Mandujano, formerly the lawyer for the maquiladora association, asks a worker to declare aloud which union he is voting for.

Tijuana, Baja California Norte, April 1995. Francisco Ortiz and his son sit in the room in which they live with Francisco's two other sons, who work in the maquiladoras in Tijuana. Their entire extended family lives in this house, including Francisco's mother and grandmother as well as an aunt, an uncle, and cousins.

Tijuana, Baja California Norte, May 1996. Women workers from the National O-Ring maquiladora demonstrate for women's rights during the May Day parade in Tijuana. Their factory was closed, and the women laid off and black-listed, after they filed charges of sexual harassment against their employer in courts in Tijuana and Los Angeles.

Tijuana, Baja California Norte, February 1998. Silvestre Reyes was a member of the executive committee of the independent union at the Han Young maquiladora. Workers at Han Young fought to organize an independent union from 1997 to 1999. The graffiti behind Reyes reads *"Libre asociación sindical"* (Freedom of union association). Over it, supporters of the company union at Han Young have painted the slogan *"Somos PRIistas"* (We are PRIistas, supporters of Mexico's governing party at the time, the PRI).

Tijuana, Baja California Norte, May 1998. Han Young striker Miguel Ángel Solorzano's right arm was injured when he fell in an industrial accident at the plant. The fractures weren't set properly, and he was forced to return to work ten days later. He still can't close his fist completely. One of the main reasons Han Young workers organized an independent union and went on strike was to improve safety conditions at the factory.

Tijuana, Baja California Norte, May 1998. Members of Tijuana's SWAT team, the Special Forces, march beside the Han Young factory as they prepare to illegally reopen the plant and bring in strikebreakers. After fighting for their union for a year, workers struck Han Young on May 22, 1998, in the first legal strike by an independent union in a maquiladora.

Tijuana, Baja California Norte, June 2000. Uciel Álvarez, a striker at the Han Young factory and a member of the independent October 6 union, moments after he and other strikers and supporters were beaten and expelled from a meeting organized by the Mexican government to discuss their right to form independent unions. Álvarez, who suffered facial cuts and bruises on his body, stands outside the doors of the swanky Camino Real hotel where the meeting was held.

Chávez and Sandoval see racism in the way indigenous people from the Mixtec, Zapotec, and Triqui towns of Oaxaca, who make up the rural workforce throughout Baja California, are targeted for prosecution. The state power structure, they say, treats these migrants as inferior and as a threat.

Thousands of indigenous families come north every year from southern Mexico to work for Baja's large landowners. Growers such as the Castaneda family and the Canelos family own thousands of hectares of land and form partnerships with U.S. corporations to grow and export tomatoes, strawberries, and other row crops. In the late fall and early spring, almost all the cilantro and green onions in Los Angeles supermarkets come from Maneadero, San Quintin, and the Mexicali Valley.

Cañon Buenavista was created during two separate land invasions by rural workers from the ranches of Maneadero, the agricultural valley just south of Ensenada.

The first invasion was led by Beníto García, a controversial figure among Oaxacan migrants. García was a charismatic leader of agricultural strikes in the early 1980s, but he was accused in later years of misusing the money and power he had amassed. In his heyday in the 1980s, however, he organized farmworkers in the Maneadero Valley, who were living in labor camps or even sleeping by the roadside, into groups that occupied fifty hectares of land on a desert hillside south of town. The state government then bought out the people who had originally claimed ownership of the land and resold it to the occupiers through a state agency, the Immobiliaria Estatal.

Julio Sandoval arrived in Cañon Buenavista in 1990 and built a home there for his family. Sandoval had already led a similar movement in San Quintin to organize a community of Triqui farmworkers, called Nuevo San Juan Copala.

Sandoval first got into trouble with the state authorities when he began telling Cañon Buenavista residents not to make payments on their lots. He had discovered that in 1973 the federal government had declared that tens of thousand of hectares in northern Baja, including the land on which Cañon Buenavista sits, were government property. As such, the land had never belonged to private owners in the first place.

Sandoval's payment boycott received a lot of support because Immobiliaria Estatal had developed a nasty reputation in Baja's poor barrios. With every increase in inflation, the agency raised the sale price and payments for each lot, even ones it had already sold. Many families never got out of debt.

Sandoval appealed to the federal government to clarify who really owned the land. Under the Constitution, before it was "reformed" by President Carlos Salinas de Gortari in the mid-1990s, Mexican citizens were entitled to settle and build homes on unused federal property. If Cañon Buenavista land had belonged to the federal government, residents would not have to continue making payments.

The ownership issue, however, has remained unresolved. This is common for landownership claims in Mexico. Agrarian reform laws were used for decades to redistribute land in Mexico, but now, as a result, multiple owners often claim the same piece of property.

That confusion was the pretext used to imprison Beatriz Chávez.

In the San Quintin Valley, four hours south of Tijuana, indigenous farmworkers in the early 1990s began settling on land belonging to the Ejido Graciano Sánchez. *Ejidos* are farm communities, originally set up by Mexico's land reforms of the late 1930s. During that era, President Lázaro Cárdenas expropriated the haciendas belonging to large landholders, creating *ejidos* of small farmers, who then held the land in common.

All that changed in 1995, when President Salinas, one of NAFTA's biggest champions, changed Article 27 of the Mexican Constitution. This act privatized the *ejido* land, making it the property of individual families, who could then buy and sell it.

In Graciano Sánchez, where Oaxacan migrants were desperate for land to settle and build homes, the *ejido* began selling lots for houses. The same lot was often sold to two or even three different people. No services, such as electricity or water, were provided.

Chávez organized the residents. "I urged people who had receipts for a lot [they had not been allowed to claim] to occupy other pieces of land. That was my crime," she recalls. "We occupied the land on December 7, 1997, and set up a tent encampment." When residents sat in at a government office, Chávez was dragged out and beaten, receiving spinal injuries that required her to have an operation in the months that followed, while a prisoner in El Cereso.

Over the next two years, organized residents forced authorities to give them electricity and water connections. Meanwhile, the fight over conflicting claims of ownership was suspended, and residents believed that the government would eventually negotiate a solution. In May 2001, however, state police swooped down on the community and arrested Chávez again. This time, instead of spending just a few days in jail, she was charged with *despojo agravado*. She was held in prison for over a year and was released only when the charge was reduced to simple *despojo*, for which she was able to make bail.

The pressure of land hunger in Baja grows every year, as more families migrate from the south. Sandoval, a Triqui, was especially interested in finding more land for other Mixtec and Triqui farmworkers. In May 2000, he led landless migrants in Mancadero in taking direct action to find a place to build homes.

Esther Murrillo was one of a group of twenty families who occupied seventy-eight hectares in the hills surrounding Cañon Buenavista. They chose May 1, the international workers' holiday still celebrated in Mexico, as the day for their action.

"There were only thirty of us at first, and the police surrounded us," she remembers. "They said they were going to burn the houses we built, but twenty of us stayed up and watched all night. We had our children inside, and we were afraid of what might happen to them. But we were all calm and wouldn't move, so there were no physical confrontations. At first, there were forty houses, and a week later fifty. Now there are about five hundred. But for a long time, the police kept coming every night to scare us."

As a result of the new land invasion, Cañon Buenavista's total population swelled to twenty-seven hundred families—about ten thousand
people. Fourteen hundred families live in the older section, about 40
percent of whom are indigenous. Of the thirteen hundred families in
the new settlement, a thousand come from Mixtec and Triqui towns in
Oaxaca.

Murrillo had no money to pay rent or buy land. Making 50 to 70
pesos a day in the fields (5 to 7 dollars) and working only during the harvest season, she couldn't survive. "We're poor. So what should we do?"
she asks.

Once they occupied the land, however, Murrillo and her fellow residents were in for a surprise. "This was just a hillside covered with weeds,
full of snakes and tarantulas, and we cleaned it all up," she says. "But
then, after we'd done the work, a lot of supposed owners suddenly
appeared."

Before 1994, no public record of any private owners can be found.
That year, the highly politicized Baja California labor board gave the
land to Pedro Corral Castro, supposedly as compensation, in a resolution of a legal dispute over unpaid work done for his brother. No evidence was ever presented that his brother actually owned the land, however. Corral then offered it to people associated with the left-wing
opposition party, the PRD, to be divided into lots. After Sandoval and
other residents occupied the seventy-eight hectares, those associates
asked authorities to charge him with *despojo* and *despojo agravado*.

Julio Sandoval was first arrested in May 2000, not long after the
occupation, as he was pulling his car onto the main highway. He was
held for four days. Then, on December 11, 2001, the police came again.
"They surrounded our house at eleven P.M.," Florentina remembers.
"Then they came inside, at first saying they were chasing a robber, and
then saying they were inspecting the pipes. But they had rifles at the
ready." They found Sandoval sitting in his house, and this time they
took him in for good. Arrest warrants are still out for seventeen others,
including Sandoval's son, but authorities seem to be making little effort
to pick them up.

Tiburcio Pérez Castro, a highly respected professor of education at the National Pedagogical University and the first Mixtec to hold that position, believes that the Baja government is manipulating different groups within its political opposition against one another—in this case, the PRD and the indigenous group led by Julio Sandoval, the Independent Indigenous Movement for Unification and Struggle (Movimiento Independiente de Unificación y Lucha Indígena). "The government has exploited these differences to disarticulate the social movement," Pérez Castro argues.

But there are even more powerful reasons why the Baja California government rules with such an iron hand. As usual, the main one is money.

Until the 1960s, Baja California Norte was a desert state with a small population. The federal government of the 1930s and 1940s actually gave away land to entice people to come and settle, fearing that a sparse population would tempt the U.S. government to lay claim to the area. But after the bracero program ended in 1964, maquiladoras began to proliferate in Tijuana, eventually drawing hundreds of thousands of workers up to the border.

Farther south down the peninsula, in Maneadero and San Quintin, a tiny handful of large growers developed an agro-industrial empire supplying the U.S. market—maquiladoras of the fields. To bring in the crops, thousands of workers were brought every year from extremely poor indigenous communities in Oaxaca. Wages were kept low in order to make Baja's strawberries and tomatoes cheaper in Los Angeles supermarkets. In 2000, the minimum wage was 37.4 pesos a day (about 4 dollars), while a kilo of meat cost 38 pesos in the local market. Wages have barely risen since.

At first, Mixtec and Triqui families returned to Oaxaca at the end of each harvest season, but as the years passed, many decided to stay in Baja. As the permanent population grew, so did discontent. In 1988, more than a thousand tomato and strawberry pickers struck in San Quintin to raise wages. Their efforts to form an independent union were broken, however, and the strike leaders fled to the United States.

In 1998, one of the local growers, the Canelos family, failed to pay workers for four weeks. When the family wouldn't come up with the money, an angry crowd of pickers set fire to their packing shed.

Growers and maquiladora owners, the two most powerful groups in the state, have the same fears and share the same desires. They fear unions, strikes, and social unrest; and they want to protect property rights and maintain a climate that encourages investment.

The National Action Party (PAN), which won control in Baja California, formed a ruling political coalition of large ranchers, maquiladora owners, and company-friendly unions that has been in power ever since. The same party elected Mexico's current president, Vicente Fox, a former Coca-Cola executive, in 2000. And while condemning the old PRI for seventy years of undemocratic rule, the PAN has been even more pro-business.

In the middle of this conflict is a unique institution: the Baja California human rights prosecutor. This position, within the state prosecutor's office, was created in the national democratic upsurge that eventually toppled the ruling party, the PRI, from power in Baja California in 1988 and in the national elections of 2000. Raúl Ramírez, the current prosecutor, was appointed by the state's legislature in 2000. Like his two predecessors, he was a member of the left opposition PRD.

Ramírez points to the government's desire to protect investment above all else as the root of the land conflicts. Speaking of settlements like Cañon Buenavista, he says, "The authorities don't care about the poverty of these communities or their social problems, like lack of housing or drug addiction. But they are very concerned with the question of the land titles of the large landholders. They want to take care of their investments. So the government uses the law, the police, even the army. They say this provides safety and stability for investors. And they abandon the poor."

Pérez Castro accuses the government of enforcing only those provisions of the law that protect private property. "There's a law guaranteeing people the right to health care, but no one has any," he notes bitterly. "There's a law which protects the right to food, but thousands of people go hungry every day. The government's interest in protecting private property has become an obsession with them, because they want to present an image that Mexico is a safe place to invest money."

No fan of the PRI, he nevertheless notes the difference in the way the PAN has chosen to resolve land occupations since achieving power in Baja. "Until a few years ago, the way people got land for housing was through land invasions," he emphasizes. "This was basically tolerated by the PRI, which would then negotiate agreements with settlers to give them legal titles. It was illegal, but the PRI would negotiate a resolution. When the PAN came in, these land invasions were no longer tolerated. They enforced the letter of the law much more strictly and refused to negotiate."

The social cost of this policy, according to Ramírez, can be found in Maneadero and San Quintin fields on any given day during the harvest season. Whole families work together, children cutting vegetables alongside the adults. Félix, a twelve-year-old boy picking cilantro in Maneadero in June, reported that his parents were making about 70 pesos a day, while he was bringing home half that. "We can't live if we all don't work," he said, in the tone of someone explaining the obvious.

"Work on the big ranches affects children's development," Ramírez counters. "They don't go to school. There are no health services for them. They're exposed to the weather and to chemicals. And the purpose is the exploitation of their labor by ranchers who profit from it. It violates their right to a childhood, their labor rights, their social rights—everything we value."

Sandoval's and Chávez's problem, he says, is that they wouldn't just shut up about it. "Because they're both leaders that create a lot of noise, the easiest thing for the government is to throw them in jail. Instead of negotiating a solution, they use the police." In Chávez's case especially, the initiative to prosecute seemed to come from the government itself. When she appeared before the judge, none of the landowners who were supposedly bringing the charges even showed up. "Who's accusing me of taking their land?" she asks. "If there's no accuser, then I shouldn't be going to prison."

Unfortunately, although the human rights prosecutor has the power to investigate cases like those of Sandoval and Chávez and, in some instances, to make recommendations, Ramírez himself has no formal power to press charges or dismiss them.

In the end, then, the rule of law itself is in question in Baja California, according to Pérez Castro, "at least insofar as it protects people, especially the poor, in the enforcement of their rights. They pass laws to protect the maquiladoras, so the rule of law exists in that sense," he admits. "But there is a danger to social stability because it's so one-sided. It's not just indigenous people who suffer from lack of legal protection. Workers do too, and even the middle classes."

For Julio Sandoval, it's even simpler. "They're not looking at the law. They're afraid of us, and all they can do is put us in jail. It's vengeance."

MACLOVIO ROJAS: LAND OCCUPATION IN TIJUANA

In October 1996, Hortensia Hernández Mendoza walked out of Tijuana's municipal jail, blinking in the bright sunlight, after she and her companions had spent two months behind bars in a fight over the land that sits underneath their homes. It was Hernández's second imprisonment in as many years. Both times, she was released after the Baja state government admitted that it had no evidence she had actually committed any crime.

Hernández, her jailmates Artemio Osuna Osuna and Juan Regalado, and thirteen hundred other people live in the barrio of Maclovio Rojas, out beyond the edge of Tijuana, on the main highway that runs east along the border to Tecate. Their homes are mostly made of scrap lumber and materials salvaged from maquiladoras—old pallets, unfolded corrugated shipping cartons, and other castoffs. The barrio sits on a dry, flat, sandy lowland, surrounded by barren, treeless hills.

The land doesn't seem any more desirable than Cañon Buenavista. But on the other side of the dirt road that leads into Maclovio Rojas from the main highway, protected by a high barbed wire fence, are hundreds of parked semitrailers. Behind them looms a warehouse belonging to the Hyundai Corporation, which has facilities and interests all over Tijuana.

The residents of Maclovio Rojas are convinced that Hyundai and other maquiladoras want their land. The companies themselves are silent, but the state government has been determined to make the people leave since 1989, when Hyundai first built its main plant in the El Florido Industrial Park nearby.

The growth of the maquiladora industry is transforming life for the 2 million people who live in what was a small, honky-tonk tourist town decades ago. Tijuana now has more than seven hundred maquiladoras, in three industrial parks and forty-two industrial zones. The devaluation of the peso and the signing of NAFTA inspired a building and employment boom. Until the economic downturn of 2001, signs advertised for workers on the gate of almost every plant.

The growth of industrial parks threatens to displace communities like Maclovio Rojas. A string of those parks extends along the Tecate highway. Just before passing Maclovio Rojas, motorists on this highway shoot by the most prominent park—El Florido—which houses the main Hyundai facility. Land pressure from these advancing factories helps to make Maclovio Rojas a thorn in the side of development. But an even greater complication is visible from the top of the hills overlooking the community. On the other side, not far from the highway, lies the railroad line, which runs along the border.

That line, built long ago by Southern Pacific and the Spreckels family, who made its fortune in the sugar industry, runs from the port of San Diego south into Mexico. It crosses back into the United States again in Tecate and winds down through the Carrizo Gorge into the Imperial Valley. There, it meets the existing trunk line in El Centro and Niland and heads east through the Southwest to New Orleans.

The rail line, owned since 1976 by San Diego's Metropolitan Transit Authority, was operated by a contractor, Kyle Properties, until mysterious fires simultaneously burned two tunnels and a trestle bridge in Carrizo Gorge in 1984. Since then, the line has been cut.

Repair work started in 1995, however, under a new contractor, Rail Tex, operating as the San Diego and Imperial Valley Railway. When the work is completed, containers unloaded in San Diego will be put on railroad cars and sent directly east, without having to move north through Los Angeles. In the short term, that will mean increased traffic in the port of San Diego, especially when line improvements are eventually made, with room enough in the tunnels for double-stacked containers.

In 2002, however, the Baja government announced the completion of plans for a new line from Ensenada to Tecate, which will change the flow of cargo substantially. In the short term, it will allow maquiladora factories in Tijuana and Tecate to move containers directly onto ships in the port of Ensenada, without entering the United States at all.

Many Tijuana maquiladoras belonging to Korean, Japanese, and Taiwanese companies would find that very convenient. Even now, rather than putting their containers on trucks for Los Angeles, where they're often delayed in the traffic bottleneck at the border, they truck them to Ensenada and put them on barges, which cross the U.S./Mexico border at sea with no delays. Once in Los Angeles or Long Beach, the containers are stacked on ocean-going vessels or on rail cars bound for the Midwest and the East Coast.

A new rail line is of special interest to Hyundai. The company already is one of the world's largest manufacturers of the containers themselves, built at its main plant at El Florido and also at Han Young and other contract facilities. But its interest goes beyond the containers. State authorities have talked to the company for years about actually building the rail line, a huge $300 million construction project, as well as about heavy industrial development on the land next to it, including a possible auto assembly plant and a basic steel mill.

Developing the line and the area around it is envisioned in the overall Plan Puebla/Panama. The Mexican government has made ambitious projections concerning maquiladora development in southern Mexico and construction of heavier industry on the northwest border, beyond the area's current assembly plants. The Plan Puebla/Panama then extends that development through Central America, along the Pan American Highway, as the backbone of a new free trade region.

The Tecate/Ensenada railroad project is part of an entirely new transportation infrastructure Mexico is developing in cooperation with U.S. and other foreign shippers. Ports are being modernized all along the Pacific coast, and intermodal links are being developed with recently privatized railroads that have increased carrying capacity. This transportation grid will serve growing industry not only in Mexico but in the United States as well, as NAFTA has eliminated much of the bureaucracy at the border.

Even U.S. longshore unions will feel the impact of this development on their bargaining leverage. If a labor dispute closes U.S. Pacific coast ports, for instance, that new transportation grid would make shipment through Mexican ports much more feasible than it is today.

Maclovio Rojas, because of its location next to the rail line amid expanding industrial parks, is an obstacle to this march of progress envisioned by government and investors. Factory investment, in other words, trumps housing for workers. But the struggle to preserve the community, whose residents are primarily maquiladora workers, has also led to labor conflict in the factories themselves.

Inside the border plants, low wages and poor working conditions provoke frequent outbursts of protest. Conflict spills over from factory to community and back.

"The struggle over the land is one thing," Hortensia Hernández says. "Here we're fighting to keep the one hundred ninety-seven hectares that we currently have in our possession. But there's also a struggle going on in the maquiladoras. Since there's no other way to survive, people have to go find jobs there. Over fifty percent of the people in Maclovio Rojas are workers in different factories. Many work at Hyundai, which wants us off this land, and at companies like Laymex, Matsushita, and others."

Maquiladora activists in Tijuana and elsewhere on the border don't see hard distinctions between what happens to people at work and what happens where they live. They're active in both areas, on both sides of the border, and have learned to move back and forth almost as freely as the companies themselves. When Hernández walked out of prison, she owed her freedom in large part to an alliance of cross-border activists, which produced a flood of telegrams from all over the United States and Mexico into the office of Baja California governor Héctor Terán Terán.

Maclovio Rojas was first settled in 1988, by people who could find no other place to live in the rapidly expanding city. The original occupation was led by the Independent Confederation of Farmers and Farm Workers (CIOAC, Confederación Independiente de Obreros Agricolos y Campesinos), a left-wing organization of rural people. CIOAC activists named the community after one of their own organizers, Maclovio Rojas, who was assassinated in the mid-1980s.

The land they chose was unoccupied and, according to the 1973 declaration, belonged to the federal government. Under Mexico's old agrarian reform law, people were entitled to settle on this land and petition the government for formal ownership.

"Tijuana was created this way," explains Tijuana barrio organizer Eduardo Badillo, general secretary of the Border Region Workers' Support Committee (CAFOR). "The government calls these settlements 'invasions,' and we call them 'possessions.' Whatever you want to call them, the law recognizes our right to settle and build homes on this land, because under the Constitution, it's our country."

At first, no one disputed that right in Maclovio Rojas. The settlers applied for title to eighteen hundred hectares, hoping to get enough land so that people could farm as well as work in the factories. They paid a hefty application fee to the federal agrarian reform administration. They built houses and organized their community.

But in 1989, Hyundai built its factory, and the land next to it became much more desirable. A nearby agricultural settlement, Ejido Francisco Villa, also made application for the land claimed by Maclovio Rojas. The government accepted this application. Even under the economic reforms of former president Salinas, *ejidos* such as Francisco Villa continue to receive priority in land distribution. In the past, however, they had to farm the land themselves; now they are allowed to sell it. Maclovio Rojas residents suspected that once the *ejido* took possession, it intended to sell out to Hyundai and other maquiladoras.

"We believe that certain state officials have made a deal with Hyundai," Hernández says.

Residents refused to abandon their homes, and the conflict grew. In 1995, Hernández was arrested for the first time. The Yorba family, Tijuana's original landowners before the revolution, accused her of illegally taking their land. While she was in jail, Hyundai officials came from the factory and took numerous photographs of the land claimed by Maclovio Rojas. After she had spent five months in prison, the Yorba family couldn't come up with documents proving their title, and Hernández was finally released.

The government, however, didn't give up. A small group of town residents began to harass and intimidate other members of the community, in an attempt to drive them out. But "the final straw that caused our arrest," Artemio Osuna says, "was when we went to the support of striking maquiladora workers."

According to Jaime Cota, of Tijuana's Workers' Information Center, Hyundai's main plant has been plagued by labor unrest. Workers complain of being hit by Korean foremen. The safety sensors on many machines have been disabled, they say, and in numerous accidents people have lost fingers and hands. "Based on the numbers on workers' ID cards, it appears that in seven years over seventy-six hundred workers passed through a plant which only employs fifteen hundred," Cota points out.

Since opening the facility, Hyundai has subcontracted out many of its operations to nearby factories, such as Daewon and Laymex. After firings and walkouts at these two plants during the summer of 1996, workers marched to the main Hyundai factory to call for a raise in pay. They were joined by residents of Maclovio Rojas, one of whom, Daniel Covarrubias, was also a leader inside the Laymex plant.

The company refused to grant the workers' demands, and Covarrubias and two others were fired. Hortensia Hernández, Artemio Osuna, and Juan Regalado were arrested the following day, accused of burning down a house in Maclovio Rojas and committing other acts of harassment that they maintain were committed by troublemakers cooperating with the government.

"In the penitentiary, one day felt like one year," Hernández recalls. "When I arrived, they gave me a little more priority, as a woman. But Artemio and Juan were just thrown into a cell, and even the prisoners there threatened to assault them and even kill them. Artemio was told three times that he could be knifed for a peso. The prison was built to hold a thousand prisoners, but there are over three thousand people there, and many of them have tuberculosis and other illnesses."

During their incarceration, 170 residents and supporters marched for eight days from Tijuana to the state capital in Mexicali to demand the release of the three prisoners. One marcher died from a heart attack, and a memorial service was held in the plaza outside the governor's office. With telegrams arriving daily from the United States protesting the imprisonment of the three, the government could still produce no evidence against them. Finally, on October 7, Governor Terán decided to release them.

Pressure from north of the border was mobilized by CAFOR and the San Diego–based Support Committee for Maquiladora Workers. Many southern California unions also contributed to the defense of Maclovio Rojas. The big El Segundo refinery local of the Oil, Chemical and Atomic Workers donated five thousand dollars for the construction of a workers' center in the settlement.

Meanwhile, the dispute over the title to the land moved through the state's court system, eventually coming before a federal judge in Mexico City in the spring of 2002. As the judge pondered his decision, pressure on the settlement's residents increased again. In mid-June, a new group of provocateurs, supposedly from within the community, the Villista Army of National Liberation (Ejercito Villista de Liberación Nacional), surfaced in the Tijuana press and denounced Hernández and other Maclovio Rojas leaders.

Police surrounded the area and threatened to arrest the leaders again. Tijuana's activist community turned out to support the residents, along with activists from north of the border, organized by a loose cross-border network called Globaliphobicos. In Los Angeles, demonstrators picketed the Mexican consulate and handed a letter of protest to the consul general. In the end, the police backed off, but the future of the community remains uncertain.

In late 2002, arrest warrants were again issued for Hortensia Hernández, Artemio Osuna Osuna, Nicolasa Ramos, Juan Regalado, and Rubén García Rocha. Nicolasa Ramos, another community leader, was arrested on December 4, 2002, and held in the La Mesa State Penitentiary without bail. The others went into hiding to avoid arrest. They were all charged with illegally diverting water from a local aqueduct over a period of several years. Maclovio Rojas had petitioned the state government years before to provide the community with drinking water, and the state public services commission had approved the petition. While community members were waiting for water service to begin, however, they did what many squatter communities do to get water and electricity—they set up their own direct connection to the main line. Even local ranchers, the police academy, and a nearby elementary school have tapped the aqueduct to get drinking water in the same way, since the state has been so slow in providing legal connections.

Human rights prosecutor Raúl Ramírez attributes the tension to the government's policy of assuring investors that property rights will be respected and its accompanying unconcern over lack of housing. "That's why there's conflict in Maclovio Rojas," he explains. "[This land is] in the pathway of the superfreeways they want to build to Tecate and the port of Ensenada for the free flow of goods, for the industry they want to see growing here. These have become very desirable lands, and they're in the hands of poor people, with few resources. And instead of resolving the question of the titles to these lands, the government itself is provoking conflicts in order to displace and dislodge the people living there. This is what we see coming."

FROM BARRIO ORGANIZING TO ELECTION CAMPAIGNS

The 2000 national elections brought the National Action Party to power in Mexico City, the first party other than the PRI to win control of the presidency. In the same elections in Baja California, however, the movements in Maclovio Rojas, Ensenada, and San Quintin combined with those of Tijuana maquiladora workers to mount the strongest opposition campaign to the PAN since 1988, when the party took control of the Baja California state government.

In 2000, the new face of politics in Baja California had Indian features—the face of Celerino García. For the first time, an indigenous candidate, a Mixtec, ran for the federal Chamber of Deputies in a state where the situation of Mixtec, Triqui, and Zapotec migrant farmworkers has been a national symbol of economic misery and social discrimination. García's candidacy, on the slate of the PRD, was part of a popular upsurge, giving notice that the state's indigenous migrants would no longer be treated as political nonentities.

García's campaign was the visible tip of a struggle for political change whose roots ran deep. From Tijuana south down the peninsula, social movements had coalesced into a power base for the left. Just eight months earlier, García and his older brother, Benito, had been sitting in a jail cell, accused by Baja's PAN government of illegally taking land. "Any act of protest here is met with repression," Celerino García declared. "The PAN here is no different than the PRI. If anything, it's worse."

The arrest of the two brothers highlighted the impact of demographic changes sweeping the peninsula as well as the long effort to organize the farmworkers of San Quintin and Maneadero independently of unions favored by the government and the ranchers. "We've been trying to gain a *registro* [government legal recognition] since 1984, but we've always been denied, first by the PRI and then the PAN," according to Julio César Alonzo, an organizer for the CIOAC, in which the García brothers have also been active.

With more agricultural workers settling in San Quintin, the pressure for housing in the valley's small towns escalated, as families tried to escape the miserable conditions in labor camps. "Over twenty thousand of us here in San Quintín have no property," García says. "We've always had to live in the camps. So we made a proposal to the state—that they set aside an area of fifty hectares, which we would divide and develop for workers. But the PAN refused to do this. In their eyes, we're strangers. They just want us to work to make the ranchers wealthy and then go back to Oaxaca."

So the CIOAC organized the workers, pooled their money, and bought a parcel of land on its own. The prospect of an indigenous voting majority in the valley (where 60 percent of the population already consists of migrants from Oaxaca), along with a push for new housing settlements and labor unrest, frightened the government and the ranchers. Police moved in, accused the Garcías of *despojo*, and sent them to jail.

According to Celerino García, "Here in San Quintín, the government associates the movement for indigenous rights with the movement to organize an independent union. They thought putting me and Benito in jail would stop us, but the opposite happened. People got angry, and our movement got bigger."

CIOAC's political allies in other Baja cities began organizing demonstrations and marches and eventually occupied state government offices in San Quintín, Ensenada, and Tijuana. Celerino and Benito were released, but others were then arrested for the sit-ins, including Beatriz Chávez, also a CIOAC organizer.

In Ensenada and Maneadero, the turmoil among farmworkers spilled over into the community of street sellers. Both groups are made up largely of Oaxacan migrants. Selling goods to tourists on the street is actually a step up from the fields—easier work, higher income, and the ability to work year-round.

In Ensenada, Ramiro Orea and Armando Reyes led efforts to organize the street sellers who hawk souvenirs and crafts to tourists on the waterfront. In 1997, the pair helped the sellers leave a government-affiliated union and form a new one. Sellers were unhappy because the old organization had been charging them numerous fees but failed to protect them against the police, who constantly tried to run them off the streets and confiscate their goods.

"Every day some of us were getting arrested," explains Filiberto Delgado, one of the sellers. Getting fined and losing all their merchandise weren't even the worst results. Delgado, like many sellers, has his three children with him when they're not in school. "I don't let them work, but I don't have money to pay for child care, either," he emphasizes, "so here they are, suffering the heat and thirst on the streets along with me." When the police picked him up, other sellers or friends would have to grab the children and take care of them until he returned.

"It's a bad life, but somehow we make it good," he says.

Through the work of Orea and Reyes, the PRD built a base among the street sellers and in the poor barrios on the hills that ring the city. According to Delgado, "Only the PRD tried to help us. They proposed to the city that we get permanent places to sell our goods, so we'd be secure and safe." Only one of Ensenada's thirteen city council members belonged to the PRD, but the party's vote totals had grown in the previous two elections. If the state PAN government hadn't changed the election laws in 1998, the PRD would have had two council members, based on the 15 percent vote they received that year, and Orea would have been one of them.

Orea and Reyes brought the street sellers union into a statewide network called ENFOCCA—the Workers, Residents, and Farmers Power Network (Enlace de la Fuerza de Obreros, Ciudadanos y Campesinos). Other members of the network included the CIOAC in San Quintin and the October 6 independent union for maquiladora workers in Tijuana. The network tried to link the PRD as a political party to social protest movements throughout the state.

"We came together to oppose the policies of the PAN state government," Orea explains. "For poor people—workers, people in the barrios—the state has refused to budget money for social services. We have terrible problems of lack of housing in Baja. In the *colonias* for workers, dirt streets turn to mud when it rains, and in many neighborhoods there are no sewers, running water, or electricity. Getting any of these services requires a big fight. So that's what we do. We fight."

When Celerino and Benito García were arrested in San Quintin, these organizations up and down the peninsula came together to mount the demonstrations that eventually freed them.

The defense effort even spread north across the border, to a radio station in Fresno, in California's San Joaquin Valley. There, Filemón López, from the same town in Oaxaca as Celerino García, hosts a radio show called the "Mixtec Hour," broadcasting in Mixtec over the Radio Bilingue chain of noncommercial community stations. López became the coordinator of the International Network of Oaxacan Indigenous People (Red Internacional de Indígenas Oaxaqueñas) and used his access to the airwaves to alert the thousands of Oaxacans living in Radio Bilingue's extensive broadcast area to the crisis in San Quintin. People responded by deluging the Baja California governor with letters and faxes demanding the release of the García brothers.

The skills and abilities people developed in the course of that campaign were then turned toward the 2000 election. The network mobilized Oaxacans living in the United States to come to the border to cast their votes for the PRD. "We're helping Oaxacans to organize in all the places we find ourselves," López says. "Being discriminated against because of being indigenous, and having our labor rights violated, has forced us to get better organized. And we've had lots of time to do it— ever since the conquest of Mexico by the Spaniards."

Another Mixtec leader, Sergio Méndez of the Binational Indigenous Oaxacan Front (La Frente Indígena Oaxaqueña Binacional), claims that Baja California is the place where life is the worst for Oaxacans. "San Diego is the most racist area of California, but the indignities which our brothers are subjected to there don't compare to those they suffer here, where the government says it's on our side," he declares. Méndez's anger was fueled by a campaign speech made by Vicente Fox, in which Fox proposed that Mexicans be trained to do gardener jobs in Los Angeles. "We aren't animals to be exported," Méndez says scornfully. "We may be exploited and treated like slaves, but we know how to think for ourselves."

The 2000 election was a contradictory test of that move toward political independence. Mexicans handed the PRI its first national defeat in seventy years, but they elected Fox, the PAN candidate, as their new democratic alternative. In Baja, where the PAN had won power more than a decade earlier, Orea predicts that there will not be much change. "The PAN's policies here are the same as the PRI's," he explains. "They both rely on our low wages to provide an incentive to foreign investors in the maquiladoras or to keep our agricultural exports cheap. Any time we try to change that, the government sees us as a threat and intervenes to try to stop us. If people in the U.S. think that Vicente Fox is going to bring about a change of policy here in Mexico, just look at what his party does here in Baja."

There was no question that many people in the state's migrant community were willing to vote for change, often against tremendous obstacles. Oaxacan migrants had to vote in special polling places, often miles from where they lived. As usual, polls in opposition areas ran out of ballots long before voting stopped. Farm laborers, especially, had to sacrifice an entire day of work, since Sunday work in the fields is often the rule. Ranchers even offered to pay them double time, for the first time in history, if they worked instead of voting. "And when workers did vote, some were fired for that alone," García alleges, "because the ranchers knew without asking which party they were voting for."

In the absence of accurate polling analyses, PRD activists speculated that the farmworker vote in San Quintin doubled the vote the party had received in the previous election to 18 percent. It was certainly enough to give activists hope that political change was in the wind in Baja California and that the PRD might prove to be the vehicle for serious challenges in years to come.

Nevertheless, the PRD coalition began to fracture even before the campaign was over. Different factions traded accusations that party leaders were motivated by the desire to win government positions. Activists associated with ENFOCCA charged that the party's leaders were reluctant to support direct action and the social movements in poor communities or to link the party to organizations of social protest.

The turmoil over the land occupation in Cañon Buenavista, followed by the arrest of Julio Sandoval, only gave strength to those accusations.

Two years later, much of that coalition had been shredded by factional division. Orea and Reyes took ENFOCCA out of the PRD and became active in the Workers' Party (Partido de Trabajo). Others, such as Badillo and Pelayo, in Tijuana's Vista Alamar neighborhood, returned to community organizing.

THE FRENTE INDÍGENA OAXAQUEÑA BINACIONAL

Despite the disappointments in the electoral route to power in Baja, at least one of the organizations involved, the Frente Indígena Oaxaqueña Binacional, has a long history both of cross-border activity and of using the PRD as an electoral vehicle.

Indigenous people from Oaxaca have been migrating within Mexico, and to the United States, for decades. Many were braceros during that program's twenty-two-year run from 1942 to 1964. In Mexican agricultural valleys from Sinaloa to Baja California, Oaxacan migrants are the backbone of the labor force that makes corporate agriculture possible.

As a result, communities of Oaxacans have settled in a broad swath leading from their state of origin through Veracruz, where they went first, as laborers in the sugar harvest; through northwest Mexico's fields of tomatoes and strawberries; into the valleys of California's San Joaquin and Oregon's Willamette Rivers; and to Washington state. Oaxacans now migrate even to Florida and the East Coast.

In Madera, California, restaurants bear Mixtec names. During meetings of Florida's Coalition of Immokalee Workers, people can be heard talking softly in the same language in the back of the room. Los Angeles furniture shops employ Zapotec-speaking workers, and Triqui speakers are an important constituency in Oregon's union for farmworkers, Northwest Treeplanters and Farmworkers United (PCUN, Pineros y Campesinos Unidos de Noroeste).

Despite this dispersal, the indigenous people of Oaxaca have found a way to unite, not only around language and their towns of origin but also around their identity as indigenous Oaxacan migrants. As might be expected from the simultaneous existence of their communities on both sides of the border, one center of activity lies in California, in Fresno, and the other in Oaxaca itself. The organization at the heart of this activity is the Frente, which began in 1987 at meetings in California's Central Valley, in Los Angeles, and in San Diego. At its founding on October 5, 1991, the organization was called the Frente Mixteca Zapoteca Binacional because the founders wanted to unite three existing Mixtec organizations and two that had been established among Zapotec immigrants.

Soon the organization began looking for a strategy that would reflect the reality of Oaxacan communities. Although Oaxacans are widely dispersed, the movement of people has created, in a sense, one larger community, located in different places simultaneously. Settlements of Mixtecs, Zapotecs, Triquis, and other Oaxacan indigenous groups along the three-thousand-mile migrant stream from Oaxaca to the Pacific Northwest are bound together by shared culture and language and by the social organizations people carry with them from place to place.

Some of the organizations among Oaxacan migrants are based on towns of origin—a not-uncommon phenomenon among immigrants to the United States from many countries. But Oaxacans have also developed the Frente, which unites different language groups in order to promote community and workplace struggles for social justice.

"Among indigenous Oaxaqueños, we already have the concept of community and organization," says Frente director Rufino Domínguez. "When people migrate from a community in Oaxaca, they already have a committee comprised of people from their home town. They are united and live very near one another. It's a tradition that we don't lose, wherever we go."

In 1984, as a young man, Domínguez left Oaxaca and migrated to Sinaloa, where he formed the Organización del Pueblo Explotado y Oprimido, the Organization of Exploited and Oppressed People, and cooperated with leaders such as Benito García and organizations such as the CIOAC in strikes among the state's farmworkers.

Conditions for migrants in Sinaloa were the scandal of Mexico, and the strikes brought them into the public eye. "We lived in labor camps [in barracks] made of steel sheets," remembers Jorge Girón, from the Mixtec town of Santa María Tindu. He now lives with his family in Fresno, but he was a farmworker in Sinaloa through those years.

"During the hot season, it was unbearable. In the morning, we would huddle around the foreman, and he would hand out buckets for the tomato harvest. Often they were irrigating, and we took off our shoes and went into the fields barefoot. In the early morning, the water would be freezing, and sometimes going in like that made you sick, but rubber boots were unknown among us. We would work from sunup to sundown. Even if we worked ten or eleven hours, we were paid the minimum."

The camp owners ran company stores that sold food on credit. "On Saturday, we would get paid, and then we would go pay our debt." As a single man, Girón slept in a room with fifteen others. Eventually, he brought his wife and children, and they shared a room with another family.

These are not happy memories for Margarita Girón. "In Sinaloa, the rooms were made of cardboard," she recalls. "Sometimes the cardboard was ripped, and you could see the other families through the holes. When you had to relieve yourself, you went in public because there were no bathrooms. You would go behind a tree or tall grass and squat. In the camps we lived in, you couldn't be picky."

There was no running water, only water from the canals and the river. "I didn't like it because there would be people bathing upstream, and further down people would be washing their clothes, and somewhere else people would be drinking the water," she says. "People would sometimes boil the water, but not always, and a lot of people became ill with diarrhea and vomiting. Others drowned after going down in the channel, because in some places it was very deep."

"Everything was bad in those times," Jorge adds. "Now there are houses made of better materials, electricity, and everything. But before, there was nothing except for candlelight. That was our only form of light." He credits the CIOAC for ending the worst aspects of their situation. "They organized most of the strikes. They wanted workers' rights to be respected, our salaries and jobs protected, better housing, running water, and transportation to and from work. And they did accomplish many of those things."

After organizing around conditions like these, Rufino Domínguez followed the migrant trail farther north, across the Gulf of California, to San Quintin on the Baja California peninsula. "I sent Benito a letter to come because there were many problems among our people there," Domínguez remembers. "We were able to organize thousands of people." In San Quintin, they mounted strikes as well.

From there, Domínguez crossed the border, winding up in Selma, California, just outside Fresno. There, he met farmworkers from his home state, who were also anxious to get organized.

"I felt like I was in my town. There were people all over, very happy, greeting me. One of them said, 'Welcome, *compañero* Rufino. Tell us, what is happening in our town? What did you do in Sinaloa and Baja California? What can you do to help us here?' I was so new that I didn't even know where to look to see the sun rise. Even so, I began to explain how we organized in Sinaloa and Baja and that we could create the same type of organization here."

One of the Frente's early forays into activity came in 1993, when it proposed that California Rural Legal Assistance (CRLA) create a staff position for an educator who would explain labor rights to Mixtec farm-workers, in their own language, in the state's Central Valley. Domínguez was the first person hired for that job.

The same year, César Chávez, founder of the United Farm Workers, died in Arizona. The Frente began a collaboration with his successor, the UFW's new president, Arturo Rodríguez. The union organized a month-long peregrination from Delano to Sacramento—re-creating its seminal march in 1967—to dramatize to California farmworkers its renewed commitment to field organizing. The pact with the Frente had a similar aim: to win support for the union among a key group in the fields, the growing community of Mixtec-speaking migrants from Oaxaca.

"We recognized that the UFW was a strong union representing agricultural workers," Domínguez explains. "They in turn recognized us as an organization fighting for the rights for indigenous migrants. That campaign was historic for us, because the union finally recognized us in a formal way." But it was an uneasy relationship, and Mixtec activists felt that UFW members often exhibited the same discriminatory attitudes toward indigenous people that were common among Mexicans back home.

Meanwhile, the nascent organization used the celebrations of the five-hundred-year anniversary of the arrival of Christopher Columbus in the Americas as a platform to dramatize its call for indigenous rights. Domínguez denounces "people who say that Christopher Columbus was welcomed when he came. They see in him a grand hero who brought good things. But they never talk about the massacres or the genocide that occurred in our villages, on the whole of the American continent. Our people were stripped of our culture, our belief in our gods. They told us that nature wasn't worth anything, when in reality nature gives us life. That different side of the story is what we wanted to tell all the people we could find. That was the object of the Frente Mixteca Zapoteca Binacional: to dismantle the old stereotype, to march, to protest."

When the Zapatista army rose up on January 1, 1994, in Chiapas, the Frente immediately organized actions to pressure the Mexican government to refrain from using massive military force against the Zapatistas and the people of Chiapas. From Fresno to Baja California to Oaxaca, Frente activists went on hunger strikes and demonstrated in front of consulates and government offices. "That binational movement helped us realize that when there's movement in Oaxaca, there's got to be movement in the U.S. to make an impression on the Mexican government. That helped us grow immensely," Domínguez says.

Soon the organization had to change its name. Triquis and other indigenous Oaxacan people wanted to participate but felt that the Frente's name excluded them. In 1995, it became the Frente Indígena Oaxaqueña Binacional.

The organization's binational character grew even stronger. In 1993, the Frente began serious organizing in Oaxaca itself. "We began with various productive projects, such as the planting of the Chinese pomegranate, the forajero cactus, and strawberries," Domínguez explains, "so that families of migrants to the U.S. would have an income to survive" in Mexico. Those efforts grew into five offices in the state and a membership base larger than that in the United States, in more than seventy towns. In 1999, the Frente allied with the PRD and elected one of its leaders, Juan Romualdo Gutiérrez-Cortez, to the state Chamber of Deputies in District 21. "For the first time, we beat the *caciques,*" Domínguez crows, referring to the local political bosses affiliated with the PRI.

The Frente's organizing strategy is based on the culture of Oaxacan communities, particularly an institution called the *tequio.* "This is the concept that we must participate in collective work to support our community," Domínguez explains. "In our communities, we already know one another and can act together. That understanding of mutual assistance makes it easier for us to organize ourselves. Wherever we go, we go united. It's a way of saying that I do not speak alone—we all speak together.

"We make efforts so that our communities don't lose their culture, their language, and their traditions. Beyond organizing and teaching our rights, we would like to save our language so that it lives and continues into the future. Even though five hundred and nine years have passed since the Spanish conquest, we still speak our language. We are conserving our way of dancing, and rescuing what we lost in terms of our beliefs—that nature is something sacred for us, just as it was for our ancestors. We want to live our culture and to ensure that it won't die."

In addition to advising workers on their labor rights, the Frente organizes communities in California's rural areas. One of them is Malaga, a trailer park outside Fresno, in which most people come from San Miguel Cuevas in Oaxaca. Residents discovered that the land under their homes had been contaminated for years by oil and toxic waste from Chevron and other oil companies. With the aid of CRLA, the Frente mounted a campaign that won a million dollars from Chevron, and 7 million more from the other polluters. The money was used to resettle the area's families. Some residents took cash, but others pooled their money and, with the Frente's help, built new housing.

The organization has also begun to change the traditional domination of community political life by men. Oralia Maceda, a twenty-six-year-old organizer from Oaxaca, came to Fresno to develop women's participation in the Frente. "At the beginning, men were the ones who would come to the organization. Before I started, there were two other women [who] lasted no more than a month. But I believe it is women's responsibility to get involved and to find out how to participate. I use different tactics to get them to come—say, a small party for Mothers' Day, with small gifts and food. But it's not really the party that gets their interest. It's letting them know how we can help them. I'll ask, who wants to become legal in this country? We talk about very basic problems like that. Really, it all starts with a small group of people."

Maceda's presence is also key to developing the participation of young people in the Frente. Given the strong pressure on children and teenagers in the United States to assimilate into the dominant consumerist lifestyle, maintaining the connection to home communities far away is very difficult. Winning the interest of youth in indigenous languages and cultural practices is even more so. Many Oaxacans are fanatical basketball players, and the Frente has used tournaments to attract young people and draw them into its activities.

Along with its bases in Oaxaca and California, the Frente also set up offices in Tijuana and San Quintin on the Baja California peninsula. "But it's been a very difficult experience," Domínguez concedes. In 2001, the organization had an internal division over the actions one of its founders, Arturo Pimentel, who had been the director of the Frente in Oaxaca. Many members accused him of not being accountable to them for the organization's finances, and many were also upset that he wanted to run for political office without a collective decision to that effect. At the Frente's congress in Tijuana in December 2001, he was expelled.

Pimentel had been an active leader in many demonstrations and marches for housing and workers' rights in Baja, and many Frente leaders on the peninsula were his allies. Following the 2000 election, the conservative PAN government in Baja California manipulated the divisions in the PRD and the Frente, and the political opposition in the state was weakened as a result.

Frente leaders such as Domínguez are not overly optimistic about the new political environment under Vicente Fox, who was the candidate of the PAN. "The political party changed, the name of the government changed, but the system continues to be the same," he says wearily. "The view of Vicente Fox is very attractive, very optimistic, and full of promises, but we're not seeing anything done. He didn't defend the proposed indigenous rights law. [Human rights lawyer] Digna Ochoa was murdered in Mexico City. There is a lot of discourse, but no definite things like electricity, potable water, and productive projects in our communities."

Nevertheless, the Frente is committed to its strategy of combining workers' rights, community organizing, and, in Mexico, electoral action. In the United States, it advocates the right of Mexican citizens to vote in Mexican elections. "The Frente should have an alliance with political parties without losing our identity and being dependent on politicians," Domínguez argues. "We have to be autonomous in relation to political parties and create alliances to win these positions. Mexican electoral laws don't permit a social organization to run independent candidates. So we have to make an alliance, not with the PAN or the PRI, but with the PRD. Within the PRD, there are a lot of divisions and internal problems, and they must resolve their internal conflicts. But it's all we have."

6

THE STRATEGIC ALLIANCE

PROLOGUE: TRABAJADORES DESPLAZADOS

Among the stereotyped ideas many people hold about the impact of free trade, one of the most pervasive is that the U.S. workers who lose their jobs as a result of free trade policies are overwhelmingly white men. Yet one key battle that offered a preview of NAFTA's effects was fought in Watsonville, California, in the late 1980s by Mexican immigrants, most of them women.

In one of free trade's great ironies, Mexican workers came north through the 1960s and 1970s, seeking good jobs and a better future. In Watsonville, they found both but then had to fight battle after battle to protect the wages and benefits that brought a certain measure of economic stability to the town's immigrant community. In the end, their employers moved those jobs to the country from which they'd come, to take advantage of the economic desperation the Watsonville workers thought they'd left behind.

By 1985, U.S. unions had suffered a series of stinging defeats, the most painful of which was the destruction of PATCO, the Professional Air Traffic Controllers Organization. In 1982, President Ronald Reagan put the military in airport towers, fired thousands of PATCO strikers, and sent their leaders to jail, ushering in a new era of labor relations. Employers understood that the permanent replacement of strikers would now receive federal protection. Unions understood that strikes would therefore become much riskier to workers. This was the accepted wisdom that Mexican immigrants in the Pajaro Valley defied in 1985.

Watsonville is that valley's economic hub, two hours south of San Francisco. It's a town of packing sheds, where for decades huge quantities of broccoli, cauliflower, spinach, and other row crops were washed, packed, frozen, and sent to supermarkets all over the United States. And throughout that time, the valley's farmworkers and their unions fought it out with growers over and over again. Watsonville's labor history is a microcosm of the state's long saga of field labor wars, from the radical strikes of the 1930s through the United Farm Workers' upsurge of the 1960s and 1970s, and, most recently, the strawberry organizing drive of the late 1990s.

During those decades, jobs in the freezer plants have been the route out of the fields, the first big step up the economic ladder for immigrants. For years, even a seasonal worker in the plants made enough money and had enough job security to get a car loan, and perhaps even to buy a house—goals that were out of reach for most field laborers.

So when the owners of Watsonville Canning and Frozen Foods, one of the valley's largest employers, tried to reduce employee benefits in 1985, the company's nine hundred workers walked out on strike. For nineteen months, they held their picket lines, watching Monterey and Santa Cruz County sheriffs protect a stream of strikebreakers who kept the plant working. Meanwhile, not a single striker went back in.

To keep the strike going, the strikers had to democratize their own union—Teamsters Local 912—and elect new leaders willing to support them. For years, the local's officers had come from a small coterie of white workers, who had been given privileged access to permanent jobs while Mexican immigrants were locked in the seasonal workforce. In the strike's first months, Local 912 members voted in a much more representative group, headed by Secretary-Treasurer Sergio López.

After a year of conflict, the company's law firm, Littler, Mendelsohn, Fastiff and Tichy, planned to implement what at the time was standard union-busting practice: filing a petition for decertification and calling for an election to get rid of the union. Only strikebreakers would have been able to vote; the strikers would have been barred from participating. But another historical irony torpedoed the company's strategy. Decades before, the Teamsters union had signed sweetheart agreements with packers all over California, in order to insulate the companies from much more radical unions such as the UFW. Relations with the plant owners grew so close that when the original Teamster contract was signed with Watsonville Canning and Frozen Foods, no one bothered to hold an election in which the workers could choose their own bargaining agent.

By 1985, however, things had changed. Many food processing giants decided that having no union was even better than having a cooperative one. In the anti-union atmosphere under Reagan, union-busting seemed easy. But the companies' attitude created a new environment inside the union. Instead of waiting for the company lawyers to file their de-certification petition, Teamster lawyers filed a motion to hold the original certification election that had been bypassed years before. In a certification election, as opposed to a decertification vote, both strikers and strikebreakers can vote. Thus when balloting began, strikers, many of whom had left Watsonville to find a way to last out the battle, returned by the hundreds, some even traveling from homes in Mexico. The Teamsters union won, according to poll watchers. But because of numerous legal challenges to the election, the votes were never counted, and the strike ground on.

Finally, the Teamsters prepared to pull its pension and benefit funds from Wells Fargo Bank, which had given the company a $32 million line of credit three weeks before the strike that allowed it to operate during the conflict. When the bank denied the company further credit, Watsonville Canning was forced into bankruptcy and sold to new owners. Negotiations for a new contract began. In a dramatic finale, after more than a year and a half on strike, workers still turned down a preliminary settlement, which they felt contained unacceptable concessions. After holding out for another week, they got a better contract, and the strike was finally over.

While the strike lasted, thousands of supporters had collected money and food, which union caravans ferried to the besieged workers. The long struggle became a symbol for militant union members who wanted to see the labor movement fight harder against concessions and strike-breaking. It also contributed to the democratic wind blowing through the Teamsters union itself, whose rank and file, at the beginning of the following decade, finally toppled a dynasty of national leaders who had been tied to organized crime and the Republican Party.

But the strike didn't usher in a new era of prosperity for Watsonville workers. Instead, the economic forces of free trade accomplished what strikebreaking couldn't—cutting labor costs and the power of workers to control conditions in the industry. This transformation was accomplished through the relocation of production.

In 1967, the Bird's Eye division of General Foods opened the first frozen food plant in the Mexican valley of Irapuato, about a thousand miles south of the U.S. border. Fifteen years later, it was followed by Pillsbury, which owned Watsonville's largest employer, Green Giant. Both plants processed broccoli and cauliflower, the primary crops of the Pajaro Valley. When Green Giant began operations in Irapuato, the number of Local 912 members in its Watsonville plant dropped from 1,400 to 850, according to Joe Fahey, who became the union's business agent during the 1985 strike and was later elected its president. "Mexico at the time wasn't even a blip on the union radar screen," he recalls.

But overcapacity in Watsonville and the movement of production south began to have an effect. Two large plants, Crosetti and John Inglis, which together employed 1,400 people in 1980, shut down operations in 1987 and 1988. Then, in 1989, Pillsbury was bought by Grand Metropolitan, a British corporate conglomerate. In 1990, the company announced that it was eliminating close to 400 jobs and would produce only specialty frozen products, mixing vegetables with sauces.

In March 1990, Fahey took his first trip to Mexico, to see where the jobs were going. He was followed by Local 912's business agent, Chavelo

Moreno. While on vacation, Moreno noticed that tomatoes sold in Mexican markets had two prices: one for those grown with clean water, and a cheaper price for those irrigated with *aguas negras*—literally, "black waters," or water contaminated with sewage. In nosing around the Irapuato plants, Fahey saw that the vegetables they were processing were irrigated with *aguas negras* and that plant discharges themselves were causing pollution problems in the barrios where their workers were living.

Fahey became one of the first U.S. union leaders to connect with the FAT, the Authentic Labor Front, when he talked to the federation's representative in Irapuato, Antonio Mosqueda. Meanwhile, in Watsonville, community and union activists were galvanized by a newspaper column written by Frank Bardacke, who had been one of the strike's leading supporters. Bardacke called for fighting the layoffs and closures instead of accepting them as inevitable. The result was the organization of Trabajadores Desplazados, the Displaced Workers, a community-based organization fighting to hold the companies who were closing plants responsible for the impact of the closures on the local community.

Both Trabajadores Desplazados and Local 912 sent delegations to Mexico to contact workers employed by the companies that were shutting down operations in Watsonville. One of the first groups was organized by Chavelo Moreno, who convinced the local to sponsor a trip with a crew headed by John Silver and the Migrant Media project. They produced a video called *Dirty Business: Food Imports to the United States*, about the contamination of Irapuato water and its effects on the local community. Another group, including Yolanda Navarro, a leader of Trabajadores Desplazados, traveled to Irapuato in cooperation with the Coalition for Justice in the Maquiladoras, on a trip sponsored by the recently elected reform leadership of the Teamsters.

The delegations and the video helped to highlight the effects of runaway U.S. employers on Mexican workers and their communities, at a time when the first proposals were being made for the North American Free Trade Agreement. They also helped to popularize the idea that workers and unions in the United States could, and should, respond by actually going to Mexico and looking for a way to cooperate with Mexican workers against common employers, rather than treating those workers as enemies who were robbing U.S. workers of their jobs.

Eventually, in 1994, Trabajadores Desplazados and the Coalition for Justice in the Maquiladoras were able to force Grand Metropolitan to meet with them and to establish pollution controls over the discharges of its Irapuato plant.

These first efforts had good intentions about establishing links between Watsonville workers and their counterparts in the Mexican plants. But contacting those Mexican workers, who knew the power of the companies to fire them, proved to be much more difficult than U.S. activists had expected. And creating new relationships with Mexican unions involved confronting very different attitudes about employers and the government.

"It was much harder for us to have any effect on wages in the Irapuato plants," Fahey says. "Bird's Eye had set an extremely low standard for wages and benefits when it had opened its plant there years before, and the government had a big stake in keeping wages low, since it was using that as a means for attracting investment. The fight we had with Green Giant, and my conversations with Mexican unionists, made me aware of a very important difference between U.S. and Mexican unions. U.S. unions tend to see the company as the enemy and think the fight should be directed against them. That's the way we think about it here [in the United States]. If we put enough pressure on a company, it becomes cheaper for them to meet our demands, and we win.

"It doesn't work that way in Mexico. Even if one company feels the pressure or wants to pay its workers more for other reasons, the Mexican government won't allow it. They won't allow upward wage competition between companies in the same industry. So the Mexican workers' movement sees the government as a bigger enemy than the individual boss, because it's the government's role to keep all wages low.

"More and more U.S. workers want solidarity with Mexican workers. But to be effective, we need to understand what Mexicans are up against and help them fight against their government."

NAFTA ON THE HORIZON

By the mid-1990s, NAFTA had become a defining issue for millions of U.S. workers and unions. But at the time President George H. W. Bush first proposed the agreement, so little was known about it that some union activists learned of its existence only from their Mexican counterparts. Frank Martín del Campo, a field representative for the San Francisco city workers union, Service Employees Local 790, took a delegation of California trade unionists to Mexico City in 1990. He says he first began to realize how important NAFTA would become by listening to the way Mexicans talked about it.

"It was obviously a critical question to them," he recalls, "and they were already engaged in an acrimonious debate over whether it would produce more jobs or lead to further loss of control by Mexicans over their own economy. They were reeling under the impact of the first wave of economic reforms, with widespread privatization and declining wages. While President Salinas was promising more jobs, even conservative unionists saw how unlikely the prospect really was for raising living standards. Most were stuck in their intimate relationship with the government and the PRI, who were using their low wages to attract corporate investment. But what was their alternative?"

Martín del Campo's delegation was one of a number of similar groups who traveled to Mexico in the late 1980s and early 1990s. They all were responding to the way recent changes in the Mexican economy were affecting U.S. workers. Many were galvanized as well by the political turmoil in Mexico, sparked by the campaign of Cuauhtémoc Cárdenas for president in 1988 and the subsequent formation of a left-wing opposition party, the PRD, in 1989. And like Martín del Campo, many of these activists were Mexican and Latino immigrants themselves— part of the Latino upsurge that transformed the leadership of many U.S. unions over the past two decades.

The 1990 California delegation was composed of unionists who had organized events on behalf of Cárdenas during his West Coast tour in the United States the year after the 1988 election. According to the report presented by the delegation after its trip to Mexico, "Cárdenas's tour made many of us realize the necessity of greater awareness of the problems faced by unionists in Mexico, and the need for solidarity between the labor movements in our two countries."

On the trip to Mexico, the group met with a broad spectrum of Mexican labor representatives, from Fidel Velásquez (head of both the CTM and the Labor Congress, to which the CTM belongs) to insurgent groups within the official unions to independent unions, social movements, and the PRD. Delegates paid their respects to Valentín Campa as well, not long before he died. Campa was a hero of the left wing of Mexican labor, having helped to organize the CTM in the 1930s and lead the national railroad strike of the 1950s (for which he was imprisoned for eleven years). When he was released from prison, Campa ran for president of Mexico as the candidate of the Mexican Communist Party.

Meeting Campa at the PRD headquarters was a statement of political independence by the U.S. delegation, for the AFL-CIO leadership at that time was still firmly committed to its global campaign against the left. Most of the cross-border activists of this period were similarly careful to maintain a degree of independence from the official structure of the U.S. labor federation, seeking to distance themselves from those cold war policies in the eyes of their Mexican counterparts. Many had been involved in solidarity campaigns with unions and movements in Central America during the 1980s and in Chile during the 1970s. Some were veterans of battles against the old destabilization programs that had been pursued by the American Institute for Free Labor Development, the AFL-CIO's foreign policy arm for Latin America. They distrusted the decades of support the federation's Department of International Affairs had given to the free trade policies of both U.S. political parties and the connection of that department to the U.S. intelligence apparatus—part of the cold war orientation.

The California delegation established its closest relationship during the trip with the Mexican Electrical Workers (SME, Sindicato Mexicano de Electricistas), the union for electric power workers in central

Mexico. The SME is one of the country's oldest and most democratic unions, with a long history of relations with the left wing of U.S. labor, especially the United Electrical Workers (UE). Members of the California delegation visited the union's workplaces and talked with its activist members for three days about the potential impact of the proposed free trade agreement. They began a relationship that has lasted for many years.

After the delegation returned to the United States in 1990, members began speaking at labor council meetings throughout northern California about the danger of NAFTA and the importance of solidarity. "As we started to give our reports, NAFTA began hitting the media. But the message lots of workers got was Ross Perot's 'giant sucking sound,' " Martín del Campo says. "So the initial reaction in many unions was fear. People were afraid they'd lose their jobs, especially since we'd already gone through a decade-long epidemic of plant closures. On the one hand, they were told that Mexican workers in Mexico were robbing their jobs, and on the other, [they heard] that Mexican immigrants in the U.S. were doing the same thing. It was a recipe for racist hysteria. But our message was different. We began saying that we all had a common enemy and that we'd only survive if we learned how to fight together."

The San Francisco group eventually joined a loose network that included the San Diego Support Committee for Maquiladora Workers, the United Electrical Workers, the Transnational Information Exchange (affiliated with the Detroit newsletter "Labor Notes"), and Teamsters Local 912 in Watsonville. Together they formed the North American Worker to Worker Network (NAWWN), whose goals were to support independent organizing among Mexican workers and to campaign against NAFTA.

In addition to NAWWN, many other U.S. and Mexican unionists also began discussing joint organizing efforts more than a year before the final vote in Congress approved the trade agreement. In their view, workers in the two countries would be whipsawed against each other as large U.S. corporations sought to lower labor costs by moving production south of the border—or by threatening to do so. Building strong unions in U.S.-owned plants in Mexico, they reasoned, would help Mexican workers win better wages and conditions and narrow the economic gulf between them and their U.S. counterparts.

In 1993, the most progressive voices in the U.S. labor movement walked away from the bruising congressional vote on NAFTA more convinced than ever that unions had to become as globally oriented as the corporations they face. Campaigning against NAFTA, many began to develop links to unions in Mexico that served as the beginning of new relationships. Those relationships in turn led to cooperative organizing projects and campaigns in factories in a number of Mexican cities.

MOVING FROM SLOGAN TO REALITY

In 1991, the organizing director of the United Electrical Workers, Bob Kingsley, attended the founding conference of the Mexican Network Against Free Trade, in response to the looming debate over NAFTA. There, he made connections with the FAT, the only Mexican union federation opposing the agreement. Kingsley began discussing with the FAT representatives the idea of a joint approach to organizing plants on the border. That connection was followed by a meeting between leaders of the two groups in Pittsburgh, where they hammered out the basic outline of a strategic organizing alliance.

Both were interested in making the alliance more than the typical ceremonial relationship in which union leaders attend each other's conventions and do little more than make flowery statements about mutual support and solidarity. The relationship the UE had sustained with the SME through the 1960s and 1970s, for example, was warm but hadn't advanced much beyond that level.

Part of the reason for the ties between the UE and the SME was their similar political history. The UE had been a leading force in the CIO during the post–World War Two period, when the left-wing federation helped to found the World Federation of Trade Unions (WFTU). In the period of the McCarthy witch hunts that followed, however, the UE and nine other unions left the CIO, which in turn accused the WFTU of being dominated by the Soviet Union.

The postwar decades also saw similar repression against the left in Mexico—Campa's imprisonment was a symbol. The SME, which had participated in organizing the WFTU, never broke its ties to that international body. Thus the relationship between the UE and the SME was an expression of political independence, even political defiance of the cold war trends in labor. It was a symbol of the mutual desire of both unions for world labor solidarity based on a vision of real workers' power. In practice, however, there was little contact between the rank-and-file membership of each union, and little common work.

The relationship between the UE and the FAT was designed to be something very different. It was launched with a tour of UE plants involving one leader from each union, who had a chance to talk directly with members on the shop floor. One of the union leaders was David Johnson, a lead organizer for the UE in Los Angeles; the other was Benedicto Martínez, general secretary of the FAT. Johnson had become one of the UE staff members responsible for developing the relationship with the FAT, in part because of his work with the mostly Mexican workforce in Los Angeles.

"We talked to workers in the plants and in meetings in our halls about free trade and why a Mexican union, the FAT, was opposed to it," Johnson said. "That turned a lot of heads, since people were being told by the media that while U.S. unions opposed NAFTA, Mexican unions were looking at the treaty as a source of jobs. That helped to change the debate about free trade in many labor councils. Up to that time, opposition to NAFTA was mixed with a lot of protectionism and nationalism. We tried to shift it to a point of view where workers could see that it wasn't a good thing for either country. Instead of calling for closing the border, we began developing support for solidarity with Mexican workers.

"It was a breath of fresh air. In a couple of councils, people told us that they hadn't known that Mexican workers were opposed to the agreement."

The pair held press conferences and met with other unions as well. New Haven, Connecticut, where the UE had conducted a drawn-out strike by immigrant workers at the Circuit-Wise plant, and Youngstown, Ohio, where steel mill closings had devastated the community, were high points of the tour. After the pair talked to workers in the break room of the GE light bulb factory in Niles, Ohio, Johnson said, Martínez told him that it all felt "just like one of our own factories." Most important, although the alliance had yet to begin picking targets, the two found enough in common in their mutual commitment to rank-and-file unionism to feel comfortable about the idea of a joint organizing program.

Following the tour, both unions researched the Mexican locations of UE-represented companies. Some shops were targeted for campaigns even before NAFTA passed through Congress and was signed by President Bill Clinton in 1993. All the national officers of each union were involved in the discussions, according to Johnson. On the UE end, Robin Alexander was given responsibility for overseeing solidarity campaigns on the U.S. side of the border, while Johnson was assigned to help on the ground in Mexico.

In developing its relationship with the FAT, Johnson emphasized, the UE tried to be sensitive to the accusation that past international relationships of U.S. unions had been marked by "racism and chauvinism toward workers in other countries." In contrast, the UE did not try to have a voice in the positions or internal policies of the FAT. "Our relationship is based on mutual respect and self-determination," he explained. "What happens in Mexico is determined by Mexicans. The key to our relationship with the FAT is its desire and ability to mount organizing campaigns and its support for real and democratic unionism."

Martínez responded that the FAT identified with the UE because "we both share a struggle for the same objectives. Each union respects the autonomy of the other. Solidarity is very important to us because the desperation of workers in Mexico is pushing them to organize. It a product of the crisis we're living in, and we have a responsibility to help them. We will be much stronger if we can face these companies together, on both sides of the border."

The FAT developed relations with other unions in the United States as well. Martínez toured California as a speaker on the Free Trade Caravan, organized and sponsored by the Teamsters union. The caravan traveled to union meetings and gatherings of workers throughout the state, to develop opposition to NAFTA. Martínez found that "some workers were concerned mostly about the possible loss of their own jobs. But when I talked about the situation of Mexican workers, U.S. unionists were very concerned about the violations of their human rights and organizing rights. We gave people a way to link their concern about their own future to concern over the situation of Mexican workers."

"It was clear from the beginning of our relationship that there would be no pretense that UE was a Mexican union," Johnson later recalled. "The FAT was the union in Mexico; we were the union in the U.S. We had a lot of similarities in our experience and approach. We were both used to a lot of employer terror against workers in our efforts to organize. But I still had to adjust to the level of that fear in Mexico, which was much greater. Workers there were facing firings, blacklists against their whole families, beatings, and a much more developed stool pigeon network."

Although Johnson was chosen in part because of his experience organizing Mexican workers in Los Angeles, he found that border workers in Mexico turned out to be quite different. "I actually found the immigrant workforce in southern California older and more worldly than maquiladora workers, with more real-life experience. Just getting to the U.S. requires a certain level of initiative and drive. In Juárez, we were talking to very young kids—sixteen, seventeen, or eighteen years old, in their first jobs."

The UE and the Teamsters began providing financial support for FAT organizers. In Juárez, across the bridge from El Paso, Texas, the UE/FAT alliance began organizing workers at General Electric's Compania Armadora plant. Farther south, in Chihuahua, the Teamsters and the FAT made contacts among workers at the home and building controls plant belonging to Honeywell Corporation.

The first efforts at General Electric seemed promising. Two days before Christmas in 1993, GE agreed to rehire six of eleven workers it had fired for union activity. Johnson charged that the company had fired the eleven immediately following a visit to the plant by a delegation of UE members from GE plants in Ontario, California; Erie, Pennsylvania; and Conneaut, Ohio. One fired worker, Manuel Gómez, had hosted a meeting with UE members in his home. Another, Fernando Castro, had spoken to U.S. reporters from National Public Radio and accused GE of using chemicals banned in the United States at its Juárez plant.

The UE credited a combination of political pressure in Washington and pressure mounted by union members in U.S. GE plants with convincing the company to rehire six of the fired workers. "President Clinton and Congress assured the American people that labor and human rights would be respected on both sides of the border," according to Amy Newell, then the UE's national secretary-treasurer, who demanded an investigation into the violation of workplace rights in Mexico.

Similar pressure, however, failed to win reinstatement for twenty workers fired at the Honeywell plant in Chihuahua. Four of the fired workers, Guadalupe and Ofelia Medrano, Anita Gutiérrez, and Carmen Delgado, said that they had been told by company personnel director Cesar Martínez and superintendent Gabriel Vargas that the factory would close before it would allow a union. They accused Martínez and Vargas of demanding the names of other workers involved in the organizing effort.

Honeywell spokesperson Linda Nordeen claimed that the workers were chosen for layoff because they violated a company rule and were away from their workstations. She refused to supply any details about the rule violations or to allow interviews with Martínez or Vargas.

The Teamsters, the UE, and the FAT asked other opponents of NAFTA, including Friends of the Earth, Clean Water Action, and Ralph Nader, to write to Clinton, asking him to pressure Honeywell into reinstating the fired workers. In San Diego, however, Lucila Conde, an organizer with the Communications Workers of America and the Support Committee for Maquiladora Workers, argued that pressuring Clinton to guarantee workers' rights in Mexico was pointless. "It was hypocritical for the president to promise such protection during the debate on NAFTA," she said. "The whole reason for the treaty was to guarantee cheap labor in Mexico, and this is what it takes."

In the end, Clinton didn't act. The firings were so intimidating to other Honeywell workers that the FAT's campaign for union representation rights was unable to proceed to a direct challenge. At Compania Armadora, there was an election, which the FAT lost.

As a result of the firings, threats, and other incidents in the companies' campaigns, the UE, the Teamsters, and the FAT filed the first two complaints under NAFTA's labor side agreement. A hearing was held by the National Administrative Office (NAO) in Washington, D.C., far from the border, making it difficult for workers to observe the proceedings or to provide testimony. Both companies refused to participate. The NAO recommended no action on the charges in both cases.

Eric Meyers, a staff member of the Coalition for Justice in the Maquiladoras, condemned the whole process. "We tried it in good faith," he asserted. "We found that even when the process is carried to its conclusion, officials of both governments are clearly unwilling to rock the boat." Robin Alexander, the UE's director of international relations, was even more bitter. She called the labor side agreement "toothless and ineffective."

THE BLACKLIST

When Alma Molina tried to organize with other workers to raise wages at Clarostat, the Juárez maquiladora where they worked, she was fired. Then she got a job working for another General Electric plant in the same city, Electrocomponentes. But she lost that job eight days later—and discovered that she had been blacklisted. Then, when Molina tried to come to the United States to describe her experiences, she was denied a visa by the U.S. consulate in Juárez.

Molina, a twenty-seven-year-old mother, was employed by Clarostat S.A., a large U.S.-owned plant making parts for the Allen-Bradley Corporation in Milwaukee, whose workers have been represented by the UE since the 1930s. After working at Clarostat for over a year, Molina and other workers began to meet to find a way to challenge the low wages. Clarostat was paying Molina the equivalent of about 86 cents an hour at the time. One of the workers tipped off the company about the meetings, however. On March 2, 1993, the personnel director called Molina into the office and told her that Clarostat's owners "will not stand for a union here." Molina was fired, and Clarostat's other workers were told that the factory would close if they tried to organize.

Bernardino Echeverría, a FAT organizer in Juárez, said that U.S. maquiladora owners generally "consider organizing a union a crime." According to Echeverría, as many as ten or fifteen workers were fired in Juárez every day during that period for seeking raises and other improvements. "Most of these efforts are spontaneous. Workers are responding to the extreme economic pressure of low wages or because their bonuses are being illegally withheld," he explained. Maquiladora wages are so low that, from the beginning of the Border Industrialization Program in the 1960s, most plants have paid a food bonus in addition to wages, a bonus that is conditional on workers' attendance.

The FAT, Echeverría said, tried to convert struggles over wages into efforts to organize unions, as workers did at Clarostat. "But the companies respond quickly, trying to cut them off at the roots."

After her firing, Molina found another job at Electrocomponentes S.A., a plant belonging to General Electric and employing fifteen hundred workers. GE paid her the equivalent of 74 cents an hour, with another 5 dollars each week for food. Twenty-three people were hired on the same day as Molina. "The company hires so many people, they can't check everyone thoroughly," she noted.

After working for eight days, she was called into the office of personnel director Roberto Sánchez. "He told me that he had a blacklist of people the companies won't hire because they're robbers or drug addicts," Molina remembered. "I could see the list in his hands. He asked me why I was on it, and I told him probably because I was fired at Clarostat. He said I couldn't continue working for Electrocomponentes.

"He knew why I was on the list. He was afraid that workers at Electrocomponentes would also try to get better benefits, and he wanted to make sure they have no leaders."

GE spokesperson Bruce Bunch, in New Jersey, denied that the company ever used a blacklist. Although he and other GE officials in Juárez and the United States refused to discuss Molina's case, Bunch called her firing "a factoid" and alleged that "this issue is being raised as a smokescreen for opposition to the free trade agreement."

Echeverría, however, countered that the existence of the blacklist has been common knowledge for many years. The list is revised and circulated among maquiladoras in Juárez on a weekly basis by the Maquiladora Associación Civil, he said.

Although anti-union firings and blacklists are illegal under Mexican law, "the law says one thing, but the practice is another," according to Benedicto Martínez. "In practice, there is no respect for the law." Martínez accused the Mexican government of not enforcing the law "because our government's policy is to attract foreign investment by maintaining conditions which the companies want, like low wages, few regulations, and no unions."

Firings, blacklists, and visa denials are old problems that unions have faced since the 1930s and before. But they are old problems with new meaning in a new era of free trade and massive relocation of production across international borders. They have become an enforcement mechanism for ensuring the investment conditions desired by foreign companies. Such obstacles are forcing unions and workers in Mexico and the United States to find new ways to cooperate more closely than ever.

Since the mid-1970s, the PRI, which governed Mexico until its defeat in the presidential election of 2000, has been deeply divided between technocrats and "dinosaurs"—the traditional local party leaders who often come out of the government-controlled unions. In border towns such as Reynosa, Matamoros, and Tijuana, the "dinosaurs" still control the party apparatus. They've been able to make an accommodation with the local authorities (even in cities where the governing party is the PAN, rather than the PRI) and the local maquiladora owners association. As a result, although maquiladoras in those cities are unionized, those unions themselves become part of the apparatus enforcing pro-investment conditions.

In Juárez, however, the local government has been run by technocrats. The city is home to more maquiladoras than any other in Mexico, with hardly any unions. The industrial growth of Juárez has made El Paso, the city's twin on the U.S. side of the Rio Grande, the seventh most polluted metropolitan area in the United States. Between 1988 and 1992, 163 children in Juárez were born with anencephaly, an extremely rare disorder in which a child is born with no functioning brain. Although city authorities blame the occurrences on malnutrition or drug use by mothers, workers and union activists such as Echeverría believe that toxic chemicals used in the plants are at fault.

In addition to their joint campaign at Compania Armadora, the UE and the FAT also tried to develop a campaign at the Electrocomponentes plant in Juárez. After Molina's firing, the UE helped to organize protests at the GE office in Boston and at the Allen-Bradley plant in Milwaukee. The demonstrations were supported by Jobs with Justice, a coalition of unions formed during the last years of Lane Kirkland's tenure as head of the AFL-CIO. Jobs with Justice aimed to develop mutual support among unions in cities around the country, to compensate for Kirkland's failure to provide effective leadership and organization and to promote a progressive political agenda in labor. Cross-border organizing was part of that progressive agenda.

Jobs with Justice invited Molina to the United States, but the U.S. consulate in Juárez refused to issue her a visa. She was told that she might become a public charge. The unions suspected complicity among the consulate, Mexican authorities, and the maquiladora owners, particularly GE.

Johnson described the use of a blacklist as commonplace. "What's surprising in Molina's case," he said, "is the blatant way they showed it to her. The companies on the border are confident they can get away with anything because the Mexican government wants foreign investment.

"In the short range," he concluded, "we have to organize actions to protect the right to organize in Mexico, as we've tried to do in Alma Molina's case, and bring to the public eye the activities of U.S. corporations." Defending labor rights in Mexican maquiladoras requires cooperation between U.S. and Mexican unions, Johnson says. "We can go to plant gates and raise money and resources from our own members. But in the long range, we have to cooperate on the larger issues. When we negotiate contracts, we have to do it in cooperation. We have to fight against NAFTA and for policies which create a decent life for workers on both sides of the border."

One of the institutions that evolved in the wake of the campaigns at Compania Armadora and Electrocomponentes was the Center for Labor Studies (CETLAC, Centro de Estudios y Taller Laboral). Both campaigns clearly showed the high degree of intimidation and fear in the plants and the difficulty in openly organizing unions, particularly when many of the workers were young and had little experience.

"Maquiladora workers are often teenagers with no previous history or knowledge of unions or even of factory work," Johnson noted. That lack of experience and union consciousness seemed in part responsible for the inability of the joint campaigns to withstand the threats and firings at GE and Honeywell. In response, CETLAC was opened in Juárez in September 1994, with the aim of increasing general knowledge and support for unions in the barrios where maquiladora workers live.

The center quickly became well known for documenting extensive hiring discrimination against pregnant women. It focused on the three FAVESA factories owned by Lear Industries, which supplied car seats to General Motors.

"When I was being hired, after the interview, they asked me when I would have my next [menstrual] period," one FAVESA worker explained. "They said I couldn't actually start work until I had my period. I was still three weeks away, so I had to wait. On the first day of my period, I came back. The nurse was there, and she said, 'Let's see it, show me the sanitary napkin.' They accepted me that same day."

CETLAC director Guillermina Solis charged that the companies don't want to hire pregnant women and will even fire women when they become pregnant, in order to avoid government-mandated maternity benefits. Her allegations were supported by the Women's Rights Project of Human Rights Watch, which issued a detailed report in 1996, titled

"No Guarantees: Sex Discrimination in Mexico's Maquiladora Sector," documenting extensive sexual discrimination in maquiladoras.

CETLAC also provided support for workers who wanted to come together, talk about their problems, and plan strategy away from the sight and hearing of company managers. In 2000, the center was used by militant activists among the twelve hundred workers at the EES plant, which produces medical supplies for Johnson and Johnson.

Trouble had been brewing at EES, and the company sought to put a lid on rising discontent there. But it didn't count on the power of a militant shop steward and his supporters.

Efraín Sosa, an intense, sharp-featured man, won the allegiance of his co-workers in part because of his direct manner—that of an *obrero*, a laborer on the line. But, to bring people together on the factory floor, he also tapped into a tradition of mutual support common among Mexican workers, farmers, and indigenous communities. When he urged them to use direct and radical action at work to solve their problems, that common culture of resistance stood them in good stead against odds that often defeat other maquila workers.

Sosa had previously been fired at another U.S.-owned plant, Cummins ReCom, where he and six hundred other auto parts workers had tried to organize a union. "For two months, we had meetings, but then the company discovered what we were doing," he recalled. "I was fired, along with about a hundred others. And when we went to the labor board, they did nothing to help us. They wouldn't enforce the law."

The EES plant where he next found a job already had a union, a *sección*, or local, of the Revolutionary Confederation of Workers and Farmers (CROC), affiliated with the PRI. But the union did little to change dangerous conditions, protect workers from unjust firings, or even help them secure their legally mandated severance pay when they were terminated. Meeting at CETLAC, Sosa and his co-workers organized a slate of candidates for offices in the CROC local union. The workers' slate won election in March 1999 by a vote of 600 to 120, and Sosa became the shop steward.

"The company wasn't used to working with a union committee that defended people's rights," he said. "Until we were elected, they just manipulated the union and did what they wanted. So the managers were not happy with us. Finally, in June, we wrote a letter to the labor board, accusing the owners of violating the contract. The labor board, instead of making an investigation, just sent our letter to the company. After they received it, I was told to report to a meeting with the human resources director, Ana Julia Núñez. Núñez told me I was fired and tried to give me a check for sixteen thousand pesos in severance pay. I told her that I wouldn't accept it and that the company had no right to fire the union representative elected by the workers.

"So she called the CROC office in downtown Juárez and made an appointment for me to see my own union leaders, who were supposed to defend us. Then our union committee was told to go to the company office, where they were held incommunicado. Meanwhile, Núñez went from department to department, telling everyone I'd agreed to quit and that the company had paid me off with fifty thousand pesos."

The head of the CROC in Chihuahua state, Luis Vidal, sided with the company. The workers went off to plan their own strategy, however.

"The next day, I went down to the factory at the three-thirty shift change," Sosa recalled. "When the time came, about two hundred workers gathered to walk inside with me. Four of them walked on each side, and in front and behind, to hide me as we went past the gate. The plant guards tried to keep us from going in. One of them even tried to put his arms around me to physically force me to leave. But by then there were five hundred workers confronting them, and there was no way they could stop us."

The company eventually called its lawyer, while workers threatened to prevent the day shift from starting work the next morning. Sosa was immediately reinstated, and Núñez removed as human resources director.

"When I went back to work the following Monday, I felt very proud of the people in the plant," Sosa concluded. "We'd been able to see beyond our own individual situation and act together to protect everyone's rights. Since then, the company treats us with more respect, and now the managers make formal agreements with us about the conditions at work. They weren't really prepared for what happened, and I don't think they believed people would respond when they fired me. The best thing is that workers at the factory now have a lot more confidence. They know that even if the labor board and the CROC leaders won't defend them and enforce the law, they have the power to do it themselves."

FREE TRADE'S REVENGE

María Villela and her husband, Raquel, spent a combined thirty-two years at Friction, an auto parts plant in Irvine, California. They were there in 1992, when the business was bought by Echlin, a Connecticut-based transnational corporation. They were leaders in the organizing drive that brought in the union in 1994; María became its president. And the Villelas, a couple in their forties and fifties, were there in the summer of 1997, when three strangers, workers from an Echlin plant in Mexico City, showed up at lunchtime.

When the lunch truck pulled into the Friction lot that day, a small group of employees took their lunches, walked out the gate to the street, and sat on the grass to hear what the strangers had to say. Like the majority of Friction's workers, who were immigrants from Mexico, Guatemala, and El Salvador, the strangers spoke Spanish. They described their own factory as nothing like the Irvine plant. Instead, they gave a Dickensian description of a history of accidents, miserly wages a tenth of those paid in Irvine, and a government-controlled union that actually prevented workers from organizing to improve conditions.

The story didn't come as a complete surprise to the workers at Friction. "We used to get boxes of parts from their plant," said Rubén Cabrera, Friction's union steward. "When we'd open them up, the parts were covered in dust." Friction workers figured the dust for asbestos, the fibrous mineral that causes mesothelioma, a kind of lung cancer, when it is inhaled. Nevertheless, "we were surprised by what they said, and some of us got pretty mad," Cabrera remembered. "The situation they described was very unjust. I felt they were being treated like slaves."

María Villela said simply, "We wanted to help the workers there win their rights."

But the company's response to their effort to support the Mexico City workers was, some came to believe, the beginning of the end of the Friction plant. In February 1999, Echlin Corporation, based in Branford, Connecticut (now a division of the Dana Aftermarket Group, the publicly traded parts giant), formally notified Villela's union, UE Local 1090, that it was closing Friction. By August 31, the factory gate shut for the last time. The ovens were turned off. The machinery that had churned out brake pads and auto parts for more than two decades was loaded onto trucks and hauled away. The plant's 110 production workers gave the boxy building a last look and moved on with their lives. Friction was gone.

Echlin spokesperson Paul Ryder denied that the plant closing was payback for the union's budding internationalism. "We have overcapacity for that product line," he said. "The closure is just the normal course of business." Local 1090 negotiated severance pay for the workers and company cooperation in efforts to assist workers in finding other jobs.

Many Friction workers were convinced that organizing their union and attempting to help Echlin workers in Mexico City were the reasons Echlin shut Friction's doors. "We think it's revenge," María Villela declared. "We worked like crazy here and made the best product in the industry. Then they said they were transferring the work to other plants."

The Friction plant is a typically anonymous, prefabricated tilt-up building on an industrial boulevard in California's Orange County. Daimler Street extends for three unimpressive blocks, between similar nameless crackerbox buildings in an aging Irvine industrial park next to the Costa Mesa Freeway. It's hard to tell what goes on in these concrete warehouses; in some, it's apparent that nothing goes on at all—real estate signs hang across their facades, advertising that the occupants have fled or disappeared.

Before the Friction plant finally closed down, a group of workers met at lunchtime and speculated that the company would sacrifice quality and efficiency by transferring the work to other plants. One pointed out that Sears Roebuck, one of Friction's principal customers, had been so pleased with the quality of the factory's product that it gave the company money to reward its employees. Each worker had taken home a hundred-dollar bonus. Chief Auto Parts had given them a similar commendation.

Another worker reported that the Virginia plant, to which some of the work was being shifted, employed eight people to work on each oven rather than Friction's two. Their conclusion: revenge was behind the plant closure, not economic motives. "I think it's likely that the company found out about the Mexico City workers' visit to Irvine and concluded that the Irvine workers had a special role in encouraging the organization of their independent union," said Bob Kingsley, the UE's national organizing director.

That conclusion was supported by conversations workers reported to union steward Cabrera. According to Cabrera, supervisors told the workers, "This is what you get for what you've done."

"What hurts isn't just the shock of losing a job," Cabrera explained. "It's losing friends and people you've known and worked with for years. I came here from a small town in Michoacán seventeen years ago. I got a job here right away, and I worked here ever since. Working at Friction was a big part of my life." Friction workers had an average of eleven years on the job.

Echlin had a well-earned anti-union reputation. On March 13, 1998, Echlin senior vice president Milton Makoski made the company's antipathy to unions perfectly clear. In a letter to Teamster union vice president Tom Gilmartin, who proposed that Echlin negotiate a corporate code of conduct, Makoski wrote, "We are opposed to union organization of our current non-union locations. . . . We will fight every effort to unionize Echlin employees who have chosen not to be represented by a union." He went on to note approvingly that, despite "sixty years of determined and relentless efforts" by unions, a majority of the company's employees were still unorganized. "There is only one [operation] in existence," he regretted, "where the employees, while they were part of the Echlin organization, have elected to be represented by a union."

That operation was the Friction plant. In the Irvine factory, the workers had formed UE Local 1090 in a fierce organizing battle in 1994. "We got tired of having supervisors tell us, 'Do this, or there's the door,'" Cabrera recalled. "If we stopped our machine just to go to the bathroom, they'd yell at us. Even those of us who had been here for years were only making six dollars an hour."

Cabrera, a heavyset, soft-spoken man, was later chosen as steward. He described conditions in the plant before the union vote carefully and slowly, with no whine in his voice—a demeanor that carried credibility even with the supervisors.

But the UE did more than rely on the credibility of leaders such as Cabrera or the bravery of workers inside the plant to overcome the company's intense opposition. It found support for them from other factories in the Echlin chain. "We put one of our organizers on the road, meeting with workers and unions at other Echlin plants," Kingsley recalled. "Workers in one Virginia factory where the Amalgamated Clothing Workers [now UNITE, the Union of Needletrades, Industrial and Textile Employees] had a contract and at various Teamster locals around the country signed petitions, sent letters of support, and wore buttons at work showing solidarity with the local in Irvine. That was the origin of what grew to be the Echlin Workers Alliance."

Two years later, during a second round of contract negotiations in the spring of 1996, unions in the Echlin alliance again sent faxes and petitions to plant managers throughout the company in support of the Irvine workers. Villela, president of Local 1090, credited the alliance's involvement with helping the local win big improvements. The second contract included five raises, totaling eighty-one cents, over two years; a bonus of a day's pay for good attendance; and two additional personal days off.

Friction workers won recognition for their union—and a certain grudging respect—from Echlin management. But it came at a price.

"They began to look at us not as the company's workers, but as its enemies," said Villela.

Then the strangers from Mexico City showed up in Irvine. They had come three thousand miles from ITAPSA, an Echlin plant in Mexico City, where, through 1996 and 1997, workers tried to shed their membership in the government-affiliated CTM in favor of the independent union STIMAHCS (Union of Workers in the Metal, Steel, Iron and Connected Industries). That effort was thwarted through the combined efforts of Echlin, the government-backed official union federation, and the local police.

Squelching independent unions in Mexico was nothing out of the ordinary. But unlike similar instances in the past, the repression at ITAPSA was met by a well-organized international response, one that broke new ground. On March 1, 1997, STIMAHCS, which is part of the FAT, helped to form a North American alliance of unions with contracts in Echlin's factories. That alliance included the Teamsters, the UE, the Paperworkers, and UNITE in the United States and the Canadian Steelworkers and Auto Workers.

The most active U.S. local in that campaign was the one at the Irvine Friction plant. Local 1090 members began by hosting the ITAPSA visitors that summer. They passed leaflets out on the production line describing what was going on in Mexico City and discussed the events at work and in union meetings. Finally, workers signed a petition demanding that Echlin stop firing workers and recognize STIMAHCS at the ITAPSA plant.

When Villela and other executive board members presented the petition to Friction plant manager Mark Levy, Villela recalled that "we could see in his face how angry he was. He told us we had drawn a line between the union and the company." Then, in February, Echlin gave the Friction workers notice of the closure.

NAFTA had been in effect for only a few months when Rubén Ruiz got a job at ITAPSA, in the summer of 1994. As his new boss showed him around, Ruiz noticed with apprehension that the machines were old and poorly maintained. He had hardly begun his first shift when workers around him began yelling out: a machine had malfunctioned, cutting four fingers from the hand of the man operating it. "I was very scared," he later remembered. "I wanted to leave." But he needed the job, and he stayed.

Accidents were only part of the problem. Ruiz later testified at a hearing concerning labor violations and health and safety problems at the plant that asbestos dust from the brake parts manufactured at ITAPSA coated machines and people alike. Workers were given X rays, Ruiz says, and later some would be fired.

Echlin claimed that its ITAPSA plant complied with Mexican health and safety laws. "Medical records indicate that since Echlin has owned the ITAPSA plant, there have been no work-related employee deaths," a company statement noted.

It seemed obvious to Ruiz, however, that things were very wrong. So when a friend asked him to come to a meeting to talk about organizing a union, he went. But as ITAPSA workers organized, they discovered that they already had one—Sección 15 of the CTM, Mexico's largest labor federation.

ITAPSA's three hundred employees had never even seen the union contract, and Mexican labor experts say that they wouldn't have been pleased if they had. Jesús Campos Linas, the dean of the country's labor lawyers, called the agreement between Echlin and the CTM a protection contract, insulating the company from labor unrest.

When ITAPSA managers discovered the union organizing effort, they began firing the leaders. In early June 1996, sixteen workers were terminated. Ruiz was called into the office of Luis Espinoza de los Monteros, ITAPSA's human relations director. "He told me he had received a phone call from the leaders of the Echlin group in the U.S., who told him that any worker organizing a new union should be discharged without further question," Ruiz recounted. "He told me my name was on a list of those people, and I was discharged right there and then."

Despite the firings, many ITAPSA workers joined STIMAHCS, and the union filed a petition with the labor board in Mexico City. A date was set for a final showdown, a side-by-side election between STIM-AHCS and the CTM: August 28, 1997.

That morning, the fired workers went to the plant, where they joined union supporters from the swing and graveyard shifts, eager to vote. But the day before, at the CTM's insistence, the labor board had postponed the election without notifying STIMAHCS. Company supervisors, looking at the off-shift workers assembled at the gate, got a very good idea of who was supporting the independent union.

"That afternoon, the company began to fire more workers," said Benedicto Martínez. He reported that fifty workers were eventually terminated—a claim Echlin disputed.

The election was finally held thirteen days later. The evening before, a member of the state judicial police drove a car filled with rifles into the plant, unloading them openly. The next morning, two busloads of strangers entered the factory, armed with clubs and copper rods. STIM-AHCS immediately tried to get the election canceled. But the labor board went ahead, even after thugs roughed up one of the independent union's organizers.

As workers came to vote, escorted by CTM functionaries, they passed a gauntlet of the club-wielding strangers. At the voting table, they were asked to state aloud which union they favored, in front of management and CTM representatives. STIMAHCS observers couldn't even inspect the credentials of many voters. People voted who were unknown to the factory's workers. Predictably, STIMAHCS lost.

The FAT and the UE filed a complaint under the North American Agreement on Labor Cooperation, NAFTA's labor side agreement, accusing Mexico of failing to enforce its laws guaranteeing workers' rights. The Echlin case alleged collusion by the Mexican government, the company, and the CTM to deny workers the right to representation by an independent union.

The charges were heard before Irasema Garza, secretary of the National Administrative Office of the U.S. Department of Labor, in Washington, D.C., on March 23, 1998. A number of ITAPSA workers submitted affidavits about the firings and intimidation. Ruiz testified. And just days after being told that her own Friction plant was closing, María Villela went to Washington to support the ITAPSA workers at the NAO hearing. "We don't regret what we did for a minute," she said. "The company is responsible for a great injustice."

Echlin never showed up to contest the testimony. On July 31, 1998, the NAO issued its report. It declared that workers "were subjected to retaliation by their employer and the established union in the workplace, including threats of physical harm and dismissal." The NAO found that the election had been marred by "an atmosphere of fear and intimidation." Workers asserting their rights "were subjected to physical attack by persons associated with the established union in the plant, and in the presence of company officials." The NAO concluded that the ITAPSA plant "may suffer serious health and safety deficiencies that are hazardous to its employees."

The NAO report vindicated the efforts Friction workers had made to help their fellow Echlin employees in Mexico. It revealed in chilling detail the obstacles confronting Mexican workers when they try to organize against poverty wages and dangerous conditions. And, by acknowledging those obstacles, the report gave eloquent testimony to the conditions that attract companies like Echlin to relocate production to Mexico in the first place.

It's strange to think of jobs that pay eight to ten dollars an hour, such as those at Friction, as high-wage jobs. Friction wages were only half of what union autoworkers earn in Detroit assembly plants. Yet wages at ITAPSA are only a fraction of those earned at the Irvine Friction plant. That wage differential leads to a movement of jobs southward, a movement that NAFTA has facilitated.

The 110 workers at Friction wound up challenging not only their own employer but the new rules of economic globalization. Those rules say that if Mexican workers want jobs, they must accept low wages and conditions far worse than those north of the border—and must be subject to firings and heavy-handed repression if they try to change them.

These rules don't affect only workers at Echlin. In hundreds of small factories scattered across the United States, job security is evaporating, as it did at Friction. These factories have become cogs within large corporations that are seeking to cut labor costs to the bone, whipsawing workers and shifting production from plant to plant, country to country, as though borders and distance have vanished.

Workers have agonized for years over the resulting devastation to lives and communities. In Irvine, however, Friction workers moved beyond complaining to action.

Villela and her union argued that NAFTA undermined their jobs by liberating the market forces that sent production to the lowest-wage areas. And NAFTA's labor side agreement, which produced the report that so clearly described the problems facing Mexican workers, did nothing to actually solve those problems. The report concluded by recommending the severest sanction available for the violation of workers' rights to form independent unions: discussions between the U.S. labor secretary and the Mexican secretary of labor and social development.

And that was all. No fines. No requirement that the company rehire the fired workers or recognize their union. Not even a rerun of the election. The NAO could recommend none of these actions because, while making it easier for companies to move money and production, the treaty contains no penalties for those who engage in the conduct reported at ITAPSA.

"We recognize there's not enough power in the process to overcome the economic incentives of free trade," said the UE's Robin Alexander, speaking of NAFTA's labor side agreement. "It's an extremely weak tool, and the lack of penalties for violating union rights is a gaping hole."

Nevertheless, the union alliance convinced the AFL-CIO, the Canadian Labour Congress, and Mexico's new independent federation, the National Union of Workers, to join the complaint against Echlin. It was the first time they had taken such action together.

"Wherever I look, I see unions making efforts to figure out how to deal with each other and face the danger of transnational corporations,"

Alexander observed. "Maybe there is no single answer, at least not yet. But we won't find any answers at all without getting out there and looking for them."

That's what the Friction workers did. Their crime, in the company's eyes, was that they didn't simply accept NAFTA's economic rules—they looked for answers. They sacrificed their jobs as a result, but they became pioneers, reaching across the border to find new ways of enforcing labor rights.

Despite doubts over the effectiveness of the process, the UE spent four and a half years following through on the complaint, in an attempt to make it meaningful. The original complaint was filed on December 15, 1997. The NAO hearing was held on March 23, 1998, followed by the NAO report on July 31. Then nothing happened for the next two years, until an agreement with the Mexican Ministry of Labor was announced on May 18, 2000. It simply mandated a seminar to discuss the issues raised in the complaint.

On June 23, a seminar on the parallel Han Young case was held at the Camino Real hotel in Tijuana. As Chapter Four described, Han Young strikers who attended were beaten for trying to participate. The UE protested to U.S. labor secretary Alexis Herman, who replied that "the UE and other interested organizations [would be] consulted on the planning of the tri-national seminar on labor boards." Louis Karesh, acting head of the NAO, agreed to hold the ITAPSA seminar in Mexico City, where it would be accessible to the plant's workers, and he welcomed the UE's suggestions for the agenda. Despite trepidations, the union submitted a proposed agenda focusing on the actions of the Mexican labor boards and the need for secret ballot elections.

Another two years passed.

Then, by accident, the UE discovered that the seminar had been moved to Monterrey, more than a thousand miles from Mexico City. Monterrey was the home of the president of the federal Mexican labor board (as distinct from the local Mexico City board, by then under the control of PRD appointee Jesús Campos Linas). The UE's suggestions for the agenda had been rejected, and the only presenters scheduled were government officials, as had been the case in Tijuana.

That was too much for the UE. In a letter to U.S. labor secretary Elaine Chao, UE president John Hovis declared bitterly that "given this history, we believe that the NAO process has deteriorated into a farce, and under these circumstances we see no value in participating further." His letter recapitulated the continuing use of open ballot elections during the four-year process, despite commitments made after the original ITAPSA hearing, noting that "Mexican workers have had their rights violated and have suffered physical and emotional abuse in connection with elections where they must still vote out loud in front of company officials and oftentimes in front of thugs." Hovis concluded acidly that "we do not choose to lend any further credibility to a process which has so totally failed to protect workers' rights."

WHAT WAS POSSIBLE?

David Johnson left the UE in the late 1990s, but he looks back at his experience in helping to build an alliance with a Mexican union with a great deal of pride. The alliance has been a high point in organized solidarity between U.S. and Mexican unions, and he had an important role in starting the process.

"I think our goal was to help the FAT organize and build a beachhead, and we were able to build a real relationship," he believes. "We put pressure on GE at the highest level, in national contract bargaining—the FAT was represented at our bargaining table. We got GE to adopt a code of conduct, which recognizes that workers have basic human rights. And in the cases of a number of fired workers, we were able to win their reinstatement."

The experience also changed the UE. In UE plants, workers who operate the same machines General Electric has in Mexico generally know not only the wage their counterparts are paid but also something about the problems Mexican workers face when they try to organize. GE workers are well aware that the company is just as opposed to independent unions in Mexico as it is to unions in its U.S. plants. That knowledge is part of the product of the strategic relationship.

"In the U.S., we paid a lot of attention to mobilizing rank-and-file support," Johnson says. "We used bulletins from the union, stewards circulated petitions protesting treatment in Mexican plants, we had rallies at the U.S. plants, we organized congressional investigations into the abuses, and we brought Mexican workers to testify in U.S. hearings."

Johnson and others understand that the union also had an advantage because of its experience in organizing Mexican immigrants in Los Angeles. The UE had a long history of condemning immigration raids and fighting employer sanctions—the section of the Immigration Reform and Control Act of 1986 that makes it a crime for an undocumented worker to hold jobs—long before the AFL-CIO finally adopted similar positions in 1999. That history won it the support of many activists in the Mexican workforce in southern California as well as the respect of human rights and labor activists in Mexico.

But the conditions for organizing in Mexico were very different, and much more difficult, than those the UE was accustomed to facing in the United States. And while the UE's membership at General Electric made the company a natural target, it was certainly not the easiest one the alliance could have chosen.

"Workers on the border in Mexico have a very low opinion of unions," Johnson adds. "That's different than the situation among immigrant workers in Los Angeles, who generally think unions are a good thing. In Juárez, when you talk about unions, you get a blank look or a negative response, and workers think they're weak. The absence of a positive example is one obstacle we haven't been able to overcome there.

"As a result, it's very difficult to organize open in-plant activity, and our experience has been that if there's no such activity, we lose the campaign. In Mexico, the fear is intense, the network of company spies is extensive, and the cost to workers who are singled out is very high. The [political] space needed for workers in Mexico is tremendous, and we've only been able to win a little. I learned that the nonunion status of their Mexican operations is critically important to U.S. companies. They won't be moved by anything short of a major explosion. We were able to do a lot of things, but not to exert that kind of power. What's required is a whole sea change in labor relations.

"But I also learned that the idea of solidarity caught fire with our members," Johnson concludes. "And ideas are extremely powerful. The difficult question is how to translate them into reality."

7

DURO MEANS HARD

MARTHA OJEDA: HELL-RAISER

There's no hotline on the border for workers who get fired for trying to organize. When people are beaten in bitter conflicts with border bosses, they can't dial 911 to get help. But there is one place they can go. They can call San Antonio, Texas, and ask for the Coalition for Justice in the Maquiladoras. Since 1989, workers have been able to find dependable allies and concrete help in the CJM office, even in the most difficult circumstances.

First headed by Sister Susan Mika when it was organized a decade and a half ago, the CJM brought together 150 Mexican, Canadian, and U.S. organizations. Even before NAFTA arrived on the political scene, these churches, unions, lawyers, lobbyists, and community groups had united to challenge the alliance of the Mexican government, foreign companies, and U.S. trade policy. Mika and a tiny staff turned the coalition into a reliable and effective force, able to back up the actions of maquiladora workers in the plants themselves with a variety of tactics to bring pressure to bear on their employers.

From the beginning, the coalition questioned corporate decisions in shareholder meetings and organized demonstrations in the United

States when companies fired workers in Mexican plants, sending waves of letters and faxes into executive boardrooms on just a few hours' notice. Consistent action over the past fifteen years has earned the coalition a grudging respect among huge transnational corporations. But its real credibility is in the cardboard houses of dozens of barrios along the border, where workers sometimes have to whisper its name, understanding that their employers fear it.

Campaigns on the ground have produced credibility in the plants. But there's another name the companies worry about, one that is also whispered house to house along those dirt streets. It's the name of one remarkable woman, Martha Ojeda, whose personal history reflects that of the coalition, which she now heads. Ojeda bears the scars of the labor war at the Sony Corporation's plants in Nuevo Laredo, scars that give the CJM much of its legitimacy as well. A decade ago in this border city across from Laredo, Texas, workers tried to raise wages and run their own union. At Sony, they were met with the most violent response in years of border rebellion. For maquiladora activists who know the history of the intense conflicts between the border plants and their workers, Sony was the big one.

Ojeda started work at Sony as a young woman, when the first plant opened in 1979 with only twenty-five employees. She grew up in the factory. While she worked on the production line, her co-workers covered for her when she needed time to study for her law degree. And over the years, she became a leader, first known on the production lines as a vocal worker-activist.

"I have very good memories of her because I always knew that Martha was a fair woman," recalls Fela Contreras, who met Ojeda on the line during those years. "She belongs to the working class. She got a university degree working at a maquiladora, and she used it to help a lot of people."

One of Ojeda's first efforts was to help workers get the housing subsidies supposedly available through the government agency Infonavit, which in practice are out of reach for most maquiladora workers. "She'd ask me, 'What about you, Fela? Don't you need a house?'" Contreras remembers. "And I'd say, 'I have one, Martha, thank God—a very poor house, but mine.' Because of Martha, many workers who didn't have housing got it. She didn't ask for herself, and she was paying rent at the time—a mother of three who had to work and leave her kids alone."

As the company grew, Ojeda eventually was elected head of the CTM *sección* (the union local) at the Sony plant. "Because she was putting pressure on them, Sony gave us a lot of benefits," Contreras says, "like buses to and from work, a ten percent pay bonus, and uniforms twice a year."

It was remarkable enough that a woman—and a maquiladora worker, at that—had become the head of the union in what had become a large plant employing thousands of people. But when Ojeda actually started winning better conditions, the CTM's protection contracts in surrounding factories looked bad by comparison. The company complained to CTM leaders in Mexico City, who finally concluded that she couldn't be co-opted and removed her from office. The union fell into the hands of people close to Sony management, and the benefits the union had won began to disappear.

By 1992, workers were ready for a change. With Ojeda's help, they began organizing in secret, outside the plant. "After we were done with our work day, we would gather in our homes with other workers," Contreras recalls. "Martha came to help us prepare for the conflict we knew was coming. We were going to change everything."

They started with elections in each department of the maquiladora, to choose new representatives. "The company realized what we were doing, and the union [in Mexico City] learned about it, too," Contreras explains. "They began firing the new delegates, along with the other workers who were going to the organizing meetings at night."

Despite the firings, Ojeda and the workers prepared for the main election, which would choose new leadership for the entire union at Sony. When the day came, workers voted on the premises of each of the four huge plants, with company management and CTM leaders from Mexico City looking on. Although the atmosphere was intimidating, and workers had to declare their choice publicly, they voted for the new slate.

"We got a big majority," Contreras remembers bitterly. "And then the representative of the CTM from Mexico City said, 'No, you lost.'

"We were outraged and left work, jeopardizing our jobs. We went out in the street to protest, to be heard. We wanted the election results respected, but nobody paid attention because we were women."

In desperation, workers sat down in the road leading to the plants. "We stopped the trucks going to the U.S., [the ones that] passed along the main street on their way to the border. We knew that by stopping exports we'd be accused of a federal crime, but we wouldn't let them pass.

"The company president came out and said, 'Please, girls, don't do this. We're going to help you—don't worry.' He promised everything and delivered nothing. So we went on strike in the main plant. We blocked the doors and didn't allow anyone to leave or enter. We made ourselves into human chains. There were no leaders—we were all equal, between eight hundred and a thousand of us."

After the workers had camped out in the plant for four days and nights, the fire department was called in and used high-pressure hoses to try to dislodge them. "When they sprayed water at us, we didn't move. We were so angry, we yelled, 'You got us wet? We don't care—just bring us soap!' " Contreras recalls.

"So they let the police into the back of the factory, and they came at us from behind and began beating us. They dragged women by the hair and hit one woman in the stomach with their clubs. And still we stayed. Finally, the state policemen, who are a lot meaner, arrived with big guns and said, 'If you don't leave, we'll kill you.' Facing that, we left. The company said, 'Girls, come back to work. Let's forget everything and start afresh.' "

Despite the conciliatory words, Sony sued the strike leaders for more money than they would ever have made in a lifetime of working at the plant. The leaders were repeatedly interrogated, and question number one was always, "Where is Martha Ojeda?" As the hunt for her spread throughout Nuevo Laredo, workers smuggled her across the bridge into Texas, hidden under the seat of a car.

"We didn't want them to find Martha. We always loved her—at least, I can say for myself that I love Martha very much. But we knew that from then on she couldn't stay in Nuevo Laredo. Martha didn't come back to Mexico for a long time."

From 1994 to 1996, Ojeda lived in Texas, while workers at Sony reorganized themselves. By this time, they had decided to try to leave the CTM and form an independent union. According to Guadalupe Carrillo, a fired striker, "The CTM just raked money off to line the officers' pockets and helped the company. We wanted to choose our own union, to win justice and real improvements in the plant."

Once again, workers sought out Ojeda. "We'd get off at eleven P.M., and we'd cross to Texas to see her," Contreras says. "We'd spend the night drinking coffee because we didn't have any money to buy food."

When the workers' committee had built enough support, several of the leaders went to the office of the state labor board and applied for a *registro* for their union. They were denied. So, together with the Coalition for Justice in the Maquiladoras, the International Labor Rights Fund, the American Friends Service Committee, and Mexico's National Association of Democratic Lawyers, they filed a complaint under NAFTA's labor side agreement—the third such complaint following the signing of the treaty.

The National Administrative Office held a hearing on the Sony case early in 1995. Unlike previous hearings in the cases of General Electric and Honeywell, which were held in Washington, D.C., and therefore were inaccessible to border workers, the Sony hearing was held on the border, and workers were able to testify. Also in contrast to the other two cases, the NAO findings in the Sony case criticized the firings, the company's intervention in the election, the police violence, and the Mexican government's refusal to give legal status to the independent union. The agency recommended a meeting between U.S. labor secretary Robert Reich and Santiago Oñate of the Mexican Labor Secretariat.

Reich and Oñate met, but they passed over the violence and the crooked election and discussed only the problem of registering new unions in Mexico. They agreed that workers' rights had been violated and that the Mexican Constitution required state labor boards to allow the registration of independent unions. Jerome Levinson, lead attorney in the case, called the agreement "cynical in the extreme," however, since it did nothing more than advise workers about the legal process that already existed on paper. His point was well taken. No enforcement efforts were recommended.

Following the Reich-Oñate meeting, workers once again tried to register their independent union. And once again the state labor board turned them down. To Ojeda, it demonstrated that "the NAFTA process favors investment but is unable and unwilling to protect workers' rights."

Ojeda was accused by both the CTM and local authorities of destabilizing the maquiladora industry by working with North American unions, who, they claimed, were using labor disputes to chase employers back over the border. "If fighting for your rights that are guaranteed in the Federal Labor Law is to be a terrorist," she responded, "if wanting to live in dignity is to be a destabilizer, then all of us are terrorists and destabilizers. I'm willing to accept these risks, and I'm ready to fight. That's the only way we can survive."

After the Coalition for Justice in the Maquiladoras spearheaded the legal case against Sony, Ojeda became the first Mexican to head the organization. Coalition members wanted to emphasize the leadership of Mexican activists in an organization dedicated to fighting for workers' rights in Mexico.

In 1997, Ojeda helped the Border Women Workers Committee (CFO, Comité Fronterizo de Obreras), a coalition member, to begin organizing Alcoa Fujikura's 13,250 workers at its plant in Ciudad Acuña. There, workers accused the company of hiding a series of gas releases, which had made many of them sick.

Ojeda and CFO took a delegation of workers to Alcoa's annual stockholder meeting in Pittsburgh, Pennsylvania. While the company might have ignored these workers and activists, it couldn't ignore another coalition member, the Interfaith Center on Corporate Responsibility

(ICCR). Bringing together religious orders that have millions of dollars invested in stocks and bonds, the center specializes in shareholder actions promoting social justice. At the Pittsburgh meeting, the ICCR forced a historic discussion of the situation in Alcoa's Mexican plants.

Ojeda spoke to the stockholders in a staccato mixture of Spanish and English, punching the air with her fists to punctuate her sentences and demolishing the stereotype of maquiladora workers as submissive women. Alcoa CEO Paul O'Neill (later to become the U.S. treasury secretary in the Bush administration) at first insisted that "you can eat off the floors of these plants." But ICCR won a commitment to investigate conditions.

The investigation subsequently concluded that a series of gas poisonings had indeed gone unreported in 1994, and Alcoa Fujikura's president, Robert Barton, was fired. For Ojeda, that was one small victory in a much longer war. "My job is to fight for the dreams of my people—for freedom, for a better living standard, for democracy and our rights."

Meanwhile, her reputation spread. Omar Gil, a worker at a Reynosa Delphi factory, recalled that he first heard about Ojeda during the Sony struggle in 1994. "For many years, Martha was a leader in Nuevo Laredo and tried to democratize the unions here," he explained. "The CTM general secretary called her an agitator and a Communist and forced her to leave. It seemed the whole world painted Martha Ojeda as a ghost to scare people and used her as an example of what could happen if they got into these problems.

"But she became well known among the workers because she tried to help them. When I was invited to join a group to talk about health and safety, I realized that it was ridiculous to believe it's bad to show workers the dangers in their jobs. The companies and the newspapers say we're putting the maquiladoras in danger, but we're just showing workers what's wrong with the way the work is organized.

"Every movement starts with just a small group, which evolves and gets bigger and bigger. Lots of people say you're just wasting your time because you'll never be able to change anything. But I say nothing will ever change if we just sit on our hands."

Fela Contreras stayed at Sony until 1998, but the job wore on her. "I was demoted, and they pushed me as far down as they could," she recalls bitterly. "The only thing that was left was sending me to sweep the floors. I thought, 'If they ask me to sweep, I'll leave.'"

In a meeting in her work area, the supervisor told the women that "we were too old, that we weren't producing as much as when we were younger. So I left my job, after thirteen years, and the company was happy. They said, 'We cannot stand this old woman anymore, stirring things up in here.'"

But losing her job was a blow, and she became very depressed. "I thought, 'I'm useless.' I'd spend the day crying, and I couldn't pass by Sony because I'd start crying again. Then Martha asked me, 'What's with you? Look back at the movement—there you were. You are useful, so get up and fight.'"

In Contreras's family, a maquiladora job has become a bogeyman used to scare her children. "My generation had no choice because we had no education," she explains. "My kids have never had to work in a maquiladora. When my son was unemployed for three months, I told him, 'You know what, son? You'll end up working in one.' He found another job. Still, any job is a good one, and no job is dishonorable. It's not a crime to be a worker, or to work in a maquiladora."

THE COALITION FOR JUSTICE IN THE MAQUILADORAS

After Eliud Almaguer's house was burned to the ground, he and his wife, Evelia, began moving from home to home, staying with friends. They rarely spent more than one night in the same place, fearing that those who destroyed their house might return to finish the job—hurting them personally or worse.

"I fear for the lives of my family," he explained.

Almaguer believed that he had been burned out in revenge. For three years before the fire in November 2000, he had led a campaign to organize an independent union at the Duro Bag plant, an effort that had earned him a lot of enemies.

Almaguer's home certainly didn't inspire any envy among his neighbors. It was typical of the houses lining a dirt street in a dusty Río Bravo barrio. The Almaguers had so little money that they used wood for heating and cooking, doing without even the illegal electrical and water hookups, which provide the only basic services for most homes in the neighborhood. Hundreds of communities of maquiladora workers all along the border have light only because they tap into power lines and then run copper wires with a thin layer of insulation to their homes, sometimes for a mile or more.

Houses in border barrios are often made of wooden shipping pallets, with unfolded cardboard boxes stapled onto them for walls. They're firetraps in the extreme—the Almaguers were lucky they weren't home and therefore weren't harmed in the blaze.

Modest as it was, however, the house had been broken into that year at least twice before, Almaguer said. "I think they were looking for union documents, since I don't really have anything worth stealing. Fortunately, we keep them in a safe place."

On the night of the fire, neighbors reported seeing a man in a blue T-shirt fleeing the scene just before flames engulfed the small dwelling. When they called the police to report the blaze, Almaguer alleged, they were told, "If it's Eliud's, let it burn." When he went to make a statement, the police refused to take one or to conduct an investigation. To no one's surprise, no culprit was ever apprehended.

Just across the Rio Grande from Pharr, Texas, the Duro Bag factory churns out the chichi paper bags sold for a buck or two at suburban shopping malls almost everywhere in the United States.

Almaguer, an intense, stocky labor activist in his thirties, got a job at the plant in 1998. There, he said, he saw people lose fingers in machines cutting the cardboard that was used to stiffen the bottoms of the bags. Safety guards, he claimed, were removed from the rollers that imprint designs on the paper lining—the extra time it took to clean rollers that had guards was treated as needlessly lost production. Almaguer recalled that solvent containers didn't carry proper danger warnings. Although workers were issued dust masks, the masks were useless for filtering out toxic chemical fumes.

"In terms of safety, well, there just wasn't any," he remembered bitterly.

The union at Duro, a *sección* of the Paper, Cardboard, and Wood Industry Union, did nothing to change matters. The union is part of the CTM, the labor federation that has been a pillar of support for the PRI since the 1940s. The *sección* had a contract with the company—a protection agreement in which union leaders were paid to guarantee labor peace.

Tired of putting up with accidents and low pay, workers in the Duro plant at first tried to have that contract enforced. In October 1998, they expelled the *sección*'s general secretary, José Ángel García Garcés, viewed as too close to company managers, and elected Almaguer as his replacement. They then brought repeated grievances before the plant's human relations manager, Alejandro de la Rosa. "We'd take [our complaints] to his office, and he'd throw us out," Almaguer said. "The company was in violation of at least fifty percent of the contract."

Wages at Duro averaged 320 pesos a week (about 35 dollars, in 1998), according to Consuelo Moreno, a Duro worker. "My daughter had to drop out of school," Moreno said, "because we didn't have the money for her to continue." Duro's vice president of manufacturing, Bill Forstrom, confirmed that wages started at 60 pesos a day (about 6 dollars). A gallon of milk in a local supermarket cost 25 pesos—almost half a day's work. Despite the hardships, "people were willing to work at bad-paying jobs," Almaguer acknowledged. "But not under those conditions."

Duro workers were unsuccessful in getting the CTM to back up their efforts. In October 1999, the company fired Almaguer, and the union in Mexico City cooperated. It invoked the notorious exclusion clause, a regulation used for decades by pro-company union officials to get rid of troublemakers. It allowed the union to exclude individuals from membership, thereby terminating their employment. Police and guards were called into the plant to enforce the firing. But after three days of turmoil, workers forced the company and the union to continue recognizing Almaguer as their leader.

Human relations manager de la Rosa alleged in Río Bravo's local newspaper, *El Bravo*, that "the workers are protesting things that aren't our responsibility. Almaguer says he's a dissident leader, but he was actually removed some time ago."

In the spring of 2000, the union contract at Duro expired, and workers drew up a list of demands for a new agreement. They asked for two pairs of safety shoes each year, work clothes, contributions to a savings plan, and a doctor at the plant to take care of injuries. "The company said it owned the factory—they would decide what would be done here," Almaguer recalled.

In April, workers stopped production to demand changes, and 150 were fired. When they still wouldn't budge, their national leaders simply ignored their demands and signed a new agreement on June 11.

On June 12, Duro managers barred Almaguer from the factory. The afternoon shift refused to go in to work, and workers voted to stop production again. By then, they had decided that better conditions were no longer enough. In front of the factory gates, they began organizing a new independent and democratic union.

"In the past, the company was always able to buy off our union leaders. Always," Moreno emphasized. "And we paid the price. We can only change things if we have a union the company can't control."

Throughout this period, Almaguer reported that his family was repeatedly threatened, starting when he began to pressure the company for changes. After he was elected the *sección*'s general secretary, a threatening individual followed him and his wife home, saying that management had paid him to follow the couple. The same person later came to their home at night and offered money.

"He told me to slow down and tell the workers not to go against the national paperworkers union and Duro, or else I would pay the consequences. That night, [he and others] came back at one A.M. and scared my daughter by knocking and kicking the door, trying to open it," Almaguer recalled.

Forstrom argued that only a minority of the plant's workers supported the independent union. Although he admitted that some workers had been injured on the job, he claimed they'd taken the guards off the machines themselves. Conditions were better in Río Bravo than at some of the company's seven U.S. plants, he asserted, and while relations with the CTM were good, the union's officials weren't pushovers. "Almaguer has had an agenda different from the company and the majority of employees," Forstrom claimed. "I think he has something to gain personally. It's fairly obvious—a job, money, status."

Evening the odds a little during their long struggle, Duro workers had help from the north, organized by the CJM. The coalition assisted the fired workers as they chased the governor of Tamaulipas, Tomás Yarrington, around the state for two months during the summer's national election campaign. Whenever he appeared in public, workers unfurled banners demanding *libertad sindical*, the right to belong to a union of their own choice. Meanwhile, determined women, often with their children beside them, confronted police outside the plant and camped out in Río Bravo's main plaza. CJM activists were arrested with them, while others mobilized a flood of letters and faxes to Yarrington and company officials.

Help also came from the National Union of Workers (UNT) in Mexico City. Cooperating with the CJM, UNT general secretary Francisco Hernández Juárez organized a public protest in August in Reynosa, a large city close to Río Bravo. The rally attracted hundreds of advocates of independent unionism from Mexico and the United States. Under the combined pressure, the Tamaulipas labor board finally granted the new Duro union legal status, although the union still did not have the right to represent workers or to negotiate.

For the UNT, supporting the fight at Duro was an important step toward a greater commitment to maquiladora workers, one that promised to give the independent federation a growing presence on the border. Employers, in response, felt threatened, fearing that if the UNT won higher wages at Duro, workers would organize independent unions in other plants as well.

In 1998, Duro was just one of 3,450 foreign-owned factories in Mexico, employing more than 1.2 million Mexican workers, according to the National Association of Maquiladoras. If those workers are able to rid themselves of the omnipresent protection contracts and run their own unions, negotiate better agreements, and raise wages, it will be very costly to foreign owners. With this nightmare in mind, COPARMEX, the Mexican equivalent of the U.S. National Association of Manufacturers, took charge of Duro's legal battle.

COPARMEX could count on government support at Duro not only because it was defending the government's policy of using low wages and protection contracts as a way of attracting foreign investment. In addition, the association's former chief, Carlos Abascal, became labor secretary in the incoming administration of President Vicente Fox, who was elected and took office as the Duro battle reached its height.

The possibilities opened by a successful independent union effort at Duro were even more threatening to those CTM/PRI union leaders who stood to lose their protected status. They accused Duro workers of being pawns manipulated by U.S. unions and the CJM.

The Río Bravo newspaper, *El Bravo*, acted as their voice, referring to Martha Ojeda as a professional agitator and accusing Almaguer of being paid to organize the work stoppage. Tamaulipas CTM leader Leocadio Mendoza Reyes accused Ojeda of mounting a "dirty war" against the CTM, to "destabilize" the maquiladoras and scare companies into relocating jobs to the United States. César Treviño Saenz, president of the local maquiladora employers association, Canacintra, alleged that a campaign was being directed from Texas to undermine maquiladora development.

"The attacks on us come from fear—the people who have benefited from this system are losing control," Ojeda declared.

Rick de la Cruz, vice president of Local 6–314 of PACE, the Paper, Allied-Industrial, Chemical and Energy Workers (which represents three Duro plants in the United States), visited Mexico with fellow unionists from his Texas plant to support the independent union. He called the charges ridiculous. "If that work leaves Río Bravo, it's not coming back to the U.S.—it's going somewhere workers have even fewer rights," he explained. "We just think everyone should have human rights, and not just in Mexico—in the U.S., too."

Duro's Forstrom admitted that the company maintains only automated production north of the border, while its labor-intensive operations are concentrated in Río Bravo. The Duro Bag Manufacturing Corporation, based in Ludlow, Kentucky, operates seven U.S. plants, all much smaller than the Río Bravo facility, and belongs to the family of CEO Charles Shor. "We're in Mexico to take advantage of inexpensive labor," Forstrom acknowledged.

By the time the Tamaulipas labor board finally organized an election for workers to choose between the independent union and the CTM, the political terrain in Mexico had changed drastically. On July 2, 2000, Vicente Fox, the PAN candidate, was elected president, upsetting seventy years of PRI rule.

The social conservatism of the PAN was traditionally derived from right-wing elements in the Catholic Church. The party was historically based among large landowning families in the north of Mexico and their business allies. The PAN came into national power with a long history of support for the PRI's economic policies, especially those designed to keep wages low to attract foreign investment (a policy that favored the business backers of the PAN). In the Mexican Chamber of Deputies and Senate in the early 1990s, the PRI even used PAN legislators to introduce economic austerity measures it viewed as too unpopular to initiate in its own name. Locally in states such as Baja California Norte, where the PAN had held the governorship for years, it implemented policies identical to those of PRI-governed states elsewhere along the border.

Nevertheless, many Mexicans hoped that the democratic upsurge that put Fox in office might lead him to support the right of workers to freely choose independent unions, discarding the old government-affiliated labor federations.

"On July 2, millions of people voted for change," Hernández Juárez of the UNT said. "They voted for democracy, not for a continuation of the system of protection contracts. They voted for union freedom. He will have to respond to people's expectations. He will not be able to maintain the old system. What sense does it make," the union leader asked, "that for the first time in history, workers could elect a president who's not from the PRI, and yet they can't elect the general secretary of their own union?"

But hopes for greater democracy, effective unions, and higher wages on the border conflicted with Fox's pro-business orientation. "To win votes, Fox made the famous 'twenty commitments,' which included union democracy," said Hector de la Cueva, who directs Mexico City's Center for Labor Research (Centro de Investigaciones Laborales y Asesoria Sindical). "But he made no effort to live up to the promise."

One key element of that promise was a government commitment that workers would be allowed to vote by secret ballot in union elections. The traditional public voting has allowed the old pro-company unions and the maquiladora owners to identify supporters of new independent unions and have them fired. Following the exposure of election abuses at Tijuana's Han Young plant and at the ITAPSA factory in Mexico City, however, the Mexican government promised to allow secret ballot voting.

That commitment was put to the test at the Duro Bag plant. And instead of creating an example of a new era of respect for workers' rights, Duro became another poster child for the abuse of those rights.

On the morning of Friday, March 2, 2001, voting began inside the factory. On the ballot were two unions: the independent Union of Duro Bag Workers and the Revolutionary Confederation of Workers and Farmers, the CROC. (By the day of the election, the CTM had grown so unpopular in the plant that it had withdrawn from the process and had been replaced on the ballot by the CROC.)

The stage had been set the day before, when observers outside the factory watched as automatic weapons were unloaded from a car and carried in through the plant gate. The following morning, workers from the swing and graveyard shifts were prevented from going home as their shifts ended. Instead, they were held behind doors blocked with metal sheets and the huge rolls of paper that fed machines on the line. A few observers from the independent union reported that they could hear cries of "*¡Déjanos salir!*" (Let us out!) until company managers began playing music at a deafening volume on the plant speaker system.

Then workers from the arriving day shift were taken in small groups into the room where voting was taking place. They were escorted by CROC organizers, who handed them blue slips of paper imprinted with the union's local number. Many workers didn't even know the name of the union they were being told to vote for. At the voting table, representatives of Mexico's national labor board asked each voter to declare aloud her or his choice, and both company supervisors and government-affiliated union representatives wrote notes.

Labor Secretary Abascal, who denied requests for a secret ballot, and the federal labor board under his control ran the election in Río Bravo. The decision to hold open voting violated the agreement negotiated between his predecessor, Mariano Palacios Alcocer, and former U.S. labor secretary Alexis Herman as part of the settlement of the Han Young and ITAPSA cases filed under the NAFTA labor side agreement.

During the election, none of the fired workers were allowed into the plant to vote, and many of those who were locked up were prevented from participating. Only 502 workers voted, in a workforce the company says numbers more than 1,400. And of those 502, only 4 workers openly declared their support for the independent union, while 498 voted for the CROC.

"The Duro election was clearly a tragic defeat for the workers and their efforts to win better wages and conditions," said Robin Alexander, director of international relations for the United Electrical Workers, which supported the independent union. Dismayed by such blatant violations, she expressed her hope that they would serve as a wake-up call.

"It shows that for both the U.S. and Mexican governments, when the chips are down, their interest in promoting investment and free trade clearly outweighs any commitments they make about labor rights," Alexander added. "Workers in the U.S. can't expect they'll be able to maintain decent standards here if a company like Duro can go across the river and violate the rights of workers in the interest of paying low wages."

And in reaction to a protest organized by the CJM outside Duro's Kentucky headquarters just before the election, company managers refused to allow the president of the PACE local at its Ludlow plant, Dave Klontz, to travel to Río Bravo as an observer.

"The Duro election strips away any idea that the NAFTA process can protect workers' rights. The side agreement is bankrupt," declared Ojeda.

THE JUNKED WORKERS

The wrecked election didn't stop the wave of efforts to organize independent unions, however. As labor war raged at Duro, another group of workers laid their case before the National Administrative Office, to be heard under the NAFTA labor side agreement.

Plant managers called these workers the *jonkeados*, the junked ones. They were workers who became so sick, so chronically disabled that they were given special jobs. But they weren't put on light duty to tide them over until they could go back to the line. Instead, they were put under even greater pressure, harassed, and assigned tasks so unpleasant "that we knew they were just waiting for us to quit and leave," according to Joaquín González, one of the leaders of this group.

In mid-December 2000, González and some of his fellow *jonkeados* went to San Antonio, Texas, for an NAO hearing. There, they testified that the Mexican government had allowed their employer, Florida's Breed Technology, to systematically violate the country's health and safety laws, casting workers aside like trash in two border factories— Auto Trim in Matamoros and Custom Trim in Valle Hermosa.

Bruno Noe Montañez López worked in the Matamoros plant for five years, gluing leather covers to automobile steering wheels, until he was fired in 1998. During that time, his son was born with spina bifida, a spinal tumor, an enlarged heart, and no kneecaps. Montáñez struggled to keep his baby alive. In an ultimate humiliation, the doctor turned him away when he tried to donate blood for the baby in the hospital. "He told me I couldn't give it since my blood was contaminated with drugs," Montáñez testified at the hearing. "I have never taken drugs. The only things I inhaled were the glues and solvents I worked with."

After six months, his baby died.

Montáñez explained that at work fumes were everywhere—so strong that they often overwhelmed him when he opened glue containers, making him so dizzy he almost collapsed. If he got glue on his hands, his supervisor told him to wash them with solvents.

Ezekiel Tinajero Martínez went to San Antonio to explain that in 1995 he, too, had a child who died—a daughter born with anencephaly. Tinajero documented a series of similar infant deaths and miscarriages among the Auto Trim workers. He went to the plant's personnel director, demanding that the company respect the rights of the workers to healthier conditions, as required by Mexican law. Instead, the director sent for a security guard, who marched him out of the factory. He was fired.

Another Auto Trim worker submitted heart-wrenching testimony describing the birth of a daughter who had no urethral opening to allow urination. The mother recalled large open containers of glue at the workplace and fumes so strong she frequently complained of headaches and dizzy spells, even while pregnant. The only protective equipment the company gave her, she reported, was an apron.

Some workers believed they became addicted to the glue, suffering withdrawal symptoms at home on the weekends. Shakes, tremors, and headaches would get so bad that they longed to go back to the production lines. When they did return, they would sometimes suffer hallucinations.

In Valle Hermosa, the situation at the Custom Trim plant was no better. Heriberto Ramos Gómez recalled a 1997 factory fire, caused when sparks from a blow dryer fell on a pool of solvents on the floor. Despite their legal obligation to do so, the plant managers refused to order even a partial evacuation.

At that plant, in May 1997, workers decided to do something about those problems. They struck for five days, demanding better health protection and an increase in their weekly wage, which was then equivalent to about thirty-five dollars. Their union, a *sección* of the CTM, signed an agreement behind their backs, ending the strike with no guarantees of better conditions. Nevertheless, workers did manage to extract a written commitment from the company not to retaliate against anyone.

It was a hollow promise. Days later, twenty-eight workers were terminated.

One of them was Isabel Morales Bocanegra, the plant nurse. She had belonged to the health and safety committee at Custom Trim, a committee the company was required to form under Mexican law. Morales tried to use the committee to document conditions, noting that in August 1996 alone, five women in the plant had suffered miscarriages. Further, the human resources manager prohibited her from making any appointments at the government's social security medical clinic for any workers who had more than one accident or injury at work and instructed her to mention only minor problems in reports sent to health inspectors. She never saw a government health and safety inspection in the two and a half years she worked there.

The fired workers went to the Tamaulipas labor board, which ruled a year later that the terminations had been illegal. It ordered the workers reinstated, with full back pay. Martha Ojeda and other experienced labor activists who had been assisting the workers suspected a trick. The decision seemed suspiciously favorable for an agency that had been notorious for bias in favor of plant owners and government-affiliated unions. She was right.

In March 1999, the first two Custom Trim workers who were slated to return to their jobs showed up at the labor board office. A board agent then accompanied them to the plant, along with one of Breed's local lawyers. But instead of going to Breed's new factory, where the work had been moved since the strike, the workers were taken to the old, closed facility. The government then declared that there were no jobs for the workers to return to and, furthermore, that the company would not be required to pay the back wages it owed (the equivalent of twenty-five thousand dollars).

That was when the workers and their allies started preparing their case under NAFTA's labor side agreement. It was not an easy decision for them to make, given the record of previous cases, which had all met similar fates. The scenario was always the same: Hearings were held. Workers testified, sometimes at considerable risk. The NAO, which hears the complaints against Mexico, concluded in almost every case that serious violations of the law had occurred.

And then—nothing.

Despite these odds, however, Custom Trim and Auto Trim workers hoped that their case would be different because, instead of focusing on union rights, it dealt only with the issue of health and safety.

The cases at Han Young and ITAPSA also charged that health and safety laws were not being enforced, but those complaints were both linked to parallel cases that charged widespread violations of union rights. "A complaint just about health conditions is new, and [it] forces the U.S. and Mexico to take this concern seriously," explained Manuel Mondragon, director of the Young Workers' Pastorate, who helped to draft it. The possible remedy also raised the stakes, since it could, theoretically, involve massive fines.

On December 12, 2000, the day of the long-awaited hearing, workers and occupational safety experts converged on San Antonio, Texas. Testimony documented the workers' experiences in the Auto Trim and Custom Trim plants, and it was backed up by Mexican health and safety expert Dr. Francisco Mercado Calderón. Mercado condemned Breed for causing irreversible injuries to workers, but he also declared that "gross negligence, or possibly wanton negligence by government authorities" had permitted the company's actions.

U.S. expert Garrett Brown went even further. "The Mexican government's failure is due to the austerity programs imposed by the International Monetary Fund, World Bank, and related institutions." Mexico's desperate need for hard currency to pay off loans has undermined its will to enforce the law and risk alienating wealthy foreign investors such as Breed, Brown charged.

U.S. unions also offered support. Lida Orta, a health expert from the United Auto Workers, flew in from Puerto Rico to testify. Breed Technologies, with $1.4 billion in sales in 1998, was represented at the hearing by a vice president for legal affairs, Stuart Boyd, but he did not present evidence.

In Washington, D.C., Tim Beaty, AFL-CIO deputy director for international affairs, was optimistic. The NAO itself was not very effective, he agreed, "but the process has provided a way in which workers can express their solidarity across borders, since these complaints are filed not in the country in which the violations occur, but by workers and unions in another one."

Once again, a flurry of accusations appeared in the Mexican press along the border, as had been the case during the Duro, Han Young, and other maquiladora campaigns. Instead of labeling Breed a foreign interloper that was violating Mexican laws and injuring Mexican workers, the newspapers accused workers at Breed of being pawns of U.S. unions.

Beaty denied that the AFL-CIO was intent on chasing work back to the United States. The federation favors economic growth in Mexico, including on the border, he said, "but only if the rules make that growth equitable. Instead, NAFTA has created a growing pattern of inequality, and the gap between rich and poor is growing, both inside Mexico and between Mexico and the United States."

In the wake of the Duro election, Ojeda called the Breed case a final test for NAFTA's labor side agreement. As a result of filing the complaint, she noted, Breed workers had been interrogated by supervisors, had lost jobs, and had received death threats. "We already know from the other cases that the treaty's supposed protections for labor rights are worthless," she said. "Now we'll see if the language on health and safety can be made to work. If there's no remedy here, we'll have to look for some other alternative."

The political terrain for that effort proved very hostile, however. On the one hand, for Vicente Fox, an effort to protect the rights and health of maquiladora workers promised to discourage companies such as Breed from building new plants. On the other hand, George W. Bush's Department of Labor was even less enthusiastic than the Clinton administration had been about imposing sanctions on Mexico over labor and safety problems in those same plants.

The Breed complaint was a good test of the new climate. In the spring of 2002, the Bush administration declined to push for any sanctions against the Mexican government in the case.

Workers and supporters, however, believed that simply exposing the conditions was a victory of sorts. "They can disguise the reality and hide the dangers we are talking about in this hearing," Mondragon told the NAO, "but what they can neither disguise nor hide are the blood and bodies of all the children left in the road."

BREAKING OUT OF THE BOX

While the NAO process failed spectacularly at Duro, Breed, Sony, ITAPSA, Han Young, and elsewhere, unions in Mexico and the United States have continued to develop relationships. Some still hope that the labor side agreement, despite its flaws, can somehow be made to work. Others, however, have tried to find ways to avoid the process entirely.

One of the first post-NAFTA union links developed between the telephone workers in both countries—the Communications Workers of America (CWA) in the United States and the Union of Telephone Workers of the Mexican Republic (STRM, Sindicato de Telefonistas de la República Mexicana). The relationship began in San Francisco, after CWA organizer Virginia Rodríguez returned from observing the disastrous election at Plasticos Bajacal in Tijuana in 1993.

At the time, Rodríguez was helping a group of women form a union in San Francisco, at a telemarketing shop run by the Sprint Corporation, called La Conexión Familiar (the Family Connection). There, 235 workers, in a classic boiler room operation, sold phone service in Spanish to the city's Latino community. La Conexión employees came from all over Latin America—Mexico, El Salvador, Guatemala, Peru, Panama, and Nicaragua. Pressure to make calls was so intense that they were even required to ask permission before going to the bathroom and were told not to drink too much water so that they wouldn't have to make too many trips.

On July 14, 1993, a week before the employees were to vote in a union representation election, they were suddenly called in and terminated on the spot. Their firing coincided with a wave of anti-immigrant hysteria in California, culminating in the electoral campaign around Proposition 187, which sought to bar undocumented immigrants from receiving health care at public facilities and to prohibit their children from attending public schools. The case of the workers at La Conexión became a symbol of the denial of rights to immigrants, and the workers themselves played an important role in the immigrant rights movements developing in California. The terminated La Conexión employees helped to organize a local march in San Francisco against Proposition 187 and sent a delegation to carry their banner and speak before more than one hundred thousand people at an immigrant rights march in Los Angeles.

In that atmosphere, the National Labor Relations Board made a decision that even the union didn't expect. The board held that the closure of the worksite violated the workers' right to join a union without retaliation and ordered Sprint to reopen it. An administrative law judge agreed. But Sprint took the case into federal court, where the property rights of the company to do as it pleased with its business trumped the rights of the workers to a union and their jobs.

The CWA sent a delegation to Mexico City, to talk to the Mexican telephone workers union. As a result, the STRM, in Mexico, filed a complaint against the United States under the NAFTA labor side agreement, alleging that the United States was failing to enforce its own labor law, which—on paper—guarantees that workers can join unions without fear of reprisal.

Reich and Oñate met to discuss the case. In settling it, however, they agreed only to hold a hearing in San Francisco on the problems of workers who were fired during organizing drives. No further government action was taken, and the workers were left without jobs.

Nevertheless, cooperation between the CWA and the STRM grew. In 1998, the CWA filed an NAO complaint over union-busting at a factory in Cananea, Sonora, that belonged to Taiwan-owned Maxi-Switch. The plant made computer keyboards and controllers for GameBoys and Nintendo products. During a union drive backed by the STRM, a company supervisor, Angel Soto, beat up the newly elected head of the workers' union, eighteen-year-old Alicia Pérez-García. The company fired a number of activists and then signed a sweetheart contract with the CTM.

In addition to filing the NAO complaint, CWA members at a Maxi-Switch warehouse operation in Arizona, which packaged the goods from the Sonora plant, visited Cananea to show support. On their return to the United States, they mobilized pressure on Maxi-Switch management in their own plant. Combined with the threat of an NAO complaint, that seemed to be enough to pressure the company into ending its relationship with the CTM and recognizing the independent union in Sonora. But suddenly Maxi-Switch closed the factory. Cananea, a tiny copper-mining town in the mountains, had no other factories, and the women working in the plant were left with few alternatives other than unemployment or emigration.

Despite the outcome, experiences such as this had an impact on the thinking of U.S. union activists. The idea of using market pressure on the U.S. side of the border began to seem like an attractive alternative to the NAO process. The power and possibilities of that alternative became clearer in 2001, at Kuk Dong, a clothing factory in Puebla.

The Mexican state of Puebla is a center for maquiladora garment production. In November 2000, a group of Korean business owners opened a new, modern plant in Atlixco, an hour from the state capital. They hired local women from surrounding villages, but they also gave jobs to individuals who had formerly worked for them at another nearby garment factory, Matamoros Garment. Among this latter group were five supervisors, including Marcela Muñoz.

At first, conditions seemed better than they had been at Matamoros Garment, where workers were often required to work forced overtime (illegal under Mexico's Federal Labor Law), sometimes without being paid for it. "Kuk Dong had new, automated machines," Muñoz recalled, "and better conditions. It seemed more secure."

But complaints soon surfaced in the new plant. Claudia Monroy, another worker, remembered that "the Koreans yelled at us, and sometimes even hit the women. The company provided food in the cafeteria, partly because the wages were so low, but it was very bad. We even saw worms in the meat, and people got sick from eating it." Muñoz and her fellow supervisors tried complaining to the managers, without effect.

The plant had an agreement with a company-selected union, a division of the Revolutionary Confederation of Workers and Farmers (CROC). When the supervisors asked the union representative to take their complaints to the company, nothing happened. So they organized a boycott.

"First we had secret meetings among ourselves, hiding among the boxes at the back of the plant," Muñoz says. Then, on December 12, they told all the plant's eight hundred workers to bring sandwiches to work the following day. To their surprise, everyone did.

The company felt very threatened. "They were angry, not because they really cared about the quality of the food, but because they could see that there was an organization among the people in the plant," Muñoz explained. "That really scared them."

Right after New Year's, on January 3, the five supervisors were fired. But instead of looking for new jobs, they continued to meet outside the plant with other workers. "We knew they'd do that to us," Muñoz says, "and we'd agreed that we'd stick up for each other and fight."

They went to the CROC office, and the union representative said not only that he couldn't help them but also that if workers continued their protest, the company would fire everyone. A week later, on January 8, everyone walked out for two hours and gave the company an ultimatum: rehire the fired workers within eight hours, and get rid of the CROC. Again, the company didn't respond, so on January 9, 2001, the workers occupied the plant.

"They were so young," recalls Huberto Juárez, a professor at the nearby Autonomous University of Puebla, who began helping them.

"Many of them were only fourteen or fifteen years old. When they began their occupation, their fathers and mothers drove down to the plant, carrying food and blankets and checking to make sure their children were okay. We live in a region of Puebla where there was a lot of militant, left-wing activity in the textile industry years ago, and some of the workers' parents had been part of it. They told their kids, 'You're doing what we did, fighting for our rights as workers.' "

Also arriving to help the workers were David Alvarado, working for the office of the American Center for International Labor Solidarity, an institution set up by the AFL-CIO to conduct solidarity work outside the United States; and Blanca Velázquez, a former maquiladora worker at the Siemens factory.

The Kuk Dong workers held out for several days. Then, on January 11, the company and local authorities sent in the *granaderos*, the local SWAT team. Armed with clubs, the police entered through a broken wall at the rear of the factory and charged the workers at the entrance. "The men were in front, and the women behind," remembers Monroy. "I saw them beating many people, who fell all around me." According to Muñoz, who was also injured, René Sánchez, the CROC representative, "was right there with the police, beating us."

Just outside the front gates of the factory is a housing project called Las Nieves, populated mostly by schoolteachers and their families. Workers fleeing from the clubs of the police ran into the community, and the teachers took them in. Three people were taken to the hospital with broken ribs, and one with internal injuries. Later, the workers all marched down to Atlixco's central plaza.

Alvarado and Velázquez told the workers that they would continue to support them. Velázquez headed the Workers Support Center (CAT, Centro de Apoyo para los Trabajadores), which began holding training sessions to help the workers set up their organization. Alvarado, who had been active in United Students Against Sweatshops (USAS) in the United States, began to make contacts with student organizations on university campuses north of the border. They identified Nike as the primary customer for the garments produced at Kuk Dong, and the company became the target for student pressure.

These efforts were supported by the AFL-CIO, whose Mexico City representative, Jeff Hermanson, had been the organizing director for the International Ladies Garment Workers Union (now UNITE, the Union of Needletrades, Industrial and Textile Employees). The strategy being developed in the Kuk Dong case was similar to the strategy UNITE had used in the United States to organize big clothing manufacturers. In Atlixco, CAT, with a grant from the AFL-CIO, paid half the wages of Muñoz and others while they continued to organize the workers.

In the United States, students on many college campuses had already fought to force university administrations to pledge not to buy clothing produced in sweatshops elsewhere in Latin America and Asia. When some of the big garment companies and the U.S. Department of Labor sought to deflect the pressure by making ineffectual promises to respect labor rights, students and their allies organized the Workers Rights Consortium. The WRC demanded more stringent commitments from companies in their codes of conduct, including protection for the right to organize. The WRC weighed in with support for the Kuk Dong workers, pointing out to Nike that the events in Puebla were a violation of the company's stated code of conduct.

When pressure mounted on Nike, the company sent investigators to Atlixco and began questioning Kuk Dong managers. At the same time, USAS students came to Atlixco to meet with the workers. Some of the fired supervisors, eventually including Muñoz, went to the United States to talk about conditions in the plant, as did Velázquez.

In a general assembly on March 28, the workers formally established an independent union. In reaction, Kuk Dong (now renamed Mex Mode) abandoned the CROC and pressed the state labor board to grant a *registro* to the independent union. In June, the labor board held an election, in which workers elected the Independent Union of Workers at Mex Mode (SITEMEX, Sindicato de Trabajadores de la Empresa Mex Mode) as their bargaining representative. After months of bargaining, the union and the company signed a contract on September 27, one of only a handful of collective bargaining agreements ever signed by an independent union in a maquiladora.

Abuse by the Korean managers stopped, and wages went up. Monroy, who'd started at 38 pesos a day, saw her salary rise to 53 pesos. "The food's still pretty bad," she said later, "but now they give us eighty-four pesos a week for lunch, so we can buy something else." Most important to Muñoz, "all the other maquiladoras in our area began giving raises to their workers, for fear they'd join us."

The Workers Support Center, born in the Kuk Dong struggle, grew quickly after the victory; a year later, it had seven people on staff. "We see our objective now as supporting and educating workers in other plants," said Blanca Velázquez, "so they can learn how to organize themselves." CAT started a theater group to agitate about workers' rights, since many of the young women drawn into the garment plants from rural areas are illiterate and thus can't read leaflets or bulletins. "We concentrate on women workers," according to Gabriela Cortez, another CAT staff member. Set up as a nongovernmental organization, CAT receives grants from the AFL-CIO's Solidarity Center, the Phoenix Foundation, and other sources. USAS sends students to intern in the CAT office, which has links to UNITE in the United States, the Maquiladora Workers Support Network in Canada, and the Clean Clothes campaign in Germany.

Following the Mex Mode struggle, CAT activists began organizing workers at the Matamoros Garment factory, from which a number of the leaders at Mex Mode had come originally. It did not prove possible, however, to replicate the conjunction of forces that came together at Kuk Dong. Once the company became aware of the organizing effort, it began to put heavy pressure on workers, according to Cortez. "Some women were threatened and followed home by armed thugs," she charged. The workers and CAT went to the labor board to get a *registro* but were denied.

CAT and the network in the United States began to put pressure on the Puma sportswear company, an important client for the plant. Puma then sent a monitor, supposedly to investigate conditions. But the monitor interrogated workers on the plant floor in front of supervisors and video cameras. "Who would be willing to tell the truth under those circumstances?" Velázquez asked bitterly.

Employment in the factory began to drop from its peak of five hundred, and eventually Matamoros Garment closed its doors in late March 2003. Strains also developed in the relationship between CAT and the union at Mex Mode, over the independence of the local union.

Nevertheless, on balance, the Kuk Dong struggle did lead to the organization and consolidation of one of the few independent unions in the maquiladoras. It improved the wages and working conditions of workers, and it did so by using the leverage of the U.S. market against the company, without becoming distracted by the ineffective process set up under NAFTA's labor side agreement. "Pressure on the label was the key," Velázquez concluded. "With the students in the U.S. using Nike's code of conduct, it was like we had them by the throat."

Muñoz agreed. "Without international support, we would never have been able to succeed at Kuk Dong," she asserted. But she was also concerned about the relationship between supporters and the workers in the factory and was insistent that the workers themselves must maintain the ability to make the basic decisions about strategy and about the activity and leadership of their union. "We want an independent relationship, in which we express our opinion, and others express theirs—but in the end, as workers in the plant, in the union, we make our own decisions. Right now, the most important thing for us is to be independent."

Independence is difficult, and it has drawbacks. The Mex Mode campaign relied on U.S. connections to help supply the resources needed to organize activities thousands of miles away from the plant. SITEMEX, which depended on the AFL-CIO and USAS for much of that help, is a local union with limited connections and resources of its own, although it has a program for building up its own electronic connections to U.S. supporters. The union does not belong to the UNT or other Mexican labor federations. In fact, Muñoz said, they asked the UNT for help early on, "and they treated us as though we were not important, as though we were just women." The powerful union at the enormous

Volkswagen plant in Puebla, which has a history of militancy and independence, does have a very close relationship with both the UNT and SITEMEX. VW workers brought help to Kuk Dong all through the battle.

Both SITEMEX and CAT eventually would like to organize workers in other garment plants, especially in the heart of the industry in another Puebla city, Tehuacán, where many factories are sewing for the big U.S. labels. But both recognize that this would require resources far beyond what they had when the first contract was signed at Mex Mode.

FIGHTING FOR A LIVING WAGE

Like unions in the United States, which have made the passage of local "living wage" ordinances a focus of activity in recent years, organizations on the border such as the CJM have also been trying to define what it takes for workers and their families to survive.

In 2001, that effort caught fire in Torreón, Coahuila, a dusty city in Mexico's northeast desert. For decades, its workers labored in the Peñoles smelter and the factories clustered around its mines and mills. Coahuila, Nuevo Leon, Chihuahua, Tamaulipas—all states along the border—were the heart of Mexico's heavy industry. Its workers were heavily unionized and well known for their militancy.

Today, most of those mills are closed. Instead, a wave of foreign-owned maquiladora assembly plants has spread out across the desert. Militant unions have been replaced by ones more amenable to the demands of investors from Wall Street or Tokyo. And wages in this northern area, once Mexico's pride, now hover slightly above the legal minimum, sometimes even dipping below it.

But history and tradition don't die easily. In the spring of 2001, Torreon's streets were filled with women chanting and shouting demands for wages that provided something better than cardboard houses and communities without sewers, electricity, or running water. The city's annual May Day parade witnessed more than two thousand women shouting, *"¡No nos callamos!"* (We won't be quiet anymore!) and *"¡Queremos una vida digna!"* (We want a decent life!).

Farther north, on the border in Ciudad Acuña, the power of the factory owners is more palpable and feared. Here, women marched with bags over their heads to hide their identities, presumably protecting themselves from firings and retaliations. But in both Torreón and Acuña, to the embarrassment of city officials and leaders of the conservative, government-affiliated unions, people along the parade routes heard the chants, cheered, and even joined in.

"In our communities, the whole family works," said Betty Robles, one of the organizers of the campaign for higher wages. "You see kids nine or ten years old bagging groceries in supermarkets or washing cars on the corners. The daughter of one of our activists was thirteen when she went to work in the factory sewing pants and shorts."

The reason is simple. A survey taken by the Service for Development and Peace-Coahuila (SEDEPAC, Servicio de Desarollo y Paz-Coahuila), the organization Robles helped to start, found that it took 1,500 pesos a week to provide food, housing, and transportation for a family of four. A normal maquiladora worker, however, made only 320 to 350 pesos. "We asked people, 'How do you survive when there's such a huge gap?' Many told us that two and three families share a couple of rooms, pooling income to cover rent and basic needs."

This income gap was extensively documented by the Center for Reflection, Education, and Action, a religious research group, in a 2001 study titled "Constitutional Wage Study/Purchasing Power Index," co-sponsored by the CJM (to which SEDEPAC belongs) and the Interfaith Center on Corporate Responsibility. At the minimum wage, according to the study, it took a maquiladora worker in Juárez almost an hour to earn enough money to buy a kilo (2.2 pounds) of rice, and a worker in Tijuana needed an hour and a half. By comparison, a dockworker driving a container crane in the San Pedro harbor, south of Los Angeles, could buy the rice after three minutes at work. Even an undocumented worker at minimum wage must labor only twelve minutes for the same result in Los Angeles.

Such a gap is a recipe for confrontation. And, in fact, the anger in the streets of Coahuila was not unique. All along the border, from Matamoros on the Gulf of Mexico to La Paz at the tip of the Baja California peninsula, economic pressure has fueled a wave of industrial unrest sweeping through the factories.

During the first year of his administration, it posed the most serious challenge yet for President Vicente Fox, who had defeated the PRI by promising greater democracy, employment, and a rising standard of living. Instead, however, Mexico's economy hit the skids. An economic downturn in the United States—the market for most of what the maquiladoras produce—created havoc in Mexico. Although Fox had promised 1.4 million new jobs, economists estimate that half a million workers were laid off during his first eight months in office. Signs soliciting workers, usually omnipresent on factory gates in border industrial parks, disappeared. Inevitably, greater competition among workers for the available jobs began pushing wages down.

In Coahuila, a cross-border solidarity effort helped to beef up SEDE-PAC's living wage campaign. Local unions in California and Oregon—including Los Angeles's Local 11 and San Francisco's Local 2 of the Hotel Employees and Restaurant Employees as well as the janitors' Service Employees Local 1877—organized a loose network called Enlace (Links) and sent organizers to help. Locals of the Longshore and Warehouse Union also offered aid.

Before the May Day march, SEDEPAC activists began setting up grassroots committees inside a number of factories, including the huge garment sweatshops run by the Sara Lee Corporation. Many of those committees were clandestine, since open activity often leads to termination.

Inside the plants, women activists were called *promotoras* because they promoted organization among their co-workers. The *promotoras* were trained to identify health and safety hazards, and they also attended workshops discussing *identidad*, self-identity. "Many of the women are migrants from indigenous communities far away and feel torn from the cultural roots which give them a feeling of self-respect," Robles explained. "They get very depressed, so we talk a lot about self-worth, to raise their expectations for better treatment and respect at work and to get them to demand their rights." Women in the factory committees in turn were linked to organizations in the surrounding communities that fight for elemental services such as sewers, water lines, paved streets, and electricity.

In 2002, SEDEPAC began a campaign at the Sara Lee plant known as Confecciones de Monclova, located in Frontera, in Coahuila state. According to Betty Robles, when the company became aware of the activity on the plant floor, many women were fired. Nevertheless, much as workers had done years before at Sony, activists at Sara Lee started trying to force the existing *sección* of the CTM in the plant to defend its own members.

In May, workers went to the local office of the labor board in Monclova, as well as the office of the state labor secretary, and demanded a copy of the contract and the by-laws of their own union. "As in most of the assembly plants, the people who do the heavy, repetitive, and routine work [sew] thousands and thousands of clothing articles that flood international markets, work twelve hours daily, and take extra jobs since they cannot survive on the money they make at Sara Lee," the union committee said in a statement appealing for international support. "The unions work in favor of the bosses. And in the case of the *compañeras* of Confecciones de Monclova, it is extreme. The workers do not even know the name of their union or the address of the union office and do not have a copy of union by-laws or union contract.... But the workers did not choose this union. They do not know anything about its contract. There has been no election."

It was the company who told the women that they'd already signed a union contract and that this union had chosen two delegates as the official representatives of the workers. By asking for a copy of the contract and the by-laws, the workers sought to expose the alliance between the company, the CTM, and the government. Their actions, they hoped, would eventually result in a free election in the factory, in which workers could choose their own union and leaders.

The year that followed, however, saw the sharpest economic crisis in the history of the maquiladoras. All along the border, thousands of workers were laid off. At Sara Lee, the company began cutting back on benefits instead of agreeing to new ones. It stopped bus service to the nearby towns where workers lived, making it harder and more expensive for the women to get to work. By making transport so difficult, the company hoped that many workers would quit, allowing Sara Lee to avoid the expense of laying them off and having to provide severance pay (as mandated under Mexican law).

Throughout this period, the Enlace network in the United States sent out appeals for support. Letters, e-mail messages, and faxes poured into the offices of company officials and government authorities. In April 2003, SEDEPAC and Enlace organized simultaneous demonstrations in Mexico and the United States.

Workers feared that the company would move beyond layoffs and actually close the plant. Five women—Carla García, Alma Martínez, Patricia Cadena, Flor Náñez, and Rafael Torres—circulated a petition demanding that the company guarantee that the factory would remain open. On April 25, the manager of the Frontera plant, Lauro Pesceira, told workers that he would post such a notice.

Given that thousands of workers had lost maquila jobs over the previous year, winning a promise that the plant would stay open was significant. Nevertheless, workers intended to continue pushing for their original demands. "The workers are still struggling for the freedom to choose their own union representation, a halt to unsafe working conditions for pregnant workers, and a living wage," an Enlace statement informed supporters.

"FLEXIBILITY" VS. ENFORCING THE LAW

In May 2000, the World Bank added to the controversy surrounding Mexico's low-wage development policy by issuing a series of recommendations to the new Mexican administration, titled "An Integral Agenda of Development for the New Era." The theme of this proposal was greater "flexibility," a word that has come to be feared by border workers, who translate it as layoffs, fewer benefits, and downward pressure on salaries.

The bank recommended rewriting Mexico's Constitution and Federal Labor Law, eliminating protections that had been in place since the

1920s. The bank suggested that companies should no longer be required to pay severance wages when they lay off workers, to negotiate over the closure of factories, to give workers permanent status after thirty days, to limit part-time work, or to abide by the forty-hour week. The bank recommended other changes that would weaken the ability of unions to represent workers and to bargain, including the elimination of the historical ban on strikebreaking. And it also urged scrapping Mexico's guarantees of job training, health care, and housing.

The recommendations were so extreme that even a leading employers' association condemned them. Claudio X. Gonzáles, head of the Managerial Coordinating Council, called the report "over the top," noting the bank didn't dare to make such proposals in developed countries. "Why are they then being recommended for the emerging countries?" he asked.

But Fox embraced the report, calling it "very much in line with what we have contemplated" and necessary to "really enter into a process of sustainable development."

Not all political parties agreed. In Mexico City, the city administration, headed by the PRD, began trying to enforce existing rights rather than eliminating them. For the first years of the PRD's administration, enforcement of labor laws had not ranked high on the agenda. But Manuel López Obrador, the new mayor elected in 2000, appointed the dean of Mexico's labor lawyers as the head of the local labor board for the region.

For decades, such appointees have been either government bureaucrats or representatives of employers and PRI-affiliated unions. But Jesús Campos Linas departed from that corporativist tradition, marking his appointment by writing a letter to the city's workers. In it, he promised to make public all the sweetheart protection contracts between the old unions and employers. And he vowed to ensure that workers could vote by secret ballot in union elections, without violence or intimidation.

On September 15, a new Web site hit the Internet, displaying a growing list of all the protection contracts in Mexico City. Campos Linas estimates that there are between seventy thousand and eighty thousand such agreements, whose existence is usually unknown to the more than

1 million workers they cover. The main function of the agreements is to keep independent unions out and ensure that workers don't organize themselves to stop production or demand higher wages.

To avoid crooked elections like the ones at Duro and ITAPSA, Campos Linas ordered all union voting to take place at the labor board office. "I was a lawyer for the workers at ITAPSA before taking my present position," he said, "and I won't permit the abuses that workers suffered there."

The PRI-affiliated unions didn't raise much fuss at first. "That's because they don't really believe we'll carry out these changes," he noted. "They think this is business as usual—that we'll just talk about changing things, while on the ground nothing happens. They're in for a big surprise."

Two separate and very different ideas about workers' rights have emerged in Mexico, and the controversies over protection contracts and the secret ballot are only its most visible symbols. The differences are much deeper, for they concern the issue of whose priorities will prevail—those of workers or those of investors with a stake in the free trade–based economy.

Campos Linas saw the World Bank proposal as a stalking horse for Mexico's largest employers and their allies among foreign corporations and financial institutions. The bank's recommendations were too drastic for the government to make itself, but they provided an extreme pole against which the government's own neoliberal proposals might seem more acceptable.

"I don't oppose reforms in general, such as those guaranteeing people the freedom to choose their own unions," Campos Linas explained. "But the changes proposed by the bank would be a gigantic step backward for workers, who would lose the stability and rights the present law gives them. They're only proposing to take things away, not to give workers anything. They don't understand that it took a revolution, in which a million people died, to get our Constitution and labor law. Our problem isn't that we need a new law—[the problem is] to enforce the one we have. That's what will make Mexican workers confident about their political system."

Campos Linas rejected the argument raised by Fox and his allies for gutting legal protections—that such actions would make the economy more competitive, attract greater investment, and create more jobs. "No labor law reform can accomplish this," he charged. "Mexico already has one of the lowest wage levels in the world, yet there's still this cry for more flexibility. The minimum wage in Mexico City is 40.35 pesos a day—no one can live on this. And now we've lost four hundred thousand jobs since January [2002] alone. Changing the labor law will not solve this problem."

A battle is brewing over which direction Mexico will take. Unlike the revolution at the turn of the twentieth century, it will not be fought mainly by farmers with guns. In large part, it will take place on the floors of the maquila plants. And since maquiladora production has spread far beyond the border, encompassing cities all over Mexico, it will be a national convulsion.

In August 2001, the CJM met in Monterrey to discuss this new reality. "We can no longer afford to be just a border-based organization," Héctor de la Cueva of the Center for Labor Research warned. "We have to be ready to assist workers in all parts of Mexico."

As if to underline the growing national character of the maquiladora movement, the meeting heard from workers in one of the most remote corners of Mexico, on the tip of the Baja peninsula. Garment workers came from La Paz to tell CJM delegates of the mass firings that had greeted their efforts to organize an independent union in three large garment factories—California Connections, Pung Kook, and Baja West. All three subcontract to U.S. manufacturers, especially ones in Los Angeles.

When they began their campaign, these workers in Baja California Sur believed that they had a big advantage. In 1998, Leonel Cota, a PRD candidate, had been elected governor of the state. Because he therefore controlled the state labor board, workers at the California Connections and Pung Kook factories won legal status in 1999 for their union, known as the Independent Union of Men and Women Workers in the Maquiladora Industry of the State of Baja California Sur (SINTTIM, Sindicato Independiente de Trabajadores y Trabajadoras de la Industria Maquiladora del Estado de Baja California Sur).

Nevertheless, eight days after that decision, every worker named in the legal documents as a union officer was fired. "We've been fighting for the right to negotiate ever since," reported union president Raquel Espinoza. "At first, Cota supported us, but now the companies say they'll close the factories if we win bargaining rights. That threat really scared him, especially in the current economic crisis."

As in Coahuila, union organizing in these factories remained clandestine as a result. Then the area's third major maquiladora, the Baja West garment factory, abruptly announced that it was going out of business, owing two weeks' wages to its workers. The governor found some subsidies that enabled workers to pay their immediate bills, but the threat frightened those workers who still had jobs in the other plants.

Because maquiladora workers have become a key part of the country's economy, the independent union movement has slowly recognized the need to devote resources to helping them. For forty years, these workers were viewed, and indeed viewed themselves, as living on the country's fringe—geographically, politically, and socially. But independent unions in Mexico will not survive if maquila workers remain marginalized. And, increasingly, workers in the border plants are affected by the same problems suffered by the rest of the country's workers.

Following the Duro election, the UNT signed a strategic alliance with the CJM, pledging a greater commitment to organize in the maquiladoras. For its part, the CJM agreed to do more to resist free trade reforms such as the continued privatization of the economy and the restructuring of Mexican labor laws.

"If the country's electrical generating system is privatized, for instance," de la Cueva reminded activists at the Monterrey meeting, "all workers will pay the price, including those in the maquiladoras. Protection contracts exist in all parts of the economy, not just on the border. And labor law reform is not a problem of central Mexico, or just of workers who belong to the old unions. Everyone is affected by the same problems, and they are forcing us all together, like it or not."

8

MEXICO'S WARS OVER PRIVATIZATION

NEGOTIATING WITH A GUN TO THEIR HEADS

The Reclusorio del Oriente, the federal prison in the eastern district of Mexico City, is the free trade prison. In 1995 and 1996, as the government of President Ernesto Zedillo overhauled the Mexican economy, it became the destination for workers and unionists who stood in the way of economic reforms. Its most famous residents were eleven bus drivers and their lawyer—the leaders of the union for Mexico City's huge Route 100 bus line, SUTAUR 100 (Sindicato Único de Trabajadores de Autotransportes Urbanos de Pasajeros Ruta 100, the Sole Union for Workers at the Urban Bus Line Route 100). On April 8, 1995, they were brought into the bare earthen compound of the penitentiary's intake section. A year later, they were still there—not integrated into the main prison population but definitely not free.

Meanwhile, demonstrations swirled outside. In front of the Mexico City municipal council building, two supporters of the unionists stopped eating for forty days and lived in an ambulance in protest. As a dramatic symbol of the government's refusal to see and hear the pain caused by its reforms, one of the hunger strikers sewed his eyes and ears closed.

The government continued to negotiate with the union's leaders over the elimination of their jobs, but those talks took place inside the prison offices, with the warden acting as a go-between. Jorge Cuellar, the union's recording secretary, called it "negotiations with a gun to our heads."

Under Zedillo and his predecessor, Carlos Salinas de Gortari, the fate of the drivers became a potent symbol for a new era of labor relations. Now even established unions in Mexico City might be treated like the upstart independent organizations on the border if they didn't conform to the demands of privatization.

The status and power of Mexican labor had fallen a long way.

In the 1930s and early 1940s, under the nationalist government of General Lázaro Cárdenas, the Mexican political structure formally recognized the existence of unions and labor rights. Mexico's largest labor federation, the CTM, was organized in that era by Communists and political radicals. Under the institutional umbrella of the Labor Congress, it was incorporated into the ruling party, the PRI, along with the older labor federations that preceded it—the Revolutionary Confederation of Mexican Workers (CROM), the Revolutionary Confederation of Workers and Farmers (CROC), and others.

The PRI was the political expression of a cross-class ruling coalition in which unions joined with the country's main farmer organizations and employer associations. The Mexican corporatist state used its control of the economy to mediate the interests of all three elements. A huge state-owned sector guaranteed employment for hundreds of thousands of workers, while the legal structure gave unions both recognition and bargaining rights. Being a labor leader became a stepping-stone into the political class.

The government administered a wide network of social services, from health care to transportation, but its role in workers' lives was far greater than that. Cárdenas's reforms were an extension of a process begun during the Mexican Revolution, intended to sever the ties that he and most Mexicans believed held their country in bondage to its northern neighbor. At the time the revolution began, U.S. companies and

investors owned oil fields, copper mines, railroads, the telephone system, great tracts of land, and other key economic resources in Mexico.
To be truly independent, the nationalists believed, Mexico had to establish an economic system in which those resources were controlled by
Mexicans and used for their benefit. The route to control was nationalization, which would both stop the transfer of wealth out of the country
and use state ownership to set up an internal market, to ensure that what
was produced in Mexico would be sold there as well. In theory, therefore, the government had a stake in maintaining stable jobs and income
so that workers and farmers could buy back what they produced.

The most powerful symbol of this economic nationalism was the
nationalization of Mexico's oil industry. Most industrial workers were
eventually employed by the state. A government food monopoly,
CONASUPO, operated chains of retail food stores that sold tortillas
and milk at low subsidized prices. CONASUPO bought corn and farmers' produce at wholesale prices that, again in theory, made it possible
for small producers to survive and stay on the land. Cárdenas also initiated land redistribution in many states, creating *ejido* communities that
owned much of the land in common. Foreign ownership of land was
prohibited.

The corporatist structure created a framework for labor rights far
different from that in the United States. On the one hand, it guaranteed
rights that U.S. unions and workers can only dream of, a system that still
exists on paper. Severance pay is mandatory if companies discharge
workers. Workers have a right to profit-sharing. During a legal strike,
the company must shut its doors until the dispute is resolved. On paper,
the government acknowledges the right of all people to education and
housing. Secret ballots for union elections were unnecessary, in theory,
because the government was obligated to defend workers and prevent
any retaliation by their employers.

On the other hand, Mexican unions gave up autonomy and control of
their own affairs. The structure of labor law was governed by a corporatist philosophy in which the government registered unions and then
oversaw their internal processes and choice of leaders. The corporatist

system never tolerated independent action by workers and unions outside its political structure. Demetrio Vallejo and Valentín Campa served
long prison terms in the 1950s and 1960s after the railroad union, which
they headed, struck against government wage policy. In the 1980s,
Rafael Galván was eventually removed as head of one of the country's
two unions for electrical workers, SUTERM, after organizing a movement called the Tendencia Democrática, the Democratic Tendency,
which aimed to democratize the country's unions. Government control
also created vast opportunities for corruption. Unions such as the one in
the oil industry eventually set up and ran businesses for the benefit of
their leaders, who often suppressed opposition viciously. More than a
hundred teachers in the state of Oaxaca alone were killed during their
long struggle to win control of their own union and to defend the
indigenous communities in which they lived.

What might have seemed like a way to ensure worker control over
economic development in the 1940s increasingly became a trap. Government control could be, and was, used to prevent independent protest
and organized labor resistance to policies that harmed workers' interests. When the government changed its basic economic policy, using
low wages to attract foreign investment and producing for the U.S.
market instead of for Mexico, the political structure punished resistance
severely.

Under Salinas, and then Zedillo, those reforms became a whirlwind,
as all the old rules and assumptions about the distribution of economic
and political power changed. The main instrument for dismantling the
old nationalist economic system was the privatization of state-owned
enterprises. And for the last years of Salinas's regime and the first years
of Zedillo's, the main target was the bus system in Mexico City.

SUTAUR 100 DEFIES THE NEW RULES

Mexico's ruling authorities began going after SUTAUR 100, the union
for the bus system's drivers, as soon as it was formed in 1981. The union
had been created by workers at a number of small private bus companies
who had pulled out of the CTM while those companies were still pri-

vately owned. In the eyes of the political establishment, the very creation of an independent union such as this was an offense. The year after SUTAUR 100 was founded, the city government therefore began moving to reestablish control by bringing the bus lines under municipal ownership. (The PRI controlled the Mexico City government until the historic election of 1996, when the PRD candidate, Cuauhtémoc Cárdenas, was elected mayor.)

Meanwhile, SUTAUR 100's reputation grew. In addition to exposing corruption among managers, the union began to pressure the city to extend bus service to the outlying areas of Mexico City, the world's largest, most spread-out municipality. That advocacy helped the union to build a base of support in the huge barrios on the city's rim, where most of the capital's poor live. Route 100 provided vital connections between these communities and the urban center at a cost people could afford.

SUTAUR 100 also acquired a reputation for political independence and a democratic structure. Unlike most Mexican unions, it was not affiliated with the PRI. The government was infuriated when the union helped to raise funds and build public support for the Zapatistas during the uprising in the southern state of Chiapas in 1994.

That fury came to a head the following year.

On April 8, 1995, at six in the morning, five of the union's top officials were suddenly arrested at their homes and charged with misusing funds. Luis Miguel Moreno Gómez, Mexico City's transport and highway secretary, then announced that the Route 100 system was bankrupt. In a ten-minute hearing before the First District Court, the government annulled the union's contract and stripped away its bargaining rights. The following day, union lawyer Ricardo Barco was also arrested.

Days later, Moreno Gómez was shot and killed. The government ruled that he had committed suicide by shooting two bullets into his own chest.

The system's twelve thousand employees were expelled from the bus yards at gunpoint, and other workers were brought in to drive the buses. The workers who were pushed out of their jobs were owed back wages and should have been paid the severance required by Mexican law, but no money was forthcoming. Finally, on June 13, during a visit to the imprisoned union leaders, six other SUTAUR 100 officials were also arrested and joined them in jail.

Meanwhile, the city announced its intention to divide the system's fleet of buses, maintenance yards, and other resources into ten new enterprises, which it planned to sell to private investors.

Growing pressure to push forward with this privatization plan at any cost began to provoke even greater bloodshed, eventually including direct attacks on the legal system itself. On June 18, Jesús Humberto Priego Chávez, a prosecutor investigating corruption in the bus line and its breakup, was shot and killed outside his home. On June 22, federal judge Abraham Polo Uscanga was also shot and killed. Despite an order by the court's president, Uscanga had refused to issue arrest warrants for the union's leaders, saying that there was no evidence to support the charges. He then agreed to testify for the union and, before his death, had taken out a full-page ad in a Mexico City newspaper calling the jailings unconstitutional.

None of the murderers were ever caught.

As violence mounted, SUTAUR 100 organized a succession of marches, demonstrations, sit-ins, and other protests, bringing tens of thousands of workers and poor barrio residents into the streets in support. While keeping the union's leaders in prison, the government met with them to negotiate a settlement. According to Jorge Cuellar, the union's recording secretary, he was told that if the unionists failed to agree to government conditions, other arrests, including his own, would follow.

When he was interviewed in prison, Gabino Camacho Barrera, the founder of SUTAUR 100, attributed the government's hostility to its fear of growing social unrest. "Our minimum wage is now twenty percent of what it was in 1970 [in terms of buying power]," he explained. "Diseases like tuberculosis, which are connected to poverty and which we thought were eradicated in Mexico, are coming back. There's never been a crisis like this. The repression against us has been terrible because the government fears people will react."

On March 25, 1996, thousands of fired bus drivers tried to back their leaders by holding an enormous rally in Mexico City's main square, the Zócalo. Earlier, drivers who had been living in an encampment there for months had been expelled by government security forces. As they gathered again in front of the national palace, drivers heard Ricardo Barco's voice echo from the walls of the plaza's ancient cathedral, over loudspeakers in a direct telephone linkup from the *reclusorio*. He condemned the city's proposal to eliminate thousands of jobs, and, with a wave of jeers and catcalls, drivers once again rejected it. After the vote, blue-uniformed riot police carrying plastic shields and wearing helmets and face masks moved into the enormous plaza. Workers and their supporters were driven into the narrow streets leading away from the city center.

While drivers confronted police in the Zócalo, two labor lawyers in an ambulance in front of the city council offices a few blocks away were surrounded and prevented from joining them. One lawyer, Ventura Galván, had lived in the ambulance for weeks while the union conducted a nonstop rally outside. In a startling protest, Galván had a friend sew thick black threads through his eyelids, pulling them together across a rolled-up gauze bandage. His ears were sewn closed the same way. His protest was directed at Mexico City's then-mayor, Oscar Espinoza Villareal, who, Galván said, wouldn't listen to the drivers or face the impact of his decisions on their lives.

On the ambulance's other stretcher lay Jorge García, another attorney, who went without food for six weeks. He fasted, he said, "because we tried all the legal ways, and the government is so intent on privatization that it's willing to violate whatever laws it thinks necessary. We're both worried about what's going to happen to our country. We're moving backward in such a drastic way that it will be difficult ever to recover."

"In our country, there are only two classes," Galván added, "the rich and the poor. Every day, the poor are more marginalized, without the right to education, health, or even food. Now they're taking away their right to public transport. The government may try to forbid public demonstrations, although our right to demonstrate is guaranteed in Article Ninety of the Constitution. But they cannot prevent us from undertaking hunger strikes or from sewing our lips closed, or our eyes. We have to say 'Enough!' to a capitalism that's crucifying us with a life with no dignity. We cannot tolerate what's happening to us anymore."

Turmoil and unrest kept the government in negotiations with the union for more than a year. In the end, it offered to give SUTAUR 100 concessions to operate two of the ten private companies it intended to create, along with 867 million pesos to cover back wages and severance pay. The city claimed that the two companies would absorb three thousand workers and that it would ensure the hiring of an additional fifteen hundred in other transport jobs. At the end of April 1996, after its leaders had been in prison a year, the union agreed to accept the two concessions, along with retraining and jobs for an additional three thousand drivers and 72 percent of the severance pay they were owed.

The drivers' challenge to the government was a focal point for popular discontent over a succession of privatizations carried out by Salinas and Zedillo. These included the Aeromexico airline, the telephone company, the petrochemical industry dependent on the state-run oil company, the Sicartsa steel mill in the port of Lázaro Cárdenas, the railroad network, many Mexican mines, and the operation of the country's ports. Other privatization plans discussed by the government included the social security system and even the operation of its world-famous archaeological sites and parks.

SUTAUR 100's leaders became the best-known prisoners of free trade, but they were not the first to go to jail for opposing privatization. That unhappy honor belonged to "La Quina"—Joaquín Hernández Galicia. For six years, he lived in the *reclusorio* hospital, an involuntary guest of his former friend Carlos Salinas de Gortari.

As one of the first acts of his administration, Salinas claimed to have "discovered" the presence of firearms in Hernández's palatial residence. In a military operation, the union leader was arrested in what was universally viewed as a message to other unions considering opposition to economic reforms. When Salinas betrayed La Quina and sent him to prison, it was as significant for Mexicans as President Ronald Reagan's decision to break the air traffic controllers' strike had been for U.S. unionists in 1983. Both actions were betrayals of union leaders who believed that the political system would never turn against them.

Hernández Galicia was the head of the oilworkers union, a position of enormous power in the national oil company, Pemex. Fearing that the government intended to privatize Mexico's largest enterprise, he gave under-the-table support to Cuauhtémoc Cárdenas's opposition campaign for the presidency in 1988. La Quina's old enemies—banned left-wing radicals—were even invited to return to speak at oilworkers union meetings.

Hernández Galicia may have been corrupt, but he saw the future with clear eyes. In the six years following his arrest, all the petrochemical plants dependent on Pemex were put on the auction block. In 1995, the income from the sale of every drop of oil was given over to Wall Street banks, where it paid for the loans arranged by President Bill Clinton in the dark days of the peso's devaluation.

During the six years of La Quina's imprisonment, others joined him. The leader of the union at Aeromexico was kept in the *reclusorio* almost as long, after he refused to quietly accept the company's privatization and the layoff of thousands of workers. The head of one of the largest *secciones* of the union representing the employees of the social security system, IMSS, also spent months there in 1995. Her crime was denouncing government plans to privatize the enormous federal pension and health care agency.

SUTAUR 100's battle over jobs attracted substantial attention among unions in the United States, because it was one of the few Mexican unions that officially opposed the North American Free Trade Agreement. Only one other union group, the Authentic Labor Front, defied the government's endorsement of NAFTA.

Cuellar appeared at the 1995 AFL-CIO convention, where John Sweeney was elected president. Latino union leaders, including United Farm Workers vice president Dolores Huerta and Jaime Martínez, a Texas leader of the International Union of Electrical Workers, shepherded through a resolution supporting SUTAUR 100. That startled many observers; resolutions rarely originate from the floor at those carefully controlled gatherings, and those that do almost never pass. But in the euphoria that surrounded Sweeney's election, support for SUTAUR 100 was symbolic of the rejection of the old cold war foreign policies pursued by his predecessors.

In the hallways outside the convention floor, many delegates explained that union repression in Mexico City wasn't only a problem for Mexican workers, nor was their support simply a case of sympathy for the downtrodden. In a new global economy, they declared, job security often depends on the fate of workers and unions south of the border. Ripples spreading out from the *reclusorio* were felt in jobs and wages from Los Angeles to Detroit. The fewer rights Mexican workers have, and the cheaper their labor gets, the more tempting it is for U.S. corporations to relocate production south.

Some unions went beyond verbal support. The San Francisco–based International Longshore and Warehouse Union (ILWU) sent a delegation to Mexico, which delivered a check for five thousand dollars during a visit to the imprisoned leaders.

In Mexico City, demonstrations by thousands of SUTAUR 100 supporters helped to fracture the close relationship between the Mexican labor movement, the government, and its ruling party. When the doddering head of the Labor Congress, Fidel Velásquez, banned union parades on May Day in 1996, thousands of workers took to the streets in defiance. Velásquez and Zedillo feared that demonstrations would give voice to popular hatred for their economic reforms and the enormous job losses they'd produced. Their fears were completely justified. Twenty-two large unions announced that the economic pain of their members was more important than protecting Zedillo. A million workers and barrio residents marched into the Zócalo, the banner of SUTAUR 100 prominent among them.

PORT PRIVATIZATION: OFFICIAL UNIONS LOSE THEIR POWER

While SUTAUR 100 was battling the privatization of public transport, the privatization of Mexico's ports offered another demonstration of the weakness of the old official unions in the face of changes in government economic policy.

Until the 1940s, the harbor of Lázaro Cárdenas was a bucolic village of fifty homes at the mouth of the Río Balsas, where families fished for a living and raised coconuts and cattle. Even the town's name was different then—"Melchor Ocampo" still appears on old maps.

But over the next four decades, the Mexican government built the country's third largest port at this location. Three blast furnaces at the edge of town today churn out steel in Latin America's largest mill. It was General Cárdenas himself who had the vision for making the city a new industrial center, which he hoped would provide Mexico with an expanded base for the nationalist economic development policy he championed. They named the city after him, and, with sixty thousand inhabitants, it's a small town no longer.

Lázaro Cárdenas is on the coast of one of Mexico's poorest states, Michoacán, which has contributed more immigrants to the United States than most others. Despite the high rates of migration statewide, it's hard to find families in Lázaro Cárdenas with relatives who have left, because for many years the development of this port supplied good jobs. Nevertheless, in the 1990s, this city also was caught up in the storms of economic reform.

Mexican port unions had been under attack for some time. Many were haunted by the events of June 1991 on the country's eastern coast, when the Mexican army took over the port of Veracruz, disbanded the country's most powerful longshore union, and installed three private contractors to manage port operations. Hourly wages of Veracruz longshore workers fell from about seven dollars to one dollar, while workers were pushed to handle forty shipping containers per hour rather than the usual eighteen.

In Pacific coast ports, the longshore union has been one of Mexico's most powerful. But even that strength provided little protection from the effects of privatization. The old political system that had given workers security and good jobs broke down, and they became politically expendable.

The fight over privatization in Lázaro Cárdenas began when the Sicartsa steel mill was privatized in 1992. Wages were cut in half, and fifteen hundred of the mill's five thousand workers were laid off. They were then rehired as temporary labor under twenty-eight-day contracts, which meant that they were no longer covered by Mexican labor law—legally, workers enjoy job rights only after they've been employed for thirty days.

Rank-and-file insurgents within the union sought to stop the changes, but the lawyers for their movement, María Estela Ríos González and María Eugenia Meza Arceo, were arrested. Under the pretext of charging them with interfering in the internal process of the union, the governor of Michoacán had the two attorneys brought under guard from Mexico City to the state capital in Morelia. Only a wave of protest by lawyers in Mexico and the United States won their eventual release. The movement to stop the reforms, however, was defeated.

Once Sicartsa was sold off, the next target in the city was its large fertilizer enterprise, Fertimex. Inside the port, the government sectioned off the dock area used by the plant. The company's new owners then hired nonunion dockworkers to load and unload ships. The decision was backed up with troops—a sign of the times.

In 1994, the Mexican Congress approved legislation transferring all ports along the Pacific coast to the Ministry of Finance, which then arranged their sale to private companies. Port terminal contracts were valued at over $200 million. Jaime Corredor Esnaola, a Mexican Transport Ministry official, claimed that privatizing the ports would lower wages and put an end to union influence, since ports would be open to private employers and competition. He was right.

Mexican ports are not sleepy banana docks or quaint fishing villages. The vast harbor area of Lázaro Cárdenas echoes to the rumble of three hammerhead cranes and four giant transtainers, moving containers that are the lifeblood of modern shipping. Huge bulk loaders unload U.S. coke from Russian vessels for Sicartsa, while other cranes load steel slabs onto Chinese freighters bound for New Orleans. In Manzanillo, row after row of new Maximas line up on the dock, bound from Nissan's assembly plant in Aguascalientes to ports in the United States, Japan, and Europe. Just as it has in San Francisco, Portland, or Los Angeles, the thunder of high-tech machinery has replaced the old cargo net.

Longshore workers who drive the cranes were traditionally well paid, by Mexican standards, their income depending on the amount of cargo they moved. Dock wages in Lázaro Cárdenas averaged between 800 and 900 pesos a week, more than 100 dollars per week, before privatization, in a country where the minimum wage at the time was about 4 dollars per day. Dockworkers had pensions, disability payments, and other benefits rare among most Mexican workers. But it was not bargaining power in the traditional U.S. sense that protected those benefits. It was the relationship between the longshore unions and the government.

On the West Coast in the United States, the ILWU had been able to protect the standard of living for dockworkers because competition between ports and workers was eliminated after the 1934 maritime strike. The union negotiated one single coastwide agreement with the Pacific Maritime Association, which represents private shipping and stevedoring companies.

Coastwide agreements don't exist in Mexico. Each port union dealt on its own with Servicios Portuarios, a government entity that employed all Pacific coast longshore workers. Once the ports were privatized, their bargaining power was fractured still further. Servicios Portuarios ceased to exist, and workers had to try to negotiate with different private terminal operators within the same port.

The Mexican government told the longshore workers that the high wages and benefits of U.S. dockworkers were the result of working for private companies, not the product of coastwide bargaining. It argued that bringing private capital into Mexican ports would increase productivity, through investment in new machinery and technology, and that a larger pie would mean a bigger slice for workers as well.

This argument had an attraction for many Mexican workers, especially those already angry at the government over its failure to invest in modern technology. Port development had historically stagnated, while corruption and rakeoffs from government enterprises by the political elite were rampant. Ensenada, an hour's drive south of Tijuana, was a good example.

Twice a week, barges would dock at the concrete breakwater in Ensenada, to be loaded with huge shipping containers destined for Long Beach, California. A cage lifted by a forklift would carry longshore workers to the top of each metal box. By hand, they'd attach the hooks and cables connected to an old dockside crane and then carefully guide each container manually to its assigned location. The workers on this job were skillful and experienced. They babied the old and obsolete equipment, coaxing the work from it. But while they were productive enough that container traffic actually increased, there was no question that the port, the Mexican harbor closest to the United States, needed to be modernized.

Ensenada's problems were typical of Mexico's Pacific coast ports, which have historically been plagued by low capacity and inadequate transportation to the country's interior. In the days when Tijuana was a wild border town of honky-tonks, Ensenada was a quiet fishing and agricultural center a hundred miles south. Its container dock lies just inside the breakwater, across the harbor from tuna boats and seafood restaurants. Barges, small container ships, and cruise vessels all vied for the same mooring space. The city had little room for expansion, and it had only two-lane roads—and no railroad—to link it to the industrial plants mushrooming in Tijuana and Mexicali, an hour north.

Today, Tijuana looks like Detroit and is one of the largest industrial centers in the country. Ensenada is destined to become a much larger port serving the growing needs of the maquiladoras on the border, eventually becoming a transportation hub for cargo coming to and from the east. In 1992, when the United States imposed a boycott on Mexican tuna, Ensenada's traditional export, authorities began looking for alternatives to boost cargo traffic. They found that they could increase container operations by offering shipping services to maquiladoras. These factories could put containers filled with finished products destined for Los Angeles on barges in Ensenada. The barges then cross the U.S./Mexico border at sea, avoiding the usual traffic back-up at the border. After they reach Los Angeles or Long Beach, the containers are transferred to oceangoing vessels or rail cars headed east. The Hyundai Corporation's large plant in Tijuana, which makes the shipping containers themselves, sends most of them out of Mexico through Ensenada.

Ensenada port authorities awarded a concession for modernizing and operating the container facility to a company from the Philippines, International Container Terminal Services. The company already operates similar concessions in Veracruz as well as in Manila, Buenos Aires, and Huangzhou. And the new concessionaire did invest in building greater capacity. Today, a hammerhead crane takes the place of the old jury-rigged setup. But while modernization undoubtedly increased productivity, it is less clear that it improved the lives of the port's workers.

The Manila company contracted with another new private entity, Estibadores de Ensenada, to take over cargo operations. When that happened, more than half the city's longshore workers lost their jobs. Seventy dockworkers used to work ships in the harbor. They belonged to a local union whose jurisdiction extended over the entire port. With privatization, however, the government required the creation of a new union, with jurisdiction over only the private concession. Just thirty longshore workers were enrolled as members when the new local was created. "Most of our older members decided to retire," explained Francisco Pimentel Peralta, the new union's secretary, "because we knew there wasn't enough work for everyone."

The pay system was changed as well. Before privatization, Mexican longshoremen were paid by the ton of cargo handled. A day's labor loading tuna in Ensenada, for instance, was worth as much as 200 to 300 pesos. Estibadores de Ensenada, however, pays by the day, at a rate equivalent to three times the minimum wage, or about 75 pesos in 1997. That's roughly twice the wage of an assembly worker in a maquiladora—a big step down from the income longshore work used to provide. In the era before privatization, a day of longshore work in Lázaro Cárdenas or Manzanillo could pay as much as the equivalent of 60 to 100 dollars a day. By comparison, a crane driver in Oakland or San Francisco working under an ILWU contract was then making more than 25 dollars an hour in wages alone.

The huge wage difference between Mexico and the United States gave U.S. shippers a compelling reason to invest in the development of Mexican ports, creating the longshore equivalent of maquiladoras on the docks. "We know these changes mean instability for us," said Alfredo Navarrete, head of the Lázaro Cárdenas longshore union at the time the port was privatized. The ILWU's president at that time, Brian McWilliams, noted that "in the long run, shipping companies want to create an integrated, intermodal system from Alaska to the Guatemala border. In the process, they want to pit longshoremen of our two countries against each other, depriving us of the leverage we need to defend our jobs and economic future."

Sealand, CSX, American President Lines, and Stevedoring Services of America (all U.S. shipping and cargo-handling companies) have operations in Veracruz and Altamira on Mexico's Atlantic coast. In Manzanillo, the largest port on the Pacific coast, a joint venture between the Mexican company Transportación Maritima Mexicana and American President Lines won the concession for operating the multiple-use terminal.

Mexican longshore unions tried to protect their members' jobs and wages through the traditional political system. Waterside unions on the Pacific coast belong to the PRI-affiliated CROM. Navarrete's brother was a PRI deputy in the Michoacán state legislature. Cecilio Lepe Bautista, head of the federation of unions in the Pacific ports, was mayor of Manzanillo in the late 1980s and senator from Colima state in the 1990s.

When the Mexican government built the port in Lázaro Cárdenas, it promised the farmers who gave up their land that their families would have good jobs on the docks for generations to come. "I went to Mexico City twice," Navarrete recalled, "and I talked to the president of the Republic. I reminded him of the promises, including to my own family, who owned a few acres of palms where the port sits now."

But when Lepe, Navarette, and other leaders like them tried to use those old political connections to overturn government economic policy, they found that they had no leverage. They couldn't stop privatization, protect the traditional wage standard, or win any guarantees that their unions would even be recognized and able to bargain with the new owners. The economic reformers within the PRI called such union leaders "dinosaurs" and saw them as obstacles to foreign investment.

Lepe complained that "although the principles of the PRI are beautiful on paper, the party is abandoning them. People are losing faith in the government and the system." In the end, however, he ran for senator on the PRI ticket, and Navarette eventually wound up working in port management. Meanwhile, Héctor Camacho Solis, interior secretary of the Lázaro Cárdenas longshore union, reported that the city now has problems with street robberies committed by people who have lost their jobs during the economic changes. "Some members are now even supporting the PRD and other opposition parties," he asserted.

The threat of port privatization did cause longshore workers from Mexico and the United States to reestablish contacts after a thirty-year lapse, however. The ILWU sent a series of delegations to Mexican ports following the signing of NAFTA to investigate the conditions of Mexican port workers. "If unions are broken in Mexican ports, and private companies take over operations, putting them into competition with U.S. ports, then we both stand to lose," said Norman Parks, a Portland longshore worker who led one delegation.

Those efforts had roots in past contacts between rank-and-file Pacific coast dockworkers from both countries. During the late 1960s, the ILWU organized a program to train Mexican longshore workers from ports all along the Pacific coast in the new container technology. In Ensenada, Manzanillo, Salina Cruz, and Acapulco, it's not hard to find older dockworkers who worked in Los Angeles and remember the experience. "It's something natural," says the union's interior secretary in Salina Cruz, Guillermo García Jiménez. "We are all longshoremen. We handle the same cargo, and we work the same ships. We're brothers."

García's view coincides with that of the ILWU. "We're all trying to protect our jobs, and there's nothing wrong with that," according to another former ILWU president, David Arián. "But we have to understand that in our present situation we have a mutual interest in working together. We're all going to go up or down together. We have to be concerned about what happens to longshoremen on the other side of the border, because it will affect us directly."

MINERS STRIKE IN REVOLUTIONARY CANANEA

One of the most bitter fights against the effects of privatization took place in the mile-high mountains of the Sonoran Desert, just twenty-five miles south of the border between Arizona and Mexico. There, at the end of the 1990s, more than two thousand miners waged an industrial war against Grupo Mexico, one of the largest of the conglomerates that grew up in the era of economic reform. Grupo Mexico operates North America's oldest, and one of the world's largest, copper mines—Cananea—in a town that has been a symbol of anti-government insurrection for almost a hundred years.

On November 19, 1998, the Cananea mine was paralyzed by a strike over the company's plans to eliminate the jobs of more than 700 of its 2,070 blue-collar employees. The strike directly challenged the Mexican government's policy of privatization, which led to those cuts, and in the process defied one of the government's wealthiest financial backers. The following February, government threats of armed intervention forced workers back to their jobs. In the aftermath of the strike, one of Mexico's oldest unions—Sección 65 of the Miners and Metallurgical Workers Union of the Mexican Republic (Sindicato de Trabajadores Mineros y Metalúrgicos de la República Mexicana)—lost much of its hard-won power. Many of its most active rank-and-file members were blacklisted.

Cananea, a small, dusty mountain town of thirty thousand residents, occupies an almost mythic place in the iconography of the Mexican Revolution. Copper has been mined continuously here since the days of the Spanish viceroys, in the late 1600s. In 1906, the mine's U.S. owner, Colonel William C. Greene, paid a lower salary to Mexican miners than to white supervisors brought from the north. Cananea miners went on strike, demanding 5 pesos for an eight-hour day and an end to the lower

Mexican wage. After they were attacked by Arizona vigilantes, the workers took up arms and were put down in a bloody fight by then-dictator Porfirio Díaz.

In Mexican public schools, children learn of Cananea as the opening shot in what became the Mexican Revolution (which officially began in 1910), much as U.S. children learn of the 1775 battles of Concord and Lexington. The 1906 battle in Cananea not only heralded the revolution to come in Mexico but also was the first strike organized by activists on both sides of the border. The Flores Magón brothers plotted the Cananea uprising in the communities of Mexican railroad workers in East Los Angeles and St. Louis. They were supporters of the Industrial Workers of the World, the early U.S. industrial union of southwestern miners and farmworkers, organized by political radicals. After the strike, the brothers spent years on the run, not only from Díaz's *federales* but also from J. Edgar Hoover, who made his initial reputation organizing the manhunt that pursued them. The brothers were eventually sent to Leavenworth prison, where Ricardo Flores Magón died.

For years, the Cananea mine belonged to the U.S.-based Anaconda Copper Company. In 1971, it was nationalized. Two decades later, after the Mexican government began implementing economic reforms, Cananea was again sold to a private company. Its new owner, Grupo Mexico, is one of the country's largest industrial corporations; its main shareholder, Jorge Larrea, heads one of the country's wealthiest families.

Larrea's industrial empire grew rapidly through his close friendship with Carlos Salinas de Gortari, the former president. Under Salinas, the Mexican government sold Larrea the Cananea and other copper mines, as well as railroads, ports, and other heavy industrial enterprises, often at a fraction of their book value. Thirteen Mexican financiers became billionaires during the Salinas administration, and Larrea was one of them.

The enterprises acquired by Grupo Mexico have been rocked by conflict over demands for drastic job cuts. In 1997, Larrea bought the 6,521-kilometer Pacific North railroad, in partnership with Pennsylvania-based Union Pacific. That year, workers throughout northern Mexico launched a series of rolling wildcat strikes over plans to reduce the railroad's workforce of thirteen thousand by more than half.

Grupo Mexico's four copper mines account for more than 90 percent of copper production in Mexico, which is one of the world's ten largest producers. When Larrea took over the Cananea mine in 1991, in partnership with the American Smelting and Refining Company, its workforce numbered more than thirty-three hundred. In six years, the mine workforce was reduced by thirteen hundred jobs. Meanwhile, production increased dramatically, from thirty thousand tons of ore per day in 1979 to eighty thousand tons in 1997.

Striker Javier Canizares explained that the job cuts were accomplished by subcontracting construction and maintenance operations: "Instead of performing those jobs with its own workers, two U.S. companies, Road Machinery and Allison Parks, brought in hundreds of workers under temporary twenty-eight-day contracts from southern Mexico." Subcontracting undermined the union and undercut wages. Sección 65, the Cananea miners union, has a militant reputation, and mine wages had averaged among the highest of the country's industrial workers—between 8 and 12 dollars an hour in 1997. Gabino Paez González, a Grupo Mexico executive in Mexico City, confirmed that subcontractors now perform many operations with contract employees.

The spark that ignited the 1998 strike was a company announcement that it would lay off 435 workers permanently, closing four mine departments. Miners charged that these closure plans would have environmental consequences. Grupo Mexico shut the smelter at Cananea, which employed 325 workers, but then began shipping the ore by train to another smelter at its nearby mine in Nacozari. The change was an effort, miners said, to avoid living up to a promise the company made when it bought the mine, to install pollution-control devices at the facility. Meanwhile, wastewater from ore concentration was held behind a large dam, but Grupo Mexico announced that it was terminating all 135 workers who maintained that tailings pond. According to striker René Enríquez León, mine runoff could reach the headwaters of the Sonora River nearby and lead to massive pollution problems in the extensive farming regions downstream. "It would be an ecological disaster," he said.

The closing of another department, the town's waterworks, provoked a further crisis for Cananea residents. The mine had been responsible for providing water to the town, as well as to its own mining operations, for eighty years. According to company official Paez, "We insisted that the city take over operations of the water system. It is their responsibility." Cananea, however, has no money or personnel to run the system. Residents accused the company of putting untreated water into the town's water supply, and Canizares claims that ten cases of hepatitis were discovered at a local school after water to its bathrooms was cut off. After the strike ended, a demonstration of four hundred women took over pumping stations, stopping the supply of water to both the mine and the town, to force the company to reassume responsibility for the system. In the countryside surrounding Cananea, local farmers supporting the women halted the operation of wells on their land, which are the water's original source. The company, however, refused to budge.

During the strike, the unionists won support from Cananea's mayor, who had worked in the mine himself for eighteen years. Popular sympathy for the miners induced the governor of Sonora and all three political parties in the state legislature, including the ruling PRI and the opposition PRD and PAN, to express verbal support. But strikers say their most important help came from copper miners and unions north of the border. Within days of walking out of the mine, they had already sent a group to Tucson to appeal for food and money. There, they found the Arizona Border Rights Project and an activist local attorney named Jesús Romo, who took the first steps in helping to organize support north of the border.

As Arizona representative of the AFL-CIO's Department of Field Mobilization, Jerry Acosta was in a unique position to publicize the miners' cause. He won union backing for the strikers by arguing that U.S. miners would be directly affected by the strike. "Because of NAFTA," he said, "U.S. corporations have moved jobs to Mexico, where they pay lower wages and aren't restricted by union contracts or environmental

regulations. If the union in Cananea is broken, efforts by Mexican workers to pull wages up and enforce their rights will be set back." Appeals
from Cananea also struck a sympathetic chord because many families,
divided by the border, have members working in the mines in both countries. "My cousins work in Cananea," Acosta explained.

In Mexico City, the representative of the AFL-CIO's Center for
International Solidarity, Tim Beaty, tried to convince the officials of the
Mexican miners union to give more support to their own strike. But
Tucson attorney Romo, who counseled the striking miners, accused the
officials of being more loyal to the government and the PRI than to
their own striking members. "Once the strike started," Romo recalled,
"they began to fear losing control over their own union. They couldn't
stop miners from seeking support north of the border without losing
their credibility, but they tried to reassign them to activity elsewhere."

Strikers charged that those who went to the United States seeking
support were targeted for firing and received death threats from police
and company guards. In mid-January, the judicial police broke into the
homes of two of these individuals, René Enríquez and Reynaldo
Palomino, terrorizing their families.

In a January press conference, another Grupo Mexico spokesperson,
José Fernando Rodríguez Correa, announced that 198 strikers had been
terminated and later threatened to lay off all Cananea workers, rehiring
only 80 percent under new arrangements. Romo charged that "workers
gathering U.S. support were all included in the termination list."

Paez denied that the company had a blacklist and asserted that some
workers weren't rehired because there was no place for them anymore
after the job cuts. But according to Canizares, who had worked at the
mine for fifteen years and was not rehired, "José Valderrama [the mine's
director of labor relations] told me that they don't want anyone working
here anymore who disagrees with their policy. They want people who
are obedient, who don't defend their rights."

The names of workers from the closed departments were not on the
recall lists, but the names of many strike activists were also missing.
"This caused a lot of turmoil," Canizares remembered. "So we had a big

meeting to discuss what had happened. And in the meeting, we decided to go in and occupy the mine. Each person was supposed to go back and occupy their job in their department.

"The day after we'd gone into the mine, there was a big mobilization of the army and all the police forces in the state of Sonora. So the mayor of Cananea, accompanied by the general secretary of the union, went into the mine and asked the workers there to leave, [telling them] that they were running the risk of repression." The workers left the mine, and the cuts went through.

Another activist, Chema Pacheco, explained that the workers believed they had no choice but to end the strike. "People finally went back to work because they couldn't survive without any income. People didn't have any more money, and they'd already fought for quite a while. They accepted the conditions because they felt they had no alternative."

Pacheco was also blacklisted. He was one of the miners who had traveled to Arizona to seek support, and he had also gone to Mexico City as a member of a commission elected by workers to try to negotiate with Grupo Mexico. When the strike ended, he attempted to return to work.

"The company posted lists for each department, of the people they were accepting back to their jobs. And when I went to look at the list for my department, my name wasn't on it. I went to the company office and spoke to the coordinator for labor relations. He said I wasn't going back. He told me it was because I was such a *grillero*, a person who always spoke out, who was always involved in the union."

But Cananea is a small town, and the mine is its main source of jobs. Being blacklisted meant that people were forced to leave the area to find work. "I had no alternative but to leave Cananea. I had to come look for work on the other side, in the U.S. I still had my house and my family, so I really didn't want to leave, but there wasn't anything else I could do."

Pacheco was so bitter that his voice cracked and he began to cry, as he explained what he then had to do. "My children and my wife are still in Cananea. We talk on the phone a lot. I don't have any papers—I really have nothing. But there's a group of us here from Cananea, friends, and we help each other. We all went to school together and then came up here together. Together we've organized this little business here. I go back and forth, but it's always a big risk, that they'll take away my passport or that something will happen to me on the road. I'd like to get some legal status here, but I don't know if it will happen. If there were an amnesty here, it would help me a lot."

Nevertheless, Pacheco would rather live in Cananea than in the United States. "I'd like to go back to Cananea, but there's nothing there for me right now. There are no jobs there. The only thing I can do right now is work here in the U.S."

Acosta was also bitter about the way the strike was suppressed. "When companies can pick up and go five miles to the other side of the border, where a miner earns less in a day than his relative on this side earns in an hour, can we find the solidarity to bridge the gap?" he asked. "If we can't find the answer, we're all going to suffer."

THE POOR FIGHT FOR THEIR UNIVERSITY,
WHILE THE RICH GO ELSEWHERE

Increasingly, it's not only workers who suffer the effects of privatization. All sectors of Mexican society, from farmers to professionals, feel its impact. In fact, one of the most determined battles to stop the reforms was fought by students rather than workers.

In February 1999, Mexico's federal government brought troops onto the campus of the National Autonomous University (UNAM) for the first time in its history, to end a student strike that had gone on for nine months. The key demand of the strikers was the repeal of a newly instituted tuition requirement. Education at the university had always been free, and the strikers claimed that the move to charge tuition was part of a larger project to begin privatizing education.

In Mexico, economic reforms demanded by the International Monetary Fund have focused on ending government subsidies for public services, especially those benefiting the poor. Under that mandate, federal administrations have for many years proposed ending free education at the university level. "We should remember who has tried to impose economic reforms on the university for the last eighteen years," said opposition leader Martí Batres Guadarrama of the PRD.

In 1998, the government announced that it intended to begin charging what it called a symbolic tuition—800 pesos a semester (85 dollars). Students and university unions, who feared that the government would go on to implement layoffs and other cost-cutting measures, called the proposal an opening wedge. But even 800 pesos was hardly a symbolic amount for many Mexicans. According to Alejandro Álvarez Bejar, an economist at UNAM, a government survey of family income from the same period found that the average five-member family in Mexico had an income equivalent to four times the minimum wage, or about 5,000 to 6,000 pesos a month. That income was based on three of the five family members working full time. Millions of families earned less.

"This really means that families aren't making enough to live on," explained Álvarez Bejar. "It's normal now that young people, when they get married, still live with their parents, since they can't earn enough to live independently. This was the key argument during the UNAM strike, and the reason why it had so much support."

According to PRD senator and economist Rosalbina Garabito, the tuition proposal at UNAM was part of a larger picture. "Since 1982, the Mexican government has been enforcing an economic policy using high unemployment and falling wages to attract foreign investment," she said. "Mexican workers have lost seventy percent of their buying power in these years. For every 10 new jobs created, 6.7 have salaries below the level workers actually need to survive."

The federal government's action in using troops to reoccupy the campus and end the strike was motivated as much by the PRI campaign to hold onto the country's presidency as it was by concern over the fate of the institution and its students. The party hoped to use a law-and-order image to appeal for votes in more conservative areas outside the capital and other major cities. In the end, however, those hopes were dashed when Mexican voters went to the polls that July and instead elected a non-PRI alternative for the first time in the party's history.

Before the election, however, the federal government's move on the campus inspired more than a hundred thousand people to march through Mexico City, protesting the arrest of strikers. The strike and the march were dramatic evidence that the huge fissures that divide Mexico—into rich and poor, urban and rural, those who benefit from economic reforms and those who are its victims—have become deeper than ever.

In 1994, the ruling PRI campaigned successfully to elect Ernesto Zedillo president, in part by identifying the PRD and its presidential candidate, Cuauhtémoc Cárdenas, with the armed Zapatista rising in Chiapas. A vote for the PRI was portrayed as a vote for social stability, against armed conflict and social unrest. In 1999, Cárdenas was once again the PRD candidate, running against the PRI's Francisco Labastida. Labastida called the student arrests a justified response to growing social chaos, much as Zedillo had characterized the attempted suppression of the Zapatista uprising in 1994.

As further proof of the PRD's alleged flirtation with social disorder, Labastida pointed to the city government in the capital. Since 1997, the PRD has governed Mexico City, the world's largest urban center. The PRI, which lost the city to Cárdenas in the city's first mayoral election in history, subsequently launched daily attacks on the municipal administration for what it called social disintegration. It was a breathtaking attempt to blame the opposition for woes the government's own economic reforms had created.

A year after winning it, Cárdenas gave up the mayor's office to campaign for president, turning the position over to Rosario Robles, who became the highest-ranking female public official in Mexico. When the federal government moved to suppress the strike, Robles was ordered to use the city police to occupy the campus and arrest students. She refused, asserting that it would violate the Mexican Constitution. Cooperation in the arrests would also have been viewed as a political betrayal of the students. Instead, the PRI was forced to use a new federal strike force intended to combat drugs, as well as army troops in police uniforms.

The strike seemed to give the PRI the opportunity to show a firm hand in a situation it claimed the PRD was unable to resolve. And perhaps it did have one unintended consequence. Although worries about the PRD kept the vote for Cárdenas low in the July election in many states outside the capital, the PRI didn't benefit from this. Instead, voter anger over seventy years of corporatist lack of democracy swept the candidate of the conservative National Action Party, Vicente Fox, into office.

And in Mexico City, a PRD stronghold, the massive arrests backfired. People were shocked by the military and police occupation of the campus, which held reminders of the violent and bloody massacre of students in 1968. Mexico, like most Latin American countries, has a tradition of university autonomy, which prohibits the presence of government armed forces on the grounds of UNAM. Most important, the move cut short a process of dialogue that sought to end the strike without confrontation and promote a national discussion over the effects and direction of neoliberal economic reforms.

Despite media allegations, the strike was not a conspiracy directed by the PRD. In fact, relations between party members and student leaders were often very difficult, even though many strike participants were sons and daughters of PRD members. The arrests united what had become a very divided opposition. "While there were many disagreements on strike strategy, the government's action brought everyone together," said then-PRD senator Jesús Martín del Campo. "No matter how we felt about other questions, we all agreed that arresting the students and occupying the campus was wrong." The most popular chant in the huge march was *"¡Ni un vota más para el PRI!"* (Not one more vote for the PRI!).

Although the arrests and the campus occupation were the immediate issues bringing together city residents, the underlying reason for the outpouring of support was economic. Since 1994, the wealth of the top 10 percent of the population has grown, according to Álvarez, while that of the remaining 90 percent has decreased. The government estimates that 40 million people live in poverty, and 25 million of them in extreme poverty, almost all in the countryside. UNAM—the place where the elite educated its children—was also the one place in Mexican society where the children of the wealthy mixed with the children of the working and middle classes. Although, with 270,000 students, UNAM remains one of the largest and most respected educational institutions in Latin America, Mexico's wealthiest families are now in the process of abandoning its premier public university. Over the past decade, they have increasingly sent their children to private universities, which have grown rapidly. These students often go on to postgraduate work in the United States, a choice unavailable to those without the money to pay for it.

Free tuition and open access to education were guaranteed in the Mexican Constitution at the beginning of the twentieth century. But the guarantee represents part of the old philosophy in which all social classes had an equal stake in society and an equal voice in its administration. The reality may be that this philosophy has gone unimplemented in the decades since General Lázaro Cárdenas promoted it. Nevertheless, the guiding principle of economic reform is to claim that the market will take care of everything and that government intervention, at least in the interests of social justice, is unneeded and unwanted.

In the wake of the student strike, this reform philosophy has been more in question than ever. According to Garabito, "We need to restore the rule of law and establish a regime which will enforce it. We need to democratize the country, not just change political parties."

Cañon Buenavista, Maneadero, Baja California Norte, November 2002.
Florentina Sandoval, daughter of Julio Sandoval, and her baby. Julio
Sandoval has been imprisoned in Ensenada for leading the land invasion at Cañon Buenavista, seeking land on which to build housing for
indigenous Oaxacan farmworkers.

Cañon Buenavista, Maneadero, Baja California Norte, November 2002. A family at work taking the husks off tomatillos in Cañon Buenavista, a community of mostly indigenous Triqui and Mixtec farmworkers, created by land invasions. Contractors bring in trucks of tomatillos, taking over streets or empty lots, where many families gather to do this work.

San Quintin, Baja California Norte, July 2000. Indigenous Mixtec and Triqui migrant workers at an election rally for Celerino García. García was nominated by the PRD as its candidate for federal deputy, the first time a member of the indigenous migrant community had run for federal office in the state.

Monterrey, Nuevo Leon, August 2001. Martha Ojeda, director of the Coalition for Justice in the Maquiladoras.

Mexico City, September 1990. Valentin Campa, a left-wing founder of the Confederation of Mexican Workers, supported independent and democratic unionism for decades. He was imprisoned for many years for leading a strike of railroad workers against the government. This photograph was taken in the offices of the PRD, which he helped to organize.

Mexico City. March 1996. Members of Mexico City's bus drivers union, SUTAUR 100, hold a giant union meeting and rally in the city's main square, the Zócalo. The police later broke up the rally and forced the drivers out of the square.

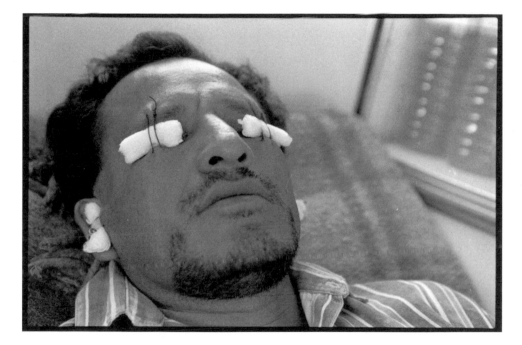

Mexico City, March 1996. Attorney Ventura Galván sewed his eyes and ears closed and spent weeks in the dark in an ambulance parked in downtown Mexico City, protesting the privatization of the Route 100 bus line in 1996. Outside the ambulance, the drivers union, SUTAUR 100, conducted a non-stop rally, twenty-four hours a day.

Cananea, Sonora, December 2001. This copper miner was still working after the Cananea mine was privatized and its new owner, Grupo Mexico, cut the number of miners drastically.

Arizona. December 2001. Chema Pacheco, an activist in Sección 65 of the Mexican miners union, was a leader of the Cananea strike against privatization and layoffs in 1998. He was blacklisted as a result and crossed the border to look for work in the United States. He found a job in a business that supplies catering trucks.

Omaha, Nebraska, May 2002. Tiberio Chávez and the organizing committee from the ConAgra beef plant hand out leaflets to workers going into the plant on the morning shift, just before voting begins. In the election held that day, workers voted in favor of the union, after a joint campaign by the United Food and Commercial Workers and the community-based organization Omaha Together One Community.

Torreon, Coahuila, November 2002. Soledad Aguilar, mother of one of the women who have either been murdered or have vanished in Juárez, marches with other mothers in Torreón, calling on Mexican authorities to investigate the cases. Most of the women murdered were young workers in the maquiladoras.

Torreón, Coahuila, November 2002. Fermina, whose daughter was murdered in Juárez.

9

TRANSPLANTED EXPECTATIONS

FROM LAND INVASION TO EMIGRATION

In 1975, when Tiberio Chávez was seventeen years old, he participated in a land invasion, just outside his hometown of Benito Juárez, Chihuahua. It was one of the formative experiences of his life.

Later, after he had spent many years as an immigrant worker in Nebraska, the land invasion still shaped his thinking. His concept of social justice, his ideas about the rights of working people, his expectations of what might be accomplished when people seek to assert those rights—all had their roots in the Almeida family hacienda, where the people took the land.

Transplanted expectations are a common thread running through the immigrant experience of millions of Mexicans and Central Americans living in the United States. People don't carry only dreams of a better life with them when they cross the border. Their culture, traditions, and forms of social organization accompany them as well, as they travel and create new communities in the north. These experiences in turn change the shape of social organization and protest in the United States.

Chávez's ideas about social justice began forming when he was a child. "My father died when I was nine years old," he remembers. His mother, a nurse, took care of the family as she moved from town to town, getting work in small local hospitals. Chihuahua in the early 1970s was in turmoil. The reforms that had redistributed much of the land in southern and central Mexico under President Lázaro Cárdenas were late in arriving in northern states closer to the U.S. border. Here, the settlement of people on the land created whole new communities. "This was the time when new towns were being formed," Chávez explains. "They needed people who could do the work my mother did, so opportunities presented themselves; and she moved with her family to these places, always looking out for our well-being."

In addition to land redistribution, the other major social change making an impression on Chihuahuan youth of that period was the emigration of thousands of residents to the United States—a development that affected every town and nearly every family. By the time he was a teenager, Chávez had serious questions about his own future and was already considering leaving for the United States. That was when the movement to take over the Almeida family estate of Pejuanez began.

"First, we held several meetings," he recalls, "mostly those people who still didn't have land after the first redistributions. Then one day, we formed a caravan and went out into the center of the Almeida estate and set up an encampment. We were there for six months—we slept there, we ate there, we didn't leave." The police came but did nothing. Since the land had been declared property of the state, under Mexican law of the time (before the Constitution was reformed in the 1990s), people with no land had the right to lay claim to it.

"We were never expelled, not one of us. We weren't afraid, because we knew that the land belonged to the people of Mexico, and we were the people." After they sent a delegation to the state capital to work out the formal titles, a redistribution took place. "All the people who didn't have land were given land to work. It gave us opportunity, our rights were respected, and it was one of the most beautiful impressions I have of my country. The land was for Mexicans who wanted to work it." As a result of his participation, the Chávez family received a few hectares.

"That event showed me that a group of people with a single goal could achieve what they wanted," Chávez concludes. "This was something that stayed with me—the idea that with unity, things are much easier, things that an individual could never do alone. That's when I understood that social justice often had to be enforced by people's action. Otherwise, our rights would just stay on paper. Many politicians and others like it to remain that way—on paper, looking good. It is up to us to put it into practice."

But dreams of social justice couldn't put food on the table. And the land the Chávez family received because of Tiberio's participation in the occupation wasn't enough to provide a future. "My brothers had land, and they worked it. But the economic situation was so bad in Mexico that everyone began abandoning their land. Plus, I could see that what we got wasn't enough for everyone. I couldn't see how I would be able to successfully provide for my own family in the future with these means. This pushed me to leave and to look for another place where I could find a future."

The place he found was south Omaha, Nebraska, in the community of workers in the meatpacking plants of the Midwest.

Chávez came to Omaha long before NAFTA was first proposed, just as millions of Mexicans have been crossing the border into the United States for more than 150 years. After all, the border north of Chihuahua, Sonora, and Baja California didn't even exist until 1848, when the United States seized the land that now makes up most of the country's western states. As many Mexicans and Chicanos point out, "We didn't cross the border—the border crossed us." And migration to the United States has been a fact of life for over a century.

Nevertheless, there's no doubt that economic reforms in Mexico have created enormous new pressures on people to emigrate to the north, and millions have done so. NAFTA was sold in part on the promise that it would ease those pressures and slow the flow. In the months leading up to its passage, Mexican president Salinas toured U.S. cities, cautioning that if the treaty was not approved, a flood of Mexicans would be forced to travel north. Only NAFTA, he assured his audiences, could create jobs and lift wages in Mexico and thereby ease the pressure on people to leave.

NAFTA didn't create jobs, however—quite the contrary. And instead of raising wages, it contributed to a steep decline.

But the flow of people northward has had social consequences unanticipated by the treaty's framers. Like Tiberio Chávez, immigrants have brought their culture and expectations with them. And they are forming a powerful force aiding movements for social justice in the United States. In fact, the revitalization of a large section of the U.S. labor movement owes much to the militance of immigrants like Chávez and the progressive social ideas they've sought to make real in the communities to which they've come.

THE KILL FLOOR REBELLION

St. Agnes Church and its sister parish, Our Lady of Guadalupe, are the heart of south Omaha. Every Sunday, hundreds of packinghouse workers—Mexicans, Guatemalans, Salvadorans—dress up in their best clothes and stream through the doors of St. Agnes on Q Street for Spanish-language mass. Mothers call out to little girls in frilly dresses who run giggling through the aisles. Men take off wide-brimmed sombreros and talk to one another with the gravity of country people.

On the last Sunday in April of 2002, a sense of anticipation ran through the normal happy chaos. As mass began, Father Damian Zuerlein spoke to the subject on everyone's mind: the coming union election at the ConAgra beef plant.

Standing at the altar, he recognized the many ConAgra workers in the congregation before him and gave his homily. "We say, there's nothing new under the sun—some people have a great deal, while others have nothing," he intoned, comparing the immigrants of Omaha with the rejected Jews of the diaspora. "Our community knows the unequal treatment of the poor, and the time has come to make a decision."

He introduced the plant's union committee. "Speak about your struggle for justice," he urged them.

Olga Espinoza, who works on the kill floor, made her way to the head of the church. Describing the accidents she had seen in her eight years on the line, she announced, "We've made our decision, and we won't take one step backward. I want everyone to stand who's for the union." A couple dozen workers slowly rose from the pews.

Disappointed, she huddled at the back of the church with Sergio Sosa, the Guatemalan organizer for Omaha Together One Community.

At the end of the mass, Espinoza came forward again to give it another try, asking workers from the plant to come to the front of the church to get Father Damian's blessing. "Don't be afraid," she urged them. "This is our moment. No one's going to stop us this time."

Slowly, out of the first pews, men and women began shuffling toward the center aisle. In a ripple spreading to the back of the church, more people stood and moved down toward the front. After a few minutes, more than a hundred workers were on their feet, some with obvious trepidation visible in their faces, but all determined that their support for the union would be a secret no longer. From that moment, Espinoza later said, "we knew if we could stand up in the church on Sunday, we could do it in the plant on Monday."

And that's what happened. The following Wednesday, just two days before the voting was scheduled to begin, the company made its final big play. Supervisors in each of the main departments ordered workers to attend a mandatory meeting to listen to a ConAgra vice president tell them why voting for a union was a bad idea.

A year before, the same speech by the same man to many of the same workers had turned the tide for the company, and a large majority had voted against the union. But this time, when the kill floor workers walked into the room, the atmosphere changed. Almost before the vice president began speaking, workers were hooting and yelling.

As he wound up his plea to them, extolling the way ConAgra had lived up to its promises of a year ago, Espinoza stood up. Earlier, she and the other activists in her department had agreed on a list of three questions they'd ask, ones they were sure the company could never answer.

She walked to the front, where the managers sat on a platform above the workers, and told them she wanted to speak. They reluctantly agreed, but she demanded the microphone as well. "I want everyone to hear," Espinoza announced at the top of her voice, pushing her way to the mike. She fired off the first question. "If you're so concerned about us, why haven't you fixed the place where Tiberio fell and was hurt?" she asked. "Are you waiting for someone else to get hurt, too?"

At first, the managers just looked at one another, each waiting for someone else to speak. Then María Valentín, the human relations director, took the microphone. "She told us she couldn't answer the question right there," Espinoza recalled, "but that she'd give the answer to anyone who came by themselves to her office later on. No one liked that, and we began chanting, 'Now! Now!' Then they told us there wasn't any more time for questions and to go back to work. We just hooted them down."

That Friday, 251 people voted for the union, with 126 against. The union won, two to one.

Later, company officials credited the St. Agnes mass with turning the tide against them. They weren't far wrong. It was a deciding moment, when the workers' culture and religious faith created a sense of safety and security that couldn't easily be broken by the normal repertoire of anti-union tactics.

But the mass was also a visible symbol of something deeper—a long-term coalition between the union and a community-based organizing project, with a goal beyond organizing that one plant. The United Food and Commercial Workers (UFCW) and Omaha Together One Community (OTOC) had come together, with the goal of reorganizing the almost entirely nonunion meatpacking industry throughout the city. And their hope was that what works in Omaha may work elsewhere too, in the dozens of small Midwest one-plant packinghouse towns, where pigs and cows are killed and sliced up into what's for dinner in America.

The people who do that work—the people on whom the meatpacking industry has always relied—are immigrants. For a hundred years, through the 1960s and 1970s, a majority of meatpacking workers were European immigrants, of many nationalities. Waves of Mexicans also traveled up along the railroads, while African Americans, especially in the South, were also an important group.

Today, the complexion of the workforce has changed. Spanish is now the language heard on the floor of almost every plant. Most workers come from Mexico, with smaller numbers from Central America. Refugees from Bosnia, Vietnam, and even the Sudan are a growing presence in some areas, but the vast majority of meatpacking workers are Latinos. A huge demographic shift has taken place in the meatpacking workforce nationally, and small towns throughout the Midwest and the South suddenly have barrios and Mexican grocery stores, and their local radio stations play *norteño* and *banda* music.

For these workers, a yawning cultural divide often makes unions seem alien and inhospitable. Union organizing in the traditional style of passing out leaflets at the plant gate only tips off the company and provokes an anti-union campaign inside the plant, which terrorizes workers. The standard speeches about wages and benefits don't inspire people to risk their jobs or to defy deportation.

The language of organizing has changed, but the problems haven't.

Tiberio Chávez recalls being approached by a worker on the line a few years before the 2002 election. "He had a piece of metal from one of the machines in his eye, and [he] asked me to go with him to the nurse. Not speaking English, he didn't think he could explain what had happened. So they washed his eye out, and I assumed it was all taken care of.

"But an hour later, he came up to me again, and by then his eye was red and inflamed. I saw the piece of metal was still there. We went to the nurse again, and this time the foreman yelled at him, saying he was just a complainer, and told him to get back on the line. It was too much for me, and I got angry and yelled back. But that's what life on the line is like. They want you to work as fast as possible, there are lots of accidents, and no one cares about the price we pay."

Chávez himself was later injured in the ConAgra plant, as he worked trying to repair broken equipment. He fell from an unsafe position near the roof, and his forearm later had so many steel pins in it that he looked like the "Terminator." An open union supporter, he was fired over the injury. ConAgra representatives declined to discuss Chávez's case, calling it a private personnel matter.

"As Hispanics," he says, "we are always being accused of not belonging here in this country. But I believe that if we work and contribute to our community, we are entitled to the same rights. They have always viewed us here as the labor force. The only right they grant us is the right to come here and work—work and produce. Often, one Mexican can produce what would take two or three other men, and the only right we have is to receive a lower salary.

"This is one of the things that disturbs me and gives me strength to find a means of organizing ourselves. I know that we can change it. The day we organize and unite, we will force them to grant us the rights we are entitled to, because all human beings have rights. Then we will live in this world in more peace and with less hardship."

New Immigrants Reinvent Old Tactics

Meatpacking unions in Omaha go back more than a hundred years, and their uneasy relationship with immigrants and workers of color is almost as old. Rebuilding unionism here will require renewed progress in resolving this historical dilemma. The relationship between the UFCW and OTOC is one key to that progress.

The city's meatpacking industry was built at the beginning of the twentieth century by eastern Europeans from Bohemia, Poland, and Lithuania. Because they were Catholics, the church had a major role in their labor battles even then. During the big strike of 1921–1922, the priest of the Polish church in south Omaha spoke for the strikers. Their main organizer, John Blaha, ran meetings in Czech as well as in English. African American workers were already a significant presence in the meatpacking plants, and some were elected officers of local unions.

The high point in Omaha unionism was the organizing drives of the United Packinghouse Workers of America (UPWA), which succeeded in unionizing the four giant meatpackers of the day—Wilson, Swift,

Armour, and Cudahy—in the late 1930s and early 1940s. The UPWA, one of the most radical unions in the CIO, relied on a tradition of rank-and-file democracy, industrial unionism, and militant struggle against employers. Master contracts covering both pork and beef processors set a wage standard above that received by most manufacturing workers. The union also pioneered the push for automatic wage increases that rose with the cost of living.

The UPWA viewed unions as a social movement, fighting both for workers' demands in the factories and for community demands outside the plant. Locals organized anti-discrimination committees to address racism on the job and to challenge the color lines that barred African Americans from many bars and restaurants in south Omaha. In the cold war hysteria of the early 1950s, those efforts were often attacked as being part of a "Communist program" of race mixing.

The ideas behind social movement unionism were the object of pitched political battles between left-wingers and their conservative opponents. Eventually, the left lost influence as the UPWA merged first with its more conservative AFL rival, the Amalgamated Meat Cutters and Butcher Workmen, and then with the Retail Clerks, to form the modern United Food and Commercial Workers. But the tradition of social and labor militancy left a lasting imprint on the meatpacking unions—and it is a tradition that the UFCW/OTOC coalition hoped to revive.

In the 1980s and 1990s, however, the industry was completely restructured. Before 1980, animals were slaughtered in urban packing-houses. Quarters of meat were then shipped to markets where skilled butchers cut them into pieces for consumers. But new companies changed that system dramatically. After slaughter, animals are now cut apart on fast-moving disassembly lines, where an individual worker might cut out one bone from each carcass, hundreds of times a day. Boxes of meat sliced into consumer-size chunks are then shipped to market. The production speed demanded of workers in the plants has increased enormously, and injury rates have skyrocketed as workers repeat the same motions over and over.

The rising giants of the restructured industry built new plants outside the cities and began slashing costs by attacking unions. Strikes rocked the meatpacking industry, as workers sought to hold on to the hard-won master agreements. Strikes against Hormel in Austin, Minnesota; IBP in Dakota City, Nebraska; and John Morrell in Sioux City, Iowa, and Sioux Falls, South Dakota, were only a few among many long, intensely bitter conflicts. Although the union continues to represent 60 percent of the meatpacking workforce nationally, according to the UFCW, labor's power to set the wage standard has been eroded drastically.

In the first half of the 1980s, the UFCW granted concessions to many companies in an effort to hold onto contracts, and packers competed to see who could get the best deal. But many older union companies couldn't compete, and, in the race to lower standards, thirty plants closed between 1980 and 1982 alone. From the wreckage emerged a new group of meat monopolies—IBP (now part of Tyson Foods), ConAgra, Cargill, Farmland, and Smithfield—which today account for 80 percent of all the cattle slaughtered in the United States and 60 percent of all the hogs. In Omaha, the old monopolies have disappeared, and new nonunion plants—ConAgra, Greater Omaha Packing Company, Nebraska Beef, and QPI—have taken their places.

By 1999, meatpacking wages had fallen to a rate four dollars below the average manufacturing wage. According to Mark Nemitz of UFCW Local 440 at Farmland in nearby Denison, Iowa, "When we gave them the cut [losing a dollar and fifty-four cents an hour and lowering wages to nine dollars an hour] in 1982, the company had four plants. Now Farmland has three beef plants, eleven pork plants, and a catfish processing operation. There was a waiting list to get a job here when I started in 1981, and I waited six months," he adds. "For the last five years, there's been a labor shortage because of the low wages."

Carl Aristón, the lead organizer assigned to the Omaha campaign by the UFCW, says that things are changing and that in the past five years, "workers in the organized plants are getting decent contracts with rates close to where they should be." Nevertheless, the packers enjoyed twenty years of flat wages.

The availability of workers willing to work for those wages is an important benefit provided to U.S. employers by NAFTA and the accompanying economic reforms in Mexico, albeit one that is rarely acknowledged. While the transfer of production south to take advantage of an increasingly cheap labor force in Mexico is widely recognized, the economic conditions in Mexico that keep labor cheap also push workers north.

The privatization of Cananea's copper mine created new opportunities for corporate investment, while the subsequent slashing of wages and jobs made it necessary for many of the town's inhabitants to leave for the north. The cabal of maquiladora operators, official unions, and government authorities has effectively created very profitable investment opportunities all along the border. But their efforts have also created a huge pool of millions of people, just a few miles south of the border, who are barely able to survive economically.

NAFTA has helped corporate America to create a huge division of labor. Some industries, such as auto parts, electronics, and garment production, are able to relocate easily and have set up plants in Mexico, where they employ thousands of Mexicans. Other industries, such as hotels or meatpacking plants, which must stay closer to their market and customers, cannot move as easily. But they too have become employers of millions of Mexican workers (along with immigrants from many other countries). Without Mexican immigrant labor, agriculture and food processing in the United States would come to a quick halt. Office buildings would go uncleaned. Residential home construction in many areas would stop for lack of workers.

The list of industries dependent on immigrant labor is a long one. And this list applies to almost every industrialized country, not only the United States. Each developed country has relationships with other nations that send workers to it. And the conditions of economic inequality in the world, supported by NAFTA and neoliberal economic reforms, act as stimuli, uprooting people and setting them into motion.

The U.S. meatpacking industry has taken advantage of that inequality and that movement of people to keep profits high and to maintain those twenty years of flat wages in the plants.

As employers sought to fill the plants while holding down wages, the percentage of immigrant workers climbed. Meatpacking companies have sent recruiting teams to Los Angeles and other established immigrant communities. They have advertised on radio stations along the Mexican border and have even sent buses to pick up recruits as workers cross over. "They're bringing people from El Paso, Durango, Zacatecas, and Chihuahua," Roberto Ceja, a worker at Nebraska Beef's Omaha plant, commented in 1999. "The companies are sending people out everywhere offering jobs."

Nebraska Beef was one of the most active recruiters. As a result, the company eventually became the focus of an Immigration and Naturalization Service (INS) enforcement operation. In 2001, the U.S. Justice Department indicted five people, including the personnel manager, the personnel director, the production manager, and another upper-level manager, for recruiting workers in Texas and giving them false immigration documents. U.S. District Judge Richard Kopf dismissed the charges in April of 2002, however, basing his ruling on the strange logic that witnesses who might have testified in the company's defense had themselves been deported in an immigration raid at the plant on December 5, 2000.

On that day, INS agents showed up at the south Omaha factory and established themselves in the company lunchroom. Supervisors stopped the production line and began herding workers upstairs, where the agents were waiting. José Guzmán remembers a supervisor coming into a cooler where he was attempting to hide and pushing people out. " 'No one can go in,' he said. The people were all trying to hide, and he was sending them back to the stairs, calling out: 'Everybody upstairs to the lunchroom.' "

Guzmán narrowly escaped by finding a hiding place in a huge air-conditioning duct. "I didn't come down from ten in the morning until seven-thirty that night, after the people had been taken away and the plant was empty," he recalls. "There was constant noise, and during all that time I was thinking about my family and my wife, who had applied for legal residency. I knew if the *migra* got me, they would deport all of us, and her application would be rejected. I couldn't even get down to go to the bathroom."

In some departments, company managers helped workers escape, according to Jaime Arias. He and his friends hid in a cooler for half an hour among the animal carcasses. "Some people stayed in the cooler for five hours, without special clothes; and when they finally came out, they were almost dead from the cold."

When Arias saw others heading for the truck bay, he followed. "We went to the shipping department and got into a truck that was loaded with broken pallets. When the *migra* came to check, someone said there were just pallets on it, and they left." A trucker drove the rig to Lincoln, Nebraska. Guzmán says that secretaries and supervisors gave the workers rides back to their homes in Omaha that night.

"They said to come back to work the following day, that there wouldn't be any problem. But some were afraid to go back and were fired."

The INS raid picked up 212 workers, out of a total workforce of slightly less than 1,000. With fewer workers, the company then increased the workload of the remaining employees, Arias says. When four women asked for higher wages to compensate for the greater workload, they were terminated.

Nebraska Beef became one of the first targets for the UFCW/OTOC alliance's unionization attempts. The company reacted to organizing efforts among its workers with an extensive anti-union campaign. "One supervisor told me that if we had a union, the company wouldn't make enough money to keep all the workers," reports Juan José Robles, one of the union's main leaders in the plant. Robles describes threats of closing the plant and blacklisting, directed particularly against people without papers and seasonal workers, and promises of wage increases to those who voted against the union.

In an election held on August 16, 2001, the union lost by a vote of 452 to 345. The National Labor Board, however, found the company's tactics so outrageous that it invalidated the results.

After the campaign was over, Robles was fired. Although the union filed labor board charges over his termination, he acknowledges, "I feel impotent. They fired me very unfairly."

Telephone calls to Nebraska Beef asking for comment were not returned.

Faced with scorched-earth opposition to union organizing, and the close relationship between immigration issues and the workers' ability to successfully resist company pressure, activists soon realized that traditional union organizing techniques were not effective. That realization led to the development of OTOC's community-based approach. The Omaha organization is a project of the Industrial Areas Foundation (IAF), begun by well-known organizer Saul Alinsky in the late 1940s among meat-packing workers in Chicago's back-of-the-yards neighborhood.

As the demographic shift transformed the composition of the meat-packing workforce, Father Damian Zuerlein became the pastor at Our Lady of Guadalupe, on Twenty-Fifth Street in south Omaha, and later at St. Agnes. "I requested to come to Guadalupe because it was a poor parish," he explains. "And I asked myself, in this community, shouldn't it be possible to prevent some of people's suffering? The only way was to help people organize. Working alone leaves no lasting impact. Besides, we all acquire greater wisdom and courage when we put our faith into action, when we put ourselves on the line."

Zuerlein saw the demographic shift taking place in his own parish. When he arrived in 1990, the church held only one Spanish-language mass, and most Latino families who were members of the church had been living in Omaha for two or three generations. But by the end of the decade, according to Zuerlein, a study of Catholic congregations that included Omaha found that 63 percent of parishioners had been living in the United States for less than five years, and another 24 percent had been in the country less than ten years. Although the older generation was jealous of the new arrivals at first, the attitudes changed when the church began organizing in the plants. Many of the older workers had been loyal union members themselves in earlier years.

Zuerlein began organizing workers at Greater Omaha Packing Company in 1996. "We were able to get them together very quickly, because the conditions in the plant were so bad," he describes. "People weren't getting bathroom breaks and even urinated in their clothes on the line. The line speed was tremendous, and lots of workers showed symptoms of carpal tunnel syndrome. But management sent spies into our group, and after a meeting with the plant manager, everyone involved in the effort was fired. We concluded that we needed to root our organizing deeper in the plant and identify and train leaders willing to make a commitment."

The activity at Guadalupe and St. Agnes provoked a reaction by the meatpacking companies, who asked the local bishop to restrain Zuerlein. They stopped donating meat to church-sponsored events, and Greater Omaha and Nebraska Beef cut off communication entirely. But the bishop quietly backed up the organizing.

Zuerlein became a magnet for people who were seeking to use liberation theology in efforts to organize Latino meatpacking workers in Midwest communities. That group included Father Stan Kasun, who eventually established a new beachhead in Madison, a tiny meatpacking town three hours from Omaha; and Jamie Loberto, who had gravitated to the church after spending two years at a radical Catholic base community in Chile. And then, in 1998, Sergio Sosa walked into the rectory looking for a job.

For over a decade, Sosa had been part of the radical movement that organized poor Mayan peasants during Guatemala's genocidal war, a war that took the lives of more than two hundred thousand indigenous people. As a seminarian, he had learned to apply the popular education theories of Paolo Freire in rural communities not unlike the home communities of many of the Mexican immigrants who had found their way into the Omaha plants. When the Guatemalan civil war ended, poor health forced Sosa to leave the seminary and the country, and he eventually immigrated with his family to the Midwest. Sosa was hired by Father Zuerlein and Tom Holler, who had started OTOC.

"I believe my political philosophy was born from what I saw and heard," Sosa asserts, recalling his experiences in Guatemala. "My conscience came by seeing injustices every day—in the news, seeing dead, and dead, and more dead. All this begins to create something inside that enrages you and makes you want to do something."

In Omaha's meatpacking plants, Sosa encountered an immigrant Latino workforce consisting of both documented and undocumented workers, often in the same families, who all formed part of a broad network of relationships. The OTOC strategy called for using those networks to organize first outside the plant—setting up soccer leagues, for instance.

He began holding one-on-one meetings with workers, "to create relations with people, discover their interests, look for talents, identify leaders, and connect those leaders in order to begin to organize"—much as he had done in Guatemala. "I think a lot of Latin Americans do this. It is part of our culture. We are all aware of what happens in the community because we weave that network together. We know where the Salvadorans live, where the Guatemalans live, or the people from Chihuahua or Oaxaca. We know who people pay attention to, and where they go on Sunday after mass. We spend time together. But I think the art is to connect this whole cultural structure of social networks with African Americans, with Anglo-Saxons and others, in order to create power. Latinos can do many things, and this is our moment. But we can't do it alone."

But the fledgling OTOC committees Sosa helped to start were initially wiped out by Operation Vanguard, a huge INS immigration enforcement scheme. In 1999, INS agents examined the I-9 forms—the forms on which every worker in the United States must declare his or her citizenship or immigration status—in the personnel records of every meatpacking plant in Nebraska and winnowed out four thousand names of people they suspected were undocumented. When the INS called in the suspected workers to verify their status, more than three thousand people quit their jobs, a result the agency termed a great success.

Afterward, Sosa and OTOC had to begin again. "But Operation Vanguard did raise the profile of the conditions in the plants, and of immigration as an issue," according to Holler. Through community forums, OTOC and community leaders pressured public officials to call for improvements and finally convinced Governor Mike Johanns to support a workers' bill of rights that included the right to organize. "We got the governor to sign on because it basically just states the law, and he's a law-and-order guy," Holler says, "but it was like Roosevelt telling workers in the thirties that the government supported their right to join unions."

While fighting for the measure, OTOC developed its relationship with the UFCW, a process that started when they both opposed Operation Vanguard.

In the period after Operation Vanguard, the UFCW was changing. At the time of the INS action, the UFCW concentrated its criticism on the agency's failure to allow the union to represent workers caught up in the sweep. In other areas of the country, some regional officials still supported employer sanctions, mandated by the immigration law that makes it illegal for an undocumented worker to hold a job. But as the national debate on immigration developed, which ultimately led the AFL-CIO to reverse its position on immigration and call for the repeal of sanctions, the UFCW's position also became clearer. At the Los Angeles AFL-CIO convention, Joe Hansen, the UFCW secretary-treasurer, spoke in favor of repeal, as did leaders of other international unions. After the experience in Omaha, many UFCW officials believed that sanctions, far from protecting labor, had become a weapon preventing immigrant workers from exercising their labor rights.

NAFTA also had an impact. Instead of seeing Mexican workers simply as low-wage job competition, many unions had been inspired by the debate over the treaty to send delegations to the border. There, they had seen the reality of the poverty that forced many Mexicans to consider emigration to the north. It was clear to many union members that building walls on the border and telling immigrants to go home not only was unworkable but also was exacerbating sharp racial divisions among workers. And the workers being displaced by NAFTA were often among those most interested in organizing unions and defending labor rights once they arrived in the United States.

Despite these changes, Omaha workers didn't automatically support the union. The OTOC committee Sosa had reorganized held several meetings in which committee members listed more than 150 questions they wanted to ask union officials, about everything from their rights as prospective union members to wages in union plants to the union's record on defending grievances.

After reducing the list to a more manageable number, twenty-one workers met with a UFCW group that included the union's regional director and chief organizer, the head of the Omaha meatpacking local, and international officials. "They spent a long time going over the questions," Sosa reports, "and at the end, although there was an expectation they'd decide to affiliate on the spot, the committee said they wanted to talk about it further." When it met, members were divided over union affiliation. When the moment of decision came, seven workers voted against being part of the UFCW and left the committee. The rest joined.

The UFCW and OTOC then went on to organize committees of workers in each of the meatpacking plants. UFCW organizer Carl Aristón credits the committee at ConAgra with the May election victory. "Our committee was united and educated and active," he emphasizes.

The UFCW assigned four organizers to the campaign, and OTOC assigned two, including former meatpacking worker Marcela Cervantes. But unlike many current union campaigns, this one was not organizer driven. Aristón says that the committee itself did most of the work of convincing individuals to sign cards and encouraging them to be active, talking inside the plant and going with organizers on house calls.

"The mass [at St. Agnes] was the workers' idea," adds Zuerlein. "They needed a spiritual space where they wouldn't be afraid.... What we're doing has a long tradition. We're showing them [that] even if they lose their jobs, they're part of a broader community that will support them."

After each committee meeting, workers got together with UFCW organizer Marco Nuñez and wrote articles for a newsletter, "La Neta" (The truth). One ConAgra worker, Jorge Ramírez, turned out to be a gifted cartoonist. His most celebrated drawing featured a worker chasing a carcass down the production line in a little car, running over another worker in his haste to keep up, while the line's speed control moves from "Fast" to "Faster" to "Over the Top." Instead of handing it out at the gate, workers took "La Neta" inside the plant. After a supervisor trashed copies that were lying on a table in the lunchroom, committee members went to the human relations department to protest.

Organizer Carl Aristón is also a former meatpacking worker who lost his job trying to organize IBP's nonunion plant in Storm Lake, Iowa. When he looks at OTOC's contribution, he sees the church. "It adds to our credibility," he says, "and that connection makes us seem more familiar to workers." Aristón put his own ideas into the mix, making arrangements for Espinoza, Chávez, and other committee members to broadcast spot announcements for the union on Spanish-language radio.

Winning union recognition at one big plant, ConAgra, and at another smaller one, the Armour-Swift-Eckrich sausage plant, was not the end of the battle. ConAgra still had to be convinced to sign a contract. In a victory for the workers, Jim Herlihy, ConAgra vice president, said that the company would not appeal the election results. "We want a motivated and satisfied workforce," Herlihy explained. "Our position is that we recognize the workers' choice." Bargaining began, and some months later, a contract was signed.

Seventy-eight ConAgra plants were already under contract, "and the company doesn't look at unions as evil," Aristón reports. That attitude differentiates it from the majority of large U.S. corporations. Certainly, if the union wins recognition at Nebraska Beef, getting a contract there may require direct action by the workers.

But beyond immediate contract problems, two larger dilemmas are apparent. As more of the Omaha plants are organized, hundreds of new Latino members will pour into UFCW Local 271. Because of the past closures of Omaha's older plants, the union had fewer than a thousand members before the ConAgra contract was signed, most of whom were not immigrants and did not speak Spanish. Its new members, almost all Latinos, joined as a result of a hard-fought campaign in which they were accustomed to making most of the important decisions. They are not likely to be content simply paying union dues as passive members.

Other unions that have made alliances with Latino workers to reorganize their industries, such as the janitors union in Los Angeles, have had problems changing internally to accommodate the desire of those same workers to make decisions and run their new organization. "These immigrant workers are going to be a challenge for the union here," Zuerlein predicts. Ariston responds that the UFCW international office is sending teams of researchers and trainers to strengthen the local's ability to win organizing drives and to establish a strong shop steward structure to defend workers on the factory floor.

Organizing drives generally raise the expectations of workers, who join unions hoping to see significant increases in their standard of living and better conditions on the production line. In meatpacking, those expectations run headlong into the industry policy of relying on immigrants to provide cheap labor. At the Omaha ConAgra plant, the starting wage was $9.20 an hour at the time of the election, not much higher than the average meatpacking wage twenty years earlier.

"It's at least partly true that wages have been flat," Ariston concedes. "Because many of these workers have had to live with a lot less, the companies believe they'll be satisfied with less. So we have to change the way the union organizes. We need bilingual organizers to communicate. We need to deal with immigration issues—workers' biggest fear. We need to respect their religious culture."

It is both an opportunity and a challenge. Clearly, if the UFCW doesn't mount a major drive for better wages and conditions, alliances such as the one with OTOC won't be enough to win the loyalty of this new workforce. But the workers' expectations, combined with new methods of organizing and raising political consciousness, can fuel a major challenge to the low-wage economy of meatpacking.

The UPWA in its heyday depended heavily on the grassroots activism of a politically educated rank and file, when it won master agreements and organized virtually the entire industry. That history may be coming to life again in Omaha.

But this time, there is an additional factor. While the meatpacking industry has historically relied on immigrants, the wave of new arrivals who have taken their places on the production lines in the past two decades have often brought strong cultural expectations about their rights as workers as well as cooperative traditions that help them organize to enforce these rights. Ironically, NAFTA, by pushing more and more people north, has created better conditions for reorganizing strong unions in the meatpacking industry than has been the case for many years.

GOING BACK HOME

The power won by Mexican and Central American immigrants as they organize unions and build a political base in the United States has profound effects on their social status and their ability to influence the policies that affect their lives. The dream of social equality and economic justice is motivating millions of people to become citizens, get organized, and participate in the political process. That transformation is already creating pressure for significant social change in all parts of the United States—and will produce even more in the years to come.

Although it was certainly not their intention, the authors of NAFTA and the free market economic reforms helped to make that transformation possible. The displacement of people and their subsequent migration, which NAFTA set into motion, have already altered California electoral politics—and other states aren't far behind.

But no one really forgets the communities from which they've come. In fact, immigration produces a new network of connections in which people themselves become the link between their new communities and the old. This human connection is more than just a yearly trip home to visit family and spend the holidays, more than nostalgia for a simpler, less competitive, and less exploitative way of life. For people like Tiberio Chávez, this connection is also one of ideas, as they seek to apply the political ideals and ways of organizing from their hometowns to the new communities they create in the United States.

The ideas of social justice that are transforming unions and politics in U.S. communities are also alive in Mexico itself. Mexican immigrants who are living in the United States are in turn significantly affecting

Mexican culture and society. The cross-border movement of people adds a new dimension to concepts of social justice. In some ways, however, this is not new; the story of immigrants returning home to participate in Mexican social struggles is as old as the border itself.

Joaquín Murrieta organized Sonoran miners on both sides of the border to defend their rights, even as the Treaty of Guadalupe-Hidalgo in 1848 put that border in place. In East Los Angeles and St. Louis, the Flores Magón brothers planned the early battles that presaged the Mexican Revolution. Mexicans in Arizona copper mines not only were the backbone of unions among hardrock miners for a century but also came to the aid of their families during strikes in the copper mines south of the border. During a 1961 strike in Cananea, for instance, Maclovio Barrajas, a Mexico-born leader of the U.S.-based Mine, Mill and Smelter Workers, led a delegation that brought food, money, and other aid to the Mexican strikers. A year later, Cananea miners responded when the U.S. union went on strike.

In 1994, Tony Castillo became a participant in this historical movement when he returned to Mexico to serve as an observer in the national elections. Castillo is a son of the Tijuana barrios, from the world of the border. As a young man, he crossed over and started a new life, mowing grass on the manicured golf courses of southern California. He went on to acquire the hardness of an industrial laborer in the factories of Riverside before his own plant shut its gates, as most California foundries did in the 1980s.

In the process, he became a union man. He crisscrossed the state, organizing help for workers who had been forced onto the street by plant closures and layoffs. He set up chapters of the AFL-CIO's constituency group for Latino unionists, the Labor Council for Latino Advancement.

Castillo is a big man, a smelter worker. Years after leaving the line, his body still holds the memory of the foundry in its breadth and heaviness. His hand is large enough to swallow up the hand of almost anyone who shakes it. A black mustache droops around the corners of his mouth, and straight black hair frames his eyes. He speaks directly, like a worker on the shop floor.

Tony Castillo was born in the central Mexican state of Michoacán. During the 1970s and 1980s, many thousands of Mexicans left Michoacán for the United States, streaming into California's foundries, fields, garment shops, and restaurants. Michoacanos became strikers and union militants, artists and community leaders. For these exiles, it was bitter irony to give up homes in some of Mexico's most beautiful countryside for the difficult lives and conditions they found on the northern side of the border.

Mexican political affairs have often swirled around Michoacán and its most prominent political dynasty, the Cárdenas family. General Lázaro Cárdenas was Mexico's well-loved president in the late 1930s, implementing the land reforms promised by the Mexican Revolution as well as wresting the Mexican oil industry from U.S. owners and nationalizing it. The general's son, Cuauhtémoc Cárdenas, once governor of Michoacán, left the ruling PRI in 1988 to run for president. Cárdenas later became the leader of Mexico's left opposition party, the PRD; and in 2000, his son was elected governor of Michoacán on the PRD ticket.

In 1994, when Tony Castillo returned to Mexico as an observer during the national elections, Cuauhtémoc Cárdenas was a presidential candidate for the second time. Despite his official status, Castillo wasn't neutral; he went home to help Cárdenas. Castillo believed that a PRD victory would make it easier for Mexico's workers to save their jobs and standard of living from the growing wave of neoliberal reform. Just seven months before the election, NAFTA had gone into effect, the peso had been devalued (drastically cutting the income of most Mexicans), hundreds of thousands of people had lost their jobs, and the Zapatista rebellion had begun. "How could I stay at home," Castillo asked, "knowing how hard my people were fighting?"

Toward the end of the electioneering, Castillo traveled to the city of Tapachula for the closing rally of Cárdenas's presidential campaign. The Mexican countryside was draped in the image of PRI presidential candidate Ernesto Zedillo—wall after wall whitewashed and covered in enormous green and red letters spelling out the slogan "Vote for peace—

PRI." Tapachula is the largest city in Chiapas, and the armed rebellion of the Zapatistas was still a reality in the mountains that rise on the city's outskirts. The PRI's message was unmistakable: a vote for Cárdenas was a vote for violence and social chaos.

The day Castillo arrived in Tapachula, the PRI held its last election rally. On the way into town, the taxi driver explained that his union, part of the solidly pro-PRI labor federation, the CTM, had promised the drivers permits for their own cabs if the PRI won. People were being bused into Tapachula's main square to provide the appearance of mass support for PRI candidates. The *acarriados*—the people bused in—were given a sandwich and some spending money and told that they'd lose their jobs if they didn't attend.

The following day, Castillo recounted his family's history as he ate breakfast at a café on the edge of Tapachula's town plaza, where brilliant morning light bounced off the gray and white stonework of the pavement. As he began to talk, a sound truck filled with Cardenistas started announcing their evening rally: "Don't let Robledo Rincón make Chiapas a place of terror, hunger, corruption, and death! Come hear General Cárdenas's son! Chiapas belongs to all of us. We will take it back!"

Around the sound truck, campaign workers began passing out leaflets with a florid appeal by Irma Serrano, an aging popular singer known as La Tigressa, who had been nominated by the PRD as its candidate for senator. Her burning eyes and heavily painted eyebrows are so well known all over Mexico that the leaflet used a drawing of them as her signature, not even bothering to print her name. Meanwhile, teenage soldiers passed by in trucks, staring nervously. Beneath their helmets and camouflage, they had the same dark, indigenous features as the Cardenistas.

The Death of Antonio Castillo

Tony Castillo's family history is bound up with the violent upheaval of Michoacán's land reform. "And it's the history of my family that brought me here," he began.

His grandfather was an *agrarista*, a militant who held to the original revolutionary promise of agrarian reform. It was the Zapatista ideal of expropriating land from the few who had it all and redistributing it to landless farmers that mobilized millions of Mexicans for the revolutionary decade of war and struggle. *"La tierra es de los que la trabaja,"* said Emiliano Zapata—the land belongs to those who work it.

Castillo's grandfather, the original Antonio Castillo for whom he was named, was dedicated to that ideal and was old enough to have participated in the bloody struggle it took to achieve it. He lived on the Hacienda de la Magdalena, owned by a Michoacán landlord, only fifteen kilometers from the town of Jiquilpán, the hometown of General Lázaro Cárdenas.

After the revolution, Antonio Castillo became the chief of police in his *municipio,* or county. In the 1930s and 1940s, this position gave him tremendous authority. "When my grandfather and his community knew someone had committed a serious crime," Castillo explained, "they didn't have a complex legal system to follow. The chief of police took the man and shot him. Antonio was a hard man in hard times. That was the way our country was."

Lázaro Cárdenas had a soft spot in his heart for his home state. He returned often and chose it as the place to begin agrarian reform. He urged Michoacanos to seek justice against landowners who, twenty years after the revolution, still lived like feudal lords. "The people of my village were taught never to look the *patrón* [the hacienda owner] in the face," Castillo said. "If they had to go with him to the village, they walked ten paces behind. If a man and a woman got married, the *patrón* had the right to spend the first night with the bride. So my grandfather began speaking to the people. He told them—'The *patrón* is a man just like we are.'"

By 1939, the expropriation of large landholdings had reached the proportions of a civil war in rural Mexican villages. Antonio Castillo led the people of Hacienda de la Magdalena in a revolt against the Cayetano Velázquez family. The landless farmers rose up and killed their *patrón,* and then they divided the land.

"My other grandfather, who also came from the same village, didn't go with Antonio, so he got no land," Castillo explained. "He worked his whole life on the land of others. The *agraristas* said only those who participated in the struggle could participate in the redistribution."

But Antonio Castillo didn't enjoy his land for long. Three years later, the foreman for the Cayetano Velázquez family, who had lost everything when the *patrón* was killed, formed a gang to seek revenge. He and his men ambushed Antonio Castillo. They found him on the street, cornered him, and shot him dead. "They say there was a bullet in every part of his body," Castillo recounted. "The foreman went up to Antonio as he lay on the ground and emptied the clip of his forty-five into his face. Then they took back Antonio's land."

Antonio Castillo believed that the revolution would fulfill its promise to redistribute land because this most fundamental right, won by Mexico's poor during the revolution, had been enshrined in the Mexican Constitution, as Article 27. In implementing it, Cárdenas had set up a system in which redistributed land was held by the families to whom it was given, grouped into *ejidos*. The land itself could be handed down from generation to generation, but it couldn't be sold. That important protection meant that rich landholders couldn't repurchase their lost land from poor rural communities and concentrate it in their hands once again.

In 1993, however, the Mexican government cut out the heart of Article 27, allowing *ejido* families to own land as individuals and also to buy and sell it. Prohibitions against foreigners owning land were also weakened.

It's no coincidence that this loss was cited by the Zapatistas as a primary reason for the Chiapas uprising. The Zapatista rebellion of poor farmers and indigenous communities has never threatened the government in a military sense, but it has threatened its historical legitimacy. The rebels called into question the government's assertion that all Mexicans would be well served by gutting Article 27, along with similar economic reforms.

"They don't care that we have nothing, absolutely nothing, not even a roof over our heads, no land, no health care, no food, no education," the Zapatistas declared in a proclamation as they announced the start of the rebellion on January 1, 1994, the day they took up arms. "Nor are we able to freely and democratically elect our representatives. Nor is there independence from foreigners. Nor is there peace and justice for ourselves and our children."

For the PRI's main opponent in that year's election, Cuauhtémoc Cárdenas, the Zapatista rebellion provided an opportunity to underline his continuing criticism of government policy, which he had been raising since his first campaign against Carlos Salinas de Gortari in 1988. Cárdenas accused the government of "violating rights won with blood, like the right of farmers and their communities guaranteed under Article 27."

From Tlatelolco to Atizapán

After attending the PRD's Tapachula rally, Tony Castillo went to Mexico City to witness election day itself with members of one of Mexico's oldest and most democratic unions, the Mexican Electrical Workers (SME). Members of this union run the electric power grid for central Mexico, including Mexico City.

In 1993, a revolt in the SME removed its president, Jorge Sánchez, who was accused of being too friendly with President Salinas and not opposing the economic reforms strongly enough. Pedro Casillas, the new SME president, was conspicuously silent when he was asked to support Salinas's hand-picked successor, Ernesto Zedillo, the PRI's 1994 presidential candidate. Most union members believed that Casillas secretly supported Cárdenas. Left-wingers in the SME then decided to run one of their own members for public office. They chose Humberto Plata, a union trustee, who became the PRD candidate for the Chamber of Deputies from Atizapán de Zaragoza, on the outskirts of Mexico City.

On the morning of election day, which by Mexican law is always a Sunday, Ignacio Plata, a retired electrical worker (and no relation to Humberto), picked up Tony Castillo in downtown Mexico City. Plata drove an old Jeep Cherokee. Before they could even get started, however, he had to change one bald flat tire for another, even older, one, right there in front of one of the city's swankiest hotels. As well-dressed businesspeople passed in and out the front door of the hotel, the doormen and the concierge rolled their eyes in embarrassment.

Plata seemed totally oblivious. Ignacio Plata is a veteran of Tlatelolco—and in Mexican politics, that counts for a lot. It makes one a veteran of the social movement, in the same sense that Antonio Castillo was in his day. In 1968, the year of the Mexico City Olympics, Mexican students had tried to use the worldwide media attention the Games attracted to highlight their call for political and social reform. That autumn, after months of student strikes and protests, they held a big rally in the Plaza of Three Cultures, Tlatelolco, not far from downtown. Government troops surrounded the plaza, and as the rally got under way, they opened fire. Hundreds of people were killed, and many more wounded. To this day, the government has provided no complete accounting of all those who perished.

Tlatelolco was a watershed event in Mexico. It became a name written in blood. It wasn't until 2002, under the first non-PRI president since the revolution, that the government finally agreed to begin investigating the "dirty war" against the country's leftists, which followed the massacre. And it still took a lawsuit by several leaders of the student protests, including Raúl Álvarez Garin and Jesús Martín del Campo, to force the investigation to begin and finally name those officials who had ordered the troops to fire. Luis Echeverría, secretary of the interior at the time and later president, became known as the "Butcher of Tlatelolco." He has been forced to give statements to the court and is accused of being the author of the killings.

When the firing began that day, Ignacio Plata was moving toward the microphone, to speak on behalf of his union. As the troops moved into the plaza, he was arrested and held in jail for weeks. Although he was released at one point, he was soon rearrested and charged, as he put it, "with everything in the book—subversion, inciting to riot—the works." Along with other figures from the political opposition, he was convicted and spent the next year and a half in prison.

His union stuck by him. When he came out, he went back to work for the Mexican Power and Light Company. He bought a house in Atizapán, in those years when workers could still afford them, and raised a family. "I could never buy my house now," he said. "Just making the payment would take more than a worker's whole salary."

It took almost an hour for Castillo and Plata to reach the city's outskirts. There, Atizapán starts in an affluent area in the flatlands, where developers have built three golf courses and a private airport. As they drove up into the hills past housing projects and *poblaciones* (slums), the communities became poorer and poorer.

At first, they passed big apartment blocks—public housing built mainly for workers. "That's the heart of our strength," Plata explained. Hundreds of electrical workers live in the apartment complexes, where residents have organized barrio committees to fight for better social services. These "solidarity committees" are the base of the PRD's strength, although most of the committee members, even those who campaigned for Cárdenas, were still afraid to join the party itself.

Castillo and Plata then reached the top of the hills, where they visited polling places in Atizapán's poorest communities. Houses in these *poblaciones* are built with cinder blocks, wood, tarpaper, and whatever else people can find. The communities have been settled by *paracaidistas*, or parachuters—people who have nowhere to live and who invade vacant land and put up homes. The houses are built along impromptu dirt roads, many of which the Jeep couldn't travel, even with four-wheel drive. Most have no electricity, no water mains, and no sewers. Every municipal service must be fought for, and sometimes the fight takes years. The PRI had a lot of power here, because local officials could promise those services—provided, of course, that residents supported the right party.

"Lots of people here," Plata added, "get subsidized milk for their children and other commodities from government programs. They have to have a credential to qualify, which the government and the PRI give them. So most people are afraid that if they support us, the credential will be taken away."

As the afternoon ended, Castillo and Plata wound up on a desolate hilltop where a polling place had been set up in front of a large house.

Under plastic tarps on poles were three tables with three ballot boxes, each with clear plastic sides, a visible symbol of the transparency of the election process. While it was easy to see that no one was stuffing the boxes, it was also easy to see how many of the ballots inside were marked.

No observers from the opposition were present at the poll, but PRI officials were out in force, directing voters to the different tables, giving instructions on how to vote. Their observers, two for each table, wore new white caps and windbreakers. Behind the tables sat the officials of the polling place, supposedly neutral parties appointed by the Federal Election Institute, but in reality well-known PRI supporters.

When voting ended at dusk, the boxes were opened, the ballots were unfolded by the officials, and the count began. It was an agonizingly slow process, and as it crept forward, the wind began to pick up and dark clouds scudded across the sky. The ballots started to blow off the tables, and finally it began to rain. The tables were carried into the front room of the house, and the count continued. Then the electricity failed, and the lights went out. "Let the PRI go buy the candles, since they're the ones ahead," someone joked, and the onlookers laughed nervously. But candles appeared, and eventually the lights came back on.

In the end, the vote count in this polling place was very close to the national results, with Zedillo far ahead. The PRI's control of television coverage and patronage politics proved unstoppable.

Plata and Castillo walked back to the Jeep after the counting was over. In the rain, the road had turned to mud. Everywhere the dust of the afternoon had been transformed, and the wet earth was covered with a dark brown, viscous soup. Plata's bald tires spun as he gunned the engine, but the Jeep wouldn't move. Residents of the neighborhood came out and put cardboard under the wheels, creating a makeshift road up the slippery hill. In the growing darkness, a dozen people grouped themselves behind the Jeep to push, and slowly the Cherokee inched back up the slope on its cardboard path. Castillo, Plata, and the neighbors ended up covered in mud.

Driving back into Mexico City, Plata was not dismayed by the national election results coming over the Jeep's radio. He'd driven the

Atizapán hills for months campaigning for Humberto Plata, Cuauhtémoc Cárdenas, and the PRD, and he knew as well as anyone the
strength of the establishment forces.

"The PRI won this election," he conceded, "but it still has no legitimacy in the eyes of most Mexicans. Our poverty will continue, because
Zedillo has the same ideas as Salinas and his predecessors. Winning an
election doesn't mean [the PRI] can continue to govern Mexico, in the
face of all our problems."

Ignacio Plata's conclusion was prescient. Three years later, in July
1997, Cuauhtémoc Cárdenas was resoundingly elected Mexico City's
mayor. And in 2000, the PRI finally did lose the presidency, though not
to Cárdenas and the PRD.

A Foot in Both Countries

Unearthing the history of Mexico's hidden dead was as much a motivation for Tony Castillo's cross-border activity as it was for Ignacio Plata
and for those who filed the suit over Tlatelolco. That history hadn't
ended with the death of Antonio Castillo in Michoacán; it had contin
ued on into Castillo's own generation as well. The day after Zedillo proclaimed his victory, Castillo recounted the last chapter.

"Lázaro Cárdenas loved the people of Michoacán so much," he
explained, "that when he expropriated the land of Chinese farmers who
had settled in the Mexicali Valley [just south of California's Imperial
Valley], he went back to Michoacán and invited the people from the
land around Jiquilpan to settle there."

Hunger for land pushed many families out of the villages where they
had lived for generations, and the expropriation of the Chinese lands
produced a large community of Michoacán exiles, living right next to
the U.S. border. From there, it was not a large step to cross that border
to look for work.

"My mother's parents had no land. First my grandfather left to work
as a bracero in California. He never came back. Then my grandmother
went after him. For years, my mother and her brothers and sisters lived
with relatives in the village in Michoacán, until they became adults. But

finally my grandmother returned. She had married a man who had settled in the Mexicali Valley and had become a prosperous rancher. She
took us with her, back to the border." For Castillo's mother and father,
life seemed brighter in the north—and after the murder of Antonio
Castillo, it seemed safer as well. As a small boy, Tony Castillo found
himself living first in the Mexicali Valley and later in Tijuana.

The favorite of the family was the youngest of Tony Castillo's aunts
and uncles, Manuel, who became an outstanding university student in
Tijuana. Manuel was a student leader in the years following Tlatelolco,
when opposition to the government resulted in left-wing youths disappearing from campuses around the country. "Like others, Manuel also
criticized and asked questions," Castillo remembered. One night he was
seen drinking with a powerful man, who became the next PRI governor
of Baja California. The next morning, Manuel was found shot dead on
the road to Ensenada.

"My grandmother went to the police," Castillo continued. "She
begged them to find the person who killed my uncle. But it was like
arguing with a stone wall. His death was a hard blow, but not knowing
was even more bitter. The government always had a hard hand behind
the nice words—if you threatened them beyond a certain point, you
never came back."

Castillo tried to investigate the death himself, but he found out nothing. "Then, years later, in 1988, when Cárdenas announced that he was
running for president, I thought maybe if he was elected, things might
change. We might be able to open those files and learn the truth about
ourselves." Castillo's grandmother had always forbidden the family to
return to the village in Michoacán, fearing more vengeance from the
death of Antonio Castillo. But Tony went back anyway. Then, in 1994,
he decided to come and lend a hand again: "With Cárdenas running
again, how could I stay away?"

Castillo wasn't the only Mexican immigrant who returned to see what
change might come as a result of the election. He traveled with a group
of others, including Eliseo Medina, another immigrant who'd become a

California union leader. Medina, whose family had come from Zacate-cas when he was a boy, was recruited by César Chávez during the first strikes of the United Farm Workers. He eventually became a vice pres-ident of the Service Employees International Union.

"There's a saying in Mexico—'*Mexicanos son muy sufridos*,' Mexicans are very long-suffering. But there's a limit to everything," Medina said. "People are getting angrier and angrier, and their problems didn't just appear overnight. That isn't going to stop just because there was an election. If you don't respond to the problems, people look elsewhere for leadership."

Medina believed that the old PRI-affiliated unions he encountered would lose their legitimacy for the same reason. "I saw those unions playing an accommodating role with the government. The question for them is, who are they going to support—the government or their mem-bers? Some unions there are working to make that change, and we need to get to know them. Ultimately, the workers in Mexico have to orga-nize themselves, but we can help them."

A third unionist traveling with Castillo, Frank Martín del Campo, grew up in San Diego after his family emigrated from Jalisco. Martín del Campo, who works for San Francisco's city workers union, also con-cluded that Mexican immigrants in U.S. unions could become a base of support for Mexican labor and political opposition. "Given our ties to Mexico—of family, of travel—we have connections to both countries," he explained. "Our interest and understanding are sometimes clearer. The very fact that we're here [in the United States] is testimony that the Mexican economy can't sustain its people. This knowledge makes it clear to us that the opposition in Mexico acts in our interest, too. Instead of feeling sorry for poor Mexicans, we know what it is to be a poor Mexican."

Living in the United States, all three of these activists faced the real-ity of challenging union leadership that for many years viewed immi-grants as a threat. To win some degree of power, they had to fight and build a base among Latinos. "We didn't arrive at our positions in the trade union movement here by inheritance," Martín del Campo con-

cluded. "Now we have to decide if we can use that base to support people in Mexico. And we know our fate is inextricably tied to theirs."

Today in union meetings in many big U.S. cities, it's not that unusual,
especially in unions where Latinos make up a significant section of the
membership, to hear discussions of the Zapatistas, language discrimination in schools, or Mexican election politics, right along with organizing
drives and civil disobedience in defense of labor rights. One California
union organizer helped high school students walk out of classes to
protest Proposition 187, which targeted undocumented immigrants; the
protesting students met in his union hall. Throughout the early 1990s in
Los Angeles, the AFL-CIO maintained an association that helped immigrant workers apply for immigration amnesty. That led not only to new
union organizing drives but also eventually to a new political base for
labor and progressive candidates in one of the country's largest cities.

These signposts mark a sea change—a huge demographic shift
sweeping through U.S. workplaces and unions. It is clear that NAFTA
and the neoliberal reshaping of the relationship between the United
States and Mexico, by increasing the flow of people across the border,
are contributing new ideas and lending new strength to the struggle for
social justice on both sides of the border.

Carlos Muñoz, retired professor of Chicano studies at the University
of California at Berkeley, believes that the culture and experiences of
immigration give new potential to social movements. "Once discrimination and low wages rub off a lot of the romance of democracy and love
for America, people get forced into activity because of their situation,"
he says. "Many immigrants already have a heritage of participation in
movements of workers in the countries they come from. Plus many
Latino workers bring with them ideas that spread through Latin America in the wake of the Cuban revolution. Immigrants will change us
more than we'll change them."

10

THE WORLD OF THE BORDER HAS CHANGED

THE SECRET MEETING IN SAN DIEGO

In early September 2002, the Coalition for Justice in the Maquiladoras put out a call to border activists, urging them to try to rescue one of the few remaining complaints under the NAFTA labor side agreement— the case of the *jonkeados*, the "junked" workers at two border plants, Auto Trim and Custom Trim. Inside the cavernous San Diego Convention Center, the CJM had learned, the temporary Binational Working Group on Occupational Safety and Health was holding a secret discussion between U.S. and Mexican government officials, supposedly to find ways of protecting the safety and health of maquiladora workers.

But just as the Han Young workers had been excluded from the Tijuana seminar on the right to form independent unions, which "settled" their NAFTA case, the Auto Trim and Custom Trim workers were barred from the San Diego meeting that was allegedly attempting to resolve their complaint. In fact, the discussion inside the convention center was really about dumping their case, not about protecting their rights. Outside, health and safety activists put tape over their mouths to dramatize how the process had effectively silenced them. The workers who had originally filed the complaint were absent—they live in Matamoros, on the Mexican side of the border and two thousand miles from San Diego. For them, the location of the exclusive get-together was an even more effective barrier to participation than secrecy.

A year before, a report issued by the National Administrative Office concluded that Mexican health and safety laws had been extensively violated in the two Breed Technologies plants, Auto Trim in Matamoros and Custom Trim in Valle Hermosa. As Chapter Seven described, workers testified about these violations in December 2000 at the hearing that produced the report, risking their jobs and ensuring that they'd be blacklisted for years. Independent health and safety experts from both Mexico and the United States submitted massive documentation. Despite bitter experience, workers and supporters had hoped that, for the first time, monetary penalties would be imposed on Mexico for health and safety violations, as the side agreement allows.

In the end, however, the secret and exclusive San Diego meeting proved to be the only actual outcome of the NAO report. The meeting was "a charade and a disgrace," declared CJM director Martha Ojeda. "Instead of specific, effective action to improve conditions at Auto Trim and Custom Trim, and throughout the maquiladora industry along the border, the injured workers are promised 'chats' between government officials whose refusal to listen and to act was the exact basis of the complaint in the first place."

Environmental activists also participated in the protest outside the convention center. NAFTA's environmental side agreement, they explained, was just as ineffective and corrupt as the labor accord. As proof, they pointed to one of the worst cases of pollution on the border—and the failure of the agreement to provide any remedy.

Metales y Derivados is a battery recycling plant, now closed, sitting on the lip of Otay Mesa, just outside Tijuana. Standing outside the plant walls on the chemical-encrusted ground, it's possible to look over the mesa's edge and see people moving about in the workers' barrio of Chilpancingo below. There, six years earlier, the Border Region Workers' Support Committee (CAFOR) and the Citizens' Committee for the Restoration of Cañon del Padre had begun to document the growing number of children born with anencephaly. After the issue began to appear in the press, two of CAFOR's Mexican organizers, Eduardo Badillo and Aurora Pelayo, along with U.S. supporters, were prevented from making annual counts of the growing number of cases. But enough data had been accumulated, they believed, to point to Metales y Derivados as a possible source of pollution causing the horrific birth defects.

In 1998, the Environmental Health Coalition (EHC) in San Diego and the Citizens' Committee in Tijuana filed a case under NAFTA's environmental side agreement. They alleged that Mexican authorities had failed to enforce environmental laws against the plant's owner, the New Frontier Trading Corporation, located in San Diego. Staff working for the North American Commission for Environmental Cooperation investigated the complaint and reported their factual findings in February 2002. Their study documented the illegal storage of seven thousand tons of toxic waste and the presence of lead, arsenic, and heavy metals in the soil surrounding the closed plant. It mentioned a limited and inconclusive survey of lead contamination among Chilpancingo residents conducted by a team from the University of California at Irvine.

But the commission staff had no power to investigate the actual health conditions in the barrio. And Mexican health authorities never conducted a health survey in Chilpancingo, which could have created a record. None of these efforts would have been difficult. César Luna, the lawyer who headed EHC's border project at the time the case was filed, found one case of anencephaly himself and heard reports from residents of at least half a dozen others.

Nevertheless, just as in the labor cases, that was it—nothing further happened. "All we got was a report, and an incomplete one at that," said EHC policy advocate Connie García. Nothing changed. "NAFTA provides no cleanup plan or enforcement mechanism, and the community continues to be poisoned," she charged. "These two landmark cases argue convincingly that NAFTA fails to protect workers or the environment. Its terms should not be reproduced in the Free Trade Area of the Americas, which President Bush is currently negotiating." The move to hold a secret hearing surprised no one, and most border activists saw it for what it was: a last gasp of the NAFTA side agreement process, sputtering to a halt.

Those side agreements, heralded as protection for labor and environmental rights as the border was opened to the flow of capital and production, had already served their purpose long ago. In 1993, their promises of protection provided political cover for liberal Democrats who wanted to vote with Clinton and thus produced the slim margin of congressional votes needed to approve NAFTA. Making the process work, however, was another question entirely.

Tangible results from the many cases subsequently filed under the side agreements were virtually invisible to the workers affected, who provided testimony and evidence at great risk to themselves. Just months before the secret hearing on Auto Trim and Custom Trim, the United Electrical Workers had labeled the NAFTA labor side agreement "a farce," after the governments of the United States and Mexico agreed to settle the ITAPSA case with nothing more than a seminar on union rights.

The last complaint filed in the United States against Mexico, lodged on June 29, 2001, involved the Duro Bag election. A final complaint under the labor side agreement, one against the New York state workers' compensation system, was filed on October 24, 2001. In all, twenty-five complaints were filed from the time NAFTA took effect in 1994 through mid-2003. By 2002, the number of new complaints had slowed to a trickle, and finally to none at all.

Under Clinton, appointees to the NAO often tried to maintain at least an appearance of commitment to workers' rights. For some, such as administrative law judge Irasema Garza, secretary of the NAO, that commitment was more than appearance. Once George W. Bush became president, however, the U.S. administration no longer bothered with pretense. The unmistakable message from the top was that any effort to restrain trade and investment was politically wrongheaded. For their part, Vicente Fox's functionaries in Mexico exhibited the same basic hostility to the process that their predecessors had shown.

The problem with the side agreement process, however, isn't the attitude of the public officials responsible for administering it, although these officials often make it plain that even an appearance of fairness depends on the political will of the administration in power. Whether liberals or conservatives hold office, in Washington, Mexico City, or Toronto, they all are committed to so-called free trade. And enforcing labor rights and environmental protections runs counter to the purpose for which NAFTA was negotiated in the first place—creating conditions favorable to investment. The Bush administration is simply more open in its embrace of those conditions, seeing nothing wrong with making money from low wages and relaxed pollution controls.

FOR MEXICAN UNIONS, LABOR LAW BECOMES A BATTLEGROUND

Despite the impotence of the side agreements, the cross-border activism of the past decade has had a significant influence on the mainstream labor movements of both the United States and Mexico. In part, NAFTA itself provoked that process of change, by creating a political debate that became a school for workers and unions in each country, forcing each to learn more about the other.

According to Benedicto Martínez, general secretary of the FAT, "In the years since NAFTA first surfaced, we've learned how to get along with workers and unions in the U.S. and Canada, how to plan together. We have cultures that are very different, so it's been a very important apprenticeship. The fact of having made any progress at all in working together is itself an achievement. We've learned to act much more rapidly, because things move today at such a speed that we're still not prepared. There's been a process of understanding and a militant commitment to solidarity among certain unions. The Steelworkers in Canada and others are just beginning to understand that the struggle is very fast, and our response has to be just as fast. That understanding didn't exist five or six years ago."

Teofilo Reyes, an organizer with the Transnational Information Exchange, contends that "the main impact of the cross-border movement has been in the change in consciousness of workers, based on their own experience. But part of the problem has been how to maintain that level of consciousness." As an example, he points to the relationship between the United Auto Workers local in Minneapolis and the Ford workers at the Mexico City assembly plant in Cuauhtitlán. "They had contact over a long period of time," Reyes explains. "The union supported the Frente Democratica de Ford [the Ford Democratic Front] and contributed money and material support. And there are still workers in both places who remember this. But the leadership of the union changed, and the relationship became dormant."

With the proliferation of maquiladoras in Mexico, official government-affiliated unions also spread, through the process of signing protection contracts. A company that is considering locating a new factory on the border is often advised by the government itself, or by the maquiladora association, to seek out one of those unions and sign an agreement in order to ensure labor peace. For Mexican workers, this has become the pattern of unionism on the border.

Mexican labor organizations and groups of workers who are interested in forming real unions to fight the companies have been forced to break that pattern. Their only means for doing so has been creating strong organizations among workers at the grassroots, in the plants. One of the most important achievements of the cross-border movement—and in particular of the efforts supported by the Coalition for Justice in the Maquiladoras—has been its focus on workers themselves, according to María Estela Ríos González. Ríos joined the coalition's executive board in the early 1990s, as president of Mexico's National Association of Democratic Lawyers (ANAD), and today is the chief legal advisor to Andrés Manuel López Obrador, the mayor of Mexico City.

"These workers risked their liberty, and even their lives," she emphasizes. "Nevertheless, our achievements were limited by the repression they've faced. Their jobs are threatened, the legal process they have to follow is very long, and it's hard for workers to last it out. Once worker-activists are marked, it's hard for them to find other jobs where they can use their experience, so often that experience is lost."

Involving people in the plants has been an enormous challenge even to democratic organizations such as the FAT and requires them to pay much closer attention to building their base. "We need to improve our methods of organizing," Martínez explains, "and work in a much more professional way. Do things more punctually. Work in accord with the characteristics of particular groups of workers. In certain industries, the process of organizing happens in a certain way, while in others it's totally different. We have to prepare, long in advance, the international relationships that will enable us to survive attacks from the government and the *charros*. We know they'll call us 'Zapatistas' or whatever they think will scare people. But there has to be an absolute respect for the right of the workers to make the basic decisions about their campaigns."

Despite the bitter rupture in relations between the FAT and the Han Young workers, Martínez pays tribute to their ability to organize effectively from the bottom up. "From the beginning, they had characteristics that aren't very common," he says. "They were very committed *compañeros*, who easily understood things. Perhaps they were this way because of the kind of heavy work they did. They also had among them people with experience of social struggle in other places. Many came from central Mexico and had definite ideas about how a union should function. But not all groups of workers are like that. With others, it's a much slower process."

For Ríos González, some maquiladora organizing drives were unsuccessful in part because they made pursuit of the *registro*, the legal recognition granted by the government, their main goal. "All of a sudden, we had two enemies instead of one—the government as well as the company," she says. "When we fight for the *registro* right away, we also put off fighting for changes in conditions—the reason why people want a union in the first place." Ríos suggests more emphasis on using the workers' organization in the factory to pressure the companies to make immediate improvements, long before the organization has legal recognition and bargaining rights. She calls this approach a *sindicato de hecho*, the union in life. "In ANAD, we've always believed that rights are best defended by exercising them."

Organizing efforts among Mexican workers can be difficult because of the anger and cynicism they often feel about the official unions, an attitude developed over decades. But that anger is only part of the picture. Martínez points out that the Han Young workers were also influenced by progressive and democratic ideas. In fact, left-wing activists and politics have a long history in Mexican unions. Much of the country's working-class left was based in heavy industry—and was consequently decimated by plant closures and privatization over the past two decades. Nevertheless, the ideas those workers propagated still have a far more widespread legitimacy than similar left ideas have had in U.S. workplaces. Mexican workers still believe strongly that they are entitled to the right to strike without being threatened by strikebreaking, that the government is responsible for providing jobs and housing, and that workers' rights should take priority over property rights. Organizing campaigns based on the cultural heritage that includes those beliefs have been strengthened, raising workers' expectations, making them more militant, and encouraging their unity. Even in the United States, organizing efforts among Mexican and Central American workers, like the one in Omaha's ConAgra plant, gain strength from tapping these progressive ideas and traditions.

One area of Mexican political life in which maquiladora organizing campaigns and cross-border solidarity efforts have had an indisputable impact is the growing debate over labor law reform. On taking office, the Fox administration proposed changing Mexican labor law to acknowledge the de facto arrangements that now exist on the border. In essence, the maquiladora model of labor relations, seen in cities such as Tijuana, would become a new legal standard.

A decade of border organizing campaigns highlights the potential cost of those new proposals. At the same time, the debate has provoked unions and their allies to propose reforms of their own, to remedy the abuses workers have experienced. In September 2002, the National Union of Workers (UNT) formally introduced a series of proposals in the Mexican Chamber of Deputies. The key reforms include secret ballot elections and the publication of all existing contracts, reforms that have already been implemented by the PRD-controlled labor board in

Mexico City. The UNT proposes to end the *toma de nota* process, in which no internal union election or contract is legal unless it is recognized by the labor board—a requirement that makes it very difficult for reformers to win control of their existing unions or to negotiate better contracts if the government opposes them. Finally, the UNT would abolish the labor boards entirely, arguing that they've become hopelessly politicized, and replace them with a system of federal judges.

"We believe it's indispensable to democratize the world of work," says UNT general secretary Francisco Hernández Juárez, "because the workers have been kidnapped by their own unions. For ninety percent of them, their unions are just a pretense. They work under protection contracts and corrupt arrangements, which are never renegotiated. In our country, Mexicans can elect a new president, but the workers can't elect their own leaders." He notes that of the 110,000 contracts in Mexico City, only 5,000 are ever renegotiated; and of the 1 million contracts nationally, only 50,000 are the result of actual bargaining.

The old system is nowhere more entrenched than along the border, and the abuses committed in defending it are more extensive there than anywhere. The many struggles of border workers produced a public outcry great enough to convince one hundred deputies to support the UNT proposals. In this debate, information and knowledge have become weapons. "[The debate has] helped educate Mexican workers, too," Martínez says, although he acknowledges that "I've seen more published in the U.S. about struggles of workers in Mexico than I've seen here about struggles of workers in the U.S. Nevertheless, we have to write more and get intellectuals more involved in denunciations [of these abuses]." In the debate over labor law reform, the stories of the campaigns at Han Young and ITAPSA, for example, have had an impact far beyond the labor movement. "If you think about all the ink used by all the people who wanted to investigate and really get at the root of what happened, you can see a great investment. Everyone's learned a lot—intellectuals and workers alike."

In the process, the sort of nationalism that has been used as a cover for protecting investors and for violating workers' rights has also been challenged. That nationalism is invariably used by the old-line unions and maquiladora owners to attack independent unions, who are accused of helping to chase jobs back across the border into the United States. In response, progressive Mexican unions have had to fight to redefine what nationalism means, or should mean. They argue that the neoliberal development model itself is wrong. Their position not only defends the historic rights of Mexican workers but also provides a basis for a common understanding with U.S. unions that are willing to defend those rights.

"We don't want to live in a country that's attracting jobs from other countries like the U.S. and Canada using the competitive advantage of low wages, the lack of enforcement of labor laws, and even [the disregard of] ecological damage," says the UNT's Hernández Juárez. "These jobs are bound to be temporary anyway. They don't give us any permanent benefit, and eventually, when there's some unfavorable event, they move to countries where the labor is even cheaper.

"The majority of Mexicans—53 million people—are being plunged into poverty. We're heading toward 75 million [living in poverty] if we continue depending exclusively on producing for foreign markets, especially the United States, and if we ignore our domestic market. We won't accept turning into a maquiladora country that's attractive simply because of its cheap labor. Through our unions, we want to establish more complex and complete labor relations that permit us to be competitive in making more sophisticated products."

Democratic Mexican unions sometimes believe that U.S. unions are primarily interested in campaigns focused on particular companies, especially ones that have U.S. connections. There's less support, they complain, for the effort to prevent Mexican labor law from being gutted—even though weaker legal protections would ultimately encourage much more job flight from the United States.

Mexican unions have some specific proposals for what they'd like to see. "What we're looking for in our relations with unions in the U.S.," Hernández Juárez explains, "is a way to make our own organizing activity stronger. We want them to talk to U.S. companies where we're organizing and ask [the companies] not to sign protection contracts and to establish contacts with the UNT instead. We offer a responsible unionism, committed to the goals of the company, but with guarantees that the union can function freely and democratically. The problem is that when companies are considering locating here, the government puts them into contact with official unions, and they sign protection contracts."

The UNT also hopes that U.S. unions can use their influence to restrain the structural adjustment policies advocated by the World Bank and the International Monetary Fund. "We want U.S. unions to try harder to influence the attitude and positions the U.S. government brings into those institutions. The U.S. has a great influence over the economies of emerging countries, and it's almost always counterproductive."

During the Clinton administration, doors were sometimes open for labor influence over trade policies. AFL-CIO president John Sweeney took that message of respect for labor rights to the White House as well as to the annual meeting of world bankers in Davos, Switzerland. With George Bush in office, however, the influence of U.S. unions over trade policy is much weaker.

Stan Gacek, who heads Latin America programs for the AFL-CIO's Department of International Affairs, would like to see equal emphasis on common organizing campaigns and political efforts to stop neoliberal reforms. "I'm not going to say that one is more important than the other. We have to do both things—not one to the exclusion of the other," he asserts. "These efforts are mutually reinforcing. [Organizing] independent and effective unions in the maquiladoras, and obtaining real representation and good contracts, obviously helps campaigns for effective labor law reform. And genuine labor law reform would help organize effective and independent unions."

That this kind of exchange is taking place is a consequence of changes in AFL-CIO policy on trade and international relations and of the inroads made by the cross-border movement. The previous AFL-CIO administrations of George Meany and Lane Kirkland provided strong support to cold war foreign policy, including neoliberal austerity programs. In contrast, Gacek explains, "it's now fair to say that it's the AFL-CIO's policy to oppose the imposition of the neoliberal economic model." Instead of making anti-Communism the litmus test for relations between U.S. unions and those in other countries, solidarity has been redefined. "It's all about finding points of coincidence and common effort, and, as in any common partnership, there are differences of emphasis. Otherwise, we wouldn't have national labor movements with national concerns. But the point is to try to reconcile these interests and have as much international solidarity as possible."

In the winter of 2002, Fox put the privatization of electricity back on the Mexican political agenda, introducing legislation in the Chamber of Deputies to encourage foreign investors to build plants and generate power. Although the Mexican Electrical Workers (SME) had defeated a similar proposal under Zedillo, Fox's initiative had much greater support. Once again, he was proposing to legalize a situation that already existed on the ground—in this case, private, foreign-owned generating stations.

Opposition to privatization is one measure of the political change occurring in both Mexican and U.S. unions. Mexican labor is no longer a monolith dominated by the CTM and Fidel Velásquez, with only a few independents around the periphery. One reason for creating an alternative center, the UNT, was to mount a much more determined fight against such neoliberal proposals, instead of the ineffective bluster (and eventual surrender) that made Velásquez notorious. "We are absolutely against the privatization of electricity," Hernández Juárez announced. "In Mexico, privatization has been a fiasco, a great source of corruption, of a few people becoming very rich. We need to explore other paths that allow national enterprises to become modernized and more efficient, but not at the price of privatization." He promised that the UNT would mobilize its members to try to stop it.

U.S. unions stayed out of previous fights over privatization, especially around electrical generation, in part because the SME is still affiliated with the World Federation of Trade Unions. The WFTU was organized when the United Nations was founded, originally with CIO

participation. But during the cold war, almost all U.S. unions abandoned it for the rival AFL-dominated International Confederation of
Free Trade Unions. The ICFTU included anti-Communist unions,
especially those in developed industrial countries, while the WFTU
included the unions in socialist countries and left-wing unions in the
third world. The competition between the federations reflected the cold
war division of the world. In Mexico, however, that cold war barrier is
now beginning to dissolve. "There's more discussion with the SME,"
Gacek says, "on a de facto basis, although not on any grand scale. But a
number of WFTU affiliates are talking to us because they've gotten
over the cold war and so have we. There are broader and more important common objectives."

Cooperation is also easier because Mexican unions have changed the
way they look at alliances. The UNT has signed cooperation agreements with the Coalition for Justice in the Maquiladoras as well as with
the AFL-CIO and even some of its affiliates, such as the Communications Workers of America. Part of the intent of these agreements is to
strengthen the ability of independent Mexican unions to challenge the
stranglehold the official unions maintain over the maquiladoras. The
UNT signed its agreement with the CJM in the middle of the campaign
for an independent union at Duro Bag. The UNT commitment to that
campaign was unprecedented, although it was chiefly limited to using
the federation's political influence to lift the repression so that the independent union could survive. That aid highlighted one important
advantage the UNT possesses. Its largest affiliate is the one to which
Hernández Juárez himself belongs: the telephone workers union, which
has locals in every state and almost every town. The UNT's ability to
hold a forum on independent unionism in the border city of Reynosa in
the middle of the Duro Bag fight relied on the participation of those
telephone locals.

That campaign became an important symbol in the debate over labor
law reform that followed. It demonstrated that democratic unions in
Mexico are beginning to provide greater resources to border workers
who are challenging the political and economic establishment in the

northern portion of the country. But they still face a perception by the political class in Mexico City that the border region is a remote area, far from the centers where decisive changes in the country's direction are made. Ríos Gonzáles believes that "local struggles on the border have never been successful in becoming national causes."

But that situation is changing, in part because of the long-term commitment made by the FAT, which has expended more effort and money on border organizing than any other independent union in Mexico. The FAT is a relatively small federation, with fewer than a hundred thousand members. Its importance lies not only in its own actions but also in the extent to which it moves the rest of Mexico's independent labor movement. "It's very important that the UNT has begun to find ways to become involved in the struggles of workers on the border," Martínez says. "They need more than their own resources. Solidarity wasn't very common in the past, but it's becoming something they can count on more now. In some of our past fights, we got more support from unions in the U.S. than we did from unions in Mexico."

He is still somewhat skeptical about what he calls "grand statements" that don't lead to real expenditures of money and personnel. "The commitment and solidarity of national centers like the AFL-CIO and the UNT are very important," he cautions. "But if we don't have the people and movement consolidated on the ground, on the local level, the rest of it just becomes publicity—denunciations and accusations. That can be useful, but it doesn't substitute for a strong movement at the base. So the main task is to create a very strong group in which the workers participate."

CROSS-BORDER TIES AND THE COLD WAR

In the United States, the influence of the cross-border movement has been more complex but equally profound. In many ways, the increasing legitimacy of the grassroots solidarity popularized by the movement provided the key challenge to the old cold war consensus in the U.S. labor establishment.

The cross-border movement is a product of NAFTA. Although the Border Industrial Program sparked the construction of maquiladoras in the early 1960s, this development received little attention from U.S. unions at the time. Free trade policies, supported for years by AFL-CIO leaders, were not a source of great controversy either. The free trade agreement negotiated with Canada in the mid-1980s, which was devastating for Canadian workers and unions, caused hardly a whisper in U.S. union halls. But the proposal for negotiating a free trade agreement with Mexico, combined with an upsurge in activity in the border plants, provoked a debate whose reverberations are still felt among millions of U.S. workers.

For most unions, that debate started with a question based on self-interest: Were Mexican workers about to steal U.S. jobs? The xenophobic image provoked by Ross Perot's "giant sucking sound" scared many working-class voters who might otherwise have slept through the 1992 election. At first, they blamed George H. W. Bush for negotiating NAFTA and for his indifference to its potential effects on workers. But then Bill Clinton, elected with those working-class votes, signed the treaty, a year after criticizing it during his campaign. As a result, many working people reexamined their own understanding of politics and the world.

California unions were particularly incensed at Democrats who voted with Clinton. The head of the state labor federation, John Henning, helped to organize meetings for the incipient Labor Party as a forum to threaten Democrats with the loss of union votes in the future. "We stand in the halls," he complained, "requesting dialogue with legislators. We lobby. We are beggars at the table of wealth." Henning, who for years had been a critic of the cold war anti-Communism of the AFL-CIO national leaders, advocated a new philosophy for international labor relations, which he called global unionism—"the creation of a new international body to arbitrate between the unions of different countries, and keep multinational corporations from pitting workers against each other in the all-out pursuit of jobs."

"The fact that there was a debate at all, or that the public was edu-cated by it, was because the labor and environmental movements made it happen," according to Ignacio De La Fuente, a representative of the Glass, Molders and Plastics Workers Union and an Oakland city coun-cil member. Trade bills typically never make it past the business pages of the newspapers; NAFTA was a two-year front-page story.

Even Mexican unionists felt the ferment. Martínez traveled through-out the United States in the Free Trade Caravan organized by the Teamsters union and spoke in many meetings of the United Electrical Workers. He remembers that "NAFTA shocked a lot of U.S. unions out of their inertia—not so much their national leaders, but people in local unions. They're the ones who began pushing the structure to move on globalization, to form new international relations and look for solidar-ity. That's what moved their leaders to pay attention to the border. It was people in local unions that began building the bridges across the border to unions in Mexico. As more local unions got involved, this movement became broader and moved their national unions."

In the post-NAFTA era, many directed their anger at treaty support-ers, especially Democrats, who had claimed that the side agreements would make it possible to organize more effective unions south of the border and would therefore take care of the income differential between U.S. and Mexican workers. Even admitting that the income differential was an issue raised questions about the real conditions and labor rights of Mexican workers. Those questions were then brought into sharp focus by the battles waged in the years that followed at Plasticos Bajacal, Sony, Han Young, and other border plants.

The NAFTA debate forced millions of workers to try to understand the ways in which they were affected by the global operations of multi-national employers and by the gulf that separates the standard of living in the United States from that in countries such as Mexico. These work-ers didn't simply absorb knowledge passively. They talked about how the difference in wages affected both sides of the U.S./Mexico border. They visited congressional representatives (and in some cases picketed them). They debated the treaty's supporters in the media and traveled to

Mexico to see conditions for themselves. And over time, they responded to Ross Perot's "giant sucking sound" with calls for solidarity with Mexican workers, both those in Mexico and those who had come to the United States as immigrants. As Frank Martín del Campo, who led delegations to Mexico during the debate, concluded, "We have to take the logical next step, to develop much closer relations between workers internationally. It would be a big mistake to let things slide back to the status quo."

That "next step" was an important one. Appeals to the perceived self-interest of U.S. workers have always been dangerously double-edged arguments, capable of mobilizing people either for progressive ends or for racist and reactionary ones. Working-class mobs organized by the Union Labor Party, for instance, were whipped into hysteria in San Francisco in the 1870s by the slogan "The Chinese must go!" Politicians campaigned by exploiting white workers' fear of losing jobs to Chinese laborers. Many Chinese immigrants, originally brought to the United States as contract labor to build railroads and drain the San Joaquin River delta, were killed and their families burned out.

But the debate over immigration and Mexican labor throughout the 1990s, while it did produce California's racist Proposition 187, also led the AFL-CIO to change its position on immigration in 1999. The federation had earlier supported the Immigration Reform and Control Act of 1986, which made it illegal for undocumented workers to hold jobs and stipulated sanctions for employers who hired them. In a reversal, the AFL-CIO called for the repeal of sanctions and for an immigration amnesty allowing undocumented workers to obtain legal residency.

Immigration and the organization of Mexican workers on the border are issues that cannot be separated. Both require U.S. workers to make a basic choice: for solidarity across racial and national lines, or for maintaining racist and xenophobic exclusion. This choice has been debated over and over throughout the history of the U.S. labor movement. The cold war orientation of the Kirkland and Meany leadership of the AFL-CIO failed to build ties across the U.S./Mexico border that could defend workers on both sides against their governments and the corporations that sought to whipsaw them against each other. That same orientation, which perceived solidarity as part of the leftist ideology it opposed, also failed to defend the rights of Mexican immigrant workers in the United States. The view of Mexican workers as foreign aliens whose exclusion could be justified led to support for the Immigration Reform and Control Act, a move most unions later came to regret bitterly.

When the NAFTA debate provoked discussion about the relationship between workers in Mexico and the United States, many union members responded by supporting efforts to organize independent unions in the border plants. "It was a kind of school," Martínez recalls. "It was not so easy anymore for someone to say that Mexicans were stealing jobs. They could see there was a real problem at the root." The Coalition for Justice in the Maquiladoras, founded in the late 1980s, began growing rapidly. Many unions slowly awoke from a slumber in which they'd left international issues in the hands of the AFL-CIO's Department of International Affairs (DIA).

Throughout the cold war, this department was widely discredited for its ties to the ultra-right and to the intelligence community, ties that were exposed in the hearings chaired by Senator Frank Church in the mid-1970s. In the early cold war period, the AFL (and, after 1953, the AFL-CIO) directly channeled money from U.S. intelligence agencies to covert labor-based operations abroad. When that activity was exposed, the department set up institutes—on the surface, independent of the federation—through which money was disbursed and activity organized in support of U.S. foreign policy goals.

One such group was the American Institute for Free Labor Development (AIFLD), whose director, William Doherty, boasted of his role in helping topple the progressive government of João Goulart in Brazil in 1964. In 1973, he also helped bring down Chile's Salvador Allende, turning the country over to fascist dictator Augusto Pinochet, who murdered hundreds of union leaders and broke the back of Chile's labor movement. In the 1966 AIFLD annual report, Doherty declared that "the key question of our time is the future road of [the Latin American] revolution: toward Communist totalitarianism or toward democracy. For the American labor movement this is one of the paramount, pivotal issues; all other questions . . . must remain secondary."

Applying this logic, the Department of International Affairs attacked unions and political parties that opposed U.S. domination and that sought deeper social changes, labeling them "radical" and "Communist." That policy began coming under fire in the early 1980s, as U.S. counter-insurgency wars raged in El Salvador and Guatemala, and intervention sought to topple the revolutionary government of Nicaragua. At the 1983 AFL-CIO convention in Anaheim, California, the presidents of the Screen Actors Guild, the International Association of Machinists, the American Federation of Government Employees, and the Amalgamated Clothing and Textile Workers attacked the DIA for supporting Reagan-sponsored intervention in Central America while the administration broke the Professional Air Traffic Controllers Organization at home. This opposition from the top level of the federation reflected activity by thousands of rank-and-file union members and local leaders across the country.

Through that decade, as U.S. foreign investment led to the loss of jobs at home, the DIA policy became even more unpopular. The department discouraged rank-and-file involvement and treated international union relations as an area in which only Washington-based paid staff could be involved. Throughout the Central American solidarity movement, however, the challenge to these policies rose from below. When the first rank-and-file delegations to Mexico were organized in the late 1980s, the DIA perceived them as a challenge, not only because they were not based on the proper anti-Communist orientation but also because they consisted of ordinary union members and local leaders, acting on their own.

In contrast, rank-and-file involvement became a hallmark of the anti-NAFTA campaign. Labor opposition wasn't based in Washington, and it wasn't an army directed by distant generals. It grew fastest in work-places, local unions, and central labor councils. It was a coalition move-ment, in which factory workers found themselves rubbing shoulders with environmental activists for the first time. This new level of activity spread across the country, into every state, into every union.

Stan Gacek, who at the time was in charge of international affairs for the United Food and Commercial Workers, felt the strength of that push for a change in direction. "NAFTA was a great catalyzing element for changing cold war assumptions about how we prioritized relationships with unions in other countries," he recalls. "Obviously, it had a tremendous effect on how we related to the Mexican labor movement. Our affiliates in fact demanded that we have as much of a relationship with the independent labor movement in Mexico as with the official labor movement."

That was one of the key battles. Under the old cold war policy, the AFL-CIO recognized the CTM and the Labor Congress to which it belonged, both headed by Fidel Velásquez, as the only legitimate union federations in Mexico. They were called "free trade unions," a phrase that identified unions supported by the AFL-CIO because of their anti-Communist orientation and their willingness to support U.S. foreign policy. Because these were the unions with protection contracts in the maquiladoras, a close relationship with them precluded support for independent unions that challenged their privileged position. DIA policy became even further discredited when the CTM and the Labor Congress, along with the rest of Mexico's officially sanctioned unions, lined up behind President Carlos Salinas de Gortari and the PRI in support of NAFTA. Along with a number of independent unions, the only labor federation to oppose the treaty was the FAT.

"Certainly there had been rhetoric in the past," Gacek explains, "which said 'Work directly with the CTM, and only with the CTM, because they are our staunch allies, and because there are other elements of the Mexican labor movement which are subversive or Communist.' But that rhetoric really sounded extremely shallow, given where the official labor movement, in particular the CTM, was on NAFTA. The relationship with the CTM was very diplomatic and, as a result, not very profound. There was no program or any activity in terms of cross-border solidarity. We did not see a whole lot in the

AIFLD program in Mexico [that] was developing cross-border links in 1993."

Gacek credits change in that overall policy to the grassroots creation of new cross-border relationships. "Cross-border linkages contributed to consideration of alternative paths for international solidarity," he says. "There's no question that they had a great effect. Eventually, the AFL-CIO found there were other voices in the Mexican labor movement, including the FAT, which were against NAFTA, a fact recognized by a number of our affiliates. The rank-and-file level and local leadership were very concerned about the impact of NAFTA."

Relations between the CTM and the AFL-CIO grew so strained that Velásquez opposed a 1994 application by the U.S. federation to open an office in Mexico City, an unheard-of expression of hostility in what had previously been almost a marriage.

The push for a new international policy gained strength from the election of John Sweeney as AFL-CIO president at the federation's New York convention in 1995 and the subsequent establishment of his New Voice administration. Sweeney's campaign was the product of many unresolved problems and crises in the U.S. labor movement, not simply the result of NAFTA. Even international union presidents believed that Kirkland was ignoring the falling percentage of organized workers and was unwilling to mobilize unions to organize on a much larger scale. Their dissatisfaction was compounded when Republicans hostile to labor gained control of the U.S. Congress in 1996. Kirkland's leadership was further discredited when fierce corporate attacks on unions at the Staley, Caterpillar, and Bridgestone plants in Decatur, Illinois, and on striking miners at Pittston Coal in West Virginia had to be fought with very little federation support. Leaders of those struggles showed up at the 1995 New York convention to push for political change, and the head of the miners union, Rich Trumka, became Sweeney's running mate.

But one of the most telling criticisms of Kirkland, leveled even by top union officers usually silent on the issue, was that he was so preoccupied with fighting Communism in Poland that he ignored the struggles of

U.S. unions to survive at home. His critics further accused him of failing to organize effective opposition to NAFTA and of ignoring Mexico generally. Jorge Cuellar, from Mexico City's beleaguered bus union, SUTUAR 100, showed up at the convention and won support from Dolores Huerta of the United Farm Workers, Jaime Martínez of the International Union of Electrical Workers, and other Latino union leaders, to the discomfiture of AIFLD operatives.

On the floor of the convention, Henning challenged Tom Donahue, Kirkland's chosen successor. He pointed out that the real sources of U.S. job losses were the development of maquiladoras on the U.S./Mexico border and the free trade policies typified by what he called "the Democratic Party's NAFTA." Existing international union bodies supported by the AFL-CIO, he charged, were worthless.

Henning's comments so enraged Tom Donahue that when Henning's allotted time ran out, Donahue, holding the convention gavel, abruptly cut off his microphone. After an outcry forced Donahue to grant an additional thirty seconds, Henning boomed across the hall: "Tom, I just want to tell you that if you want to save this nation, and save your own soul, you'll get behind global unionism." Afterward, Henning expressed relief at Sweeney's election. "I think that as a result of the departure of Kirkland, we'll have a more progressive approach," he predicted. "We were associated with some of the very worst elements ... all in the name of anti-Communism. But I think there's an opportunity to review our foreign activities. The basic thing is that we should stop the cannibalism, the global competition for jobs among the trade unions of the world."

After Sweeney was elected, Trumka voiced the direction of the new policy for international relations, saying that he saw "an absolute need for a change in [AFL-CIO] foreign policy," which had been geared toward the cold war. "But the cold war has come and the cold war has gone," he declared. "It's over with. What we want is to be able to confront multinationals as multinationals ourselves. If a corporation does business in fifteen countries, we'd like to be able to confront them as labor in fifteen different countries. It's not that we need less international involvement. But international involvement should be focused toward building solidarity on both sides of the border . . . you're talking about helping workers achieve their needs and their goals back here at home."

Under the Sweeney administration, the direction of international relations did shift, although not always at the same speed and to the same degree in relation to all countries. The association of the AFL-CIO with major figures plotting an abortive 2002 coup against Venezuela's anti-imperialist president, Hugo Chávez, indicates that the change in direction is not at all complete. Even earlier, after the September 11, 2001, attacks in New York and Washington, the progressive movement in the AFL-CIO on foreign policy had begun to slow and fracture. Some union leaders spoke out against the war in Afghanistan, but most remained silent. The AFL-CIO leadership warned against rising anti-immigrant hysteria in the United States, but when fifty thousand airport baggage screeners were fired en masse in 2002, many of them immigrants, there was almost no protest. Then, as Bush began his drive toward war in Iraq, a number of international unions, labor councils, and union leaders came together as U.S. Labor Against the War (USLAW) to oppose it. The Sweeney administration at first condemned the flimsy pretexts used to justify the invasion as well as the domestic use of "national security" as a pretext for union-busting and a pro-corporate economic agenda. But once the war started, the federation fell in line to support the troops, with only a mild warning about the devastating economic implications of the war for U.S. workers.

In Mexico, opposition to the war in Iraq was almost universal—and extremely vocal. The UNT and the FAT participated in joint statements with the Communications Workers of America and other unions active in USLAW, opposing military intervention. But with further military adventures proposed by the Bush administration and increasing tension over national security at home, it seemed possible that the new international labor policy based on solidarity might become a battleground again.

Nevertheless, in relation to Mexico, the political change in direction in the AFL-CIO has been far-reaching and has developed deep roots and extensive relationships with Mexican unions. Independent unions in Mexico feel it. "The AFL-CIO now has a more pluralistic relation with Mexican unions," observes the FAT's Martínez. "It's not just exclusively with one group, the CTM . . . it now has relations with the UNT and everyone. I think they've realized that the Labor Congress isn't good for much of anything. Before Sweeney, the AFL-CIO saw the world in terms of the cold war. When the leadership changed, new people came in that we'd already identified in the trenches as more progressive."

Gacek was brought in to work at the DIA by Barbara Shailor, Sweeney's appointee to head the department. "When I came, in February of 1997," he says, "it was very clear that there was a great interest in Mexico because of the anti-NAFTA movement and cross-border campaigns. I didn't find the upsurge surprising—I could see it emerging and growing. The raising of consciousness about NAFTA, the putative end of the cold war, the greater interest among affiliates in Mexico as a result of NAFTA, the Sweeney administration and the new leadership coming in—all these elements were interacting causes for the AFL-CIO pushing an anti-neoliberal program more aggressively."

Gacek had developed a reputation as a progressive when he supported the Brazilian union federation, the Central Única dos Trabalhadores (CUT), at a time when Doherty and the AIFLD refused to speak to its leaders, calling them Communists. At the AFL-CIO, Gacek helped to establish a new policy in which the cold war barriers began to come down and discussions started with unions belonging to the WFTU. "One example would be the General Confederation of Peruvian Workers," he explains. "Whether you like it or not, it's the biggest of the labor centrals there. We also now talk very actively with the wing of the CUT in Chile which is more aligned with the Communist Party. That's very important in getting a consensus within the whole CUT [in order] to arrive at a common statement with the AFL-CIO on a future free trade agreement with Chile. All of the tendencies in the CUT have said that including enforceable labor rights within the body of any treaty is an indispensable precondition to any trade agreement."

This change would not have been possible if the cross-border movement, in response to NAFTA, had not pushed for a reexamination of the way U.S. unions see international solidarity. "The New Voice administration," Gacek notes, "provided a space for us to systematically rethink and redefine the relationships we had with the *officialistas* in Mexico, the so-called *charros*, and particularly with the CTM. If you look at the New Voice platform, there's a reference about international unionism and recognition of the serious need to rethink international affairs and make them serve our membership. We need the most reliable and militant partners to leverage multinational companies and to make labor rights and sustainable development a precondition to trade."

Along the border, activists have experimented with new ways to organize workers. "Cross-border work means working with community organizations which are not formally tied to unions," Gacek says," but which cooperate in organizing workers. It requires developing an authentic unionism through effective alliances with other organizations, including community and religious organizations. I believe it breathes new life into the old phrase 'We shall be all.' It is a way of confronting the globalized economy with the hemispheric social alliance—creating effective resistance and an alternative to the dominant Free Trade Area of the Americas, NAFTA idea. We need to see that organizing the border is not a marginal issue, and [we need to] overcome the vast imbalance in resources between workers and what they're up against."

Currently, however, the activities of the DIA and the American Center for International Labor Solidarity, as well as AFL-CIO programs in almost every country, are funded by the U.S. government. Most of the money comes through grants from the Agency for International Development and the National Endowment for Democracy. It is unlikely that the federal government, especially under the Bush administration, will finance a vast increase in resources devoted to undermining the very conditions it seeks to foster through NAFTA and free trade policy.

Canadian unions fund a large part of their operations with solidarity funds collected from members through dues checkoff. That gives them much greater independence in the programs they choose to undertake and makes it more difficult for the Canadian government to use funding to force compliance with its foreign policy.

In the United States, this has been a subject of great controversy, especially because the foreign policy of the U.S. government is much more interventionist and anti-labor than the foreign policy of Canada. State labor federations in California and Washington, as well as numerous central labor councils, have passed resolutions calling on the AFL-CIO to "come clean" on the intelligence operations in which it cooperated in the cold war era and to report completely on the activities it currently undertakes with government funding.

The idea of funding international activity through members' dues has been raised in the United States. Many international unions now have their own programs abroad and provide minimal levels of support to organizations on the border. It is still unclear, however, how the DIA will respond to these calls for greater financial independence. According to Gacek, "Given the intense interest in Mexico among our affiliates, there was a perception by the Solidarity Center and the International Department as early as 1997 that we should look at the possibility of starting independent funding. We thought of going directly to affiliates and seeing if they would contribute to an independent foundation. Those discussions began, but unfortunately they haven't ended or produced this independent fund. In addition, major affiliates have moved in their own directions in many ways and spent their own funding. It's a discussion we still have to continue."

NAFTA and the cross-border solidarity movement not only helped to create the need for this discussion (among many others) but also changed the politics of the U.S. labor movement so that the discussion became possible. That is a good indication of one important long-term effect of this movement: it has opened up political space for discussing what was unspeakable during the cold war era. International working-class solidarity, formerly a forbidden ideological concept, has become a set of practical and political problems confronting workers in the border plants themselves. And a powerful support movement has been organized to help them solve these problems.

Yet this process of change is incomplete. There remains a gross inequality of power between workers and unions on one side, and corporations, governments, and international financial institutions on the other. Unions in both countries often still see international solidarity as a general good but as less critical than the negotiation of their next contract.

Further, throwing off the suffocating mantles of the cold war and of official corporatist and business union politics is a complex process that takes time. But the border movement's other lesson is that this process is, ultimately, not driven by labor functionaries in Washington or Mexico City, but rather by ordinary workers themselves. So long as they continue to organize and seek answers, they will generate the necessary pressure for change.

THE CONFRONTATION TO COME

The political message of repression and low wages, made plain to maquiladora workers every day, carries an increasingly disturbing subtext. Residents of the border are being treated as throwaway people, whether they're the "junked" factory laborers in the Custom Trim and Auto Trim plants or the residents of Chilpancingo living in a plume of toxic waste. In Juárez, this attitude has reached an extreme, with the murder or disappearance of hundreds of women workers since 1993. Despite a climate of fear and hysteria in the working-class neighborhoods of Juárez, Mexican authorities have been unable to locate suspects or motives for these crimes or to find any of the missing women. For the U.S. authorities, these are simply unfortunate occurrences on the other side of the border.

Rosario Acosta is the mother of one of the missing women and a leader in Nuestras Hijas de Regreso a Casa (Our Children Must Return Home), an organization started by many of the mothers. Since 1996, according to Acosta, 284 women are known to have been murdered, and 450 have simply disappeared. Sixty percent of them were workers in the maquiladoras, and the rest were university and secondary school students, even girls as young as ten and twelve. Their average age is sixteen.

"It has to do with the opening of the big door, which is our border to the U.S., in order to allow big multinationals—more than four hundred of them—to settle in our city," Acosta says. "We gave them a permit to do absolutely everything. They don't guarantee the most elementary security measures to their female workers who commute back and forth from their homes." She also cites poverty and the lack of elementary social services, such as running water and electricity in their homes. "A poverty that doesn't allow people to have access to material things beyond those [that are] absolutely basic causes people to be blind and unaware of their rights, so that they don't know how to fight for themselves," she concludes. "These women have been vulnerable to these assassinations and disappearances precisely because they are people blind to their rights, due to their economic situation."

Acosta and the other mothers hold the state government responsible and accuse it of using repression to silence denunciations of the murders. "The state . . . doesn't recognize this as a serious social problem," she explains. And because authorities can't or won't solve the murders, they've stirred up hostility toward the thousands of migrants who have come to Juárez from states in the south looking for work. Acosta accuses authorities of inciting hysteria by claiming that "immigrants to Juárez were responsible for the increasing insecurity in our city."

The bitter truth is that maquiladora development relies on the labor of these thousands of young women who travel north from cities, small villages, and rural areas in central and southern Mexico. But they are important to industry only as productive workers, not as human beings. If they disappear, they can and will be easily replaced.

"This low value for the lives of women [reflects] the value that the government has given them," Acosta emphasizes. "The lack of response to this cry for justice, the inability to stop the crimes, is a way of saying, in other words, in attitudes, 'We don't care that women keep disappearing and being murdered.' It places a low value not only on women's lives but on the basic right to live for everybody."

But murders and the devaluation of workers' lives by the government and the plant operators haven't weakened efforts to achieve better conditions, either in the factories or in the communities. People don't view themselves as worthless. In fact, the border region has become a hotbed of walkouts, in-plant protests, community-based movements, and political ferment, from one end to the other.

Some observers predicted that protest might be dampened by the economic crisis that swept through the maquiladoras in 2001, bringing massive layoffs in its wake. The companies, all too aware of continued discontent, attempted to use the flattened economy as a further instrument to suppress dissent, putting their own propaganda spin on economic crisis. The layoffs, the maquiladora association warned, could become a permanent fact of life if production left the border and headed to China and East Asia.

For decades, U.S. workers have been told that their wages were too high—and that higher labor costs would force their employers to move to Mexico. Now Mexican workers are on the receiving end of the same threat, and this time the bogeyman is China. Beginning with the Asia Pacific Economic Conference, hosted by Mexico in Cabo San Lucas in November 2002, a rising media chorus in both Mexico and the United States has argued that Mexico is losing the low-wage competition with China and that plants have closed and moved away as a result. "With the advances of the giant Asian power," Rolando González Barrón, national president of the Maquila Export Industry Association, stated at a Matamoros press conference in April 2002, "all these companies are trying to compete with China with cheap labor." He advised factory owners to move to southern Mexico, where wages are much lower. "The border has no possibility of competing with China."

There is no doubt about the extent of the sharp economic crisis affecting border plants. González announced in April 2002 that three hundred thousand workers had been laid off on the border in 2001 and the first months of 2002. Marco Antonio Tomás of Mexico City's Center for Labor Research (CILAS) put the number of layoffs at four hundred thousand, as of November 2002. Until the crisis hit, the maquiladora industry had employed more than 1.3 million workers, according to the association.

Nevertheless, only two actual plant closures have been cited as evidence of flight to China. One, a factory making computer monitors for

Phillips North America in Juárez, shut down during the summer of 2002, costing about six hundred jobs. Production moved to Suzhou, China. In another case, Canon closed an older facility making inkjet printers, moving production to southeast Asia. Phillips, however, has another twelve border plants, including ones that make televisions, and the company increased its investment in many of them in the same year. The other big television manufacturers, including Sony, Samsung, and Thomson, also continue to produce in Mexican plants.

Relocating much of maquiladora production to China would not be practical or economical. Mattel, for instance, which produces many small toys in China, produces its "large-cube" items, such as jungle gyms and tricycles, in Mexico. Thomas Debrowski, Mattel vice president for operations, quoted in the *New York Times* on March 2, 2003, told reporter Daniel Altman that "if you want to be competitive in large-cube products, and you want to source it in China, you're going to go broke pretty quick," given the cost of transporting the items.

Although some media estimates repeat employer assertions that maquiladora workers earn $2.00 to $2.50 per hour, and compare this to 35 cents an hour in China, the actual average maquiladora wage is generally about $6.00 to $8.00 per day. Meanwhile, a study by the Economics Faculty of the National Autonomous University in Mexico City reported that Mexican wages had lost 81 percent of their buying power. Thus in the early 1980s, the minimum wage could pay for 93.5 percent of a family's basic necessities, whereas by 2002 it bought only 19.3 percent.

Alcoa Fujikura played the China card directly, after workers at its factory in Puebla sent a solidarity message to their co-workers at the Alcoa plant in Piedras Negras who were involved in a bitter conflict with the company. Jake Siewart, vice president of Alcoa Fujikura Limited in Pittsburgh, Pennsylvania, passed along to the Puebla workers a letter from company executive Alan Belda, which enthused that "all the automotive operations of Alcoa Fujikura Limited in Mexico offer attractive pay and benefits packages." Belda went on to warn, however, that the company's "Mexican workers earn approximately $3,300 a year, not counting benefits . . . [while equivalent] Chinese workers make about $2,000."

The union at the Puebla plant, which supplies wire harnesses to the nearby Volkswagen assembly facility, analyzed the company's claims, with the help of Huberto Juárez, a professor at the Autonomous University of Puebla who has studied the auto industry in Mexico for two decades. First, they found that labor costs in Mexico make up only 7.4 percent of the total cost of sales. In other words, even if what Belda said was true, the actual difference in total cost was very small.

But they also discovered that the company's wage figures for its Mexican workforce simply weren't true. The wage scale at Alcoa Fujikura in Puebla ranges from 58.46 to 121.71 pesos a day. At the rate of exchange in January 2003 (a little more than 10 pesos to the dollar), the average worker makes $43.10 a week, which is $6.16 a day, or 89 cents an hour. That gives them a yearly average salary of $2,241.20, or only about 10 percent more than the company itself quoted for equivalent Chinese wages. Given that the company had as much of a motive to underestimate Chinese wages as it did to overestimate Mexican ones, the difference could easily be even less.

In fact, the union noted that a thousand Alcoa Fujikura workers in Puebla (about 40 percent of the plant's workforce) earn less than the average, bringing their wages even closer to the Chinese estimates. "We know that the companies are beating the drum about the 'wage race to the bottom,' using the Chinese as a threat to put downward pressure on wages in many parts of the world," the union study explained. "But the low salaries are here [in Mexico], earned by workers who without any doubt are producing at a world-class level. But they don't live, as the company pretends they do, in world-class conditions."

The study also profiled the average Alcoa Fujikura worker in Puebla, whom it described as a young woman between the ages of eighteen and twenty-eight. Only about 30 percent of the workers are married; the rest are single, and many of them are single mothers. Considering that about three-quarters of them earn less than 76 pesos a day, their wages "are not enough to offer a decent life," the study concluded. Ninety-five percent of the workers surveyed were supporting at least one dependent and reported that their earnings weren't enough to cover the basic necessities for their family. Their diet consisted of tortillas, beans, pasta soup, vegetables, bread, and milk. Only 23 percent of the workers ate chicken three times a week; 9 percent could afford chicken only twice a week, while 41 percent reported that they ate it once a week.

Nevertheless, when the companies play the China card, maquiladora workers say they get the message.

Nelly Benítez, who worked at one of Sony's three huge plants in Nuevo Laredo, said that the company openly threatened to move to China if workers didn't accept cuts in wages and benefits. "The company began threatening to move to China when they began lowering the wages and benefits in 2001," she recalled. "Weekly salaries were reduced from about eight hundred pesos to six hundred pesos [for a six-day week]. We used to get a ride to and from work on company buses, since almost no one owns a car, and often we get off work late at night. Now we can only get a ride one way, not both."

Benítez noted that Sony was still bringing new machines into the plant in late 2002 to make batteries and microcassettes. But, after starting production, the number of people working each machine would then be cut. "For example, if they start with five on a machine, they'll eventually fire three, and the other two have to continue running it."

Sony also transformed its workforce. Until the recession hit, each of its four plants employed about twenty-six hundred people, who were permanent company employees. But by November 2002, said Benítez and CILAS's Tomas, the number in each plant had been reduced to fifteen hundred. The majority were temporary hires, laid off right before they were slated to acquire permanent status (under Mexican law, at the end of thirty days). "They never became permanent employees," Benítez said, and therefore had no right to severance pay, housing benefits, or status under labor law.

According to Martha Ojeda, director of the Coalition for Justice in the Maquiladoras, the China threat was being used far beyond the maquiladora industry, in particular to justify the reforms in labor law that were being proposed by the World Bank and the Fox administration. "They're promoting a policy of fear, in which workers are told that it's better to see five pesos in wages cut to three than to lose their jobs entirely," Ojeda explained. "This is combined now with an effort to change the labor law itself. If we don't accept their reforms, the companies say they'll take their investment elsewhere."

The proposed reforms under discussion include the kinds of changes that have been made at the Sony plant. "Companies want the unlimited ability to hire temporary workers, who never acquire seniority, benefits, or labor rights," Ojeda added. "This is what already exists in the maquiladoras. They're using the maquiladoras as the model for what they want to do with workers in the rest of the economy."

Rising anti-Chinese hysteria in the maquiladora industry, however, obscures a basic fact. The border industry has tied the Mexican economy so tightly to the U.S. market that when consumers in the north stop buying, workers from Tijuana to Matamoros lose their jobs by the thousands. When the U.S. economy catches a cold, the saying goes, Mexico comes down with pneumonia. These terminations have been caused overwhelmingly by reduced demand for the goods maquiladoras produce. The market is in the United States—when consumers there stop buying, production lines in Tijuana, Juárez, and Matamoros slow down and eventually stop.

While the maquiladora industry would like workers to look east to China as the source of their problems and participate in a wage-cutting race to the bottom, Benítez concluded that "where we really need to look is north." But the threat of relocation serves an important purpose. It trumpets a strident message to workers: Shut up and work harder. You're already too expensive. If you ask for more, if you organize a union and strike, if you demand costly ventilation and pollution-control equipment—factories will move offshore. No labor is cheap enough. If you lose your jobs, it's not because of the economics of the system and the increased dependence of the Mexican economy on production for the U.S. market. Rather, you have no one to blame but yourselves.

Economic crisis and the collapse of NAFTA's side agreement process are both important political markers. They signal the completion of a stage in the development of the maquiladora industry and the cross-border solidarity movement that was organized to respond to it. At the end of a decade of activity, it's possible to measure the changes this movement has brought about—the extent to which it has influenced public policy and its success in using the state apparatus to enforce improvements in labor conditions.

When we look back to the world of the mid-1980s, one political shift has become very clear. The border itself now plays a much more important role in the political life of the United States and Mexico. When the bracero program ended in 1964, the border region was still very sparsely populated. In fact, the Mexican government began the Border Industrialization Program in part to find employment for the thousands of migrants who had journeyed north to the United States as part of the bracero program but then found themselves pushed back into Mexico as the program ended. New plants employing this pool of labor could serve to head off potential social unrest among the unemployed. The workforce attracted by these new industries could also help to boost the population of the border region—a goal of nationalist governments in Mexico for many years, who feared that the United States would take advantage of the region's remoteness to further annex pieces of it.

Today, the problem of depopulation has become its opposite—the region now suffers from overcrowding and lack of housing. Cities such as Juárez and Tijuana are home to millions of people; they have become megacities on the order of other important metropolitan centers elsewhere in the world. And, like other huge cities, they have created their own regional economy, a unique culture, and their own political dynamics.

The migrants from the south who make up the population of these border cities brought with them more than simply the economic desperation that factory bosses have tried to use to create a pliant and willing labor force. Just as the workers at Han Young carried with them the knowledge of unions gained in the oil districts of Veracruz, other migrants have come with experience of land occupations, strikes, and other forms of social struggle. In addition, border workers hold the same expectations about the rights of workers generally, and their legitimate place in society, that are shared among Mexicans as a whole. They believe, for instance, that during a legal strike, an employer should shut down the factory. Hiring strikebreakers, in their view, is a violation of their rights and of the law itself. And, in fact, Mexican law supports this view. This understanding gives border workers expectations that were driven out of the consciousness of workers in the north fifty years ago.

Nevertheless, the border region is an area where those rights are increasingly in question, regardless of what the law says. Maquiladora development has depended on a political arrangement created decades ago among factory owners, compliant official unions, and pro-investment political authorities. In that arrangement, workers' rights have been sacrificed in the interest of labor peace, in an effort to encourage foreign investment. With maquiladora development now extending throughout Mexico, this dangerous arrangement is spreading as well. As a consequence, the challenge to the constitutional provisions protecting labor has grown stronger, while the legitimacy of the rule of law has been weakened, as working people become cynical about how the law is enforced.

The economy of the border rests on this development policy. If and when workers successfully challenge it, they will not simply raise their own wages. They will change the political structure that holds the arrangement in place.

A unique economy has created a new workforce, with its own characteristics and problems. It is a mixed workforce, in which people speaking indigenous languages from all parts of Mexico mix with those who have always spoken Spanish. Workers with many different cultural traditions find these traditions to be a source of both strength and difficulties. Many people, for instance, still maintain strong links to the towns and regions from which they come, and to which they return, even if only to visit. Hometown connections and family relationships thus often provide an initial network for organizing. But in order to organize a simple work stoppage in a plant, workers also have to overcome regional differences.

And often the traditions and structures that exist in their hometowns, which transfer cultural and political understanding from one generation to the next, are absent on the border. In their place, people must organize new institutions, from barrio committees to independent unions to political parties. As one might expect, it will take time before these institutions grow strong enough to challenge the existing political and economic order. But if the past ten years of activity are evidence, that day will come.

NAFTA liberated the movement of money and production but made it harder for people to move themselves. In economic terms, it increased the division, especially the differential in income, between one side of the border and the other. But a new social movement not only is confronting those difficulties but also, over time, is making deep and lasting changes in the political lives of both countries.

Since the Bush administration came to power, the challenge has become much greater. This administration is much more hostile to basic workers' rights and to anything that interferes with corporate profit-making. It has also developed a pretext for intervention against working people that will inevitably affect any activity on the border. Since the September 11, 2001, attacks, national security has become a justification for stopping strikes and any interruption of economic activity in airlines and among dockworkers. It has been invoked as a rationale for eliminating unions for tens of thousands of federal workers. National security has become an excuse for increasing immigration raids and for the firing of hundreds of immigrant workers in a new campaign of draconian immigration enforcement in the workplace.

Along the border, upheavals of workers in maquiladora plants that produce for the U.S. market will meet the same hostility. Furthermore, efforts to cross the border to support workers as they battle U.S. companies will inevitably draw the same charge of disloyalty. In a heightened atmosphere of national security, political support for these efforts will have to be much more effective than in the past; even actions such as Representative David Bonior's pioneering invocation of the Han Young strike to stop Clinton's proposal for fast track trade negotiating authority will not be enough.

Meanwhile, new plans for border development, part of Mexico's Plan Puebla/Panama, call for the creation of heavy industrial plants in the northwest, along the rail line from Tijuana and Tecate to Ensenada. U.S. electrical utilities are already building power plants there, maquiladora electrical generators for the U.S. market. This situation creates new possibilities. Heavy industry and power generation have been historical strongholds of the left in Mexican labor. Expansion of these sectors on the border will do more than give the government a greater stake in ensuring labor peace to investors—potentially, they may also create a base of workers who will be in a better position to challenge neoliberal labor policies.

Despite the economic crisis, border development is not going to disappear. The number of factories and workers will continue to grow, although their jobs may well be transformed. And, as the demographics of the border workforce change, the workers' ability to challenge the economic order may grow, too. Tijuana and Juárez are reminiscent of what Detroit must have looked like to the early organizers of the first auto unions in the 1920s. Low wages, toxic pollution, and a corrupt political establishment have combined to place workers in a pressure cooker, closing off any alternative other than radical social movements to challenge the status quo.

In the face of an increasingly unbearable situation, that pressure cooker is getting hotter, waiting to blow.

Abascal, Carlos, 197, 200
Acosta, Jerry, 243–44, 246
Acosta, Rosario, 313–14
A&E Plastics (Calif.), 64
Aeromexico, 230, 231
Afghanistan: war in, 307
AFL-CIO, 9, 11, 90, 160; alliances of,
    180, 297; appeal to, 119–20; cold war
    stance of, 51, critique of, 302–3; free
    trade policy of, 158; government-
    sponsored unions recognized by,
    304–5; immigration amnesty sup-
    ported by, 284, 301; NAO function
    and, 205; New Voice administration
    of, 305–7, 309–11; policy change in,
    267, 295, 306–11; right-wing covert
    activities of, 302–3; Task Force on
    Trade, 46; workers' strike supported
    by, 211. See also American Center for
    International Labor Solidarity; Labor
    Council for Latino Advancement
African American workers, 57–58
age: of average maquiladora worker,
    169; concerns about old, 70–71; of
    garment workers, 210, 215. See also
    children and youth
Agricultural Association of Vegetable
    Producers of the Mexicali Valley
    (Asociación Agricola de Productares
    de Hortalizas del Valle de Mexicali),
    36

Agricultural Labor Relations Act
    (Calif., 1975), 25
agriculture. See farm industry
Ahn, Peter, 113–14
AIFLD (American Institute for Free
    Labor Development), 158, 302–5, 308
Albina Garabito, Rosa, 53, 114
Alcoa Fujikura plants: in Ciudad Acuña,
    190–91; in Puebla, 316–18
Alexander, Robin: on Duro Bag elec-
    tions, 200–201; on labor alliances,
    180–81; on strike settlements, 117,
    120; UE/FAT alliance and, 162
Alinsky, Saul, 264
Allende, Salvador, 302
Alliance for Responsible Trade, 27
Allied Signal, 28
Allison Parks (company), 242
Almaguer, Eliud, 192–97
Almaguer, Evelia, 192–93
Alonzo, Julio César, 138
Altman, Daniel, 316
Alvarado, David, 210–11
Álvarez Bejar, Alejandro, 8–9, 246–50
Álvarez Garin, Raúl, 9, 11, 278
Amalgamated Meat Cutters and
    Butcher Workmen, 259
American Center for International
    Labor Solidarity, 210–11, 244, 309
American Federation of Government
    Employees, 303

American Friends Service Committee, 189

American Institute for Free Labor Development (AIFLD), 158, 302–5, 308

American Metal Products, 28

American President Lines (shipping company), 238

American Smelting and Refining Company, 242

American United Global, 77

Amphenol plant, 28

Anaconda Copper Company, 241

Anderson, Sarah, 9, 11, 27, 47

anti-immigration sentiment, 15, 57; firings and, 207; Proposition 187 and, 207, 284, 301; union support for, 51. *See also* immigrants

Arian, David, 239–40

Arias, Jaime, 263

Ariston, Carl, 260, 268, 269, 270

Arizona Border Rights Project, 243

Armenta, Emeterio, 82–85

Armour (meatpacker), 259

Armour-Swift-Eckrich (meatpacker), 269

Atizapán: housing in, 279–80

Authentic Labor Front (FAT, Frente Auténtica de Trabajo), 15, 55, 85, 87–90, 166, 307; alliances of, 155–56, 160–65, 176, 298; disagreements with, 98–99; disappointment in strike settlement, 117; NAFTA opposed by, 93, 231. *See also* United Electrical Workers/Authentic Labor Front alliance

automobiles, 234–35, 317

Auto Trim factory (Matamoros), 201–2, 204–6, 285

A&W Brands, 28

Axiohm Transaction Solutions Corporation, 109–10

Ayala, Antonio, 29

Ayala, Luz María, 29–30, 42

Badillo, Eduardo, 44, 74, 134, 287

Bagdasarian (grape grower), 26

Baja California (Mexico): children's education in, 34; elections in, 138, 142–43; human rights violations in, 32; maquiladora industry in, 221–22; monetary concerns of, 127–30; population growth in, 125, 126, 127–28, 138–39. *See also specific locales and towns*

Baja West plant, 221–22

Baltimore Aircoil, 28

Barco, Ricardo, 227, 229

Bardacke, Frank, 155

Barrajas, Maclovio, 272

barra (mud), 43

barrios: organizing efforts in, 138–41. *See also* community; food; housing

Barron, Jorge, 62

Barton, Robert, 191

Basla, Mark, 110

Batres Guadarrama, Marti, 247

Bautista, John, 29

Baxter International, 27–28

Beaty, Tim, 205, 244

Beckman, Steve, 53

Belda, Alan, 316, 317

Benítez, Nelly, 318, 319

Binne, William, 66

Bird's Eye plant, 154, 156

blacklists, 3, 165–72; of Han Young workers, 84, 111; of ITAPSA workers, 117; of miners, 240, 244–45; workers' response to, 24

Blaha, John, 258

Bluestone Farming Company, 25–26, 28

Bonior, David, 91–92, 100–101, 322

border, 253; as symbol of NAFTA, 48–49. *See also* cross-border movements

Border Industrial Program, 299, 320

Border Region Workers' Support Committee (CAFOR, Comité de Apoyo Fronterizo de Obreros Regionales), 44, 134; alliances of, 73–74; on health and safety violations, 286–87; protests against activists' arrest, 136

Border Women Workers Committee (CFO, Comité Fronterizo de Obreras), 190

Boscovitch, Phil, 29
Boscovitch Farms (Perris), 28–29, 36, 42–43
Bossidy, Lawrence, 28
boycotts: against cafeteria food, 209; against grape growers, 21–25; against land payments, 123–24. *See also* demonstrations and protests; strikes
Boyd, Stuart, 205
bracero program, 44, 127, 320
Breed Technology (Florida), 204–6. *See also* Auto Trim factory (Matamoros); Custom Trim factory (Valle Hermosa)
Bridgestone tire industry, 305
Bronfenbrenner, Kate, 53
Brown, Garrett, 94–97, 204–5
Brown, Harry, 48
Brown, Jerry, 25
Brunch, Bruce, 166–67
Bush, George H. W., 157, 299
Bush, George W.: anti-unionism of, 52, 295; NAFTA supported by, 12, 206, 322; opposition to, 307; trade agreement negotiations and, 287–89

Cabrera (union steward), 174, 175
Cadena, Patricia, 218
CAFOR. *See* Border Region Workers' Support Committee
California: family income in, 57; NAFTA debates in, 299–300; political changes in, 271; Proposition 187 in, 207, 284, 301; unemployment claims in, 27. *See also specific cities*
California Connections plant, 221–22
California Rural Legal Assistance (CRLA), 146–47, 148
Calleros, Rivera, José, 113
Camacho Barrera, Gabino, 228
Camacho Solis, Hector, 239
Camino Real (Tijuana establishment), 114–18
Campa, Valentin, 10, 158, 161, 226
Campbell, Bruce, 11
Campos Linas, Jesús, 81, 177, 219–20
Canacintra, 197

Canada: cross-border movements and, 212, 289; economy of, 16; jobs lost in, 47; solidarity funds in, 310; U.S. free trade agreement with, 299
Canadian Labour Congress, 180
Canadian Steelworkers and Auto Workers, 176
Cananea (Mexico): mining industry in, 240–46, 261; water in, 243
Canizares, Javier, 242–45
Cañon Buenavista: homes in, 121–22; land occupations in, 123–27, 129; Maclovio Rojas compared with, 130–31
Canon Business Machines, 28, 316
Cárdenas, Cuauhtémoc, 273; campaign of, 106, 157, 231, 273, 276–77, 281, 282; educational privatization and, 248–49, 250; election of, 86, 227; U.S. tour of, 157–58
Cárdenas, Lázaro, 273, 275; land expropriation by, 124, 281; reforms and labor unions under, 224–25, 230, 252
Carey, Ron, 24
Cargill plant, 260
Carlisle Plastics (Boston), 64, 66. *See also* Plasticos Bajacal (Tijuana)
Carrillo, Guadalupe, 189
Casillas, Pedro, 277
Castillo, Antonio, 274–77
Castillo, Ingracia: grape boycotts and, 22–25; NAFTA's impact on, 19–20
Castillo, José: grape boycotts and, 22–25; NAFTA's impact on, 19–20; unemployment assistance for, 25–26
Castillo, Manuel, 282
Castillo, Tony, 14–15, 274–77, 281–82; national election observed by, 277–81; as union organizer, 272, 273–74
Castro, Fernando, 164
Caterpillar Corporation, 305
Catholic Church: PAN linked to, 198; as venue for organizing, 254, 255, 268–69
CAT (Centro de Apoyo para los Trabajadores; Workers Support Center), 210–13

Cavanagh, John, 11, 47
Ceja, Roberto, 262
Center for Labor Research (Centro de Investigaciones Laborales y Asesoria Sindical, Mexico City), 199
Center for Labor Studies (CETLAC, Centro de Estudios y Taller Laboral), 169–70
Center for Reflection, Education, and Action, 8, 215
Central Intelligence Agency (CIA), 58–59
Central Unica dos Trabalhadores (CUT, Brazil), 308
Centro Nacional de Desarollo Social (National Center for Social Development), 9
Centro Patronal (employer association), 64
Cerna, Samuel, 32
Cervantes, Marcela, 268
CETLAC (Centro de Estudios y Taller Laboral; Center for Labor Studies), 169–70
CFO (Comité Fronterizo de Obreras; Border Women Workers Committee), 190
Chao, Elaine, 182
Chávez, Beatriz: imprisonment of, 122, 124, 129–30, 139; organizing efforts of, 125; on racism, 122–23
Chávez, César, 20, 22–23, 29, 146, 283
Chávez, Hugo, 307
Chávez, Jovita, 63–64
Chávez, Tiberio: immigration of, 253–54, 271; injury of, 256; land invasion by, 251–53; radio broadcasts of, 269
Chavistas, 20, 283. See also Chávez, César
Chevron Corporation, 148
Chiapas. See Zapatistas
child care, 38
child labor, 16, 30–39, 129: call for eliminating, 40–41, 43;129; pervasiveness of, 215
children and youth: Frente's concerns about, 149; limited education for,

31–35, 71, 194; with medical conditions, 74, 168, 201–2, 287; murdered, 15, 313–14; "of NAFTA," 16–17. See also child labor
Chile: grape harvests in, 20–21
Chilpancingo (neighborhood), 73–74
China: as employers' trump card, 315–19
Chung, Ted, 113
Church, Frank, 302
CIA (Central Intelligence Agency), 58–59
CIOAC (Confederación Independiente de Obreros Agricolas y Campesinos; Independent Confederation of Farmers and Farm Workers), 134, 138–39, 140, 145–46
CIO (Congress of Industrial Organizations), 10, 160. See also AFL-CIO
Circuit-Wise plant (New Haven, Conn.), 161–62
Citizens' Committee for the Restoration of Cañon del Padre, 286–87
Citizens Trade Campaign, 27
CITTAC (Centro de Información para Trabajadoras y Trabajadores Asociación Civil; Workers' Information Center), 62
Civic Alliance (Alianza Civica), 84
CJM. See Coalition for Justice in the Maquiladoras
Clarostat S.A. plant (Juárez), 165–66
Clean Clothes campaign (German), 212
Clifford, Jim, 89
Clinton, Bill: complaints about, 164, 165; on free trade, 118–19; loans and, 231; on NAFTA extension, 91–92, 93, 322; NAFTA signed by, 162, 299; rhetoric of, 27, 45, 164, 288; on "safety net," 19–20
Coachella Valley (U.S.): farm industry in, 20–25
Coalition for Justice in the Maquiladoras (CJM, San Antonio), 14, 16, 185–86, 190–92, 221, 302; alliances of, 222, 290, 297; complaints filed by, 189; Duro Bag workers supported

by, 196; investigative trip to Mexico, 155–56; junked workers and, 285
Coalition of Immokalee Workers (Fla.), 143
Cobe Renal plant, 109–10
cold war ideology: challenge to, 52–59; cross-border union alliances and, 10, 298–302; labor federations reflective of, 296–97; right-wing covert activities and, 302–3; union rejection of, 232, 295–96; union support for, 51
Columbus, Christopher, 147
Communications Workers of America (CWA), 206–8, 297, 307
community: cooperation within, 148; garment workers strike and, 210; and gender, 149; role in organizing efforts, 255–58, 264–71, 309–11; role in social change, 28–29, 279
Compania Armadora plant (GE), 163–65
ConAgra packing plant (U.S.): elections at, 254–55; as monopoly, 260; organizing efforts at, 14–15, 264–69; union recognition at, 269–70
CONASUPO (food monopoly), 45, 225
Conde, Lucila, 164
Confecciones de Monclova, 217
Confederation of Mexican Workers (CTM, Confederación de Trabajadores Mexicanos), 10, 102, 187, 224; AFL-CIO recognition of, 304–5; corruption of, 189; independent unions as threat to, 197; on Mary Tong, 104; pocket of resistance in, 103; PRI'S link to, 194, 224, 274; protection contracts of, 101, 177, 189, 194–95, 203, 208, 217; rejection of, 176, 189
Confederation of Revolutionary Workers (COR, Confederación de Obreros Revolucionarios), 65–68
consciousness: changes in, 51–52; development of, 6–7; maintaining heightened, 289–90
Constitution, Mexican: child protection laws in, 32; as defense, 248; on free

education, 250; labor laws in, 104, 114, 190; land laws in, 124, 252, 276; World Bank's recommendations on, 218–21
Contreras, Fela, 186–88, 189, 192
Convention 138 (ILO), 40
Convention 32 (U.N.), 40–41
COPARMEX, 68, 100–101, 112, 113, 197
COR (Confederación de Obreros Revolucionarios; Confederation of Revolutionary Workers), 65–68
Cordoba, Norberto, 97–98
Corona, Bert, 29
Corona, Luz Elena, 62–63
Corral Castro, Pedro, 126
Correedor Esnaola, Jaime, 234
Cortez, Gabriela, 212
Cosio, Jesús, 101–3, 104
Cota, Jaime, 62, 68, 135
Cota, Leonel, 221, 222
Cota, Mario, 32, 36
cotton harvest, 39
Covarrubias, Daniel, 135–36
crime: upsurge in, 239. See also murders
CRLA (California Rural Legal Assistance), 146–47, 148
CROC. See Revolutionary Confederation of Workers and Farmers
CROM (Confederación Revolucionaria de Obreros Mexicanos; Revolutionary Confederation of Mexican Workers), 61, 63–64, 65, 81, 224
Crosetti plant, 154
cross-border business ventures, 6–8, 37–38, 42–44. See also maquiladora industry
cross-border movements, 10–15, 49–52, 289; cultural implications of, 320–23; example of, 143–50; land occupations and, 137; NAFTA as impetus to, 16; social justice concept impacted by, 271–84; solidarity in, 50–51. See also Coalition for Justice in the Maquiladoras (CJM, San Antonio)

Cross Border Organizing Committee (Portland, Ore.), 108
cross-border union alliances, 53, 76, 157–60; achievements of, 290–91; cold war ideology and, 298–302; difficulties of, 156, 290–98; examples of, 206–7, 210–13, 216–18, 239–40; implementation of, 160–65; implications of, 182–84; during NAFTA debates, 61–62, 64–66, 86; NAFTA's role in forming, 298–305; necessity of, 155–56, 159, 168–69, 300–301; possibilities in, 13–14, 119–20
CSX (shipping company), 238
CTM. See Confederation of Mexican Workers
Cudahy (meatpacker), 259
Cuellar, Jorge, 224, 228, 231–32, 306
culture, 292; cross-border movements' implications for, 320–23; of labor activists, 1–5; organizing efforts in context of, 255–58, 264–71
Cummins ReCom, 170
Custom Trim factory (Valle Hermosa): health and safety violations of, 201, 202–3, 204, 285; strike against, 203
CUT (Central Unica dos Trabalhadores, Brazil), 308
CWA (Communications Workers of America), 206–8, 297, 307
Daewon (plant), 82, 114, 135
Daifullah, Nagi, 24
Day, Mike, 66
Debrowski, Thomas, 316
de hueso colorado, 20
de la Cruz, Juan, 24
de la Cruz, Rick, 197–98
de la Cueva, Hector, 199, 221
De La Fuente, Ignacio, 300
de la Rosa, Alejandro, 194, 195
Delgado, Carmen, 164
Delgado, Filiberto, 140
Delgado, José, 76
Democratic Tendency (Tendencia Democrática), 226

democratization, 291–93, 298; of Teamsters, 152
demonstrations and protests: against activists' arrests, 136–37, 141; for bus transport workers, 228–30; CJM-organized, 185–86; against devaluation of peso, 75–76; for Duro Bag workers, 196–97; on housing needs, 139–40; against Hyundai, 90–91, 107–8; for junked workers, 285–86; against Plasticos Bajacal, 62–66; against Sony, 188; against student arrests, 248. See also boycotts; strikes
despojo agravado (crime), 122; people charged with, 125, 139. See also land invasions
Deupree, Cliff, 63–64
devaluation of peso: demonstrations against, 75–76; effects of, 38, 47, 71, 231; forced, 45–46
Díaz, Porfirio, 241
Díaz, Victor, 71, 72
Dirty Business (video), 155
discrimination: by EDD, 29–30; in neoliberalism, 13; organizing against, 259; against pregnant women, 169–70
disease: of children, 74, 168, 201–2, 287; failure to document, 286–87; return of tuberculosis, 228
Doherty, William, 302, 308
Domínguez, Araceli, 9, 105–6
Domínguez, Rufino, 144, 146–50
Donahue, Tom, 306
Duro Bag factory (Río Bravo), 8; elections at, 198, 199–201; firings at, 194–95; organizing efforts at, 192–93, 195–96; outside support for organizing workers at, 196–98; wages at, 194; workers' injuries at, 193–94
Duro Bag Manufacturing Corporation (Ludlow, Ky.), 198, 201

Echeverría, Bernardino, 166, 167
Echeverría, Luis, 278

Echlin (company): alliances against, 180–81; anti-unionism of, 174–75, 176; complaints filed against, 178–82; Friction plant bought by, 172; on health and safety, 177; solidarity across plants of, 175–76

Echlin Workers Alliance, 175

economic development, 56–57

Economic Policy Institute (D.C.), 11, 47

economy, global: Canada, Mexico, U.S. bound together in, 16, 319; critique of, 58–59; everyday experience of, 3–4; Mexican labor unions in context of, 232; NAFTA debates and, 300–301; recession in, 15; transformation of, 53

economy, Mexican: crisis in, 38–39, 44, 216, 217–18, 315, 319–23; decline of, since NAFTA, 107; insecurity of, 57–59; neoliberalism's impact on, 13, 157; U.S. workers impact by, 157; workers' rights discarded in, 204–5. *See also* devaluation of peso

education: child laborers and, 31–35, 71, 194; privatization of, 246–50

EES plant, 170

EHC (Environmental Health Coalition), 287

Ejido Francisco Villa, 134–35

ejidos, 124

El Bravo (newspaper), 195, 197

election process (unions), 60–61, 67–68. 87; change in locale, 220; complaints filed on, 208, 288–89; in meatpacking plants, 254–55, 263–64; organizing efforts in, 141–43; reopening of, 87–88; secret ballot denied in, 199–200, 225

electrical workers union, 226

electricity: privatization of, 296

Electrocomponentes S.A. plant (Juárez), 165, 168

electronics factories, 3, 28, 208. *See also* Sony plants; *other specific plants*

El Mañana (newspaper), 9

El Mexicano (newspaper), 9, 105–6

Elorduy, Eugenio, 64

El Salvador: war in, 303

employment: promises of, 26–27, 157; retraining for, 46; undermining of, 180. *See also* job losses

Employment Development Department (EDD, Calif.), 25–26, 29–30

ENFOCCA (Enlace de la Fuerza de Obreros, Cuidadanos y Campesinos; Workers, Residents, and Farmers Power Network), 140, 143

Enlaces (Links), 216, 218

Enríquez León, René, 242–43, 244

Ensenada (Mexico): port of, 235–37; protests in, 139–40

Environmental Health Coalition (EHC), 287

Escobedo Jiménez, Luis Manuel, 85

Espinoza, Olga, 255–56, 269

Espinoza, Raquel, 222

Espinoza de los Monteros, Luis, 177

Espinoza Villareal, Oscar, 229

Estibadores de Ensenada, 237

Exportadora de Mano de Obra, 77–79

Factor X (organization), 64

factory relocations, 6: list of, 28; to Mexico vs. Asia, 27; nonunionized status and, 183–84; as threat, 315–19; workers impacted by, 3–4. *See also* child labor; cross-border union alliances; maquiladora industry

Fahey, Joe, 154–55

Falcon, Raniel, 115

farm industry: conditions in, 2–3, 129, 140, 142, 144–46; crop prices and, 20, 37, 38; extent of, in Baja California, 123, 127; grower contracts in, 36–39; job relocation in, 12–13; packing places for, 152–56; relocation of grape growing, 22–26; relocation of green onion growing, 28–41. *See also* child labor

Farmland (meatpacking), 260

farmworkers: discrimination against, 13;
food processing plant workers com-
pared with, 152–56; housing needs
of, 138–43; movements of, 2–3,
42–44; NAFTA's immediate impact
on, 19–20
FAT. *See* Authentic Labor Front
FAVESA factories, 169–70
Feigan, Ed, 79, 90
Fertimex plant, 234
Field Institute (Calif.), 57–58
Fighting for Our Lives (film), 24
Filipino workers, 22–23
Flood, Greg, 37
Flores Magón, Ricardo, 241
Flores Magón brothers, 50–51, 241, 272
food: of average Alcoa worker, 318; as
bonus, 166; boycott against cafeteria's, 209; company stores for, 145;
contamination of, 155; costs of, 35–36,
71; decontrolled prices for, 45, 46;
nationalization of supply of, 225; U.S.
government's attitude toward, 55
food processing plants: conditions in,
152; relocation of, 154–56
Ford plant (Mexico), 290
foreign investment, 39, 167; challenging
system of, 104–5; encouragement of,
72, 97, 201; increase in, 48; protection contracts for, 81–82, 101, 177,
189, 194–95, 203, 208, 217; reliance
on, 44–45. *See also* free trade;
neoliberalism
Formglas plant, 28
Forstrom, Bill, 194, 196, 198
foundries: succession of immigrant
groups in, 3
Fox, Vicente: appointments by, 197;
campaign promises of, 199, 205–6;
election of, 128, 198–99, 249; free
trade under, 288; Frente's view of,
150; on job training, 141–42; on labor
law reform, 292, 318–19; privatization under, 296; wages under, 216;
on World Bank's recommendations,
219, 220–21

Frank Capurro (grower), 36
Freedman (David Freedman Com-
pany), 21–22, 24–25
free trade, 151, 172–82, 208–9; accep-
tance of, 299; as priority, 201. *See also*
NAFTA; neoliberalism
Free Trade Area of the Americas: alter-
native to, 309–11; current negotia-
tions on, 287–88; as extension of
NAFTA, 12
Free Trade Caravan, 162–63, 300
"free trade unions" concept, 304–5
Freire, Paolo, 265
Frente Democratico de Ford (Ford
Democratic Front), 290
Frente Indígena Oaxaqueña Binacional
(Binational Indigenous Oaxacan
Front), 141; alliances of, 146–47,
148, 150; geographical dispersal
and, 143–44; indigenous rights as
focus of, 147; organizing tactics of,
148–50
Fresh Choice (grower), 36, 37
Fresno area (Calif.): migration to, 146;
Oaxacan group's activities in, 144,
148
Friction plant (Calif.): challenges by
workers at, 179–82; closure of,
173–74; ownership of, 172; union rec-
ognized in, 175–76; wages at, 179

Gacek, Stan, 308–9; on AFL-CIO's pol-
icy, 295, 296, 304–5; on cross-border
organizing, 15; on funding, 310
Galván, Rafael, 226, 229
Gambro Healthcare (Colorado), 109–10
Garabito, Rosalbina, 247, 250
García, Benito, 123, 138–39, 141
García, Carla, 218
García, Celerino, 138–39, 141, 142
García, Connie, 287
García, José, 229
García Estrada, Federico, 32–33, 39–40
García Garcés, José Ángel, 194
García Jiménez, Guillermo, 239–40
García Rocha, Rubén, 137

garment workers: age of, 210, 215; conditions for, 3, 208–9; firings of, 221–22; organizing efforts of, 212–13; strikes of, 209–12

Garza, Irasema, 94, 99, 178–79, 288

gender: job losses and, 151; in political life, 149

General Confederation of Peruvian Workers, 308–9

General Electric Corporation: blacklisting at Mexican plants of, 165–67; Compania Armadora plant of, 163–65; light bulb factory of, 162; profits from Mexican plants, 48; protests against, 168, 182; solidarity across plants of, 182–83

General Foods: Bird's Eye plant of, 154, 156

Gephardt, Richard, 91, 93

Gil, Omar, 191

Girón, Jorge, 145–46

Girón, Margarita, 145

Glickman, Dan, 55

Globallphobleos, 137

globalization: differential effects of, 57–59. See also economy, global

global unionism, 299, 306

Gómez, Manuel, 164

Gonzáles, Claudio X., 219

González, Antonio, 60–61

González, Jesús, 29

González, Joaquín, 201

González Barrón, Rolando, 315

González Hernández, Pedro, 33–35, 39–40

Gore, Al, 93, 101, 118

Goulart, Joao, 302

Graciano Sánchez, Ejido, 124

Grand Metropolitan Corporation, 154, 156

grape growing industry: expansion of, 20–21; strikes in, 22–25; unionization in, 21–22

Greater Omaha Packing Company, 265–66

Greene, William C., 240–41

Green Giant plants, 154, 156

green onion growing industry: child labor in, 30–35; conditions in, 35–39

Grupo Mexico, 8; enterprises of, 241–42; strike against, 240, 242–46

Guatemalan civil war: activists in, 265–66; U.S. right-wing and, 303

Gutiérrez, Anita, 164

Gutiérrez-Cortez, Juan Romauldo, 148

Guyana: destabilization of, 58–59

Guzmán, José, 262–63

Hansen, Joe, 267

Han Young de Mexico strikes, 80–84, 93–94, 105–7; bargaining rights and, 98–99; breaking of, 114–20; court decisions on, 111–12, 113, 116; democratization and, 291–92; effects of, 6, 109–11; firings and, 84–85, 97–98; first legal, 99–105; implications of, 13, 91–93; police force in breaking, 102, 104, 108–9, 112–13; settlement of, 116–17; voting and, 86–91, 101–3; walkouts at, 84–86, 91, 93, 97; working conditions and, 92–93, 94–95

Hathaway, Dale, 9–10

health and safety issues: asbestos as, 177; at Duro Bag, 193–94; at Han Young, 92–93, 94–98; secret gas releases as, 190; toxic chemicals as, 73–74, 168, 202, 287; among workers, 201–6, 285–86. See also workplace injuries

Henning, John, 299, 306

Herlihy, Jim, 269

Herman, Alexis, 116–17, 118, 181, 200

Hermandad Mexicana Nacional (Mexican National Brotherhood), 28–29

Hermanson, Jeff, 211

Hernández, Armando, 89

Hernández, Enrique, 84, 92, 98–99, 101–2, 110, 112; on AFL-CIO, 119; beating of, 115–16, 118; on electoral opportunities, 107; on free trade, 93–94; on Han Young elections, 90, 101; legal charges against, 104, 109, 113, 114

Hernández, Inocencia, 109–10
Hernández, Javier, 62, 66
Hernández, José Luis, 118, 119
Hernández Díaz, Juan Pablo, 36, 38–39
Hernández Galicia, Joaquín ("La Quina"), 230–31
Hernández Hernández, Rocardo, 108
Hernández Juárez, Francisco, 15, 196–97; on cross-border alliances, 294–95; on democratization, 293; on Fox's election, 199
Hernández Mendoza, Hortensia, 130, 133, 134, 135–37
Holler, Tim, 265, 266–67
Honeywell Corporation, 163–65
Hoover, J. Edgar, 241
Hormel (meatpacker), 260
Hotel Employees and Restaurant Employees union, 216
hours: of farmworkers, 35–36; increase in, 57–58; labor laws on, 208–9
housing, 123, 125, 126; burned for revenge, 192–93; Cañon Buenavista vs. Maclovio Rojas, 130–31; demonstrations concerning, 139–40; descriptions of, 69–70, 121–22, 279–80; government subsidies for, 186–87; materials of, 130; for migrant farmworkers, 144–46; payments for, 123–24, 126; utilities and, 125, 137, 243
Hovis, John, 118, 182
Hudspeth, Lionel, 46
Huerta, Dolores, 22–23, 231–32, 306
Hughes Aircraft, 28
human rights, 164–65, 198
Human Rights Watch, 169–70
hunger strikes, 6, 223, 229
Hyundai Corporation: in Cañon Buenavista, 8, 131, 133, 134–35; court decision against, 113–14; in Maclovio Rojas, 134–35; as model, 89; new railway and, 132; picketing against, 90–91, 107–8; supplier for, 81, 89; transportation by, 237. See also Han Young de Mexico strikes

IAF (Industrial Areas Foundation), 264
IAM (International Association of Machinists), 66, 303
Ibarra, María, 70, 71, 72
Ibarra Estrada, Jesús, 112
IBP (meatpacker), 260
ICCR (Interfaith Center on Corporate Responsibility), 8, 90, 190–91, 215
ICFTU (International Confederation of Free Trade Unions), 297
ILO (International Labour Organization): Convention 138 (ILO), 40
ILWU (International Longshore and Warehouse Union), 8, 232, 235, 237, 239–40
IMF. See International Monetary Fund
immigrant rights movement, 207
immigrants, 1, 2, 3, 307; as influence on U.S., 284; Mexican labor organizing linked to, 301–2; transplanted expectations of, 251–54; U.S. companies' dependence on, 261–62; workers' unions of, 14–15. See also anti-immigration sentiment; Mexican workers in U.S.
Immigration and Naturalization Service (INS), 262–63, 266–67
Immigration Reform and Control Act (1986), 183, 301–2
Immobiliaria Estatal, 123, 124
IMSS (social security system), 231
Independent Confederation of Farmers and Farm Workers (CIOAC, Confederación Independiente de Obreros Agricolas y Campesinos), 134, 138–39, 140, 145–46
Independent Union of Men and Women Workers in the Maquiladora Industry of the State of Baja California (SINTTIM, Sindicato Independiente de Trabajadores y Trabajadoras de la Industria Maquiladora del Estado de Baja California Sur), 221–22

Independent Union of Workers at Mex Mode (SITEMEX, Sindicato de Trabajadores de la Empresa Mex Mode), 211–14
indigenous people: cross-border group for, 143–50; election of, 138–39; geographical dispersal of, 143–44; government's fears of, 122–23, 128–30, 139; land occupations by, 123–27; unionization and, 127–28
Industrial Areas Foundation (IAF), 264
industrial parks: growth of, 131
Industrial Workers of the World (IWW), 51, 241
Infonavit (government agency), 186–87
Institute for Health Policy Studies (Calif.), 57–58
Institute for Policy Studies (D.C.), 9, 11, 47
Interfaith Center on Corporate Responsibility (ICCR), 8, 90, 190–91, 215
Interhemispheric Resource Center (Albuquerque), 48
International Association of Machinists (IAM), 66, 303
International Brotherhood of Electrical Workers, 47
International Confederation of Free Trade Unions (ICFTU), 297
International Container Terminal Services, 237
International Independent Tribunal Against Child Labor, 40
internationalism: as influence, 1–2
International Labor Rights Fund, 189
International Labour Organization (ILO): Convention 138 (ILO), 40
International Longshore and Warehouse Union (ILWU), 8, 232, 235, 237, 239–40
International Molders Union, 2
International Monetary Fund (IMF): accountability in health violations, 204–5; attempt to influence, 295–96;

loan conditions and, 54–55; mandates of, 45–46, 246–47; reforms expected by, 295–96, 318–19; structural adjustment programs of, 39–41, 54–55
International Network of Oaxacan Indigenous People (Red Internacional de Indígenas Oaxaqueñas), 141
Iraq: war in, 52, 307
irrigation water: clean vs. black, 155
Irvine (Calif.). See Friction plant
ITAPSA plant (Mexico City), 8; challenges by workers at, 182; conditions at, 176–77; firings at, 177–78; strikes settled at, 116–17; wages at, 179
ITT Cannon plant, 28
IWW (Industrial Workers of the World), 51, 241

Jagan, Cheddi, 58–59
janitors union, 270
Jiménez, Jorge Alberto, 106
JNCA. See Junta Nacional de Conciliación y Arbitraje
job losses, 151; cross-border, 53; factors in, 19, 46–48, 51–52; increases in, 54, 110–11; post-2002, 221; and uncertified workers, 27–28. See also blacklists
Jobs with Justice, 168
Johanns, Mike, 267
John Inglis plant, 154
John Morrell (meatpacker), 260
Johnson, David: on blacklist, 168–69; reflections of, 182–84; UE/FAT alliance and, 161–62, 163
joint ventures, 33, 37–38, 42–44. See also foreign investment
jonkeados, 201
Juárez (Mexico), 167–68, 183–84,323; blacklisting in, 165–66; labor board and employers linked in, 170–72; murders of women in, 15, 313–14; population growth in, 320–21

Juárez Núñez, Huberto, 11, 209–10, 317
Junta Nacional de Conciliación y Arbi-
    traje (JNCA): vote certification
    refused by, 89–90; votes certified by,
    101–3; voting overseen by, 60–61,
    87–89. *See also* state labor boards

Kalmijn, Jelger, 64–65, 66
Kang, Won Young, 90, 96, 98, 103, 104
Karahadian (grape grower), 22–24
Karesh, Louis, 118, 119, 181
Kasun, Stan, 265
Kendall International, 69, 71–72
Ken-Mex (medical products, Tijuana),
    69, 70, 71–72
Keytronic (keyboards), 28
Kingsley, Bob, 160–65, 174
Kirkland, Lane, 168, 295–96, 305–6
Klontz, Dave, 201
Kopf, Richard, 262
Korea Fund of Scudder, Stevens and
    Clark, 90
Korean Confederation of Trade
    Unions, 90
Kozlowski, L. Dennis, 72
Kuk Dong (Mex Mode) plant (Puebla),
    11; conditions at, 208–9; strike
    against, 209–12; violence against
    women at, 209, 210
Kyle Properties, 132
Kyocera International, 28

Labastida, Francisco, 248
labor activists, 1–5, 255–58, 291–94;
    beatings of, 115–18, 119; firings of, 65,
    82, 84–85, 97–98, 105–6, 110; on land
    and work, 133–34; market pressure as
    tool of, 208–13; setbacks for U.S.,
    151–56; transplanted from Mexico to
    U.S., 282–84. *See also* cross-border
    union alliances; unionization efforts;
    specific people
Labor Congress (Congreso de Trabajo),
    74–75, 85–86
Labor Council for Latino Advance-
    ment, 272

labor laws, Mexican: battle over reform-
    ing, 292–98, 318–19; on blacklist, 167;
    on child labor, 32; corporatist
    approach to, 225–26; flexible use vs.
    enforcement of, 218–22; on hours,
    208–9; legal strikes under, 99–105,
    114; limits of, 63, 97, 117–18, 234; on
    plant closings/reopenings, 109; on
    profit sharing, 82; on registering
    new unions, 189–90; on strike
    notification, 63; on voting, 68, 88;
    on working conditions, 96–97
labor laws, U.S.: failure to enforce,
    207–8
labor unions: demographic changes in,
    264, 269–71; exclusion clause of,
    194–95; history of, 10, 224–26,
    258–64; immigration tied to Mexi-
    can, 301–2; independent, 213–14, 222,
    233, 302–5; international activities
    funded through, 310; NAFTA's
    impact on U.S., 267–68, 271–84;
    spread of government-affiliated,
    290; U.S. vs. Mexican, 156. *See also*
    specific unions
LaBotz, Dan, 9
La Conexión Familiar (Family Connec-
    tion), 206, 207
La Frontera (periodical), 115–16
La Jornada (newspaper), 9
land invasions: by indigenous migrant
    people, 123–27, 130–37; as long-term
    influence, 251–53, 275–76
land ownership: conflicting claims of,
    124–26; redistribution of, 124, 225,
    281. See also *despojo agravado* (crime)
Larrea, Jorge, 241
Latino workers, 57–58
laws: on child protection, 32; environ-
    mental, 287; failure to enforce,
    76–79, 287; on land claims, 124, 252,
    276; selective enforcement of,
    128–29; on unused federal property,
    124; weakened, 6, 130; World Bank's
    recommendations on, 218–21. *See also*
    labor laws

Laymex plant, 82, 114, 135
Lázaro Cárdenas (Mexico): port of,
234–38
Lear Industries, 169–70
Lee, Ho Young, 109
leftists, 292; AFL-CIO attacks on, 303;
investigating "dirty war" against,
278; repression of, 160–61. *See also*
labor activists
Lepe Bautista, Cecilio, 238–39
Levinson, Jerome, 190
Leviton Company, 47
Levy, Mark, 176
liberation theology, 265
libertad sindical, 115–16
Littler, Mendelsohn, Fastiff and Tichy
(law firm), 153
Lizarraga, Santos, 67
Loberto, Jamie, 265
Lombardo Toledano, Vicente, 51
Longshore and Warehouse Union, 216
longshore workers, 14, 133; cross-border
alliances of, 239–40; Hyundai pick-
eted by, 107–8, privatization's impact
on, 235; wages of, 237–38
Lonidier, Fred, 82–83
López, Filemon, 141
López, Sergio, 152
López Limón, Gema, 30; labor investi-
gations by, 31–33, 35, 43; on struc-
tural adjustment, 39–40
López Obrador, Andrés Manuel,
290
Los Angeles, 132–33, 137
Luna, César, 287

MacArthur, John R., 11
Maceda, Oralia, 149
Maclovio Rojas (barrio, Tijuana), 82,
133; Hyundai factory in, 134–36; land
values in, 130–31; provocateurs in,
136–37
Makoski, Milton, 174–75
Malaga (Calif.): organizing in, 148
Mandujano, José, 61, 68
Maneadero (Mexico): protests in, 139

Manríquez, Blas, 75
Manzanilla (Mexico): port of, 237–38
Maquiladora Associación Civil, 167
maquiladora employers, 8; associations
for, 64, 197; blacklist of, 167; China
card of, 315–19; protection contracts
for, 81–82, 101, 177, 189, 194–95, 203,
208, 217; UNT feared by, 196–97;
workers bought out by, 98. *See also*
violence
Maquiladora Health and Safety Support
Network, 95
maquiladora industry, 4–5, 192, 197,
221–22, 321, 322–23; conditions in, 13,
36, 92–93, 94–95, 133–36, 176–77,
208–9, 265; increased production in,
44–48; independent union bargaining
agreements in, 211–12; layoffs by,
27–29, 155, 315; low wages as critical in,
50; poor people feared by, 122–23, 128;
revenue from, 45–47. *See also* factory
relocations; *specific industries and plants*
maquiladora workers, 43–44, 313–14;
age of, 169; firings of, 84–85, 97–98,
164, 177–78, 187–88, 194–95, 203,
207, 221–22; "junked," 201–6, 285–86;
Mexican workers in U.S. compared
with, 163; murders of, 15; permanent
vs. temporary, 318–19; persistence of,
314–15; from U.S., 48–49. *See also*
child labor; farmworkers; garment
workers; labor activists
Maquiladora Workers Support Network (Canada), 212
market pressure: as labor strategy,
208–13
Martín del Campo, Frank: on international cooperation, 301; on NAFTA
debates, 159; visit to Mexico, 157–59,
283–84
Martín del Campo, Jesús, 249, 278
Martínez, Alma, 218
Martínez, Benedicto, 15: on blacklist,
167; on cross-border cooperation,
289, 302, 308; on economic development and social concerns, 56; on

Martínez, Benedicto, (*continued*)
    firings, 178; on organizing methods,
    291–93, 298; UE/FAT alliance and,
    161–62; U.S. tour of, 162–63, 300; on
    U.S. media, 90
Martínez, César, 164
Martínez, Jaime, 231–32, 306
Martínez, Pedro, 113
Martínez, Presiliano, 34–35
Martínez, Rubén, 11
Matamoros Garment factory, 208–9,
    212–13
Matsushita (televisions), 28
Mattel Corporation, 316
Maxell (cassette tapes), 70, 72–73
Maxi-Switch plants (Mexico and U.S.),
    208
May Day: fear of mobs on, 74–75; inde-
    pendent celebrations of, 75–76;
    parades banned for, 232; women's
    marches on, 214–15
McWilliams, Brian, 238
Meaney, George, 295–96
meatpacking plants, U.S.: changing
    organizing tactics in, 264–71; elec-
    tions in, 254–55; history of unions
    in, 258–64; immigrant workers in,
    253, 256–57; INS investigations of,
    262–63; union recognition in, 269
Medel Torres, Gerardo, 111
media, 9, 293: on anencephaly occur-
    rences, 287; on farmworkers, 19; on
    foreign interference at Breed, 205;
    Han Young strikes and, 101–2; on
    NAFTA, 161; on police harassment,
    112; pro-labor, 8; on union election, 90
Medina, Eliseo, 282–84
Medrano, Guadalupe, 164
Medrano, Ofelia, 164
Mejia, Marcantonio, 112
Melendez, Dan, 77–78
Méndez, René, 84
Méndez, Sergio, 141
Mendiola, Leticia, 63, 65, 68
Mendoza Reyes, Leocadio, 197
Mercado Calderón, Francisco, 204

Metales y Derivados plant (Tijuana),
    286–87
Mexicali (city, Mexico): growth of, 33
Mexicali Valley: child labor in, 30–35;
    crops in, 29; grower contracts in,
    36–39; structural adjustment's impact
    on, 39–41
Mexican Electrical Workers (SME,
    Sindicato Mexicano de Electricis-
    tas): alliances of, 158–59, 160–61, 297;
    members of, 277–79; privatization of
    electricity and, 296
Mexican government: bonds for, 45;
    housing subsidies from, 186–87;
    Labor Ministry of, 116; land owned
    by, 123–24; poor people feared by,
    122–23, 128–30; privatization's impact
    on, 55; secret U.S. meetings with, on
    junked workers, 285–86; strike set-
    tlements by, 118–20; strikes feared
    by, 89–90; subsidies from, 54; televi-
    sions stopped by, 90; wage increase
    offer of, 110–11. *See also* Constitution,
    Mexican; laws
Mexican Network Against Free Trade,
    160
Mexican Revolution, 44, 50–51, 241,
    272, 273
Mexican workers in Mexico: corporatist
    structure and, 49–50; impact of
    Mexican workers in U.S. on, 271–84;
    unionization of, 54
Mexican workers in U.S., 11, 151, 161,
    179–80, 270–71; companies' depen-
    dence on, 261–62; grape strikes by,
    22–23; increased number of, 48–49;
    maquiladora workers compared
    with, 163; in meatpacking plants,
    256–58; Mexican workers at home
    impacted by, 271–84; NAFTA's
    impact on, 260–61; union organizing
    by, 64; visits to Mexico, 277–84. *See
    also* immigrants
Mexico: bailout of, 45–46; class system
    in, 229–30; as economic experiment,
    45; electoral politics of, 106–7,

277–82; May Day celebrations in, 74–76, 214–15, 232; registering new unions as problem in, 189–90. *See also* Mexican government

Mexico City: labor unrest in, 85–86; Olympics in, 278; Tlatelolco massacre in, 11, 278; transportation workers in, 223–26. *See also* ITAPSA plant (Mexico City)

Mexico Moderno (CROM-affiliated): company support for, 63–64, 65; competition for, 67–68; voting on, 60–61

Mex Mode. *See* Kuk Dong (Mex Mode) plant (Puebla)

Meyers, Eric, 165

Meza Arceo, María Eugenia, 234

Michoacán, 273, 281; violence in, 275–76

Migrant Media project, 155

Migrant Watch International, 57

migration, global, 57. *See also* immigrants

Mika, Susan, 185

Miners and Metallurgical Workers Union of the Mexican Republic (Sindicato de Trabajadores Mineros y Metalúrgicos de la Republica Mexicana), 240

mining industry: attacks on U.S. unions in, 305; organizing in early, 272; privatization of, 240–46, 261

Missouri: jobs lost in, 46–47

Mixtec people: election of, 138–39; geographical dispersal of, 143–44; homes for, 125, 126; as organizers' target audience, 146–47; unionization and, 127–28

Moctezuma Barragan, Javier, 114–16, 118, 119, 120

Molina, Alma, 165–69

Molina, Pedro, 67–68

Mondragon, Manuel, 204, 206

Monroy, Claudia, 209, 210, 212

Montañez Lopez, Bruno Noe, 201–2

Morales Bocanegra, Isabel, 203

Moreno, Chavelo, 155

Moreno, Consuelo, 194, 195

Moreno Gómez, Luis Miguel, 227

Morones, Luis, 81

Mosqueda, Antonio, 155

Muñoz, Carlos, 284

Muñoz, Marcela, 208–9, 210, 211, 212, 213

Muranaka Farms, 30–31, 36, 37

murders: of labor activists, 150, 201–2, 227, 228, 274–77; of teachers, 226; of women workers, 15, 313–14; workers' response to, 24

Murrieta, Joaquín, 272

Murrieta Llaguno, Fernando, 103

Murrillo, Esther, 126

NAFTA (North American Free Trade Agreement): alternative to, 309–11; border as symbol of, 48–49; children of, 16–17; and cross-border union alliances, 298–305; debates on, 4, 11, 156, 299–301; effects of, 6–9, 12–15, 42–49, 201, 205, 261–62; extension of, 12, 52, 91–92, 287–88; fatal flaws of, 120, 190, 287–89, 319–23; opposition to, 29, 49, 86, 92, 159–60, 161–63, 165, 231; passage of, 162; rhetoric of, 12, 253–54; support for, 118–19; U.S. labor unions and, 267–68, 271–84; workers' rights and, 91–93. *See also* free trade; neoliberalism; North American Agreement on Labor Cooperation

NAFTA-TAA (Trade Adjustment Assistance): applications for, 28–29; claims certified by, 47; claims denied by, 25–28; failures of, 98

Nañez, Flor, 218

NAO. *See* National Administrative Office (NAO, U.S.)

National Action Party (PAN, Partido de Acción Nacional): constituents of, 128; critique of, 138, 140; on foreign investment, 105; Garcia opposed by, 32; land occupations and, 129; manipulations by, 149–50; miners' strike and, 243; opposition to, 106, 140–41; social conservatism of, 198–99; victory of, 59, 198. *See also* Fox, Vicente

National Administrative Office (NAO, U.S.), 99, 165; and Breed plants, 201, 204–6, 285–86; and Duro Bag, 208, 288–89; failure of, 182, 206; and Friction, 181–82; and Han Young, 90–91, 93–98, 116–17; and ITAPSA, 178–81; and Sony, 189. *See also* North American Agreement on Labor Cooperation

National Association of Democratic Lawyers (Mexico), 90, 189, 290

National Association of Maquiladoras, 197

National Autonomous University (UNAM), 246–50

National Endowment for Democracy, 301

nationalism, 293–94

nationalization: of mines, 241; of oil industry, 225, 273; process of, 224–25; reversal of, 226

National Labor Relations Board (U.S.), 207

National O-Ring Corporation, 77–79

National Union of Workers (UNT, Union Nacional de Trabajadores), 54, 86, 110, 119, 296–97, 307; alliances of, 180, 222, 297–98; Duro Bag workers supported by, 196–97; labor law reforms proposed by, 292–93; strike supported by, 106; women workers disregarded by, 213–14

Navarrette, Alfredo, 238–39

Navarro, Yolanda, 155

NAWWN (North American Worker to Worker Network), 66, 159

Nebraska Beef (meatpacker), 260, 262–64, 269

Nemitz, Mark, 260

neoliberalism, 13, 93–94. *See also* free trade; NAFTA

Newell, Amy, 164

New Frontier Trading Corporation, 287

New Jersey: unemployment in, 28

New York state: workers' compensation in, 288

Nicaragua: revolution in, 303

Nike Corporation, 210–11

Nintendo, 28, 208

Nissan plant, 234–35

Nordeen, Linda, 164

North American Agreement on Labor Cooperation, 14, 206; complaints filed under, 90–91, 178–80, 189; jobs undermined by, 180; lack of enforcement of, 116–18, 180–82; on secret ballot, 200; on U.S. union formation, 207–8. *See also* National Administrative Office

North American Commission for Environmental Cooperation, 287

North American Free Trade Agreement. *See* NAFTA

North American Worker to Worker Network (NAWWN), 66, 159

Northwest Treeplanters and Farmworkers United (PCUN, Pineros y Campesinos Unidos de Noroeste), 143

Nuestras Hijas de Regreso a Casa (Our Children Must Return Home), 313–14

Nuevo Laredo. *See* Sony plants

Nuevo San Juan Copala, 123

Nunes, Tom, 37–38

Nunes Farms, 36–38

Núñez, Ana Julia, 171

Núñez, Marco, 268

Oaxaca: centrality of, 144, 147–48; teachers killed in, 226

Obrador, Manuel López, 219

Ochoa, Digna, 150

October 6 Union for Industry and Commerce (Sindicato 6 de Octubre para Industria y Comercio), 109, 117, 140; bargaining rights of, 98–99; opposition to, 102–3; strikes declared by, 99–102, 111–14. *See also* Han Young de Mexico strikes

Oil, Chemical and Atomic Workers, 8, 136

oil industry, 225, 231, 273
oilworkers union, 231
Ojeda, Martha, 14, 186, 191; accusations against, 197; on Breed case, 205, 286; as Coalition head, 190–92; in hiding, 188–89; as housing activist, 186–87; organizing efforts of, 187–88; on threat of jobs lost to China, 318–19; worker firings and, 203
Olympics (1968), 278
Omaha (Neb.), 264, 269–71; immigration to, 251–54; meatpacking history in, 258–64
Omaha Packing Company, 260
Omaha Together One Community (OTOC): alliances of, 256, 258, 267–71; organizing efforts of, 255; strategies of, 264–67
Oñate, Santiago, 189–90, 207–8
O'Neill, Paul, 191
Operation Vanguard, 266–67
Orea, Ramiro, 139–40, 142, 143
Organizacion del Pueblo Explotado y Oprimido (Organization of Exploited and Oppressed People), 144–45
Orta, Lida, 205
Ortiz, Antonio, 88
Ortiz, Francisco, 69–70, 71
Osuna Osuna, Artemio, 130, 135–36, 137
OTOC. See Omaha Together One Community (OTOC)
Our Children Must Return Home (Nuestras Hijas de Regreso a Casa), 313–14
Oxford (shirts), 28

PACE (Paper, Allied-Industrial, Chemical and Energy Workers), 197–98
Pacheco, Chema, 245–46
Pacific Maritime Association, 235
Paez González, Gabino, 242, 243, 244
Palacios Alcocer, Mariano, 116, 200
Palomino, Reynaldo, 244
PAN. See National Action Party
Pandol, Jack, 20–21

Paper, Allied-Industrial, Chemical and Energy Workers (PACE), 197–98
Paperworkers, 176
Parks, Norman, 239
Parrada, Luis, 84
Party of the Democratic Revolution (PRD, Partido de la Revolución Democrática), 76, 128, 138, 157; alliances of, 148, 150; barrios organized by, 140–43; California delegation's meeting with, 158; educational privatization and, 248–49; Han Young strikes and support for, 105–7, 112; land offered to, 126; miners' strike and, 243; social services and, 279–80; whisper campaigns of, 98–99
Party of the Institutionalized Revolution (PRI, Partido de la Revolución Institucional), 105, 167; alliances of, 82, 194, 224, 274; campaigns of, 273–74; critique of, 138–39; defeat of, 59, 119, 128, 142, 148; miners' strike and, 243; PAN compared with, 198; power of, 224, 227; privatization and, 239, 247–49
PATCO (Professional Air Traffic Controllers Organization), 151–52, 230–31, 303
PCUN (Pineros y Campesinos Unidos de Noroeste; Northwest Treeplanters and Farmworkers United), 143
Pelayo, Aurora, 107, 287
Pemex (Mexican government owned), 54–55
Peñaflor Barrón, José, 84, 98, 99; criminal charges filed by, 113; on despojo agravado, 122; on Han Young elections, 101; legal charges against, 104, 108, 109, 114; on strike settlements, 117–18; on union efforts, 86–87
Peñoles smelter (Torreon), 214
Pérez Astorga, Carlos, 89
Pérez Castro, Tiburcio, 127, 128–30
Pérez Cruz, Carlos, 92
Pérez-García, Alicia, 208

Perot, Ross, 159, 299, 301
Perris: Boscovitch Farms in, 28–29, 36,
    42–43
Pesceira, Lauro, 218
Philippines: Mexico compared with, 72
Phillips North America plant (Juarez),
    316
Phoenix Foundation, 212
Phoenix Vegetable Growers, 36
Pillsbury Corporation: Green Giant
    plants of, 154, 156
Pimentel, Arturo, 149–50
Pimentel Peralta, Francisco, 237
Pinochet, Augusto, 20, 302
Plan Puebla/Panama, 132–33, 323
Plantronics plant, 28
Plasticos Bajacal (Tijuana), 8; elections
    at, 7, 60–62, 66–68; organizing
    efforts at, 6, 73–74; protests at,
    62–66
Plata, Humberto, 277–81
Plata, Ignacio, 277–81
Plaza of Three Cultures: Tlatelolco
    massacre in, 11, 278
police, 193: attacks on striking garment
    workers, 210; to break Han Young
    strikes, 102, 104, 108–9, 112–13; firing
    enforced by, 194–95; harassment by,
    112–13, 140; land occupations and,
    126–27; violence against Sony work-
    ers by, 186, 188–89. See also violence
Polo Uscanga, Abraham, 228
Poniatowska, Elena, 11
poor people and poverty, 249–50; gov-
    ernment's fears of, 122–23, 128–30;
    increases in, 16, 57–58, 294
ports, Mexican: modernization of,
    235–36; pay system of, 237–38; priva-
    tization of, 232–35, 238–40
ports, U.S.: rail line and, 132–33
PRD. See Party of the Democratic Rev-
    olution
PRI. See Party of the Institutionalized
    Revolution
Price Pfister plant, 6
Priego Chávez, Jesús Humberto, 228

prisons: Chávez in, 122, 124, 129–30, 139;
    conditions in, 136; Sandoval in,
    121–22, 129–30; SUTAUR 100 mem-
    bers in, 223, 227, 230; for those
    opposed to privatization, 223,
    226–32; Vallejo in, 226
privatization, 14; beginnings of,
    44–46; of buses, 228; of education,
    246–50; of *ejido* land, 124; of elec-
    tricity, 296; imprisonment for
    opposition to, 223, 226–32; of min-
    ing industry, 240–46; policies fos-
    tering, 54–55; of ports, 232–40; of
    railroads, 241–42; resistance to, 222;
    violence in, 223–26
Professional Air Traffic Controllers
    Organization (PATCO), 151–52,
    230–31, 303
Progressive Asset Management, 90
promotoras, 216–17
Prudential Insurance, 25
Puebla (Mexico), 210. *See also* Kuk
    Dong (Mex Mode) plant
Puente, Julian, 117
Puma plant, 212–13
Pung Kook plant, 221–22

QPI (meatpacking), 260

Raat, W. Dirk, 11
racism, 159; and indigenous migrant
    people, 122–23, 128–30; in San Diego,
    141–42
Radio Bilingue, 141
radio broadcasts: accusations on, 164;
    on activists' arrests, 141; as docu-
    ments, 7; for meatpackers, 269
railroads, 131–33, 241–42
Rail Tex (company), 132
Ramírez, Jorge, 268–69
Ramírez, Raúl, 114, 128, 129–30, 137
Ramos, Nicolasa, 137
Ramos, Raymundo, 9
Ramos Gómez, Heriberto, 202–3
Rascón, Armando, 112
Reagan, Ronald, 151–52, 153, 230–31, 303

Reclusorio del Oriente (federal prison), 223

Regalado, Juan, 130, 136, 137

Regency Packing (grower), 46

Reich, Robert, 19–20, 189–90, 207–8

religious beliefs: liberation theology and, 265; and organizing efforts, 255–56, 268–69. See also Catholic Church

Retail Clerks (union), 259

Revolutionary Confederation of Mexican Workers (CROM, Confederación Revolucionaria de Obreros Mexicanos), 61, 63–64, 65, 81, 224

Revolutionary Confederation of Workers and Farmers (CROC, Confederación Revolucionaria de Obreros y Campesinos), 224; activists' use of, 170–72; in Duro Bag elections, 199–200; opposition to, 83–84; protection contracts of, 81–82, 97, 209; voting for, 85–89; workers attacked by, 210

Revolutionary Union of the Working Class (Sindicato Revolucionario de la Clase Obrera), 92–93

Reyes, Armando, 139–40, 143

Reyes, Magdaleno, 65, 100, 101–2

Reyes, Silvestre, 112–13

Reyes, Teofilo, 289–90

Reyes Colin, Pedro Fernández, 113

Rhode Island: jobs lost in, 47

Río Bravo barrio: housing in, 193. See also Duro Bag factory (Río Bravo)

Ríos González, María Estela, 15; arrest of, 234; on child labor, 40–41; on cross-border union alliances, 290; on site of labor struggles, 298

Road Machinery (company), 242

Robeson, Paul, 1–2

Robles, Betty, 215

Robles, Juan José, 263–64

Robles, Rosario, 248

Rodríguez, Arturo, 146

Rodríguez, Virginia, 67, 68, 206–7

Rodríguez Correa, José Fernando, 244

Rojas, Maclovio, 131

Romero, Gus, 26

Romo, Jesús, 243, 244

Ruiz, Honorina, 31

Ruiz, Rigoberto, 31

Ruiz, Rubén, 176–79

Ruiz Barraza, Jesús, 105–6, 107

Ryder, Paul, 173

safety. See health and safety issues

"safety net," 19–20, 26

Salas, Carlos, 11

Salinas de Gortari, Carlos: alliances of, 241; critique of, 277; imprisonments by, 230–31; jobs promised by, 157; on NAFTA, 253–54; reforms under, 124, 226; transportation workers under, 224

Samet, Andrew, 118

Samsung plant, 316

Sánchez, Jorge, 277

Sánchez, Miguel Ángel, 104, 112–13

Sánchez, René, 210

Sánchez, Roberto, 166

Sánchez Murillo, Miguel, 108

San Diego and Imperial Valley Railway, 132

San Diego (Calif.): racism in, 141–42; secret meeting in, 285–86; Tijuana compared with, 43–44

San Diego Support Committee for Maquiladora Workers, 65–68; alliances of, 73–74, 159; Han Young strikes and, 83, 90–91; legal suit filed by, 78–79; protests against activists' arrest, 136; voting observed by, 87–89

Sandoval, Florentina, 121, 126

Sandoval, Juana, 121

Sandoval, Julio: imprisonment of, 121–22, 129–30; land occupations of, 126–27; payment boycott of, 123–24

Sandoval Silva, Jonathan Abel, 121

sanitation: absence of, 145, 193. See also water supply

San Joaquin Valley (U.S.): grape strikes in, 22–25

San Quintin Valley: *ejidos* in, 124; elections in, 142; growth of, 138–39; land occupations in, 122, 125

Sanyo plant, 73

Sara Lee Corporation (garment sweatshops), 28, 216–18

schools. *See* education

Scott, Robert, 11

Screen Actors Guild, 303

Sealand (shipping company), 238

Secretariat for Labor and Social Benefits (STPS, Secretaria de Trabajo y Previsión Social, Mexico), 96–97

Secretariat of Labor and Social Forecasting (Mexico), 33

Secretariat of Public Education (Mexico), 33

SEDEPAC (Servicio de Desaeollo y Paz-Coahuila; Service for Development and Peace-Coahuila), 215, 216–18

September 11 attacks, 52, 307, 322

Serrano, Irma, 274

Service Employees International Union, 7, 283

Service for Development and Peace-Coahuila (SEDEPAC, Servicio de Desaeollo y Paz-Coahuila), 215, 216–18

Servicios Portuarios, 235

Shahid, John, 77–78

Shaiken, Harley, 44, 45

Shailor, Barbara, 308

Shor, Charles, 198

Sicarsta steel mill, 234

Siewart, Jake, 316

Silicon Valley, 3, 5

Silver, John, 155

Sinaloa (Mexico): migrants in, 144–46

sindicato de hecho (union in life), 291

SINTTIM (Sindicato Independiente de Trabajadores y Trabajadoras de la Industria Maquiladora del Estado de Baja California Sur; Independent Union of Men and Women Workers in the Maquiladora Industry of the State of Baja California), 221–22

SITEMEX (Sindicato de Trabajadores de la Empresa Mex Mode; Independent Union of Workers at Mex Mode), 211–14

SME. *See* Mexican Electrical Workers

Smithfield (meatpacking), 260

social justice: civil war as influence on, 265–66; land invasions as influence on, 251–53; migration's role in spreading, 271–84

social movements: border development's implications for, 320–23; silences in, 5–6; veterans of, 278

sociopolitical change, 6–7; economic development linked to, 56–57; as electoral context, 138–39; Mexican workers in U.S. as influence on, 271–84; organizing for, 141–42

solidarity, 53, 56–57, 184, 301; across plants in same company, 175–76, 182–83; Canadian funds for, 310; challenge to, 58–59; committees for, 279; cross-border, 50–51; discourse opened on, 310–11; redefinition of, 296, 298

Solidarity Center (AFL-CIO), 212

Solis, Francisco, 111

Solis, Guillermina, 169–70

Solorzano, Miguel, 95–96

Sony plants (Nuevo Laredo), 316; firings at, 187–88; hiring status changes at, 318, 319; older women forced from, 192; violence by police against workers at, 186, 188–89

Sosa, Efrain, 170–72

Sosa, Sergio, 255, 265–71

Soto, Angel, 208

South African Trade Unions, 56

South Carolina: unemployment in, 27

Special Forces (Fuerzas Especiales), 102, 104

Sprint Corporation, 207. *See also* La Conexión Familiar

Staley (corporation), 305

standard of living: decline of, 46–47; economic development linked to, 56–58; subsidies related to, 54. *See also* food; hours; housing; wages

state labor boards: complicity with employers, 203–4; new union rejected by, 189–90; UNT proposals on, 292 93

steel mills, 234

Steinberg, Lionel, 21–22, 25

Stevedoring Services of America (shipping company), 238

STIMAHCS. *See* Union of Workers in the Metal, Steel, Iron, and Connected Industries

STPS (Secretariat for Labor and Social Benefits; Secretaria de Trabajo y Prevision Social, Mexico), 96–97

strawberry organizing drive, 152

street sellers, 106, 139, 140

strikes: against Duro Bag, 195–96; against farmwork conditions, 144–45; against grape growers, 22–25; against health and safety violations, 203; by indigenous migrant workers, 127–28; against Kuk Dong, 209–12; against meatpacking plants, 260; against mining industry, 240–41; notification before, 99; by PATCO, 151–52. *See also* boycotts; demonstrations and protests; Han Young de Mexico strikes

STRM (Sindicato de Telefonistas de la Republica Mexicana; Union of Telephone Workers of the Mexican Republic), 206–8

structural adjustment, 39–41, 295; unemployment due to, 54–55. *See also* devaluation of peso

students: market pressure utilized by, 210–13; massacre of, 278–81; privitization of education and, 246–50

Support Committee for Maquiladora Workers. *See* San Diego Support Committee for Maquiladora Workers

SUTAUR 100 (Sindicato Unico de Trabajadores de Autotransportes

Urbanos de Pasajeros Ruta 100; Sole Union for Workers at the Urban Bus Line Route 100), 223, 226, 227–32

SUTERM (electrical workers union), 226

Sweeney, John, 295, 305–11

Swift (meatpacker), 258–59

Tapachula (Mexico): campaigning in, 273–74

Tapia, Alfredo, 70

teacher *(maestro):* connotations of, 33–34

Teamsters: alliances of, 163, 164–65, 176; cooperation of, 85; Free Trade Caravan of, 162–63, 300; renewal of, 154; sweetheart agreements of, 153; UFW vs., 21–22, 24

Teamsters Local 912: alliances of, 159; democratization of, 152; investigations by, 154–55; strike tactics of, 153–54

tequio concept, 148

Terán Terán, Héctor, 88, 134, 136

theater group, 212

Thomson plant, 316

Tijuana (Mexico): approach to post-NAFTA, 13; border crossing at, 48–49; conditions in, 64–65, 68, 80; Detroit compared with, 236, 323; land occupation in, 130–37; number of maquiladoras in, 72; population growth in, 127, 131, 320–21; San Diego compared with, 43–44; street sellers association in, 106; unrest in, 112–14; weakened rule of law in, 6. *See also* Maclovio Rojas (barrio, Tijuana); Plasticos Bajacal (Tijuana)

Tinajero Martinez, Ezekiel, 202

titularidad (right to bargain) concept, 98–99

Tlatelolco massacre, 11, 278

Tomás, Marc Antonio, 315, 318

Tong, Mary: deportation of, 89; injured workers and, 66; on labor laws, 91; on NAFTA, 93; opposition to, 98–99; organizing tactics of, 83;

Tong, Mary (*continued*)
on toxic chemicals, 74; on UAW
contract, 79; on union opportunities,
86; warnings to, 103–4
Torreón (Mexico): women's marches in,
214–15
Torres, Rafael, 218
Trabajadores Desplazados (comm.
org.), 155, 156
Trabajo y Democracia Hoy (Work and
democracy today, magazine), 9
Trade Research Consortium, 27
Transnational Information Exchange,
159, 289–90
Transportación Maritima Mexicana
(shipping company), 238
transportation: of people, 43–44, 63, 70,
72, 187, 226–32; of products, 131–33.
See also ports, Mexican; SUTAUR
100
Treaty of Guadalupe-Hidalgo, 272
Treviño Saenz, Cesar, 197
Triqui people, 143–44. *See also* San-
doval, Julio
Trumka, Rich, 305, 306–7
tuberculosis, 228
Tyco Corporation, 71–72

UAW (United Auto Workers), 8, 79,
205, 290
UE. *See* United Electrical Workers
UFCW. *See* United Food and Commercial Workers
UFW. *See* United Farm Workers
union
UNAM (National Autonomous University), 246–50
unemployment assistance, 25–28. *See
also* job losses
unionization efforts: in context of privatization, 55–56; conversion to, 23;
independence in, 86–87; opportunities for, 85–86; suppression of, 6
Union of Duro Bag Workers, 199–200
Union of Needletrades, Industrial and
Textile Employees (UNITE, earlier

Amalgamated Clothing Workers),
175, 176, 211, 212, 303
Union of Telephone Workers of the
Mexican Republic (STRM, Sindicato de Telefonistas de la Republica
Mexicana), 206–8
Union of Workers in the Metal, Steel,
Iron, and Connected Industries
(STIMAHCS, Sindicato Trabajadores de la Industria Metal-
Mecanica): alliances of, 176; request
to join, 85–86; vote to join, 87–90, 178
unions, 49, 61–62; bargaining rights of,
98–99; cross-border solidarity of,
50–51; demonstrations against,
75–76; divisions among, 21–22, 24;
independence and, 86–87; official,
74–75; in postwar vs. current Mexico, 54–55; pro-government (*sindicato charro*), 81
United Auto Workers (UAW), 8, 79,
205, 290
United Electrical Workers/Authentic
Labor Front alliance, 13–14, 16,
160–61; complaints to NAFTA filed
by, 178–83; implications of, 182–84;
investigations by, 161–62; organizing
efforts of, 168–69
United Electrical Workers (UE):
alliances of, 85, 159, 160–65, 176;
complaints filed by, 181–82; disappointment in strike settlement, 85,
117; NAFTA and, 288, 300; organizing for, 2, 4
United Electrical Workers (UE) Local
1090, 175–76
United Farm Workers union (UFW):
Frente's collaboration with, 146–47;
grape strikes by, 22–25; organizing
for, 2, 4, 21–22, 283
United Food and Commercial Workers
(UFCW), 259; alliances of, 256, 258,
267–71; concessions of, 260; union
organizing by, 64
United Nations: Convention 32 (U.N.),
40–41; World Federation of Trade

Unions (WFTU), 160–61, 296–97, 308
United Packinghouse Workers of America (UPWA), 258–59
United Professional and Technical Employees, 64
United States: cross-border union alliances as influence on, 298–302; as economic policy influence, 54–55; exports from, 46–48, 55; failure to enforce labor laws of, 207–8; labor movement rejuvenated in, 254; military budget of, 52; problems of, 319; protests against activists' arrests, 136
United Students Against Sweatshops (USAS), 210–12
UNITE (Union of Needletrades, Industrial and Textile Employees; earlier Amalgamated Clothing Workers), 175, 176, 211, 212, 303
university: privitization of, 246–50
UNT. See National Union of Workers
UPWA (United Packinghouse Workers of America), 258–59
Uribe Vasquez, Manuel, 87–88
U.S. Agency for International Development, 301
U.S. Department of Labor, 27, 118
U.S. Labor Against the War (USLAW), 307
USA·NAFTA (business coalition), 26–27, 28
USAS (United Students Against Sweatshops), 210–12
U.S./Mexico border, 4, 5, 43, 320. See also cross-border movements

Valderrama, José, 244
Valdez, Carmen, 64
Valentín, María, 256
Vallejo, Demetrio, 10, 226
Vargas, Gabriel, 164
Vasquez, Yolanda, 76, 77, 79
Vavi, Zwelinzima, 56
Vega de la Madrid, Francisco, 113
VegaMix (grower), 36

Velasquez, Fidel: AFL-CIO's relation to, 304–5; California delegation's meeting with, 158; death of, 86; on May Day celebration, 74–75; union parades banned by, 232
Velazquez, Blanca, 210–11, 212, 213
Velazquez, Eustolia, 67
Veracruz (Mexico): military takeover of, 233; workers hired from, 92–93, 97
Verastegui, Eleazar, 100, 103
Vidal, Luis, 171
Villagomez Guillon, María Lourdes, 103, 104
Villela, María: on NAFTA, 180; organizing efforts of, 172–73, 175–76, 179
Villela, Raquel, 172–73
Villista Army of National Liberation (Ejercito Villista de Liberación Nacional), 136–37
violence: accusations of, 100–101; increase in, 53; against students, 11, 278; against women, 209, 210. See also murders; police
visa denials, 165, 168
voices, 2, 11–15; broadcasts of, 7–8; of child labor, 40; of Han Young workers at hearing, 94–98
Volkswagen (Puebla), 214, 317

wages: average, 316, 317; concessions on, 46–47; decline of, 57–58; disparities in, 53; maintenance of low, 38, 50, 127, 156; in green onion growing (Mexico), 35–36; inadequacy of, 70, 194; "living," 214–18; of longshore workers, 237–38; in meatpacking plants, 260–61, 270; NAFTA debates and, 300; offered increase in, 110–11; organizing to increase, 165–66; privatization's impact on, 237–38; promised vs. real, 92; structural adjustment's impact on, 39–41, 46; U.S. vs. Mexican, 44, 53–54, 179; World Bank's recommendations on, 218–21
walkouts: at Han Young, 82–84; workers fired for, 82

water supply: for drinking, 137, 243; for
    irrigation, clean vs. black, 155
Watsonville (Calif.), 151; strike in,
    152–56
Watsonville Canning and Frozen
    Foods, 152–56
wealth, 249–50
Weiss, Larry, 118
Welch, Jack, 48
Wells Fargo Bank, 153–54
WFTU (World Federation of Trade
    Unions), 160–61, 296–97, 308
Williams, Rob, 46
Wilson, Pete, 26–27
Wilson (meatpacker), 258–59
women: average Alcoa worker as, 317–18;
    bikini contest expected of, 77–78;
    demonstrations by, 76; legal suit filed
    by, 78–79; May Day march of, 214–15;
    miscarriages of, 203; murdered, 15,
    313–14; organizing efforts of, 187–88,
    190. See also garment workers
Woolrich (sportswear), 28
Workers, Residents, and Farmers
    Power Network (ENFOCCA,
    Enlace de la Fuerza de Obreros,
    Cuidadanos y Campesinos), 140, 143
Workers' Information Center (CITTAC,
    Centro de Información para Traba-
    jadoras y Trabajadores Asociación
    Civil), 62
Workers' Party (Partido de Trabajo),
    143–44
workers' rights: different ideas about,
    220–21; discarded, 204–5; exercising
    of, as best defense, 291; human
    rights and, 164–65, 198; ignored,
    313–14, 320; pledge to protect, 12;
    poor outlook for, 201
Workers Rights Consortium
    (WRC), 211
Workers Support Center (CAT, Centro
    de Apoyo para los Trabajadores),
    210–13
working-class social movements: indus-
    trial basis of, 4–11, 292. See also
    cross-border movements

workplace injuries, 201–6, 285–86; com-
    pensation for, 66; at ITAPSA plant,
    176–77; in meatpacking plants,
    255–56, 257–58, 259; protests in
    response to, 62–64; responsibility for,
    196. See also health and safety issues
World Bank: accountability in health
    violations, 204–5; on flexibility,
    218–21; loan conditions of, 54–55;
    reforms expected by, 295–96, 318–19
World Federation of Trade Unions
    (WFTU), 160–61, 296–97, 308
World Food Summit (Rome, 1996), 55,
    58–59
World Trade Organization (WTO), 57,
    118–19
WRC (Workers Rights Consortium), 211
Wright, Carisa, 37
WTO (World Trade Organization), 57,
    118–19

Xentrek, 28

Yañez, Guadalupe, 84
Yarrington, Tomas, 196
Young Kang, Won, 89
Young Workers' Pastorate, 204
Youn Lee, Ho, 89
youth. See children and youth
Zapata, Emiliano, 275
Zapatistas, 55, 276; election and, 273–74;
    NAFTA denounced by, 19; support
    for, 147, 227
Zapotec people, 143–44
Zedillo, Ernesto: campaign of, 273–74;
    election of, 277–81; IMF reforms and,
    45–46; labor conditions under,
    114–15; on May Day celebration,
    74–75; privatization and, 248; reforms
    under, 71, 223, 226, 230; strikes and,
    107; transportation workers under,
    224; wage increase offer of, 110–11
Zenith plant, 28, 46–47
Zuerlein, Damian: on demographic
    changes, 264, 270; organizing efforts
    of, 264–65, 268; on union election,
    254, 255

Compositor:	Impressions Book and Journal Services, Inc.
Text:	10/15 Janson
Display:	DIN Mittelschrift
Printer and binder:	Thomson-Shore, Inc.